S0-AJD-791

A New Order of Things

The story told here is a critical yet unknown chapter in the creation of the American republic. Claudio Saunt vividly depicts a dramatic transformation in the eighteenth century that overturned the world of the powerful and numerous Creek Indians and forever changed the Deep South. By 1800, some Creeks, whose most valuable belongings had once been deerskins, owned hundreds of African American slaves and thousands of cattle. Their leaders, who formerly strove for consensus, now ruled by force. New property fostered a new possessiveness, and government by coercion bred confrontation. *A New Order of Things* is the first book to chronicle this decisive transformation in America's early history, a transformation that left deep divisions between the wealthy and poor, powerful and powerless.

Claudio Saunt, formerly a Mellon Fellow in History at the Society of Fellows, Columbia University, is an Assistant Professor of History at the University of Georgia. His research has been supported by major awards from the Research Institute for the Study of Man and the National Endowment for the Humanities.

CAMBRIDGE STUDIES IN
NORTH AMERICAN INDIAN HISTORY

Editors
Frederick Hoxie, University of Illinois, Urbana-Champaign
Neal Salisbury, Smith College

Also in the series

RICHARD WHITE   *The Middle Ground: Indians, Empires, and Republics in the Great Lakes Region, 1650–1815*

SIDNEY L. HARRING   *Crow Dog's Case: American Indian Sovereignty, Tribal Law, and United States Law in the Nineteenth Century*

COLIN G. CALLOWAY   *The American Revolution in Indian Country: Crisis and Diversity in Native American Communities*

FREDERICK E. HOXIE   *Parading through History: The Making of the Crow Nation in America, 1805–1935*

JEAN M. O'BRIEN   *Dispossession by Degrees: Indian Land and Identity in Natick, Massachusetts, 1650–1790*

A New Order of Things

Property, Power, and the Transformation of the Creek Indians, 1733–1816

CLAUDIO SAUNT

University of Georgia

CAMBRIDGE
UNIVERSITY PRESS

PUBLISHED BY THE PRESS SYNDICATE OF THE UNIVERSITY OF CAMBRIDGE
The Pitt Building, Trumpington Street, Cambridge, United Kingdom

CAMBRIDGE UNIVERSITY PRESS
The Edinburgh Building, Cambridge CB2 2RU, UK   www.cup.cam.ac.uk
40 West 20th Street, New York, NY 10011-4211, USA   www.cup.org
10 Stamford Road, Oakleigh, Melbourne 3166, Australia
Ruiz de Alarcón 13, 28014 Madrid, Spain

© Claudio Saunt 1999

This book is in copyright. Subject to statutory exception
and to the provisions of relevant collective licensing agreements,
no reproduction of any part may take place without
the written permission of Cambridge University Press.

First published 1999

Printed in the United States of America

Typeface Ehrhardt 11/13 pt.   *System* QuarkXPress [BTS]

*A catalog record for this book is available
from the British Library.*

Library of Congress Cataloging-in-Publication Data

Saunt, Claudio.
A new order of things: property, power, and the transformation of
the Creek Indians, 1733–1816/Claudio Saunt.
p.   cm. – (Cambridge studies in North American Indian
history)
Includes bibliographical references and index.
ISBN 0-521-66043-2 hb. – ISBN 0-521-66943-X pb
1. Creek Indians – History.   2. Creek Indians – Cultural
assimilation.   I. Title.   II. Series.
E99.C9S28   1999
975'.004973 – dc21   99-12567   CIP

ISBN   0 521 66043 2   hardback
ISBN   0 521 66943 X   paperback

Contents

Illustrations and maps

Abbreviations

AGI   Archivo General de Indias, Seville, Spain. Microfilm copies in PKY.

AGN   Archivo General de la Nación, Mexico City, Mexico. Microfilm copies in PKY.

ASPFR   *American State Papers, Class I: Foreign Relations.* 6 vols. Washington, D.C., 1833–1859.

ASPIA   *American State Papers, Class II: Indian Affairs.* 2 vols. Washington, D.C., 1832.

CIL   "Creek Indian Letters, Talks, and Treaties, 1705–1839." Edited by Louise F. Hays. Typescript in GDAH.

CO   Colonial Office

CRG   *Colonial Records of the State of Georgia.* Edited by Allen D. Candler. Atlanta: Franklin Printing, 1904–1916.

CRG   Colonial Records of the State of Georgia. Edited by Allen D. Candler. Typescript in GDAH.

DIASC   *Documents Relating to Indian Affairs, Colonial Records of South Carolina.* 2 vols. Edited by William L. McDowell, Jr. Columbia: South Carolina Archives Department, 1958.

EF   East Florida Papers, National Archives, Washington, D.C. Microfilm copies in PKY.

FO   Foreign Office

GDAH   Georgia Department of Archives and History, Atlanta

LBH   *Letters, Journals, and Writings of Benjamin Hawkins.* 2
             vols. Edited by C. L. Grant. Savannah: Beehive Press,
             1980.

LBH   "Letters of Benjamin Hawkins, 1797–1815." Edited by
             Louise F. Hays. Typescript in GDAH.

LOC   Lockey Collection, PKY

LTB   "Unpublished Letters of Timothy Barnard, 1784–1820."
             Edited by Louise F. Hays. Typescript in GDAH.

MIPAFD   *Mississippi Provincial Archives: French Dominion.* 5 vols.
             Edited by Dunbar Rowland and A. G. Sanders. Jackson:
             Mississippi Department of Archives and History, 1927.

PC   Papeles Procedentes de Cuba. Archivo de Indias, Seville,
             Spain. Microfilm copies in PKY.

PKY   P. K. Yonge Library of Florida History, University of
             Florida, Gainesville

PRO   Public Record Office, London, England

SCG   *South Carolina Gazette.* Only the later date of each
             weekly newspaper is cited.

SD   Santo Domingo Papers, Archivo de Indias, Seville, Spain.
             Microfilm copies in PKY.

ST   Stetson Collection, PKY

USS   United States Serial Set. These citations refer to con-
             gressional documents and are given in the standard bib-
             liographic form as used by the Congressional Information
             Service.

WO   War Office

Acknowledgments

In the course of writing this book, I have become indebted to many people. Over the past several years, numerous friends and acquaintances have shared with me their thoughts about history, Native Americans, and the Deep South. A list of these individuals would be too lengthy to include here, but I wish to thank them for their assistance, whether offered at conferences, seminars, archives, or dinner tables. Bruce Chappell at the P. K. Yonge Library of Florida History deserves special mention for his kindness during my long stay in Gainesville. He shared with me his remarkable knowledge of the Spanish archives and made my research as productive and trouble-free as possible.

At different times, three organizations provided financial support for this undertaking. The Research Institute for the Study of Man subsidized its early stages with a dissertation grant, and the National Endowment for the Humanities sponsored its completion. Thereafter, a Mellon Fellowship in History at the Society of Fellows in the Humanities, located at Columbia University, afforded me the time and space to turn my dissertation into a finished manuscript. I am grateful to these institutions for their support. I also thank the editors at Cambridge University Press for their assistance in producing this book.[1]

When I was in the final stages of writing, Lil Fenn generously took time from working on her own manuscript to offer much-appreciated editorial advice. Peter Wood, above all others, has helped shape this

[1] Portions of this book have previously been published in Claudio Saunt, "'The English has now a Mind to make Slaves of them all': Creeks, Seminoles, and the Problem of Slavery," *American Indian Quarterly* 22, nos. 1 and 2 (1998): 157–180; and Saunt, "'Domestick . . . Quiet being broke': Gender Conflict among Creek Indians in the Eighteenth Century," in *Contact Points: North American Frontiers from the Mohawk Valley to the Mississippi, 1750–1830*, eds. Fredrika J. Teute and Andrew R. L. Cayton (Chapel Hill: University of North Carolina, 1998).

project. Throughout its development (and in fact even before its inception), he has shared with me his incisive knowledge of history. The enthusiasm and insight that he brings to the study of early America first drew me to the subject, and the breadth and clarity of his thought continue to inspire me. I thank him for his intellectual and personal generosity.

Paulette Long and Jerry Long have provided immeasurable support both during this project and in the many years preceding it. I wish I could thank them enough.

Introduction

On the Flint River in June 1801 in what is now Crawford County, Georgia, a United States Indian agent named Benjamin Hawkins spoke to Creek leader Efau Hadjo about a pressing problem: obtaining "supplys for those who from age and old habits could not be immediately benefitted by the new order of things." His concerns reflected a confidence in the future. He would attempt to smooth a rough road – to feed and clothe those lagging behind – but no matter how many were lost on the way, he was certain of the destination. Not all Creeks shared his conviction. Efau Hadjo told the agent that the "old Chiefs and their associates in opposition" not only failed to benefit from the "new order of things," but they in fact hoped to destroy it.[1] This book is about the rise of the new order, a great transformation that overturned Creek lives in the three decades following the American Revolution.

Order and things, or power and property, are its subject. Before the Revolution, individual Creeks neither claimed nor asserted coercive power over their neighbors. Leaders created political order by persuasion rather than force. By the second decade of the nineteenth century, in contrast, a "national council" composed of a few dozen men asserted its rule over every Creek person. The council executed those who disobeyed its orders. A similarly dramatic change occurred in the realm of property. Before the Revolution, Creeks did not strive to accumulate significant amounts of material possessions or to protect and defend their belongings from their neighbors. Yet by the 1810s, a few people had thousands of dollars and hundreds of cattle and slaves. The kind

---

[1] Benjamin Hawkins to Henry Dearborn, 1 June 1801, in C.L. Grant, ed., *Letters, Journals, and Writings of Benjamin Hawkins* (Savannah: Beehive Press, 1980), 1:359 (hereafter cited as *LBH*).

as well as the quantity of these new possessions reshaped the lives of Creeks.

In a general sense, the conflict between Creeks over the new order of things might be described in terms of assimilation and tradition, but these two oft-used words in Native American history obscure rather than clarify the tensions in Creek society. The simple dichotomy they present does not reflect the real problems that Creeks confronted. Creeks did not choose between moving forward or backward, or between "white" or Creek cultures. Instead, they faced complicated questions about how they should rule themselves and what kind of economy they should pursue. These fundamental problems extended into all areas of Creek life. Changes in power and property posed difficult questions about Creek identity, aggravated long-standing tensions between women and men, and fomented controversy over the responsibility of individuals toward an inchoate Creek "nation." These and other related themes shape the chapters that follow.

One particular subject deserves to be mentioned at the outset. I argue that Creek mestizos had a profound and disruptive impact on Creek society, and consequently on occasion I point out that individuals had European and Indian heritage.[2] In so doing, I do not mean to imply that culture and biology are linked. Nevertheless, it appears incontrovertible to me that Creeks who were familiar and comfortable with the market economy, coercive power, and race slavery of colonial settlements were disruptive, and that more often than not these Creeks had acquired that familiarity and comfort from their European forebears.[3] Not all mestizos were disruptive, of course. Some rejected the influence of their Scottish fathers (two of the staunchest opponents of the new order were mestizos), and others never knew their fathers in the first place. Likewise, not all disruptive Creeks had European parentage. But despite these qualifications, a strong correlation exists between the response of Creeks to the new order and their family background. To illustrate this point, I use "mestizo" to refer solely to the children of European and

---

[2] One of the few books on Indian history to address the disruptive role of mestizos, albeit in a later period than the one examined here, is Melissa L. Meyer, *The White Earth Tragedy: Ethnicity and Dispossession at a Minnesota Anishinaabe Reservation, 1889–1920* (Lincoln: University of Nebraska, 1994).

[3] Stephen Aron points out that people who lived between American and Indian worlds were as much "cultural breakers" as "cultural brokers." Aron, "Pigs and Hunters: 'Rights in the Woods' on the Trans-Appalachian Frontier," in *Contact Points: American Frontiers from the Mohawk Valley to the Mississippi, 1750–1830*, ed. Andrew R. L. Cayton and Fredrika J. Teute (Chapel Hill: University of North Carolina, 1998), 189.

Native American parents, understanding that early childhood influences rather than genetic material led many mestizos or Scots Creeks to become planters and ranchers.

Geographically, this book covers the broad region of the Deep South occupied by Creeks in the eighteenth century. This region – Creek country – stretched from the ridge dividing the Alabama and Tombigbee rivers east to the Savannah River, and south down the Florida peninsula, an area roughly defined by the present-day states of Alabama, Georgia, and Florida (see Fig. 1). To the north, beyond Creek country, lay the mountainous lands of the Cherokees; to the east, the encroaching settlements planted by Georgians; and to the west, the lands of the Choctaws and Chickasaws. To the south, sparsely populated settlements at St. Augustine and Pensacola gave the Spanish a tenuous but politically significant presence in the region.

Creek country for the most part has fallen under the rubric of Spanish borderlands history, a field pioneered by Herbert Eugene Bolton in the early twentieth century.[4] Bolton found a frontier unexamined by other historians who, influenced by Frederick Jackson Turner, imagined a westward-moving line between "wilderness" and "civilization." Exploring long-neglected archives, Bolton recovered from historical anonymity a lost section of the continent, one stretching from California to Florida. Yet, despite Bolton's efforts, Florida remained neglected by traditional colonialists who rarely strayed far from New England or the Chesapeake. Spanish borderlands history in fact became as historiographically marginal as its subject appeared to be geographically, though any map would reveal that California, Texas, and Florida, to name three areas of the "borderlands," occupy a significant portion of North America.

Following Bolton's lead, I found that the rich records of the Spanish empire still remain relatively unexplored. Spain claimed rights to Florida from 1513, when on Pascua Florida, or Easter Sunday, Juan Ponce de León landed on the unmapped "island," to 1821, when it finally ceded the last of its much-diminished territory in the Southeast. Spanish officers left behind thousands of letters and reports documenting the colonization of this region. These records, familiar to historians of Spanish Florida, but scarcely used by scholars of Indian history and of the early Southeast, reveal new information

---

[4] John Francis Bannon has edited a useful selection of Bolton's works: Herbert Eugene Bolton, *Bolton and the Spanish Borderlands* (Norman: University of Oklahoma, 1964).

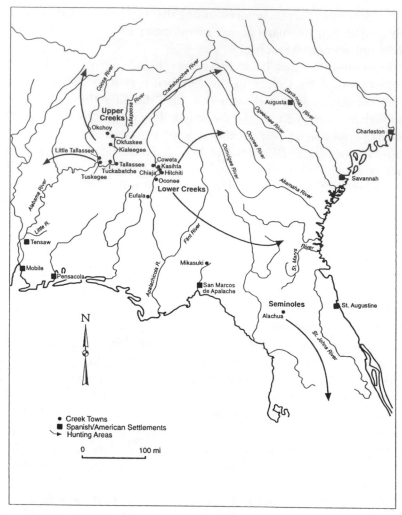

Figure 1. Creek country in the late eighteenth century. Map drawn by Mike Feeney, Campus Graphics and Photography, University of Georgia.

about the Creeks and Seminoles and have yet to divulge all of their secrets.

It is perhaps only the language of the sources that makes the southeastern borderlands "Spanish." Though Spain played a significant role in the history of the area, so too did France, Britain, and the Creeks. The Spanish-speaking population in Florida during the period here under

study fluctuated between 2,500 and 3,500, while Native Americans numbered as many as 16,000 at the end of the eighteenth century.[5] Clearly,
the region was not in any significant sense Spanish. Nor was it a borderland, except from the narrow perspective of Spanish officials in
Mexico City or slaveowners in Charleston, South Carolina. An early
American history that includes native peoples must adopt less biased
language.

Another tradition of scholarship, whose inheritors now call themselves
ethnohistorians, has long recognized the presence of the people who
populated Alabama, Georgia, and Florida before the nineteenth century.
One leading figure in the study of southeastern Indians was John
Swanton, an anthropologist active in the early twentieth century. His
extensive work remains an important source of ethnographic data,
though it scarcely recognizes historical change.[6] Other scholars with a
more chronological bent soon followed Swanton's lead, focusing primarily on Creek removal in the 1830s and its aftermath.[7] Those few who have
given the eighteenth century an intensive examination have generally

[5] Stephen Folch, "Journal of a Voyage to the Creek Nation from Pensacola in the year 1803," 5
May 1803, Papeles Procedentes de Cuba (hereafter cited as PC), Archivo General de Indias (hereafter cited as AGI), Seville, Spain, leg. 2372, 1, reel 436, P. K. Yonge Library of Florida History
(hereafter cited as PKY); Peter H. Wood, "The Changing Population of the Colonial South:
An Overview by Race and Region, 1685–1790," in *Powhatan's Mantle: Indians in the Colonial
Southeast*, ed. Peter H. Wood, Gregory A. Waselkov, and M. Thomas Hatley (Lincoln: University of Nebraska, 1989), 38. When Spain evacuated Pensacola and St. Augustine in 1763–1764,
about 3,700 people were living in the two outposts. In the Second Spanish Period, between 1781
and 1821, the population was close to 2,500. Robert L. Gold, *Borderland Empires in Transition:
The Triple-Nation Transfer of Florida* (Carbondale: Southern Illinois University, 1969), 66–69,
101; David J. Weber, *The Spanish Frontier in North America* (New Haven: Yale University, 1992),
276. For a detailed analysis of the population of Pensacola between 1784 and 1820, see Pablo
Tornero Tinajero, "Estudio de la Población de Pensacola," *Anuario de Estudios Americanos* 34
(1977): 537–562. The low Spanish-speaking population in St. Augustine led this historian to apol-
ogize. "One should say that the small number of residents should not be surprising since Florida,
both East and West, was practically unpopulated" (241n22). He neglected to consider Native
Americans living in the region.
[6] Among his many works, see John R. Swanton, *Early History of the Creek Indians and Their
Neighbors*, Bureau of American Ethnology Bulletin 73 (1922); *Social Organization and Social
Usages of the Indians of the Creek Confederacy*, 42nd Annual Report of the Bureau of American
Ethnology (1928): 23–472; and *Indians of the Southeastern United States*, Bureau of American
Ethnology Bulletin 137 (1946).
[7] Grant Foreman, *The Five Civilized Tribes* (Norman: University of Oklahoma, 1934), and
Foreman, *Indian Removal: The Emigration of the Five Civilized Tribes* (Norman: University of
Oklahoma, 1952); Angie Debo, *The Road to Disappearance: A History of the Creek Indians*
(Norman: University of Oklahoma, 1941). More recently, Michael D. Green has provided
an insightful analysis of Creek politics in the two decades preceding removal. His study begins
with a concise and suggestive summary of Creek history in the eighteenth century. Green, *The
Politics of Indian Removal: Creek Government and Society in Crisis* (Lincoln: University of
Nebraska, 1982).

failed to follow Bolton to the Spanish archives.[8] Their work has suggested
new areas of research, but historians have been slow to travel down the
unfamiliar paths leading into the heart of Alabama, Georgia, and Florida.

Once Creek country is rescued from the obscurity of the borderlands,
we can begin to recognize the relevance of its history to the larger story
of colonial expansion in North America. The transformation of the
Deep South paralleled changes in regions throughout the continent and,
to think even more broadly, throughout the Atlantic world. Historian
Daniel Usner, for example, has described the frontier exchange economy
in the lower Mississippi valley and pointed to its collapse beginning in
1763, and Richard White has written suggestively about the destruction
of the "middle ground" in the Great Lakes region during the same time.[9]
The connections between these two transformations are distant, yet real.
After the Seven Years' War, trade became increasingly commercialized
in both regions, leaving Indians dissatisfied in Louisiana and the Great
Lakes.[10] The dictates of empire came to control events, politically and
economically. And in both regions, political and economic imperialism
paralleled the expansion of biota – European migrants, wheat, white
clover, and cattle around the Great Lakes, and European and African
peoples, indigo, and sugarcane in Louisiana.[11] By the end of the eighteenth century, the rapid pace of change around the Atlantic world was
overturning earlier political, economic, and social relationships in the
Great Lakes region and lower Mississippi valley.

[8] David Corkran has thoroughly explored English-language sources in his work, *The Creek Frontier, 1540–1783* (Norman: University of Oklahoma, 1962). So too has Kathryn E. Holland Braund in her excellent monograph on the deerskin trade, *Deerskins and Duffels: The Creek Indian Trade with Anglo-America, 1685–1815* (Lincoln: University of Nebraska, 1993). J. Leitch Wright, Jr., used Spanish sources in his survey, *Creeks and Seminoles: The Destruction and Regeneration of the Muscogulge People* (Lincoln: University of Nebraska, 1986), but did not do so systematically. Historian Howard F. Cline, working in 1959 for the Department of Justice to defend the United States in litigation brought before the Indian Claims Commission, also used Spanish sources, especially the East Florida Papers. Howard F. Cline, *Florida Indians I: Notes on Colonial Indians and Communities in Florida, 1700–1821* (New York: Garland, 1974); and Cline, *Florida Indians II: Provisional Historical Gazetteer with Locational Notes on Florida Colonial Communities* (New York: Garland, 1974).

[9] Daniel H. Usner, Jr., *Indians, Settlers, and Slaves in a Frontier Exchange Economy: The Lower Mississippi Valley before 1783* (Chapel Hill: University of North Carolina, 1992); Richard White, *The Middle Ground: Indians, Empires, and Republics in the Great Lakes Region, 1650–1815* (New York: Cambridge University, 1992). Peter C. Mancall similarly describes the transformation of the upper Susquehanna region in *Valley of Opportunity: Economic Culture along the Upper Susquehanna, 1700–1800* (Ithaca: Cornell University, 1991).

[10] Usner, *Indians, Settlers, and Slaves*, 274; White, *The Middle Ground*, 264–266.

[11] Usner, *Indians, Settlers, and Slaves*, 281–282; White, *The Middle Ground*, 493. More generally, see Alfred W. Crosby, Jr., *Ecological Imperialism and the Biological Expansion of Europe, 900–1900* (Cambridge: Cambridge University, 1986). Regarding white clover, see Crosby, *Ecological Imperialism*, 158.

Creek country is part of this larger story of dramatic change and disruption. Like other peoples around the Atlantic world, Indians in the Deep South were inextricably linked to far-reaching population movements and economic forces. Consequently, unexpected parallels exist between the experiences of diverse groups of Native and nonnative Americans in the late eighteenth century. When an expanding Atlantic economy pushed into the Carolina piedmont in the 1760s, for example, white hunters and subsistence farmers came under attack by "regulators" who demanded a more ordered market economy. Creeks later felt some of the same pressures when the Deep South fell under the pull of the Atlantic economy after the American Revolution. Tellingly, in the 1790s, the rhetoric of Creek proponents of the new order mirrored that of South Carolina regulators.[12] The same economic pressures were felt all through the Atlantic world.[13] It is not a coincidence, then, that in the 1780s, when a London locksmith named Joseph Bramah developed the first lock with movable wards,[14] Creeks were among those feeling an increased need for such extra security. And it is not surprising that in the 1810s some Creeks divided their Indian neighbors into the "idle" and the "industrious," words familiar to London dock workers in the late eighteenth century.[15] Long after the 1783 Treaty of Paris between Britain and the United States, the forces that propelled the American Revolution continued to disrupt the lives of Creeks.[16] From this broad perspective, the rise of the new order of things in the Deep South is as much a part of the creation of the American republic as is the more familiar history of the independence of the first thirteen states.

[12] Rachel N. Klein, *Unification of a Slave State: The Rise of the Planter Class in the South Carolina Backcountry, 1760–1808* (Chapel Hill: University of North Carolina, 1990).

[13] Peter Linebaugh and Marcus Rediker, "The Many-Headed Hydra: Sailors, Slaves, and the Atlantic Working Class in the Eighteenth Century," *Journal of Historical Sociology* 3 (1990): 225–252.

[14] Peter Linebaugh, *The London Hanged: Crime and Civil Society in the Eighteenth Century* (New York: Cambridge University, 1992), 365.

[15] Ibid., 221–223.

[16] Edward Countryman, "Indians, the Colonial Order, and the Social Significance of the American Revolution," *William and Mary Quarterly* 53 (1996): 359–362.

PART I

Power and property before the new order, 1733–1783

1

Fair persuasions:
Power among the Creeks

In early summer 1735, nearly fifty Native Americans from the Chatta-hoochee River, which now separates the states of Georgia and Alabama, set out for a bluff near the mouth of the Savannah River where new-comers had established an outpost two years earlier. Already familiar with the Georgia colonists, they undertook the 300-mile trip only after a specific request from these new British neighbors. The colonists oblig-ingly gave them "presents" on their arrival, but not before performing a military parade to reassure themselves and convince the Indians that the blankets and shirts were gifts rather than tribute. With ensigns flying and drums marking time, grenadiers and "gentlemen" volunteers marched into the central square of Savannah and fired forty-seven cannons.[1] The guests then responded with their own story about power and authority. Before an audience of "Sundry Gentlemen and Free-holders," Chigellie and Antioche, who both lived in Coweta town, where Columbus, Georgia, now sits, held forth with a story that lasted for two days.

The meaning of the story was lost on the audience, even though Chigellie and Antioche sent an English translation, carefully written in red and black ink on a buffalo skin, to the Georgia trustees in London.[2] One listener described the content of the narrative as the "Rise and some

---

[1] Thomas Causton to the Trustees, 20 June 1735, in Kenneth Coleman, ed., *Colonial Records of the State of Georgia: Original Papers, Correspondence to the Trustees, James Oglethorpe, and Others, 1732–1735* (Athens: University of Georgia, 1982), 20:398–403 (hereafter cited as *CRG*. Type-script editions in the Georgia Department of Archives and History will be cited as CRG).

[2] Scholars long thought that this now-lost buffalo skin featured a pictograph of the history of the Kasihtas, but historian Rodney M. Baine has shown conclusively that it recounted the narrative in English. Baine, "Note and Document: The Myth of the Creek Pictograph," *Atlanta History* 32 (1988): 43–52. For a structural analysis of this myth, see Amelia Bell Walker, "The Kasihta Myth," *Anthropology Tomorrow* 12 (1979): 46–63.

Particular adventures of the Cussitaws," but the story actually told about the present politics of the inhabitants of the Deep South (including the Cussitaws or Kasihtas).[3] In the 1730s, a growing population of 8,000 people, most of whom spoke a language now known as Muskogee, lived in as many as forty towns in what is today Alabama and Georgia. The neighboring French and Spanish colonists, in contrast, occupied a few small outposts and struggled to keep their free and slave populations from dwindling. Spanish Florida, whose key towns were St. Augustine and Pensacola, had only about 2,000 non-Indian residents in the 1730s, and the French settlements in the lower Mississippi valley, notably New Orleans and Mobile, counted a little over 3,700 inhabitants, more than one-third of whom were slaves.[4] In Georgia, the initial 100 colonists who disembarked in 1733 grew to only 1,000 a decade later. Not until the 1760s would the separate colonial populations in the lower Mississippi valley and Georgia surpass the Native American population in the Deep South. In Florida, it would not do so until annexation by the United States in 1819.[5]

Pressing the colonial outposts against the Atlantic and Gulf coasts, the Native American towns of the Deep South lined the banks of two great river systems.[6] One drains what is now central Alabama, where the

---

[3] Thomas Causton to the Trustees, 20 June 1735, *CRG*, 20:398–403. Anthropologists and historians have tried unconvincingly to glean the early history of the peoples of the Deep South from this story. Frank T. Schnell, "The Beginning of the Creeks: Where Did They First 'Sit Down'?" *Early Georgia* 17 (1989): 24–29.

[4] Wood, "The Changing Population of the Colonial South," 38; Usner, *Indians, Settlers, and Slaves*, 48–49.

[5] Wood, "The Changing Population of the Colonial South," 38; Usner, *Indians, Settlers, and Slaves*, 108–115; Weber, *The Spanish Frontier in North America*, 276–278; Kenneth Coleman, *Colonial Georgia: A History*. (New York: Scribner, 1976), 36–54, 223–230. The first territorial census of Florida in 1825 reported a population of 13,544. Five years later, the population had boomed to 34,730. Charlton W. Tebeau, *A History of Florida* (Coral Gables: University of Miami, 1971), 134.

[6] Peter H. Wood suggests that there were about 11,000 Indians in the Deep South in 1730, while J. Anthony Paredes and Kenneth J. Plante estimate there were a little over 7,000 Native Americans in the Deep South. The difference arises from Wood's inclusion of 21 peripheral Indian villages from a 1715 South Carolina census. Paredes and Plante, "A Reexamination of Creek Indian Population Trends: 1738–1832," *American Indian Culture and Research Journal* 6:4 (1983):9; Wood, "The Changing Population of the Colonial South," 38, 58–9. The most precise, if not most accurate, estimate of the Native American population at this time, a town-by-town census taken by the Spanish in 1738, lists 2,073 warriors, or about 7,255 men, women, and children. Given the common relocation and division of towns, it is probable that some settlements were omitted from this accounting. The 1715 census (used by Wood in his estimate) lists 42 towns, for example, while the 1738 Spanish census lists only 33. The average population per town in the 1715 census is 174 people, while for the 1738 census it is 220, so if the Spanish had indeed left out nine towns, the 1738 census may have undercounted as many as 2,000 people. Governor of Havana to Secretary Torrenueva, 28 May 1738, Stetson Collection (hereafter cited as ST), bnd. 5731, 87-1-3/48, Santo Domingo 2593, PKY.

Coosa and Tallapoosa rivers join to form the Alabama River some 150 miles before it empties into Mobile Bay. Though a few towns were located far up and down the lengths of these rivers, most of them clustered just north of the confluence of the Tallapoosa and Coosa, especially along the thirty-mile stretch of the Tallapoosa before it turns north. The other great river system lies to the east. There, the Chattahoochee, which begins near the headwaters of the Savannah, cuts southwest across the present-day state of Georgia and then runs nearly due south. Seventy miles before its waters drain into the Gulf of Mexico, it meets the Flint River of western Georgia to become the Apalachicola. Again, most towns lay in one area, the thirty-mile section of the Chattahoochee River below the site of the present-day city of Columbus.

Native Americans who lived along these rivers had no single word to describe the residents of the Deep South. Outsiders, by contrast, created, borrowed, and transferred names in order to refer conveniently to these peoples. The Spanish, borrowing words from neighboring Indian groups, referred to the residents on the Chattahoochee-Flint as Uchizes and to those on the Coosa-Tallapoosa as Talapusas. "Talapusa," apparently a Muskogee term, is perhaps derived from a word that means "stranger," suggesting that Indians on the Coosa and Tallapoosa did not give it to themselves.[7] Similarly, "Uchize," meaning "people of another language," is an imposed name used by Hitchiti speakers who lived in the Deep South to refer to those who spoke Muskogee.[8] Like the Spanish, the British also distinguished the residents of the Coosa and Tallapoosa from those of the Chattahoochee and Flint, calling them Upper and Lower Creeks. Rather than denoting the respective latitudes of their towns (which in fact were nearly all between the thirty-second and thirty-third parallels), this nomenclature referred to the fork of a trading path from Charleston whose southern or lower branch dropped off toward the Chattahoochee. The term "Creek" itself originally had been the English name for Native Americans living on Ochese Creek, a tributary of the upper Ocmulgee River in Georgia, but traders, retaining only the second word, began applying it to every native resident of the Deep South.[9] In the late eighteenth century, Native Americans in the

[7] Albert Samuel Gatschet, *A Migration Legend of the Creek Indians with a Linguistic, Historic, and Ethnographic Introduction* (Philadelphia: D. G. Brinton, 1884–1888), 145.

[8] Swanton, *Indians of the Southeastern United States*, 219; William C. Sturtevant, "Creek into Seminole," in *North American Indians in Historical Perspective*, ed. Eleanor B. Leacock and Nancy O. Lurie (New York: Random House, 1971), 97–98.

[9] Verner W. Crane, "The Origin of the Name of the Creek Indians." *Mississippi Valley Historical Review* 5 (1918): 339–342; Sturtevant, "Creek into Seminole," 98. On the problem of

region would adopt it as their own along with another name imposed from without, Muskogulge or Muskogee, meaning "people of the swampy ground," a word of Algonkian origin.[10]

Though native residents lacked a word even to express the idea of a nation, Indian and European outsiders did not wholly fabricate the ties binding together the inhabitants of the Deep South.[11] The inhabitants themselves also acknowledged a common bond. They recognized too, as did outsiders, that those living on the Chattahoochee often had interests and priorities different from those living on the Tallapoosa. Though they did not divide themselves into upper and lower groups in the mid-1700s, the useful distinction between Upper and Lower, Talapusa and Uchize, recognizes these differences and locates the residences of Indians in the Deep South. "Upper" and "Lower Creek" and "Muskogee" will be used here as shorthand to refer to these native southerners, the first two terms referring to the geographic distinctions just described and the last referring more generally to the Creeks. Over the course of the eighteenth century, the nature of the bond among these peoples would change dramatically. To understand its composition in the mid-eighteenth century, before a new order swept through Creek country, we should turn to the words of the people themselves. The British, Spanish, and French found their political identities in the person of their monarchs; to illustrate the point, they marched behind standards bearing their kings' arms, as the Creeks witnessed in Savannah. Native Americans in Creek country had a more difficult story to tell about a political system based on persuasion.

Only a brief synopsis exists of the two-day story recounted by Chigellie and Antioche.[12] Though it is shorn of detail and of the performance that shaped its meaning, it conveys important information about the Creeks. Chigellie and Antioche described how their ancestors and those

---

nomenclature in Creek history, see Joel W. Martin, *Sacred Revolt: The Muskogees' Struggle for a New World* (Boston: Beacon, 1991), 6–13; and Wright, *Creeks and Seminoles*, 1–6.

[10] Gatschet, *A Migration Legend of the Creek Indians*, 58–62. Though English, French, and Spanish translations of Creek speeches usually retained the names of different ethnic groups, not one recorded a Creek Indian saying "Muskogulge" in the eighteenth century. Like "Creek," it appears to be a word used by outsiders. Kathryn Holland Braund notes perceptively that since the Creeks "claim to have originated in the drier lands to the west, their designation as *Muskogee* is a relatively new one." Braund, *Deerskins and Duffels*, 193n1.

[11] *Itálua*, the closest word to "nation" in Muskogee, referred to a group of people associated with a ceremonial town center. Sturtevant, "Creek into Seminole," 93, 97; Gatschet, *A Migration Legend*, 156.

[12] The following account is based on Talk of Creek leaders, 11 June 1735, *CRG*, 20:381–387.

of their neighbors and relatives from Kasihta town had emerged from a mouth in the ground and gone east in anger because the earth ate them. After joining with three other peoples and crossing a "red bloody river," they spotted red smoke emerging from a white fire. They took the white fire and mixed it with red and yellow flames from the north. At the source of the conflagration, they discovered four medicinal herbs of war and purification as well as a hissing, burning stick that became their "wooden Tomihawk." While men took the "Physick," or herbal medicine, and went to war, women made fire by themselves, "and learned thereby to be separate at certain times." The four peoples then competed for scalps in a war against their enemies to see who would be the most senior. Not surprisingly, considering the source of the story, the Kasihtas were victorious. Continuing east, they killed a man-eating bird, colored blue, and then followed a white path, "beleiving it might be for their Good." After killing a vicious lion whose bones were red and blue and destroying a town that had returned their peaceful offers of white arrows with red ones, they encountered the "people they had So long travell'd to See," the ancestors of the Apalachicolas, who "told them their Hearts were white, and they must have white Hearts." The "bloody-minded" Kasihtas "Strove for the Tomihawk, but the Pallachucolla people by fair persuasions gain'd it from them and Carried it under their Cabin," a burial of arms that symbolized peace. The Apalachicolas then gave the warriors white feathers and told them they should "be all one with their people." Ever since, "they have liv'd together and shall always live together and bear it in remembrance."[13]

These "Particular adventures" portrayed the identity of the Creeks in broad strokes. Red (and its correlates, black and blue) – as in the bloody river, red fire, red- and blue-boned lion, and red and black letters in which the story itself was recorded – warned the English that the storytellers' people were warriors. James Adair, who began his thirty-year career as a trader with southeastern Indians in 1735, described how warriors stretched human scalps, the "trophies" of battle, on small wooden hoops, and painted "the interior part of the scalp, and the hoop, all round with red, their flourishing emblematical colour of blood."[14] At least one Georgia colonist had already recognized the significance to his neighbors of certain colors. In early 1735, the storekeeper of the

---

[13] Ibid., 386.
[14] James Adair, *Adair's History of the American Indians* (1775; reprint, Johnson, TN: The Watauga Press, 1930), 415–416.

Savannah settlement reported to the trustees that the Carolina agent to the Creeks had "carried Red Colours with him" on a recent journey into the interior of the Deep South. "We find it a Materiall part of the Story," he explained, "because it seemed to them a To[ken] of Warr, and encreased theer Suspition."[15]

"Red hearts," Chigellie and Antioche suggested, were central to the identity of Creek men. If Georgia colonists did not understand, examples were soon to come. In early 1741, Creeks reportedly intended to "roast" one or two Cherokee captives they had taken in battle.[16] Two years later, Creek warriors presented five Spanish scalps and a severed and gloved hand to their English allies, who had been alerted to their success from afar "by the melancholy Notes of their warlike Death-houp."[17] The Chickasaws, ancient Creek allies, according to the Coweta storytellers, shared their admiration for violence. In 1740, they had presented the head of a Spanish soldier to a "disgusted" James Oglethorpe, who refused the gift. One Chickasaw leader responded that if he had carried the head of an Englishman to the governor of Florida, "he should have been used by him like a Man, as he had been now used by the General like a Dog." The Chickasaws departed soon afterward.[18] Having learned from past experience, Oglethorpe received the severed hand from his Creek allies more graciously.

Much as the mythic Kasihtas had established authority and power by bringing home more scalps than their allies, Creek warriors went to war to secure honor and respect. The Lower Creeks, the parish priest in St. Augustine explained in 1760, "respect only the leading warriors."[19] Feats of battle earned young men war titles, such as Itcho Fiksiko Tassikaya (Deer Heartless Warrior) or Itcho Hadsho Tassikay (Deer Crazy Warrior).[20] Luis Milfort, a French adventurer who entered the Deep South in 1776 and lived with the Creeks for some twenty years, reported that in order "to occupy any place whatsoever," men had to take scalps.

[15] T. Causton to the Trustees, 20 January 1735, *CRG*, 21:70–74.
[16] William Stephens, "A Journal of the Proceedings in Georgia," 6 and 7 February 1741, *CRG*, supplement to vol. 4, 85–86.
[17] Edward Kimber, *A Relation, or Journal, of a Late Expedition to the Gates of St. Augustine on Florida . . .* , ed. John Jay TePaske (Gainesville: University of Florida, 1976), 15–16.
[18] Depositions of William Steads, Captain Richard Wright, and Lieutenant Bryan, 13 March, 28 March, and 25 May 1740, in *The St. Augustine Expedition of 1740: A Report to the South Carolina General Assembly*, ed. John Tate Lanning (1742; reprint, Columbia: South Carolina Archives Department, 1954), 116, 129, 125.
[19] Juan Joseph Solana to Secretario Arriaga, 9 April 1760, ST, bnd. 6447, 86-7-21/91, Santo Domingo 2584, PKY.
[20] Gatschet, *A Migration Legend of the Creek Indians*, 160–161.

On returning with his first scalp, he stated, a warrior received a war name in place of the one given by his mother; only then could he begin the search for a wife.[21] According to James Adair, Creeks knew well "the fickle and ungovernable temper of their young men, and ambitious leaders, when they had no red enemies to war with, to obtain higher war-titles by scalps."[22] Years later, a Chickasaw warrior would tell his Creek counterpart, "When men say We are men and waryears I should think they would not care how many Enemies they had."[23] Europeans who described "fickle, rapacious, and vicious" Creeks, as did the governor of Florida in 1734, almost never understood the violence they observed, but despite their ignorance and prejudices, they expressed a kernel of truth.[24]

Notwithstanding the recurring red, blue, and black themes of their narration, Chigellie and Antioche concluded that "they still find the white Path was for their good." White – the path chosen by the story-tellers and their ancestors and the color of the feathers the Kasihtas accepted from the Apalachicolas – symbolized peace. Chigellie and Anti-oche meant to assure the Georgia colonists of their friendship, but they also intended to alert the newcomers to the political alliance that held together the towns of the Deep South. The white path had led the Kasi-htas and Apalachicolas, as well as neighboring peoples, to "be all one." The storytellers suggested that this alliance, whose members claimed diverse ancestries and spoke different languages, existed by choice, not by "ethnic" or linguistic determination.[25] Moreover, it existed by "fair persuasions" rather than coercion. Their conclusion that they "still" chose to be at peace implied that they might change their minds. It warned the English, but also presented an open question to Creeks about which path they should follow in the future.

In the past, political organization in the Deep South had been dramati-cally different from the conditional alliance described by Chigellie and Antioche. Over the previous 300 years, people there had experienced

---

[21] Luis Milfort, *Memoir; or, A Cursory Glance at my Different Travels and my Sojourn in the Creek Nation* (1802; reprint Chicago: R.R. Donnelley, 1956), 109–110.

[22] Adair, *Adair's History of the American Indians*, 299.

[23] Opaymingo to the Creeks, 7 September 1795, ST, PC, leg. 203/49.

[24] Copy of letter from Francisco del Moral Sánchez to the King, 8 June 1734, Santo Domingo Papers (hereafter cited as SD), leg. 844, 264, reel 15, PKY.

[25] Vernon J. Knight, Jr., "The Formation of the Creeks," in *The Forgotten Centuries: Indians and Europeans in the American South, 1521–1704*, ed. Charles Hudson and Carmen Chaves Tesser (Athens: University of Georgia, 1994), 373–375.

as much change as had any Europeans. Its inhabitants had lived in centralized, hierarchical societies in the sixteenth century. Traveling up the Savannah River in 1776, the naturalist William Bartram described "remarkable Indian monuments," the vestiges of these bygone chiefdoms:

> These wonderful labours of the ancients stand in a level plain, very near the bank of the river, now twenty or thirty yards from it. They consist of conical mounts of earth and four square terraces, &c. The great mount is in the form of a cone, about forty or fifty feet high, and the circumference of its base two or three hundred yards, entirely composed of the loamy rich earth of the low grounds.[26]

In Bartram's time, no Creek could remember who had built these enduring structures. Still visible today throughout the South, these mounds testify to the long and varied history of the region's native inhabitants.

Archaeological evidence suggests that hierarchical societies, capable of organizing and directing the labor of large numbers of people, had begun constructing some of the earthworks in the Deep South 500 years before Columbus arrived in the Americas.[27] When the Spanish expedition under Hernando de Soto explored the region from 1539 to 1543, survivors from the *entrada* reported seeing chiefs borne on litters and thousands of subjects at the command of their leaders, observations confirmed by later Spanish explorers.[28] Other evidence also testifies to social stratification in these chiefdoms. A privileged few, for example, were buried next to or in the mounds, and some were interred with valuable objects such as stone axes and copper headdresses or necklaces. In mounds along the Tennessee and Little Tennessee rivers, skeletal evidence from the fourteenth and fifteenth centuries shows that elites were better nourished and more sedentary than commoners.[29]

By the late fifteenth and early sixteenth centuries, these chiefdoms

---

[26] William Bartram, *Travels of William Bartram*, ed. Mark Van Doren (1791; reprint, New York: Dover, 1928), 265. For an excellent annotated collection of Bartram's writings on Native Americans, see Gregory A. Waselkov and Kathryn E. Holland Braund, eds., *William Bartram on the Southeastern Indians* (Lincoln: University of Nebraska, 1995).

[27] Marvin T. Smith, *Archaeology of Aboriginal Culture Change in the Interior Southeast: Depopulation during the Early Historic Period* (Gainesville: University of Florida, 1987), 89–90. A brief overview of Mississippian chiefdoms can be found in Charles Hudson, *Knights of Spain, Warriors of the Sun: Hernando de Soto and the South's Ancient Chiefdoms* (Athens: University of Georgia, 1997), 11–30.

[28] Smith, *Archaeology of Aboriginal Culture Change*, 87.

[29] Ibid., 89–112, 243–244; David J. Hally, "The Chiefdom of Coosa," in *The Forgotten Centuries*, 244.

had collapsed. European diseases such as smallpox decimated the population of the Southeast in the sixteenth century, perhaps destroying the elaborate political, economic, and social hierarchies in the region.[30] But, in the destruction of the chiefdoms, internal dynamics may have been equal to if not more important than the viruses introduced by European and African intruders. In fact, the populations of some chiefdoms began dispersing before Old World viruses made their first journey across the Atlantic.[31] War may have undermined the authority of ruling chiefs by interrupting trade in the prestige goods that legitimized their status. Alternatively, famine, brought on by population growth and soil exhaustion, may have forced residents to abandon mound sites.[32] Whatever the ultimate cause of dispersal, by the end of the seventeenth century, inhabitants of the Deep South had regrouped into towns and villages and had begun forming alliances with each other.[33]

By the eighteenth century, residents of the Deep South identified with their families and towns more than with any larger political organization. Every town was home to several networks of families traced through the female line – "matrilineal clans" in the parlance of anthropologists – each one with an imagined progenitor such as Wind, Deer, or Bear.[34] These kin relations formed a significant part of a person's identity. Deer people identified themselves not as Creeks, but as Deer people. A "hieroglyphick painting" recorded in the early 1770s, for instance, pictures a successful attack by Deer people against a group of Choctaws. The "scalp in the stag's foot," explained the British surveyor who copied the painting, "implies the honour of the action to the whole family" (see Fig. 2).[35]

While Creeks tried to honor their clans, they also drew honor from them. Leaders garnered power from the strength of their kin. The Tiger clan, for instance, was reportedly one of the largest in Creek country.[36] All people in the "Tyger Family are of royal Descent," Emistesigo, a Creek

---

[30] Smith, *Archaeology of Aboriginal Culture Change*, 54–85.
[31] Mark Williams, "Growth and Decline of the Oconee Province," in *The Forgotten Centuries*, 190–191.
[32] Knight, "The Formation of the Creeks," 382–383; Patricia Galloway, *Choctaw Genesis, 1500–1700* (Lincoln: University of Nebraska, 1995), 69–74.
[33] For differing views on the process of the formation of the Creeks, see Vernon J. Knight, Jr., "The Formation of the Creeks," 386; and Smith, *Archaeology of Aboriginal Culture Change*, 129–142.
[34] Swanton, *Social Organization*, 107–110.
[35] Bernard Romans, *A Concise Natural History of East and West Florida* (New York: Printed for the author, 1775), 102.
[36] William McIntosh to Patrick Tonyn, 29 May 1777, enclosed in Tonyn to Germain, 18 September 1777, Public Record Office (hereafter cited as PRO) 5/557, p. 607, reel 66-C, PKY; Arturo O'Neill to Estevan Miró, 21 July 1788, PC, leg. 38, 217, reel 191, PKY.

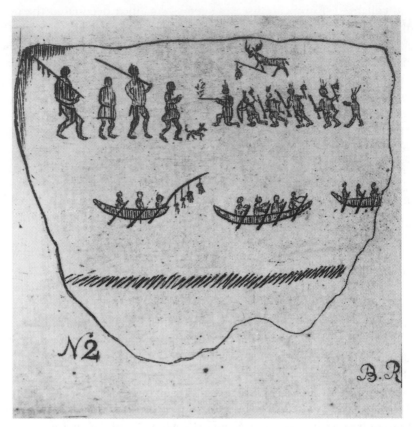

Figure 2. Bernard Romans made this copy of a Creek "hieroglyphick painting" in the 1770s. Courtesy of the Hargrett Rare Book & Manuscript Library, University of Georgia Libraries.

leader, proclaimed to the governor of Georgia in 1768, adding that he was a member of that clan.[37] He did not mean to say that the Tiger clan had a special standing among other clans. Rather, he meant to link himself to the "great King over the Great Water" who, Creeks believed, was also "of the Tyger Family." The lioncel on the Hanoverian bearing had apparently suggested the king's lineage.[38] Aside from the identification with British

[37] Emisteseegoe to James Wright, 5 September 1768, *CRG*, 10:580–582.
[38] Head men and warriors of Upper Creeks to James Wright, 1 May 1771, enclosed in Memorial of James Wright to the Lords of Trade, 1771, CRG, vol. 28, 2:806–815, Georgia Department of Archives and History, Atlanta (hereafter cited as GDAH). Years later, a leader of the Eagle clan would claim a similar relationship with the eagle of the United States. Benjamin Hawkins, "Journal of Occurrences in the Creek Agency from January to the Conclusion of the Conference and Treaty at Fort Wilkinson by the Agent for Indian Affairs," *LBH*, 2:419.

royalty, Emistesigo's reference to the Tiger clan illustrates that his power came from the numerous relations he had throughout the Deep South. In fact, Creek leaders often identified their clans as a source of power. Mortar stated in 1765 that he was "king of the ancient bear family," for example, and Alexander McGillivray wrote in 1777 that his "powerful clan" would lend him influence.[39] Large clans assured Creeks of allies in cases of conflict. In one instance in 1764, British officials pressured Creek leaders to punish a number of Creeks guilty of murdering colonists. The *South Carolina Gazette* observed that the murderers were "all men of such note and influence in the nation (chiefly of the Bear family, one of the greatest in it) that we can have little or no hopes of seeing them punished."[40] The threat of retaliation by numerous kin prevented outsiders, whether of a different clan or country, from punishing the murderers. When at war, observed English visitor Thomas Campbell in 1765, Creeks "never ask any but their own family or clan to go with them." But even within the clan, power was rooted in persuasion rather than coercion; "and these," Campbell continued, "they only acquaint they are going out against such a nation and will remain a certain time at such a creek or hill where those who have a mind will find them."[41]

Despite their particularity, clans did not divide the Creeks against each other. Rather, these imagined kinship networks extended from town to town, uniting residents on the Tallapoosa River with those on the Chattahoochee. "The strongest link in their political and social standing as a nation is in their clanship or families," George Stiggins, the son of a Virginia trader and Natchez woman, would write in the 1830s, explaining that all Creeks are "linked, harmonized, and consolidated as one large connected family." There "is not part of the nation," he would observe, "but a man can find his clansmen or their connection."[42] Moreover, every Creek married someone outside of his or her clan, and though no one switched clan identity, these marital ties created a dense network of interrelationships throughout the Deep South.[43]

[39] "At a Congress held at the Town of Pensacola . . . By His Excellency George Johnstone Esquire Governor of the said Province, and John Stuart Esquire . . . and the Several Chiefs and Warriors of the Creek Indians," 26 May 1765, Lockey Collection (hereafter cited as LOC), PRO, Colonial Office (hereafter cited as CO) 5/582, PKY; copy of a letter from Alexander McGillivray to John Stuart, 25 September 1777, Sir Guy Carleton Papers, reel 58A-4, doc. 677, PKY.

[40] *South Carolina Gazette* (hereafter cited as SCG), 28 January 1764.

[41] Robin F. A. Fabel and Robert R. Rea, "Lieutenant Thomas Campbell's Sojourn among the Creeks, November, 1764–May, 1765," *Alabama Historical Quarterly* 36 (1974): 108.

[42] "A historical narration of the genealogy, traditions, and downfall of the Ispocoga or Creek tribe of Indians, written by one of the tribe," Draper Manuscripts, reel 146I, PKY.

[43] Ross Hassig, "Internal Conflict in the Creek War of 1813–1814," *Ethnohistory* 21 (1974): 255, 264–265.

Native Americans in Creek country also identified themselves by town. Once a year when the annual corn crop ripened (late July or August, according to the Gregorian calendar), town members gathered together for the *Poskita*, or busk, a week of celebration and purification. The *Poskita* focused on the town's square ground, or ceremonial center, where leaders kindled a new fire that women then carried to each household hearth, uniting individual families to the larger community of the town.[44] William Bartram noted significantly in the 1770s that "every town celebrates the busk separately, when their own harvest is ready."[45] Occasionally, Creeks identified with large "ethnic" groupings, as well, but these groupings were declining in importance, as suggested by one native resident in 1753. Conflating ethnicity and geography, he explained that the towns in the region were "divided into three different Parts, that is, we live upon three different Rivers, viz., the Cowetas, the Abecoes, and the Talepooses."[46]

Creek towns and clans were joined by their common commitment to the white path that existed in constant tension with the red. In the words of the Coweta storytellers, Creeks could never completely "leave their red Hearts which tho' they are white on the one Side, are Red on the other." In fact, Creeks divided their towns between red and white groups, or "moieties" in the language of anthropologists.[47] Though both red and white towns made war, white towns appear to have striven more consciously for peace. "As I am one of the White Towns, I am pitched upon to give an answer," the Captain of the Okfuskees told the British when he delivered a message of good will in 1760.[48] The tension between red and white towns and between and even within individuals made alliances conditional and negotiable and made persuasion the root of power. When Creeks discussed treaties, for example, their antagonists heard from leaders from both red and white towns.[49] The rhetoric of British,

---

[44] For historical and modern descriptions of the *Poskita*, see Swanton, *Social Organization*, 546–614.
[45] Bartram, *Travels*, 399.
[46] Proceedings of the Council Concerning Indian Affairs, 28 May 1753, *Documents Relating to Indian Affairs, Colonial Records of South Carolina*, ed. William L. McDowell, Jr. (Columbia: South Carolina Archives Department, 1958), 1:394 (hereafter cited as *DIASC*). J. Leitch Wright presents a different view in *Creeks and Seminoles*. He argues that much of Creek history in the eighteenth and nineteenth centuries can be explained by the division between Muskogee and non-Muskogee speakers.
[47] Swanton, *Social Organization*, 156–166.
[48] *SCG*, 29 March 1760.
[49] See, for example, "At a Congress held at the Fort of Picolata in the Province of East Florida . . . ," 9 December 1765, PRO, CO 5/548, p. 113, in "British Colonial Office Records," 2:574, PKY.

Spanish, or French officials influenced which side would prevail. Relations between Creek towns worked in the same way. When Chigellie claimed he would make the rest of the Creeks "comply" with the peace with Georgia colonists in 1735, his method rested on words: "I have a strong mouth," he said.[50]

The tension between red and white emerged in relations between young people and elders and between men and women. Creeks commonly attributed violence to youth. In 1734, an old warrior explained his initial reluctance to be at peace with the English: When "he was Young, he took delight in War and hunting, and did not mind the Instructions of the Old Men."[51] Similarly, in 1752 Coweta leaders told the English that "they were very sensible that their young People were very ungovernable and committed a great many mad Actions which they ought not to do."[52] Eight years later, Upper Creeks gave the same explanation, that assaults were committed "by a few young fellows, without consulting the headmen of the nation."[53] Having reached "the Years of Knowledge," one Creek leader stated in 1760, he took "great Pains to rule his young People."[54]

On the surface, intergenerational relations could often look frayed. In 1760, when South Carolina and the Cherokees were at war, for example, many young Creeks who wanted to assist the colonists "kept out of the Way of their Headmen," according to the *South Carolina Gazette*, whose editors believed that the Creeks were bitterly divided against one another.[55] Sempoyaffe (Fool Harry), according to the *Gazette*, had even lost the allegiance of his son and nephew, who both went to war against his advice. These young men reportedly told Governor Ellis of Georgia in April that "they could not bear the Sound of War without participating in it, and if [Sempoyaffe] was displeased, they would adopt the English for their Fathers."[56] As the *Gazette* closely followed the apparently divisive debate over neutrality or alliance, Creeks were actually conforming to their usual pattern of decision-making. They would not follow a single path, but would instead explore all forks until one route

---

[50] Talk of Creek leaders, 11 June 1735, *CRG*, 20:386–387.
[51] Journal of the Trustees for Establishing the Colony of Georgia in America, 3 July 1734, *CRG*, 1:177–178.
[52] Journal of Thomas Bosomworth, July–October 1752, *DIASC*, 1:268.
[53] *SCG* (Supplement), 21 June 1760.
[54] A Journal of the Proceedings and Minutes of the Governor and Council of His Majesty's Province of Georgia, 8 November 1760, *CRG*, 8:419–422.
[55] *SCG*, 22 March 1760.
[56] *SCG*, 10 May 1760.

clearly seemed more advantageous than the others. By May 1760, Sempoyaffe had found that path. He arrived in Savannah with twenty warriors and declared his readiness to set out against the Cherokees.[57]

Francisco Luis de Caracas, a Christian Indian, had tried to explain the relationship between young warriors and elders to the governor of Florida, Manuel de Montiano, in 1745. The frustrated governor sought to understand why Lower Creeks continued to attack Spanish subjects despite professions of friendship from their leaders, but Caracas's explanation probably only added to his confusion. Caracas appeared to be of two minds about the matter, and he spoke in contradictions. Creek chiefs, he first suggested, had the power to put an end to the violence and consequently were "guilty of inaction." Yet, Caracas said, "despite that stated above," the chiefs remained "in friendship" with the Spanish as indicated by their refusal to accompany the English against Florida. Caracas then added another layer of ambiguity: Perhaps the reluctance of the Creeks to fight alongside the English reflected a position of neutrality.[58] Caracas's explanation – suggesting one possibility, then the other, leaving the contradiction unresolved – illustrates the tension between young and old, war and peace, a tension that Creeks sought to maintain rather than dissolve, and one that lent strength rather than weakness to their peoples.[59]

Another Christian Indian explained to a Spanish official in the 1750s that a peace concluded with a Creek leader was a peace with that individual only, not with his people. Creek leaders, he stated, "do not have the authority that our governors have."[60] No single Creek chief formulated and promulgated policies toward Spanish, English, or French colonies; rather, young warriors and experienced elders daily negotiated the balance between white and red, one side weighing more heavily than the other according to political circumstances. In 1760, the parish priest

---

[57] *SCG*, 17 May 1760.

[58] Governor of Florida to the King, 17 February 1745, ST, bnd. 6151, 58-2-13/17, SD 862, PKY. Historian David Corkran insightfully writes about the Creek policy of neutrality in *The Creek Frontier*, but does not place it in the context of Creek culture.

[59] According to historian Richard White, Choctaws also found strength in their factionalism. Factionalism allowed them to balance and play off European powers. White, *The Roots of Dependency: Subsistence, Environment, and Social Change among the Choctaws, Pawnees, and Navajos* (Lincoln: University of Nebraska, 1983), 64–68.

[60] Andres Escudero to Castilla y Lugo, 6 July 1759, in "Testimonio de los autos fechos a contesta del coronel Don Miguel Roman de Castilla y Lugo . . . en que da quenta al movimiento de guerra que los Indios infieles Talapuses intentaron," 10 November 1761, Marina, Archivo General de la Nación (hereafter cited as AGN), v. 17, exp. 10, f. 157, reel 144G, PKY.

of St. Augustine, frustrated by constant Creek raids, lost all patience for subtlety: The Lower Creeks, he wrote, "know no subjection, not even to their chiefs, everyone is master of his own actions."[61]

Like elder men, women also whitened the red hearts of young warriors. In 1757, for instance, Daniel Pepper, South Carolina's agent to the Creeks, refused to relay the colonial assembly's decision to grant rewards for the scalps of the French and their Indian allies. Pepper had learned from a Creek leader that "such a Thing might breed a good Deal of Disturbance in the Nation, particularly with the Women, who would alledge that I forced them by such Encouragement to a War."[62] Karl Kroeber, a scholar of American Indian literatures, suggests that one Creek tale about greed and violence, apparently traditionally recounted by women, has an element of "feminine ridicule of masculinity." Women perhaps used such ridicule to control warriors whose rash behavior often endangered entire communities. The opposition of Creek women to the power of young warriors may explain why they often interposed when Creek men threatened to kill traders or other whites in the Deep South.[63] According to one Indian, in the 1740s when Creeks were raiding Spanish and Indian settlements in Florida and returning with scalps, "the wise Indians and the women spoke to them thus: Since now you come to kill some who do not harm us, and who give us food, clothes, and munitions for free when we go to see them, why don't you go to make war against enemies who are the English and leave our friends and relatives in peace."[64] Though Europeans observed only inconstancy and disorder, Creeks saw a healthy tension between female and male, old and young, and peace and war.

If the white path mentioned by Chigellie and Antioche kept Creeks at peace with one another, it did not establish a clear hierarchy of power among or within towns, despite the intentions of some storytellers. Brims, an Indian from Coweta who was styled the emperor of the Creeks by the English in the 1720s, for example, could influence other towns through persuasion, but his power went no further. He had little

---

[61] Juan Joseph Solana to Secretario Arriaga, 9 April 1760, ST, bnd. 6447, 86-7-21/91, SD 2584, PKY.

[62] Danll. Pepper to Governor Lyttelton, 7 April 1757, *DIASC*, 2:363–365.

[63] For two such instances, see "A Journal of the Proceedings and Minutes of the Governor and Council of His Majesty's Province of Georgia," 26 May 1760, *CRG*, 8:314–317; *SCG*, 31 May 1760; *SCG*, 7 March 1761; *SCG*, 14 March 1761. Also see Jean Bernard Bossu, *Jean Bernard Bossu's Travels in the Interior of North America, 1751–1762*, ed. and trans. Seymour Feiler (Norman: University of Oklahoma, 1962), 139.

[64] Governor of Florida to the King, 17 February 1745, ST, bnd. 6151, 58-2-13/17, SD 862, PKY.

recourse when in 1725 his Yamasee allies, a non-Muskogee people, suffered an attack by a party of Creeks from Kasihta, who lived just below
him.[65] Later, when Brims decided to break with the Yamasees, some
Creek towns near Coweta warned them of the impending assault.[66]
Brims himself recognized the flexibility of the ties binding Creeks
together. "The Tallapoop's and Abecas may do as they please," he said
in 1725, referring to the recent reconciliation of his Upper Creek allies
with the Cherokees, "But we have Nothing of Makeing a peace."[67] If
Brims was an emperor, his authority extended only to the limits of his
own town.

Even within towns, a rigid hierarchy did not exist. James Oglethorpe,
the head of the new Georgia colony, noted that "there is no coercive
power in any of their nations; their kings can do no more than to persuade."[68] "All the power they had," he said of Creek leaders in the 1730s,
"is no more than to call their old men and captains together and to pro-
pound to them the measures they think proper; and after they have done
speaking, all the others have liberty to give their opinions also; and they
reason together with great temper and modesty till they have brought
each other into some unanimous resolution."[69] In 1734, after England
had promoted a Coweta Indian as head of all of the Creeks with a "crown
and scepter and clothes of his position," a Spanish clergyman observed
that "those Indians do not want to become acquainted with so absolute
a master."[70] Creeks who held otherwise felt the disapproval of their relatives. At the end of 1752, for example, an Upper Creek Indian named
Tunape traveled to Coweta to present papers he had obtained in England
making him the king of all the Creeks. Tunape told his audience that the
British monarch would build forts in their towns, well supplied with
arms, munitions, and troops, to defend them against their enemies, and
that they would enjoy "all the freedoms, benefits, liberties, distinctions,
and privileges" of other English subjects. The Cowetas responded
that they wanted nothing to do with the English and gave the pretender

[65] Corkran, *The Creek Frontier*, 68–71; Tobias Fitch, "Journal of Captain Tobias Fitch's Mission
from Charleston to the Creeks, 1726," in *Travels in the American Colonies*, ed. Newton D. Mereness (New York: Macmillan, 1916), 182.
[66] Fitch, "Journal of Captain Tobias Fitch's Mission," 194; John J. TePaske, *The Governorship of
Spanish Florida, 1700–1763* (Durham, NC: Duke University, 1964), 205–206.
[67] Fitch, "Journal of Captain Tobias Fitch's Mission," 182.
[68] Quoted in Charles C. Jones, *Historical Sketch of Tomo-chi-chi, Mico of the Yamacraws* (Albany:
J. Munsell), 45.
[69] Quoted in ibid., 44–46.
[70] Conde de Montijo to Secretary Patino, 19 November 1734, ST, bnd. 5380, 87-1-1/13, SD 2591,
PKY.

a dose of poisonous herbs, leaving him "totally crippled, unable to move."[71]

To most southeastern Indians, the power and privilege of colonial authorities made little sense. In 1754, for example, a Cherokee headman told a party of Creeks that "he hoped it would never be in the Power of one Head Man to create a War Betwixt their Two Nations." When a Creek murdered a Cherokee, he stated, the Cherokees would ask the Creeks for satisfaction "or they would take it of the particular Person who committed the Offence or at least of his Town, but that they never would involve the two Nations in a War."[72] In 1759, after the governor of Florida provoked a number of Creek raids, a Creek leader asked the Spanish:

> Why didn't they kill the micco [governor] as many innocent
> people had to pay for such a bad man, for in their land in
> having someone who was so, everyone would join together
> and kill him.[73]

The Spanish interlocutor responded that "here one cannot because His Majesty had appointed him and ordered that they obey him."[74] With examples of centralized hierarchy so close at hand, most Creeks were certain that they preferred their own system. When the governor of French Louisiana promoted the leader of Coweta as the head of the Indians along the Alabama River, they consequently objected, "claiming that one chief over each village was enough." "In brief," noted a French officer in 1759, "they were unwilling to make any changes at all in their form of government."[75]

Servitude, the companion of power and privilege, also disturbed the Creeks. They had long feared the contamination of their towns by the

---

[71] Copy of letter from Alonzo de Arrivas to Fulgencio García de Solis, 17 July 1754, Historia, AGN, v. 436, exp. 4, f. 6, reel 144G, PKY; Fulgencio García de Solis to Conde de Revillagigedo, 27 July 1754, Historia, AGN, v. 436, exp. 4, f. 1, reel 144G, PKY.

[72] Information of George Johnston, 2 October 1754, *DIASC*, 2:12. Joint military expeditions between Indians and colonists sometimes foundered on the conflicting views about power and privilege that the participants held. Such was the case in 1756 when horrified Cherokees watched a Virginia officer flog a soldier. Gregory Evans Dowd, "'Insidious Friends': Gift Giving and the Cherokee-British Alliance in the Seven Years' War," in *Contact Points: American Frontiers from the Mohawk Valley to the Mississippi, 1750–1830*, ed. Andrew R. L. Cayton and Fredrika J. Teute (Chapel Hill: University of North Carolina, 1998), 128–129.

[73] Juan Joseph Solana to Secretary Arriaga, 9 April 1760, ST, bnd. 6447, 86-7-21/91, SD 2584, PKY.

[74] Ibid.

[75] *Jean Bernard Bossu's Travels*, 152–153.

coercive order they witnessed during their visits to South Carolina, Spanish Florida, and Georgia. In the early eighteenth century, they had observed with alarm the settlement and development of slave colonies around the fringes of Creek country.[76] They were well aware that southeastern Indians had been enslaved on the earliest English plantations in the region and exported regularly to the West Indies in exchange for African slaves.[77] During a particularly tense time in British–Creek relations in 1747, Creek leader Chigellie recalled the words of his father, "that the English were come from the East, to settle upon our Lands, the Spaniards towards the South, and the French towards the West. . . . I wish you may not see the Day when they will be for taking your Lands from you, and making Slaves of your Wives and Children."[78] Other Creeks, such as the Mortar of Okchoy, expressed similar concerns. In 1756, he returned from the Cherokees with a talk "which is that the English has now a Mind to make Slaves of them all, for [they] have already filled their nation with English Forts and great Guns, Negroes and Cattle."[79]

At times, Creeks manifested a deeper, inner fear of slavery. In August 1739, Quilate, a leading warrior from the town of Apalachicola, informed the Spanish commandant at Fort San Marcos in Apalache (in the Florida panhandle) that "the English had gone with more than 100 Negroes to construct a fort; that these had risen up and killed all the English."[80] In fact, there had been no such uprising.[81] But Quilate's report reflected the rumors and fears swirling through the towns of the Deep South. South Carolina was at the same time rife with rumors of slave conspiracies and would in a few weeks experience its most serious slave uprising of the century. When Creeks had visited Carolinians during their winter hunts

---

[76] The sentiments of Creeks in the eighteenth century mirrored those of the Osage in the early nineteenth century. In 1820, Big Soldier, an Osage, stated to his American audience: "You are surrounded by slaves. Everything about you is in chains, and you are slaves yourselves. I hear I should exchange my presents for yours. I too should become a slave." Quoted in Willard H. Rollings, *An Ethnohistorical Study of Hegemony on the Prairie-Plains* (Columbia: University of Missouri, 1992), 67.

[77] Peter H. Wood, *Black Majority: Negroes in Colonial South Carolina from 1670 through the Stono Rebellion* (New York: Norton, 1974), 39; William Little Ramsey III, "'Heathenish Combination': The Natives of the North American Southeast during the Era of the Yamasee War" (Ph.D. diss., Tulane University, 1998), chap. 5.

[78] A Speech made by Malatchi Opiya Mico to Alexander Heron, 7 December 1747, CRG, 36:322, GDAH.

[79] Creek Traders to Governor Lyttelton, 31 July 1756, *DIASC*, 2:152.

[80] Manuel de Montiano to Juan Francisco de Güemes y Horcasitas, 19 August 1739, East Florida Papers (hereafter cited as EF), bnd. 37, 157, reel 15, PKY.

[81] Manuel de Montiano to Juan Francisco de Güemes y Horcasitas, 20 November 1739, EF, bnd. 37, 167, reel 15, PKY.

earlier in the year, they had likely been exposed to the climate of oppression and fear that had already settled on the colony.[82] Moreover, James Oglethorpe and a retinue of about twenty-five people were at the time of Quilate's report visiting Coweta and Kasihta to confirm a Creek alliance with Georgia.[83] Lower Creeks welcomed their guests, but at the same time proclaimed their own authority and independence. At Coweta, they greeted Oglethorpe with a dance, illustrating their war exploits, and in the subsequent negotiations they asserted the land rights of their people "who have maintained Possession of the said Right agst all oposers by Warr and can shew the heaps of Bones of their Enemies Slain by them in Defence of their Lands."[84]

Other Creeks shared Quilate's fears. In 1756, Creeks reportedly felt the "great Terror" that spread among the Cherokee Indians when a "large Quantity of Iron" was transported from Charleston to Fort Prince George on the east bank of Keowee River near the Cherokee town of Keowee (eleven miles southwest of modern Pickens, South Carolina). According to the fort's commander, the Cherokees, who sent word of the shipment to the Creeks, imagined that the iron was "brought up on Purpose to put them in Irons and make them Prisoners."[85] Most Creeks "look upon the Words Fort and Slavery as synonomous Terms," an English agent explained.[86]

The social oppression that Creeks witnessed on the rice plantations of South Carolina made them particularly wary of the numerous and expansive English relative to the small Spanish outpost at St. Augustine. In 1738, Lower Creek leaders agreed that they preferred that the masters of the land be the Spanish who "enslave no one as the English do."[87] One Spanish officer recalled that when eight Crecks had visited Governor Francisco del Moral y Sánchez in St. Augustine in the mid 1730s, they said that "trade with the English was not what they most desired, nor did it agree with them that they went in their towns, fearing that with the passage of time they could subjugate them, resulting in the

[82] Wood, *Black Majority*, 308–314.
[83] Phinizy Spalding, *Oglethorpe in America* (Chicago: University of Chicago, 1977), 90–91.
[84] "A Ranger's Report of Travels with General Oglethorpe, 1739–1742," in *Travels in the American Colonies*, 220; Proceedings of the Assembled Estates of all the Lower Creek Nation, 11 August 1739, *CRG*, 26:485–489.
[85] Captain Raymond Demere to Governor Lyttelton, 12 September 1756, *DIASC*, 2:200; Headmen of the Upper Creek Nation to Governor Lyttelton, 9 August 1756, *DIASC*, 2:153–154.
[86] Daniel Pepper to Governor Lyttelton, 21 December 1756, *DIASC*, 2:297–300. Also see Daniel Pepper to Governor Lyttelton, 30 November 1756, *DIASC*, 2:295–297.
[87] Governor of Havana to Secretary Torrenueva, 28 May 1738, ST, bnd. 5731, 87-1-3/48, SD 2593, PKY.

injury of enslaving them." Another Spanish officer familiar with the
Creeks reported that they believed the English encouraged them to make
war with the end of "subjugating the few who remain and enslaving
their women and children."[88] These fears explain the behavior of a party
of Spanish-allied Indians who captured a "settlement Indian" from
Georgia in 1742. The captive later reported that "they kept him Prisoner five days but as he spoke Indian and pretended to be a Slave they
intrusted him with Arms telling him they were Freinds to all Slaves and
He under pretence of hunting made his escape."[89]

Creeks, who did not use bondage as a form of social control, noted
how different were their European neighbors. In 1735, during a visit to
Creek country, Indian agent Patrick MacKay wrote to the storekeeper
of Savannah, "Please Send by my Express 4 pair Cuffs with Small
Padlocks. I find a great many Saucey Villians in this Country that dont
incline to Submitt to any Government, and their is an absolute Necessity to make Examples of some for the Terror of others."[90] MacKay had
in mind disobedient traders, but his handcuffs and padlocks frightened
the Creeks as well. In 1725, distrust and apprehension perhaps had led
the leader of Palachuckaly on the Chattahoochee to untie a fugitive
African American recaptured by Tobias Fitch, an agent from South
Carolina. The "King of the Town Cutt the Rope and threw it into the
fire and the King of sd Town Told the White men that they had as good
Guns as they, and could make as good use of them."[91] A few days later,
Fitch complained in the square ground of Coweta that another recaptured fugitive slave had escaped on the return to South Carolina. The
slave fled to an Indian named Squire Mickeo "who Imediatly assisted
him with Cunnue and provissions sufficient to Carry him to Saint
Mallagoes." "Now there Sitts the Squire," an angry Fitch accused; "Let
him Denie it if he dares."[92] But Squire Mickeo apparently had other
concerns. He did not want the social oppression of the colonies to contaminate Creek square grounds. Twenty-five years later, a successor to

---

[88] Governor of Florida to the King, 17 February 1745, ST, bnd. 6151, 58-2-13/17, SD 862, PKY.
[89] The Declaration of Nottoway a Settlement Indian in Georgia, 22 November 1742, CRG, 36:54,
      GDAH.
[90] Patrick Mackay to [Thomas Causton], 27 March 1735, *CRG*, 20:290–291.
[91] Fitch, "Journal of Captain Tobias Fitch's Mission," 205–206. In 1730, one Cherokee expressed
      the difference between Native American and colonial slavery in a vivid image: Objecting to a
      treaty article that stipulated the return of fugitive slaves, he stated, "This small rope we shew
      you is all we have to bind our slaves with, and may be broken, but you have Iron Chains for
      yours." Quoted in Wood, *Black Majority*, 262n85. See also Patrick Riordan, "Seminole Genesis:
      Native Americans, African Americans, and Colonists on the Southern Frontier from Prehistory
      through the Colonial Era" (Ph.D. diss., Florida State University, 1996), 242.
[92] Fitch, "Journal of Captain Tobias Fitch's Mission," 211.

Fitch named Thomas Bosomworth encountered similar resistance. English visitors had recaptured a fugitive slave "sculking about" a Creek town, but the slave escaped and made his way back to Coweta where he disappeared, likely with the assistance of Indians.[93] Even as recently as the twentieth century, a Seminole Indian conveyed the foreignness of captivity in a story he recounted. Indians who went on a journey to the "Breath-maker's home," the residence in the sky of the supreme being, found a panoply of exotic and alien items, including iron chains.[94]

Given the dispersed nature of power among Indians in the Deep South, Creeks had to rely on storytelling to maintain order and unity among their towns. Storytelling, the province of the oldest and wisest members of Creek towns, allowed elders to negotiate with the young. Edmond Atkin, the future British superintendent to the southern Indians, wrote in 1755:

> The old Head Men of Note, who being past the fatigue of War and constant Hunting for their Livelyhood, but on Account of their Age held in great Veneration for their Wisdom and Experience, spend the remainder of their days almost intirely in the Town Round Houses, where the Youth and others daily report; relating to them the History of their Nation, discoursing of Occurrences, and delivering precepts and Instructions for their Conduct and Welfare.[95]

Unlike the stories written in history books, spoken stories are performed before responsive audiences. The storyteller can emphasize certain themes and even alter content according to the reactions of listeners. When political circumstances change rapidly, overnight or even during the course of a narration, storytellers can adapt immediately. Storytelling consequently allowed Creeks to maintain the constant tension between red and white. Authority rested on negotiation as much as control.[96]

Governor James Glen of South Carolina witnessed the Creek

[93] Second Journal of Thomas Bosomworth, October–December 1752, *DIASC*, 1:272, 320. For a discussion on black–Indian contact in the Southeast in the early eighteenth century, see Wood, *Black Majority*, 260–263.

[94] Ethel Cutler Freeman, "A Happy Life in the City of Ghosts: An Analysis of a Mikasuki Myth," *The Florida Anthropologist* 14 (1961): 27–28, 30.

[95] Edmond Atkin, *The Appalachian Indian Frontier: The Edmond Atkin Report and Plan of 1755*, ed. Wilbur R. Jacobs (1954; reprint, Lincoln: University of Nebraska, 1967), 10.

[96] Karl Kroeber, a scholar of ethnopoetics, argues convincingly that myths, and more generally spoken stories, foster rather than constrain the reassessment of "tradition." Kroeber, "Unaesthetic Imaginings: Native American Myth as Speech Genre," *Boundary 2* 23 (1996): 171–198.

political process in 1753, but could not grasp its meaning. He complained about the conduct of Creek leaders:

> They behave unworthy and inconsistent with the Character of Head Men. They dare not speak their own Sentiments even when they are sensible they are in the Right, for Fear of giving Offence to their People, and must say Nothing but what they permit them. Thus instead of acting like Head Men, the Guides and Instructors, they degrade themselves, and put the People in their Place.[97]

Care not to offend and attention to the wishes of the audience are indeed the qualities of face-to-face communication between friends. These Creeks were acting like headmen, not guiding or instructing, but negotiating and persuading. Compared with the great distance between colonial officials and their subjects, Creek leaders and their people, as Glen observed, did occupy the same place.

At a meeting between Muskogees and the commandant of Pensacola in 1758, Acmucaiche, the leader of Tuckabatche, situated on the Tallapoosa some twenty miles upriver from its junction with the Coosa, explained the importance of storytelling as negotiation and social control. Several months earlier, bands of "young Creek men" had raided Pensacola and Fort San Marcos in Apalache despite the existence of a treaty between the two sides. At that treaty, Acmucaiche recalled, they had, like the Apalachicolas in Chigellie and Antioche's story, broken and buried arms beneath the very table upon which the Spanish had written the articles. He explained that since they had "neither books nor letters" to inform the younger generation, their children learned from the "memory that is maintained between the chiefs and leaders."[98] Because memory "customarily becomes confused with time," Acmucaiche continued, the Creeks decided to travel to Pensacola to renew it. He recognized that the symbolic action of the breaking and burying of arms as well as the penning of letters were mnemonic devices, and both had to be preserved. On the present occasion, he gave the governor "a pipe of red stone and two fans of white feathers so that these three tokens are kept in the archive of this government and serve forever as instruments that accredit this firm reconciliation and obligate them to fulfill it."[99] The same sense

---

[97] Proceedings of the Council Concerning Indian Affairs, 28 May 1753, *DIASC*, 1:412.
[98] "Testimonio de los autos fechos a contesta del coronel Don Miguel Roman de Castilla y Lugo . . . en que da quenta al movimiento de guerra que los Indios infieles Talapuses intentaron," 10 November 1761, Marina, AGN, v. 17, exp. 10, f. 157, reel 144G, PKY.
[99] Ibid.

of memory and of loss led the Wolf King to tell British Indian superintendent Edmond Atkin in 1759, "Notwithstanding we have not the
Sense, or Wit of our Forefathers, who tis certain talked good Talks with
the white People, and loved them a great deal, yet we their Offspring
now alive, strive to keep up a good Understanding with them, as well as
we can."[100]

Creek leaders not only told stories but regularly reenacted them and
condensed them into symbolic gestures. When Oglethorpe and his
colonists disembarked in 1733, for example, a Creek Indian had greeted
them, "dancing in Antick Postures with a spread Fan of white Feathers
in each hand as a Token of friendship." "The man with his feathers came
forward dancing and talking," reported an English witness, "which I am
informed was repeating a Speech, the Acts of their Chief Warriours."[101]
Similarly, in 1748, a Creek leader sent the wing of a white heron to the
governor of Florida to confirm a recently concluded peace.[102] In a
meeting in Fusache in 1759, Creek leader Acmucaiche, using "fair persuasions," asked warriors why they would attack Spanish settlements
when the governor "looked on them as sons, satisfying them in every
way possible." After seeing their errors, the warriors washed the red
paint from a fan of white feathers and sent it to the Spanish governor,
much as their mythic ancestors had given and received white feathers to
"be all one."[103] Another Creek leader explained in 1768 that regular visits
tended "to keep up a Remembrance of old Treaties." He, "on that
Account, had visited the Governour of Pensacola, and presented him
with the Tail of a white Eagle."[104]

Storytelling held Creeks together as long as they were listening to one
another, but beginning in the mid-eighteenth century, young warriors
began reporting less frequently to town roundhouses. Warfare and the
growing deerskin trade kept "our young People from coming home,"
Creek leaders stated in 1756.[105] In addition, epidemic disease killed many

---

[100] SCG, 5 January 1760.
[101] Thomas Causton to his wife, 12 March 1733, CRG, 20:15–18.
[102] Manuel de Montiano to the King, 15 March 1748, SD, leg. 845, 561, reel 17, PKY.
[103] Andrés Escudero to Castilla y Lugo, 6 July 1759, in "Testimonio de los autos fechos a contesta
   del coronel Don Miguel Roman de Castilla y Lugo . . . en que da quenta al movimiento de guerra
   que los Indios infieles Talapuses intentaron," 10 November 1761, AGN, Marina, v. 17, exp. 10,
   f. 157, reel 144G, PKY.
[104] Emisteseegoe to James Wright, 3 September 1768, CRG, 10:566–571.
[105] Headmen of the Lower Creeks to Governor Lyttelton, 13 October 1756, DIASC, 2:212–213.
   Kathryn E. Holland Braund ably discusses the effects of the deerskin trade on eighteenth-

of the older Creeks responsible for telling stories to young warriors.[106] Storytelling became less effective as a form of negotiation and social control, and consequently in the 1760s some Creeks, later known as Seminoles, began to settle in Florida away from the storytelling of their elders. The flexible and conditional nature of Creek political organization allowed for such events, but the disruptions of European trade, warfare, and disease encouraged them.

As early as 1725, Creek leaders had noticed that the new sources of wealth supplied by French and English traders were increasing the tension between young men and town elders. Any "young Fellow," complained Brims, who "goes Down and Tell[s] a Find [fine] Story they [get] a Commission and then they Come here and they are head Men and at the Same Time No more [fit] for it than Doges."[107] Coweta leaders echoed Brims's complaint a quarter-century later: The English made "Captains and great Men by Commissions granted them who had no Right to command, which made great Confusion in their Nation."[108] The "old men complain," wrote Atkin in 1755, "that our Traders, who confine their kindness and Civility almost wholly to the Young Hunters for the sake of the deerskins, shew Slights to them which lessen them in the Eyes of their People."[109]

Despite the efforts of leaders such as Acmucaiche to control their warriors, the disruptions of warfare, trade, and disease proved too great. In the 1750s and 1760s, wayward Creeks began to form separate settlements in the Alachua prairie, where the University of Florida and the

---

century Creeks in *Deerskins and Duffels*, 131. The increased emphasis on hunting led Creeks to change the architecture of their houses both to accommodate the storage of large numbers of deerskins and to adapt to new residence patterns. Once Creeks extended their hunting season and spent less time in town, the semi-subterranean winter houses, which demanded a substantial investment in labor, became unnecessary. See Gregory A. Waselkov, "The Macon Trading House and Early European-Indian Contact in the Colonial Southeast," in *Ocmulgee Archaeology, 1936–1986*, ed. David J. Hally (Athens: University of Georgia, 1994), 195. Willard H. Rollings finds that among the Osage Indians in the eighteenth century, there occurred a similar increase in the power and prominence of individual warriors. Rollings, *An Ethnohistorical Study*, 40, 154, 157, 159–168.

[106] At least two epidemics struck the Creeks in the eighteenth century before the outbreak of the American Revolution, one between 1728 and 1733, the other in 1760. Henry F. Dobyns, *Their Number Become Thinned: Native American Population Dynamics in Eastern North America* (Knoxville: University of Tennessee, 1983), 15; Charlesworth Glover to [Middleton?], 17 March 1727/8, Records in the British Public Record Office Relating to South Carolina, 13:116–117, in the South Carolina Department of Archives and History; *SCG* (Supplement), 21 June 1760.

[107] Fitch, "Journal of Captain Tobias Fitch's Mission," 194.

[108] Journal of Thomas Bosomworth, July–October 1752, *DIASC*, 1:305.

[109] Atkin, *The Appalachian Indian Frontier*, 10–11.

suburban malls of Gainesville now sit.[110] The Spanish believed that these
new settlers, who continually harassed them, were renegades, and consequently called them "*cimarrones*," or runaways, perhaps the root word
of "Seminoles." (Alternatively, "Seminole" may originate from the
Muskogee term *ishti semoli*, meaning "wild men.")[111] Manuel de Montiano, the governor of Florida, noted in 1744 that "disobedient" Creeks,
supported by English trading posts, were "not subject to the town governments."[112] Alvaro López de Toledo, a former commandant of Fort
San Marcos below present-day Tallahassee, confirmed this commonly
held belief. The hostile Creeks, he claimed, were "those who, for not
being subject to the government of their towns, are more frequently with
the English, who influence them with their presents."[113] Similarly,
Miguel de Ribas Rocafull, who also served at Fort San Marcos, learned
from Lower Creeks that those who committed raids were "*cimarrones*
who were not subject to their government."[114]

In calling these Indians *cimarrones*, Spanish officers failed to recognize the normal tension between white and red in Creek society, and,
anxious to absolve themselves of responsibility, they too readily believed
the excuses of Creek leaders who told them that their antagonists were
uncontrollable. Nevertheless, they touched on a truth: At some point in
the mid-eighteenth century, the Florida Creeks did become runaways in
the eyes of Creek leaders. The ambiguities of cultural and linguistic
translation obscure the chronology of this process. In the 1740s, for
example, an Ocmulgee leader reportedly complained that the Florida
Creeks were "*cimarrones*, and badly intentioned, similar to those there
are also among the whites whose captains cannot command them, and
that for him it was the same." "As he was no more than one, and the disobedient many," he continued, "he had difficulty bringing about what
he wished."[115] Yet the Ocmulgee leader may not have believed that his
relatives had crossed the flexible bounds of Creek political organization;
a Spanish interpreter had colored his Muskogee words, and he perhaps

---

[110] Creeks had been hunting and warring in Florida as early as 1680. See Verner Crane, *The Southern Frontier* (Durham, NC: Duke University, 1928), 79–81; and John H. Hann, *Apalachee: The
Land between the Rivers* (Gainesville: University of Florida Press, 1988), 264–283.
[111] Sturtevant, "Creek into Seminole," 105; Cline, *Florida Indians*, 1:205–214. The earliest recorded
use of "Seminole" in English is from 1765.
[112] Cédula to the Governor of Florida, 11 February 1744, ST, bnd. 6108, 58-1-25/123, SD 838,
PKY.
[113] Governor of Florida to the King, 17 February 1745, ST, bnd. 6151, 58-2-13/17, SD 862, PKY.
[114] Ibid.   [115] Ibid.

meant not to indict his friends but to describe the normal balance of power among Creeks. Conversely, he might have intended to condemn the Florida Creeks. Leaders recognized that they could not establish working relations with their colonial neighbors without reining in young warriors. Malache, the head of the Cowetas, faced this dilemma in 1754 when he sent word to the governor of Florida: "[I]f by chance the *cimarrones* who go about there say anything to Your Lordship, do not mind them, because if before I made war there, now I am at war with no one."[116] Cowkeeper, a leader of the Florida Creeks, indicated the extent of the distance between his people and the Chattahoochee and Tallapoosa Creeks when he told the governor of Georgia in 1757 that he "had not been in the Nation these four Years." He added that "he was a Stranger to the State of Affairs in the Indian Nation having been so long absent."[117]

By 1763, the governor of Florida recognized that those Creeks now permanently settled in the Alachua region maintained only peripheral relations with their relatives along the Chattahoochee and Tallapoosa rivers. He explained that a recent treaty with the Lower Creeks would ensure peace were it not for the Seminole "towns" of Santa Fe, La Chua, and Satile, which "form a separate community because of their proximity."[118] Florida Creeks and their relatives in the Deep South doubtless had a more complex understanding of their relationship, as indicated by Seminole leaders. In 1767, Cowkeeper said that Upper and Lower Creeks called him "a Wild man," but nearly thirty years later, his successor would still refer to his "mother towns" on the Chattahoochee.[119]

The flexible and conditional nature of Creek political organization confused European observers who struggled to apply familiar terms – nation, confederacy, and king – to an unfamiliar people. We must carefully interpret and question such descriptions. If our language lacks the words to describe the Creek peoples, we might best return to the metaphors of Chigellie and Antioche: Those who buried arms and

[116] "Testimonio de la declaración del Indio Antonio Muono, del decreto y de la carta del Chiquile, o Emperador de las provincias de los Uchizes," 26 September 1754, Historia, AGN, v. 436, exp. 2, f. 11, reel 144G, PKY.

[117] A Journal of the Proceedings and Minutes of the Governor and Council of His Majesty's Province of Georgia, 13 September 1757, CRG, 7:626–630.

[118] Intendente-Gobernador Melchor Feliú to Secretario Arriaga, 20 February 1763, ST, bnd. 6507, 86-6-6/88 SD 2542, SD 2542, PKY.

[119] Cowkeeper to Patrick Tonyn, 27 March 1774, PRO 5/554, p. 55, reel 66-B, PKY; Chief Payne to Juan Nepomuceno de Quesada, 1 July 1795, EF, bnd. 115K9, reel 43, PKY.

followed the white path were Creeks. To understand Creek political organization, we must also refrain from "upstreaming," the term anthropologists use to describe the practice of deducing the past customs of a people from later descriptions. "Upstreaming" tells us that the Creeks had a national council, a police force, and a preeminent leader. But these were innovations that lay in the future. They point to the dramatic changes that would occur in the years following the American Revolution.

2

"Martial virtue, and not riches": The Creek relationship to property

Recalling his travels among the Creeks in the 1770s, William Bartram wrote,

> If one goes to anothers house and is in want of any necessary that he or she sees, and says I have need of such a thing or things, It is only a polite way of asking for it, & the request is forthwith granted, without ceremony or emotion; For he knows he is welcome to the like generous & friendly return, at any time.[1]

To this day, Europeans and Americans have caricatured, idealized, and even invented Indians in order to critique Western civilization. Bartram was not immune from the practice. This collector of plants and seeds who was given the name Puc-Puggy, or flower hunter, by his Creek hosts, surely had in mind in this passage the selfishness and one-upmanship of his Philadelphia brethren.[2] Bartram, however, was too keen an observer to fabricate his description. Despite its romantic overtones, his account suggests that Creeks and colonists had notably different relationships to property. The Creeks' generosity did not create an Edenic world – their enthusiasm for torturing and killing enemies dispels such notions – but it did set them at odds with the expanding colonial settlements. In Creek country, where the possession and accumulation of things meant so little, property could not command people.[3]

---

[1] Bartram, "Observations on the Creek and Cherokee Indians," in *William Bartram on the Southeastern Indians*, ed. Gregory A. Waselkov and Kathryn E. Holland Braund (Lincoln: University of Nebraska, 1995), 160.

[2] Bartram, *Travels*, 218.

[3] Some Native Americans, in contrast to the Creeks, were extremely possessive of their personal belongings. The work of anthropologist A. L. Kroeber in the early twentieth century revealed

Compared with their colonial neighbors, Creeks possessed few material goods in the first half of the eighteenth century. Englishman Thomas Causton, observing the inappreciable difference between the clothing worn by Creeks and their leaders, noted in 1733 that they "maintain very little Distinction." Compared with the Georgia colonists, common Creeks were "almost naked," according to Causton. Leading men wore only "Coats and Drawers and a piece of Cloth tied about their Legs like Boots," while leading women donned "Common printed Calicoe, Jacket and Petticoat without any Head Cloaths."[4] In 1768, Emistesigo assured the governor of Georgia that he indeed was a Creek leader despite his appearance: "[I]n Regard to Indians," he explained, "they are not known by their Dress a King being scarce to be distinguished from a common Man."[5] In addition to clothing, Creek possessions included jewelry, agricultural instruments, cooking utensils, weapons of war, and animal hides. In 1733, when Muskogees welcomed James Oglethorpe to the Savannah River, they sent a gift of deerskins, which, the *South Carolina Gazette* clarified, "is their Wealth." After presenting the hides to Oglethorpe, a Creek emissary explained that "those were the best Thing they had."[6]

Creek houses, owned by the matriarch of each family, also reflected the Creeks' indifference toward possessions. When Tomochichi visited London in 1734, he wondered aloud why short-lived men would erect such long-lived buildings, an attitude that extended to other kinds of excessive property acquired by intensive labor.[7] In contrast to the brick edifices in London, Creek houses were built to last only a few years. William Bartram noted that the residence of Cowkeeper, the leader of Cuscowilla town near the present-day city of Gainesville, Florida, "stood on an eminence, and was distinguished from the rest by its superior magnitude, a large flag being hoisted on a high staff at one corner."[8] Though clearly set apart from other houses, this habitation nevertheless differed

---

that, among the Yuroks on the Klamath River, individuals possessed groves of trees, fishing sites, and even songs. Arnold R. Pilling, "Yurok," in *Handbook of North American Indians: California*, ed. Robert F. Heizer (Washington: Smithsonian Institution, 1978), 8:145–146.

[4] Thomas Causton to his wife, 12 March 1733, *CRG*, 20:15–18. Archaeological evidence confirms Causton's observation that Indians "maintain very little Distinction." See Waselkov, "The Macon Trading House and Early European-Indian Contact in the Colonial Southeast," 194–195.

[5] Emisteseegoe to James Wright, 5 September 1768, *CRG*, 10:580–582.

[6] *SCG*, 2 June 1733.

[7] Jones, *Historical Sketch*, 68. Tomochichi's ancestors, who constructed permanent earthen mounds, had different ideas about labor and material wealth.

[8] Bartram, *Travels*, 163.

only in its size, a reflection of prestige but not riches.[9] Because their
houses were made of tree branches and mud and built on plentiful
land, Creeks did not need land title, sawyers, carpenters, glaziers, and
bricklayers to raise them. The absence of a significant division of labor
beyond that between men and women meant that anyone with the desire
to do so could construct a house as large as Cowkeeper's. Housing, in
short, did not reflect unequal access to labor or building materials.

Some personal possessions, particularly ceremonial clothing and
jewelry, did reflect riches of a kind, as British surveyor and engineer
Bernard Romans recognized when working in Florida in the 1770s. Displaying the temperament of his profession, he calculated the number of
deer hooves adorning the leggings worn by Creek women in a dance,
counting 493 "claws" in one example. With nine dancers each wearing
two leggings, he reasoned, eight hoofs to an animal made a total of 1,110
deer. Romans concluded he had witnessed "an instance of luxury in
dress scarcely to be paralleled by our European ladies."[10] In the normal
course of four years of hunting for meat and deerskins, however, one
man easily could have collected the hooves to adorn a pair of leggings.
Most British, in contrast, could not have acquired in a lifetime of labor
enough money to purchase the silver necklace of a London gentle-
woman. Moreover, because the exchange of goods in Creek country
depended more on kinship, religion, and politics than on the dictates of
supply and demand, valuables such as ceremonial leggings could not
purchase the labor of other people.[11]

Creeks also did not accumulate land. Because the shortage of labor
rather than the scarcity of land proved the greater impediment to
extracting wealth by hunting or farming, Creeks claimed exclusive rights
to acreage only when they were using it. Within each town, women
worked individual plots and took the produce – in the eighteenth
century, gourds, peanuts, sweet potatoes, melons, and rice – for their
families.[12] They claimed rights to the crops their labor produced, not to

---

[9] In societies with dramatic inequalities in wealth, elite housing will be qualitatively different from
common housing. David B. Guldenzopf, "The Colonial Transformation of Mohawk Iroquois
Society" (Ph.D. diss., State University of New York at Albany, 1986), 89–90, 97.

[10] Romans, *A Concise Natural History*, 95.

[11] By comparison, see Richard White's discussion of the neighboring Choctaws. "There was no
market," White writes. "Instead, economic exchange was deeply embedded in the larger cultural
framework of kinship, religion, and politics." White, *The Roots of Dependency*, 41–42.

[12] Daily reports of the two pastors, 9 July 1751, *Detailed Reports on the Salzburger Emigrants who
Settled in America . . . edited by Samuel Urlesperger*, ed. George Fenwick Jones (Athens: University of Georgia, 1993), 15:101–102. This report seems to conflate the individual plots of land in
town and the lands worked in common on the outskirts. Bartram drew the distinction more

the land itself. When towns moved to more fertile locations after the soil had tired, Creeks abandoned any claim to the produce – what scholars call "the rights of usufruct" – on their old plots.[13]

Outside of town, Creeks followed a different practice. "They have large fields around their towns, which they have prepared by communal work," the residents of New Ebenezer on the Savannah River reported learning from Creek visitors in 1751.[14] William Bartram elaborated after visiting the Deep South in the 1770s. On the outskirts of towns, he noted, families had individual plots but farmed them communally.[15] This land, worked in common but harvested in severalty, was not owned as much as used. On an occupant's death, the land returned to public possession. In 1755, after the Upper Creeks had confirmed and reconfirmed a land cession to Mary Bosomworth, they added that she "was an old woman and by the course of nature could not live long," a statement that seemed irrelevant to Georgia officials but that jibed with the Creek practice of ownership by usufruct.[16] The Kasihta King explained in 1771 that "our Land is like our Flesh, but that we could not cover the whole Land ourselves, and that when any Person died they could only rot on one spot of it."[17]

In the case of hunting grounds, Creek towns had certain areas most convenient for the chase, but these were not clearly delineated except when bordering colonial settlements.[18] Bartram wrote, "Every individual inhabitant has an equal right to the soil and to hunt and range over this region, except within the jurisdiction of each town or village, which

---

clearly, stating that in town each house had a small plot for corn, rice, and squash, which was planted earlier to provide food before the general crop came in. William Bartram, "Observations," 158–160.

[13] William Cronon writes of New England Indians that land ownership was based on usufruct. That is, they owned not the land itself but its products. It appears that Creek land use was based on the same principle. Once a plot was abandoned, it thus was senseless to claim any right to it. William Cronon, *Changes in the Land: Indians, Colonists and the Ecology of New England* (New York: Hill and Wang, 1983), 62–67.

[14] Daily reports of the two pastors, 9 July 1751, *Detailed Reports on the Salzburger Emigrants*, 15:101–2.

[15] William Bartram, "Observations," 158–160. See also Bartram's *Travels*, 400–401. John Pope further noted, "Those who live in Townships are Tenants in Common of large extensive Fields of Corn, Rice and Potatoes, which commonly lie on the flat low-Grounds of some River convenient to their Towns." John Pope, *A tour through the southern and western territories of the United States of North America; the Spanish dominions on the river Mississippi, and the Floridas; the countries of the Creek nations; and many uninhabited parts* (1792; reprint, Gainesville: University of Florida, 1979), 60.

[16] Abstract of Proceedings at a Conference, 15 December 1755, CRG, 27:451–456, GDAH.

[17] Head men and warriors of Upper Creeks to James Wright, 1 May 1771, enclosed in Memorial of James Wright to the Lords of Trade, 1771, CRG, vol. 28, 2:807–808, GDAH.

[18] Much has been written on Indian ownership of hunting grounds, but the scholarship has focused with few exceptions on Algonkian peoples in the Northeast. For a succinct review of the literature, see William Cronon, *Changes in the Land*, 227–228.

I believe seldom extends beyond its habitations and planting grounds."
He noted that the Uchees (who lived on the Chattahoochee River),
claiming exclusive property, were possibly an exception.[19] There are
several references scattered in the written sources to the hunting areas
of different towns, but nothing indicates that these were owned in any
other sense than that specific towns customarily visited them.[20]

"Martial virtue, and not riches, is their invariable standard for prefer-
ment," James Adair observed of southeastern Indian men in the mid-
eighteenth century. He continued, "For they neither esteem, nor despise
any of their people one jot more or less, on account of riches or dress."[21]
In the 1760s, however, two factors would begin to change the minds of
some Creeks. The deer population would show signs of decline, forcing
hunters to look for alternative economic pursuits, and a generation of
mestizo Indians, ready to apply the commercial acumen learned from
their British fathers, would come of age.

Before the 1760s, the deerskin trade did little to alter the relationship
between Creeks and property.[22] The trade operated in the context of
long-established Creek subsistence practices. Men hunted as they had
always done, and women continued to farm. With the trade, they participated in commercial exchange to secure some goods, but the market
existed between them and outside traders, not between Creeks. Moreover, Creeks established kin relationships with traders, making the
exchange of goods reciprocal and obligatory rather than purely commercial.[23] In 1745, Spanish officials in St. Augustine, investigating the
activities of their British rivals in the Deep South, found that trade and
marriage were indissoluble. The Spanish learned that they could not
excel at the first without agreeing to the second. Some Creeks explained
that they would not have permitted British men to marry into their fam-

[19] Bartram, "Observations," 146.
[20] See, for example, Governor of Florida to the King, 17 February 1745, ST, bnd. 6151, 58-2-13/17,
SD 862, PKY; Major William Forbes to the Secretary of the Board of Trade, 29 January 1764,
PRO 5/582, p. 189, f. 107, reel 66N, PKY; and "At a Congress held at the Town of Pensacola
. . . By His Excellency George Johnstone Esquire Governor of the said Province, and John Stuart
Esquire . . . and the Several Chiefs and Warriors of the Creek Indians," 26 May 1765, LOC,
PRO, CO 5/582, PKY.
[21] Adair, *Adair's History*, 7.
[22] On the impact of the deerskin trade on Creeks in the eighteenth century, see Braund, *Deerskins
and Duffels*, chaps. 4 and 7.
[23] Despite the concerted efforts of white traders, Native Americans throughout the continent used
kinship to turn commodities into gifts. See, for example, Thomas Hatley, *The Dividing Paths:
Cherokees and South Carolinians through the Revolutionary Era* (New York: Oxford University,
1993), 43–44; and White, *The Middle Ground*, 97–119.

ilies had the Spanish been more active traders.[24] Because goods regularly passed between relatives, these marriages integrated the deerskin trade into long-standing patterns of exchange. Even when actual kin relations did not exist, Creeks, like other southeastern Indians, used the language of kinship to establish mutual ties of obligation among "brothers," "children," and "fathers."[25] These ties demanded that allies exchange gifts rather than commodities. Manuel de Montiano, the governor of Florida, recognized as much in 1748, though he mistakenly blamed the profligacy of the French and English for accustoming the Creeks to expect presents. "The wheel of their disposition turns only on the axis of gifts," Montiano wrote.[26]

Foreign-manufactured goods in and of themselves did not alter the Creek attitude toward riches, though these items replaced some local products, reducing the need for women's labor.[27] Muskogees certainly desired trade goods, as a Creek leader named the Mortar stated in 1765: "In former times, we were entirely unacquainted with the customs of the white people, but since they have come among us, we have been clothed as they are, and accustomed to their ways, which makes it at this day absolutely necessary that we should be supplied with goods."[28] Yet, even with this increasing dependency on foreign goods, Creeks still did not see any reason to accumulate possessions.

With few exceptions, they made conscious decisions to retain practices that prevented the concentration of wealth in the hands of a few people. During the yearly *Poskita* celebrating renewal, for example, they burned their worn-out belongings, and at burials of the dead, they interred the valued possessions of the deceased, at least through the 1760s.[29] As the white husband of one Creek woman learned in the 1770s,

<hr />

[24] Governor of Florida to the King, 17 February 1745, ST, bnd. 6151, 58-2-13/17, SD 862, PKY. See the testimony of Antonio Solana, Laureano Solana, and Francisco Luis de Caracas.

[25] Patricia Galloway, "'The Chief Who Is Your Father': Choctaw and French Views of the Diplomatic Relation," in *Powhatan's Mantle*, 254–278.

[26] Manuel de Montiano to the King, 15 March 1748, SD, leg. 845, 561, reel 17, PKY.

[27] The reduced importance of women's labor, a significant aspect of the deerskin trade that facilitated the later development of a market economy by weakening kin relations, will be discussed in Chapter 6.

[28] "At a Congress held at the Town of Pensacola . . . By His Excellency George Johnstone Esquire Governor of the said Province, and John Stuart Esquire . . . and the Several Chiefs and Warriors of the Creek Indians," 26 May 1765, LOC, PRO, CO 5/582, PKY.

[29] Bartram, *Travels*, 399; Fabel and Rea, "Lieutenant Thomas Campbell's Sojourn among the Creeks," 111. For examples of burials, see L. Ross Morrell, "The Woods Island Site in Southeastern Acculturation, 1625–1800," *Notes in Anthropology* (1965): 1–68; and David L. Dejarnette and Asael T. Hansen, "The Archaeology of the Childersburg Site, Alabama," *Notes in Anthropology* (1960): 2–65.

Muskogees also insisted on sharing goods with their kin. She "drained him of all his possessions," William Bartram wrote, by distributing them "amongst her savage relations."[30]

In 1749, the apathy of some North American Indians toward the accumulation of goods became a subject of parliamentary debate in Britain. The Cree Indians northwest of Lake Superior, members of parliament learned from Hudson's Bay Company traders, responded unpredictably to price incentives. Rather than prompting Crees to bring in more furs, lower-priced trade goods encouraged them to hunt less since fewer furs now yielded the same return. Crees did not have an insatiable demand for property and saw no reason to accumulate more than they needed for the year.[31] Though similar detailed information about the hunting practices of Creeks does not exist, their reluctance to accumulate property strongly suggests that they ignored rational economic incentives much as the Crees did.

Despite the Creeks' indifference toward property, concerted efforts by colonial officials enriched some leaders. Muskogees who accepted bribes and gifts, however, quickly become alienated from their people by relying on outsiders. In 1735, after Tomochichi returned from a visit to England, for example, Creeks took exception to their leader's growing wealth.[32] One colonist noted of Tomochichi that other Indians seemed "to Envy him very much," though "resent" might have been a more suitable word. He explained:

> They say he has Sold them to the English for the presents he
> has received and what he tells them of the Grandeur & People
> of our Nation is a Lye to keep them in Awe, and indeed I
> must Say I could wish Tomichichi and his Wife would Com-
> municate some of his Presents to his People.[33]

---

[30] Bartram, *Travels*, 110. Bartram reported that the Creeks condemned this woman for her character, but, according to Bartram's observations elsewhere, her vice could not have been the compunction to share possessions.

[31] E. E. Rich, "Trade Habits and Economic Motivation among the Indians of North America," *Canadian Journal of Economics and Political Science* 26:1 (1960), reprinted in *Sweet Promises: A Reader in Indian-White Relations in Canada*, ed. J. R. Miller (Toronto: University of Toronto, 1991), 168–177. Closer to Creek country, the Choctaws also lacked the economic motivations expected by Europeans. White, *The Roots of Dependency*, 57–58. See also Cronon, *Changes in the Land*, chap. 4, for an incisive discussion of the difference between the wants of Indians and Europeans in colonial New England.

[32] The Georgia trustees had explicitly made it their policy to promote Tomochichi's authority among the Creeks. Harman Verelst to Thomas Causton, 18 July 1735, CRG, 29:140–3, GDAH.

[33] Thomas Christie to the Trustees, 19 March 1734/5, *CRG*, 20:269–273.

Apakowtski, who had accompanied Tomochichi overseas, remarked that he "makes himself greater than he Should be."[34] Though local Georgia officials recognized the ineffectiveness of enriching Tomochichi, the London trustees reproached them for distributing goods to other Creeks: "You are to know farther that Tomochachi Mico is the Person whom the King, and by his Orders the Trustees intend to employ to all the Indian Nations; & for this purpose it is necessary to give him as much weight as may be amongst his Country Men." The trustees "positively commanded" the Savannah storekeeper "to deliver every Parcel whatsoever of the said Presents to Tomochachi for they belong to him."[35]

Twenty years later, a warrior revealed displeasure at the prospect of leaders who accepted bribes. If European colonies enriched some of the headmen and made them "hearty in their Interest," he stated, "we that are (the Back of the House People) or the People in general might go naked, and of course very miserable."[36] Similarly, in 1757, a Creek woman expressed concern that Creek leaders were putting their own self-enrichment before the interests of the people. Most Creeks believed that these men supported the English, she said, solely because "they frequently went to Charles Town and received great Presents, but as for them they were obliged to buy what they wanted of the Traders at a most extravagant Price, when the French would supply them with Necessaries and take Oil, Meat, and other Trifles in Payment."[37]

More serious threats to the relationship between Creeks and property did not arise until the 1760s when a generation of Creek mestizos came of age and the deer population began to show signs of decline. The children of European men and Creek women had long lived in the Deep South, but not in significant numbers until the mid-eighteenth century. Early traders working out of Carolina do not appear to have spent enough time in Creek towns to have imparted their values to their children. With the settlement of Georgia in 1733, however, Savannah and Augusta traders soon married into Creek families, and by the 1760s, their sons were appearing in public forums, identified as mestizos by outsiders if not by other Creeks.[38] The settlement in Muskogee towns of some 600

[34] Ibid.
[35] Harman Verelst to Thomas Causton, 18 July 1735, CRG, 29:142, GDAH. A similar French policy among the Choctaws also failed. White, *The Roots of Dependency*, 50.
[36] Journal of an Indian Trader, 1755, *DIASC*, 2:70.
[37] Talk of Oxinaa to Captain Raymond Demere, 8 April 1757, *DIASC*, 2:410.
[38] The testimony of Antonio Solana, Laureano Solana, and Francisco Luis de Caracas suggests that marriage between traders and Creek women was a relatively recent occurrence in the 1740s.

whites during and immediately after the American Revolution rein-
forced the Anglo heritage of these rising mestizos.[39] Their influence was
"sufficient to contaminate all the natives," one visitor would conclude in
1791.[40]

The emergence of mestizos attuned to the commercial practices of
European colonists corresponded with the encroachment of colonists
and cattle on Creek lands. These intruders, Muskogees believed rightfully or not, were responsible for ridding the forests of deer.[41] Between
1745 and 1760, the white population in Georgia more than quadrupled,
from roughly 1,400 to 6,000, and by 1775, it had risen to approximately
18,000.[42] White people "spoils our hunting Ground and frightens
away the Deer," Lower Creeks stated in September 1756, repeating their
grievance the following month as well.[43] Three years later, an elderly
leader from Coweta told the governor of Georgia that whites who "have
Guns that will kill Deer as far Distant as they can see them" were "wandering all over the Woods destroying our Game, which is now become
so scarce that we cannot kill sufficient to supply our Necessities."[44]

Cattle presented an equally serious environmental threat by driving

Governor of Florida to the King, 17 February 1745, ST, bnd. 6151, 58-2-13/17, SD 862, PKY.
Documents that identify individuals as "half-breeds" include *SCG*, 22 March, 24 May, and 19
July 1760; At a Meeting of head men at Little Talsey, 10 April 1764, enclosed in James Wright
to the Lords of Trade, 5 July 1764, CRG, vol. 28, 2:86–92, GDAH; At a General Council held
of the chiefs of Fourteen Towns of the Tallapusays and two of the chiefs of the lower Creeks,
enclosed in John Stuart to Thomas Gage, 19 December 1766, Thomas Gage Papers, American
series, reel 140F, PKY; John Ritchy to General Haldimand, 22 September 1767, Haldimand
Papers, MG21/B11, BM 21671, 243/328, reel 59D, PKY.

[39] Governor Vicente Manuel de Zéspedes of East Florida reported, from "reliable sources," that
600 white men had moved into Creek country during the American Revolution. Vicente Manuel
de Zéspedes to Domingo Cavello, 22 June 1790, EF, bnd. 22I2, 114, reel 8, PKY. Historian
Kathryn Braund suggests a lower number, between 300 and 400 white immigrants. Braund,
Deerskins and Duffels, 180.

[40] Caleb Swan, "Position and State of Manners and Arts in the Creek, or Muscogee Nation in
1791," in *Information Respecting the History, Condition and Prospects of the Indian Tribes of the
United States*, ed. Henry Rowe Schoolcraft (New York: Paladin Press, 1855), 5:263. In the 1830s,
Creeks would maintain that their "innate passions and morals" had been "corrupted by the white
men residing among and those having an intercourse with them." "A historical narration of the
genealogy, traditions, and downfall of the Ispocoga or Creek tribe of Indians," PKY.

[41] Richard White illustrates that political, social, economic, and cultural factors all affect the way
humans interact with the environment. The decline of the deer population in Creek country
surely had causes as complex as those outlined by White in Choctaw country, now the state of
Mississippi. White, *The Roots of Dependency*, 83–96.

[42] Wood, "The Changing Population of the Colonial South," 38.

[43] Headmen of the Lower Creeks to Governor Reynolds, 17 September 1756, *DIASC*, 2:191–2;
Lower Creeks to Governor Reynolds, 13 October 1756, *DIASC*, 2:239–40.

[44] A Journal of the Proceedings and Minutes of the Governor and Council of His Majesty's
Province of Georgia, 10 October 1759, *CRG*, 8:160–167. See also At a meeting of the head men
of the Upper Creek nation, 5 April 1763, *CRG*, 9:71–72.

off bear and deer and destroying the canebrakes and grasses that attracted indigenous animals. By the 1750s, South Carolina, with about 100,000 head of cattle, had become overstocked, and ranchers began expanding into the neighboring colonies of North Carolina and Georgia.[45] These large herds soon pushed into Creek country, despite the objections of Muskogees. At the same time, cattle expanded rapidly around Pensacola and Mobile.[46]

Cattle not only threatened the ecology of Creek hunting grounds but also represented a new and prolific kind of private property that could be accumulated in vast quantities. Both as new possessions and as intruders, cattle threatened the very identity of Creeks. If hunting became less viable and Creek men began to abandon the chase for the more sedentary pursuit of ranching, then they would no longer wield the "wooden Tomihawk" described by Chigellie and Antioche. The "old Head Men of Note" whom Atkin had observed in the 1750s would have to earn their "great Veneration" from material riches rather than from "War and constant Hunting." Similarly, women would have to face the intrusion of men into their fields and households.

The complaints of Creeks about cattle reveal a deep anxiety about the potential threat of ranching.[47] In 1771, Emistesigo and other Upper Creeks informed Governor James Wright of Georgia that the Indian trader Lachlan McGillivray had assured that "Cattle should go no farther than your own yards." McGillivray had "came very young to our Nation, and knew well how we lived," Emistesigo said, and "the white people was obliged to be satisfied with the same coarse food that we used."[48] He meant not to extol the virtues of venison over beef but rather to point out that the impact of cattle went far beyond the dinner table. Some nine months later, Indian agent David Taitt reported that "beaver Tooth King and Mad Dog" had complained to him about

---

[45] John S. Otto, "Open-Range Cattle-Herding in Southern Florida," *Florida Historical Quarterly* 65 (1987): 331–332. For an overview of cattle-ranching in the Old Southwest, see Thomas D. Clark and John D. W. Guice, *Frontiers in Conflict: The Old Southwest, 1795–1830* (Albuquerque: University of New Mexico, 1989), 99–116.

[46] Ibid., 102–103.

[47] Tom Hatley notes that Cherokees also used cattle to distinguish themselves from settlers. Deer and cattle "became critical to Cherokee identity," Hatley writes. The rejection of cattle "had at its core the rejection of borrowed elements of material culture, and a return to simpler traditional ways and clarity in human-animal relationships." Hatley, *The Dividing Paths*, 162–163, 214–215. Quote on 214. By comparison, see James Taylor Carson, "Native Americans, the Market Revolution, and Culture Change: The Choctaw Cattle Economy, 1690–1830," *Agricultural History* 71 (1997): 1–18.

[48] Head men and warriors of Upper Creeks to James Wright, 1 May 1771, enclosed in Memorial of James Wright to the Lords of Trade, 1771, CRG, vol. 28, 2:806–815, GDAH.

cattle owned by traders. "The mad Dog is very much against it," Taitt
noted, "and says they were poor before the white people came amongst
them, and they will remain poor, and if the Traders were not poor
they would not come amongst them, therefore if they do like not their
method of living they may return to their own Country again."[49] Like
Emistesigo, who contrasted ranching with "how we lived," these Creek
leaders also suggested that domestic livestock overturned "their method
of living."

In two treaties between the Creeks and Britain in 1763 and 1765, the
spread of cattle was a major Creek grievance. The Mortar of Okchoy
complained in April 1763 that the west side of the Savannah River was
"settled all over the Woods with People Cattle and Horses, which has
prevented them for some Time from being able to supply their Women
and Children with Provisions as they could do formerly, their Buffalo,
Deer and Bear being drove off the Land and killed."[50] Okchoy King,
with a subtle sense of irony, registered his objection to English encroachments by refusing to attend the 1763 Treaty of Augusta. "All the reason
he had for his not coming," a trader explained, "was, that the governor
would not send him a negro boy, to mind his stock."[51] The excuse had
some basis in truth, for Okchoy King did own a few cattle.[52] But at the
same time, he intended to draw attention to the rapid expansion of slave
plantations and cattle ranching. The extent of his irony became clearer
the following year. In 1764, Okchoy King oversaw a meeting in which
the Upper Creeks agreed to cede land to Georgia only on condition that
"you keep your slaves & Cattle within that Bounds."[53] Other Creeks
protested with actions. In 1763, Creeks were accused of "wantonly
killing the people's cattle" during treaty negotiations in Augusta, though
they had been "amply supplied with provision."[54] Two years later, at a
meeting in Picolata near St. Augustine, a Creek named Captain Aleck
registered his protest vocally, insisting that "People may be kept within

---

[49] Taitt, "David Taitt's Journal," 539.
[50] At a meeting of the head men of the Upper Creek nation, 5 April 1763, *CRG*, 9:71–72.
[51] *Journal of the Congress of the Four Southern Governors . . . with the Five Nations of Indians, at
     Augusta, 1763* (Charlestown: Peter Timothy, 1764), 21.
[52] In 1752, Gun Merchant, who was likely the same person as Okchoy King, offered to host a con-
     gress at his town. He stated he "had Cattle enough to kill if the Head Men would wait they
     should be welcome to the best Entertainment his House could afford." Second Journal of
     Thomas Bosomworth, October–December 1752, *DIASC*, 1:312.
[53] At a Meeting of head men at Little Talsey, 10 April 1764, enclosed in James Wright to the Lords
     of Trade, 5 July 1764, CRG, vol. 28, 2:87, GDAH.
[54] *Journal of the Congress of the Four Southern Governors . . . with the Five Nations of Indians, at
     Augusta, 1763*, 42.

bounds cattle cannot, but the owners must endeavour however to keep them within bounds."[55]

Cattle and people continued to encroach on Creek lands, however. In 1771, Creeks recalled that "it was promised that no more Cattle should be drove thro' our Nation but that the Path should be always kept Green," a statement that had a literal as well as metaphorical meaning.[56] Paths were usually described as red or white, crooked or straight, according to the hearts of Creek warriors, but this one had been green until muddied by cattle. That same year Emistesigo complained that several traders were driving cattle through Creek country.[57] Soon after, in early 1772, he again objected to the "good Many Cattle in the Country," and a visitor to Tallassee and Tuckabatche on the Tallapoosa River reported seeing 150 head in these two Upper Creek towns.[58]

Leaders such as Mad Dog, Beavertooth King, and Emistesigo perhaps expressed themselves with urgency because the threat of change came from other Creeks as well as from outsiders. "Indians begin to be fond of cattle," Governor James Grant of East Florida explained in 1767.[59] Most but by no means all of these Creek ranchers were mestizos whose notions of property they had inherited in part from their British fathers, though the declining deer population encouraged others to take up the practice. For example, the Wolf King of Muclasa (near present-day Montgomery, Alabama) had 200 black cattle in the mid-1760s.[60] He claimed that "his bowels were interwoven with those of the white people," suggesting that he considered himself metaphorically, if not literally, of European descent.[61] During the American Revolution, ranching became even more common in Creek country.[62] In the 1770s, British

---

[55] "At a Congress held at the Fort of Picolata in the Province of East Florida . . . ," 9 December 1765, PRO, CO 5/548, p. 113, in "British Colonial Office Records," 2:574, PKY.

[56] Head men and warriors of Upper Creeks to James Wright, 1 May 1771, enclosed in Memorial of James Wright to the Lords of Trade, 1771, CRG, vol. 28, 2:811, GDAH.

[57] "At a Congress of the Principal Chiefs and Warriors of the Upper Creek Nation," 29 October 1771, LOC, PRO, CO 5/589, PKY.

[58] Taitt, "David Taitt's Journal," 504, 508.

[59] James Grant to the Board of Trade, 31 October 1767, PRO, CO 5/549, p. 13, in "British Colonial Office Records," 2:706, PKY; Taitt, "David Taitt's Journal," 539.

[60] Black cattle were descended from Spanish stock. Fabel and Rea, "Lieutenant Thomas Campbell's Sojourn among the Creeks," 108; Joe A. Akerman, *Florida Cowman: A History of Florida Cattle Raising* (Kissimmee, FL: Florida Cattleman's Association, 1976), 13. See also Taitt, "David Taitt's Journal," 539. Twenty years later, in 1772, the Upper Creeks agreed to "let what Cattle the Traders have in this nation Remain alive, but no more to be brought amongst them." David Taitt to John Stuart, 4 May 1772, in Mereness, *Travels in the American Colonies*, 552.   [61] *SCG* (Supplement), 21 June 1760.

[62] Benjamin Hawkins, "A Sketch of the present state of the objects under the charge of the principal agent for Indian affairs south of the Ohio," March 1801, *LBH*, 1:352.

surveyor Bernard Romans observed that the Lower Creeks had "plenty of beef" and raised an "abundance of small cattle, hogs, turkeys, ducks and dunghill fowls."[63] A Spanish visitor to St. Augustine similarly noted after the Revolution that many of the Indians had "formed plantations where they cultivate the soil and raise stock with a portion of slaves that they bought in St. Augustine during British rule, and in Georgia."[64] In fact, in 1776 in revolutionary Georgia, the members of the Council of Safety recommended that Indians be paid in cattle "for their good offices." "We are of opinion this step would answer many valuable purposes," they declared, "and would have a tendency not only of attaching them to our interest from gratitude, but would also be a means of civilizing them, and by fixing the idea of property would keep them honest and peaceable with us for fear of reprisals."[65]

In addition to cattle, African American slaves began to fix Creeks with the idea of property in the 1760s. The slave population in the region surrounding Creek country rose dramatically in that decade. In 1751, Georgia was opened to slavery, and in 1763, English planters began moving into Florida after Britain took control of the colony.[66] Between 1760 and 1775, the black population in Georgia and Florida more than quadrupled, from 4,100 to roughly 18,000, rapidly surpassing the estimated 14,000 Creeks in the vicinity.[67] The weight of numbers dictated that blacks and Native Americans would meet more often. Moreover, the blockades and embargoes of the American Revolution, coupled with the decline in the deer population, forced Creek warriors to pursue new economic activities, including smuggling slaves across their land.[68] Though Creeks had long taken prisoners and disposed of them, either by adopting captives as full family members, killing them to offset the

---

[63] Romans, *A Concise Natural History*, 92–93. William Bartram also described seeing "several herds of cattle" belonging to a Seminole leader in the 1770s. Bartram, *Travels*, 167.

[64] José del Río Cossa, *Descripción de la Florida Oriental hecha en 1787* (Madrid: Sociedad Geográfica Nacional, 1935), 10.

[65] Journal of Council of Safety, 5 July 1776, *Revolutionary Records of the State of Georgia*, ed. Allen D. Candler (Atlanta: Franklin-Turner, 1908), 1:154.

[66] See Wilbur H. Siebert, "Slavery and White Servitude in East Florida, 1726–1776," *Florida Historical Quarterly* 10 (1931): 3–23; and Siebert, "Slavery and White Servitude in East Florida, 1776–1785," *Florida Historical Quarterly* 10 (1932): 139–161.

[67] Wood, "The Changing Population of the Colonial South," 38.

[68] On the disruption of the deerskin trade during the American Revolution, see Braund, *Deerskins and Duffels*, 165–170; Martha Cordary Searcy, *The Georgia-Florida Contest in the American Revolution, 1776–1778* (Tuscaloosa: University of Alabama, 1985), 115, 132.

murder of a relative, or, for a brief period in the first decade of the eighteenth century, trading them to the burgeoning slave colony of Carolina,
they had not significantly exploited the surplus labor of their captives.
By the 1760s, however, a small number of Creeks, often the same people
who took up ranching, began keeping slaves.

The Creeks' abhorrence of coercion coupled with their disinterest in
accumulating property meant that the vast majority of Muskogees
adopted the growing number of runaways who reached them in the
1760s. Formal adoption into a Creek clan gave the newcomer full rights,
but most fugitives received a less inviting welcome, at least until they
had put down roots among the Creeks. Whites described these people as
slaves, but they more closely resembled dependents. When Muskogees
took captives in their battles against Florida Indians, reported a
Salzburger minister from Georgia in 1760, they "killed the old ones and
led the young ones as slaves to their tribe, where they receive the same
treatment as the other Indians and in time marry into the Indian families."[69] In the 1770s, William Bartram reported seeing "more or less"
slaves in every town he visited, but they "were free and in as good circumstances as their masters." All captives were liberated upon marry-
ing Creeks, he said.[70] Until such time, however, Muskogees did not
hesitate to sell their dependents. Blue Salt, for instance, traded David
George, a fugitive from Essex County, Virginia, back to George's master
for rum, linen, and a gun. When George fled to another Creek town,
King Jack took and sold him to a trader.[71]

While the slave colonies continued to expand, colonial officials worked
to "prevent the Indian country [from] becoming an asylum for
negroes."[72] Their struggle suggests the difficulty of discouraging blacks
from fleeing to a place where "slaves" and "masters" could scarcely be
distinguished. After assuming control of East and West Florida in

---

[69] Daily reports of the two pastors, 15–21 October 1760, *Detailed Reports on the Salzburger Emi-
grants*, 17:262–264. See also Manuel de Montiano to the King, 20 July 1747, SD, leg. 866, 534,
reel 46, PKY; Theda Perdue, *Slavery and the Evolution of Cherokee Society, 1540–1866*
(Knoxville: University of Tennessee, 1979), 3–15; Peter H. Wood, *Black Majority*, 38–40; J.
Leitch Wright, *The Only Land They Knew: The Tragic Story of the Indians in the Old South* (New
York: Free Press, 1981), 137–150; Riordan, "Seminole Genesis," chap. 5.

[70] Bartram, *Travels*, 183.

[71] "An Account of the Life of Mr. David George," in *Unchained Voices: An Anthology of Black
Authors in the English-Speaking World of the Eighteenth Century*, ed. Vincent Carretta
(Lexington: University of Kentucky, 1996), 334.

[72] John Stuart to Thomas Gage, 26 September 1767, Thomas Gage Papers, American series, reel
140H, PKY.

1763–1764, British agents asked Creeks not to shelter Englishmen "whether blacks or whites."[73] But Muskogees did not always honor the request. In 1766, James Grant, the governor of East Florida, noted the favorable result of a recent treaty with the Creeks by recounting "a late Instance of their good will." "Our negroes run away from a Plantation," he explained, "crossed the River St John's, and got into the Indian Country, where they fell in with some Indian Hunters, who were very fond of them, and employed them as Servants, but immediately gave them up when they were applied for."[74] Yet the governor of West Florida, George Johnstone, gave a less rosy assessment of affairs only two months later, charging that the Creeks daily stole cattle and were harboring slaves and deserters.[75]

In late spring 1767 in Augusta, British Indian agent John Stuart won a promise from the Creeks to return fugitive slaves.[76] A few months later, however, he still had reason to complain that Muskogees "protect in their country a number of fugitive slaves from the settlements." Stuart instructed Roderick McIntosh, the British agent to the Upper Creeks, to "renew his applications" on the subject.[77] McIntosh met with Upper Creek chiefs several weeks later and received assurances from all but one, who was holding five fugitive slaves, that they would return the runaways.[78] At the same time, Stuart sent word to the Lower Creeks to ask for the "restitution of the fugitive slaves from Georgia who have taken refuge in their towns."[79] By July 1768, Stuart had secured what was from his point of view a successful resolution: McIntosh succeeded in "obtaining restitution of such negro slaves as could be taken, being seven, belonging to this province and Georgia who had taken refuge in the Creek town." Nine others fled from the Creeks, and one was recaptured and scalped by a warrior. "This cannot fail of having a very good

[73] "At a Congress held at the Town of Pensacola . . . By His Excellency George Johnstone Esquire Governor of the said Province, and John Stuart Esquire . . . and the Several Chiefs and Warriors of the Creek Indians," 26 May 1765, LOC, PRO, CO 5/582, PKY.

[74] James Grant to the Board of Trade, 26 April 1766, PRO, CO 5/541, in "British Colonial Office Records," 1:223, PKY.

[75] George Johnstone to Henry Seymour Connay, 23 June 1766, PRO 5/583, 609, reel 66Q, PKY.

[76] John Alden, *John Stuart and the Southern Colonial Frontier: A Study of Indian Relations, War, Trade, and Land Problems in the Southern Wilderness, 1754–1775* (London: Oxford University, 1944), 233.

[77] John Stuart to Thomas Gage, 26 September 1767, Thomas Gage Papers, American series, reel 140H, PKY.

[78] Roderick MackIntosh to John Stuart, 16 November 1767, enclosed in Stuart to Gage, 26 December 1767, Thomas Gage Papers, American series, reel 140H, PKY.

[79] John Stuart to Thomas Gage, 27 November 1767, Thomas Gage Papers, American series, reel 140H, PKY.

effect," Stuart concluded, "by breaking that intercourse between the negroes and savages which might have been attended with very troublesome consequences had it continued."[80]

British officials such as John Stuart wanted to believe they were getting a handle on a very worrisome situation, but Creeks and African Americans continued to encounter one another in the Deep South. In late 1769, for example, whites in the Creek nation captured a fugitive slave, later described in the *Georgia Gazette* as a "new negroe fellow . . . of the Bumbo country." He had learned Muskogee while living among the Creeks and reported in that language that he had run away from Pensacola twelve months earlier. During his residence in Creek country, he had fetched firewood for a "man with a big belly," a task that the African probably preferred to the activities he would have performed in Pensacola, such as felling trees, clearing swamps, cutting roads, planting rice, and making staves.[81] Two years later, Lieutenant Governor John Moultrie of East Florida noted:

> It has been a practice for a good while past for negroes to run away from their masters and get into the Indian towns from whence it proved very difficult and troublesome to get them back. When the Indians were spoke to on that head, they said they only gave them victuals, but that their masters or other white men might come and tie them, which was not to be done easily as they were sometimes sequestered, or recused when attempts have been made to take them.[82]

Like Stuart, Moultrie, who had recently secured the return of seven slaves, commended himself for his successful management of affairs, writing, "I dare say this transaction will soon put a stop to run away slaves, flying into their towns; for they will not seek shelter there when they see that the Indians assist in bringing them back."[83] But even Moultrie must have been skeptical of continued cooperation on the part of the Creeks. For he and other officials surely noticed that several past agreements had failed to put an end to African–Creek relations.[84] As his

---

[80] John Stuart to Thomas Gage, 2 July 1768, Thomas Gage Papers, American series, reel 140H, PKY.

[81] Quoted in Robin F. A. Fabel, *The Economy of British West Florida, 1763–1783* (Tuscaloosa: University of Alabama, 1988), 28–29.

[82] John Moultrie to the Board of Trade, 29 June 1771, PRO 5/552, reel 66B, PKY.

[83] Ibid.

[84] In 1774, Governor James Wright of Georgia concluded a treaty with the Creeks providing for the return of fugitive slaves. In exchange, Wright offered sixty pounds of leather or the equivalent in goods for every wayward slave brought to Savannah, and fifty pounds of leather for slaves

letter reveals, Creeks often had their own ideas about what to do with fugitives.

During the American Revolution, some Creeks began to run a slave trade through the Deep South and to establish plantations. Many hunters participated in the trade to compensate for the collapse of the deerskin market. They had long sold fugitives back to colonists, and the traffic in slaves conveniently met their needs: blankets, firearms, and rum.[85] Other Creeks, by contrast, resembled war profiteers rather than hunters. They took advantage of the disorder engendered by the Revolution to accumulate as much wealth as they could. In some cases, their fathers had given them starting capital. A trader named Sullivan, for example, left his "half breed Indian Boy," some "Negroes & a Stock of Cattle" in the early 1760s, though his son died in 1762 before he could profit from the inheritance.[86] Similarly, in 1776, trader George Galphin drew up a will leaving forty-seven slaves and their offspring to his three mestizo children.[87] (Galphin would not die until 1782.)

These offspring of mixed marriages occupied a different position in the economy of the Deep South than did most Creeks and Seminoles. They worked as traders and factors and thus were one step higher on the chain of debt that extended from London to the trading houses in Pensacola and Georgia, to the traders in the Deep South, and to Creek and Seminole hunters. By virtue of their ancestry and upbringing, they had greater cultural, social, linguistic, and geographic ties to the colonial settlements, traveling periodically to Pensacola and the Georgia trading posts to unload their skins and pick up more trade goods. For these reasons, they knew the price of a black slave better than most Creek and Seminole hunters, and they could more readily purchase or sell slaves in colonial settlements.[88] Moreover, the commodity value of a slave

delivered in Creek country to whites. "At a Congress held at Savannah in the Province of Georgia," 20 October 1774, CRG, vol. 38, 1:343, GDAH.

[85] For example, in 1771, Emistesigo reminded the governor of Georgia that Creeks had been promised one rifle and three blankets for every captured fugitive slave. Head men and warriors of Upper Creeks to James Wright, 1 May 1771, enclosed in Memorial of James Wright to the Lords of Trade, 1771, CRG, vol. 28, 2:808, GDAH. In 1776, the South Carolina Council of Safety considered paying Creek warriors to hunt down and kill slaves who had "deserted" during the war. Peter H. Wood, "'The Facts Speak Loudly Enough': Exploring Early Southern Black History," in The Devil's Lane: Sex and Race in the Early South, ed. Catherine Clinton and Michele Gillespie (New York: Oxford University, 1997), 10–11.

[86] James Wright to the Lords of Trade, 20 February 1762, CRG, vol. 28, 1:604, GDAH.

[87] George Galphin's will, dated 1778, "Creek Indian Letters, Talks, and Treaties, 1705–1839," ed. Louise F. Hays (hereafter cited as CIL), 1:8–15, GDAH.

[88] In the 1790s, for example, a mestizo slaveowner named John Cannard would purchase several slaves in Savannah to work on a plantation he was establishing near the Spanish Fort San Marcos

was more important to them than it was to most Indians. It allowed them to dispose of debts or accumulate hard currency or luxury goods. Scots Indians (the children of Scottish deerskin traders and Creek women) and European American merchants were put out of business if they could not obtain goods on credit.

For Creek hunters, in contrast, debt burdened rather than enriched them. As their obligations mounted, they had as much reason to evade as to satisfy their creditors. Hunters also were less familiar with hard currency, and though they desired some of the same luxury goods as Scots Indian and European American traders, they ultimately had different aspirations. A young hunter, for example, might have valued the prestige that came with the scalp of an African American more than he would have cared for the silver coins that the same African American garnered in Pensacola or St. Augustine. Or, rather than putting a slave to work, he might have preferred to exchange that slave for something more befitting a warrior. As Governor James Wright learned in 1779, while older, more established Creeks intended to hold on to the slaves they had captured during the Revolution, some "of the young or Inferior Indians being in great want of Horses have Exchanged some Negroes for Horses."[89]

The Scots Indian named Boatswain or Bosten, also known as James Latson (Lawson), represents a typical Creek war profiteer.[90] William Bartram used the case of Boatswain to enlighten "those prejudiced, ignorant, obstinant people, that assert that it is impossible for the Cricks to be brought over to our modes of civil society."[91] Boatswain was one of the few Muskogees who owned "Private plantations," located near Hitchiti, a Lower Creek town on the Chattahoochee River, below present-day Columbus, Georgia. From Bartram's 1774 description, it is clear that the mestizo's residence combined the "square ground" layout and open shelters of his mother's Creek world with the frame dwellings familiar to his father:

> There were Three oblong uniform Frame Buildings, and a Fourth Four Square fronting the principal House or Common Hall, after this manner encompassing an area: The Hall was his Lodging House, &c – large & commodious – The

in Apalache. Few other Indians had the motivation or experience to buy slaves in coastal slave markets. William Laurence to William Panton, 15 August 1798, Cruzat Papers, PKY.

[89] At a Council held in the Council Chamber at Savannah, 26 July 1779, CRG, vol. 38, 2:186, GDAH.

[90] Arturo O'Neill, 31 May 1783, EF, bnd. 195M15, doc. 1783–1, reel 82, PKY.

[91] Bartram, "Observations," 157–158.

> two wings were, – one, a Cook House, & the other Skin
> Houses, or Ware Houses – and the large Square One was a
> vast Open Pavillion supporting a canopy, or cedar roof, by two
> rows of columns, one within the other.[92]

During his visit, Bartram and his companion "had excellent Coffee
served up in China Dishes by Young Negro Slaves" and "plenty of excellent Sugar, Honey, Choice Warm Corn Cakes, Venison steak, & Bar-
bacued." Boatswain's fortune had been made in trade, for he carried
deerskins, furs, hides, tallow, oils, honey, wax, and other Native American goods to the Altamaha River, shipped them downriver to Frederica,
and from there sometimes continued on to Sunbury and Savannah. In
the European American settlements, he purchased sugar, coffee, and
"every other kind of goods suitable to the Indian Markets."[93]

Boatswain farmed over 100 acres of fenced land with the help of his
"family" of thirty people, including fifteen black slaves. The slaves,
Bartram recounted, remained in servitude until they married Indians, at
which time they "become Indians, or Free Citizens."[94] Boatswain purchased African Americans in Creek country where they were less expen-
sive than in colonial settlements; few other Muskogees had any use for
them. In 1780, for example, a group of Indians stole a slave named Will
in New Orleans and carried him into Creek country. Eventually, they
"gave" him to Boatswain, likely receiving "gifts" such as cloth, gunpowder, or rum in exchange.[95]

Boatswain had neighbors who pursued wealth just as diligently as
he. John Cannard, a Scots Indian who lived between the Flint and
Chattahoochee, ninety miles below Kasihta and Coweta, would have
"forty valuable negroes, and some Indian slaves" by 1791, as well as
nearly 1,500 head of cattle and horses and between $5,000 and $6,000,
property accumulated "entirely by plunder and freebooting, during
the American war, and the late Georgia quarrel."[96] Boatswain's and
Cannard's economic and cultural ties, like those of other European
American and Scots Indian traders, made them more disposed to profit
from the influx of African Americans into the interior during the un-
stable years of the American Revolution.

[92] Ibid., 156.   [93] Ibid., 156–157.   [94] Ibid., 156.
[95] Estevan Miró to Arturo O'Neill, 16 November 1784, PC, leg. 3A, 694, reel 154, PKY; Arturo
O'Neill to Estevan Miró, 1 December 1784, PC, leg. 36, 1020, reel 184, PKY. Will ran away
shortly afterward and by the end of 1784 was in Pensacola where the commandant had put him
to work on the launches. Loyson, Will's owner, submitted a claim for him, and he was returned
to New Orleans in December of that year.
[96] Swan, "Position and State of Manners," 260–261.

If Boatswain represented for Bartram "our modes of civil society," we can imagine a visit by the naturalist to the abode of a more common Indian in the nearby town of Hitchiti, one who might have participated in the contraband slave trade as a hunter rather than profiteer. His residence, according to Bartram, would consist of "a large oblong house, which serves for Cook-room, eating house & lodging rooms, in 3 apartments under one roof." Another building, set eight to ten yards away, would be two stories high and serve as the granary or provision house.[97] Bartram would be served by his host on an earthenware vessel, not china, and the naturalist would describe not a private plantation of 100 fenced acres, but a public plantation worked in common by the town and divided according to the size of each family. Unlike Boatswain's plantation, Hitchiti had no fences until after the turn of the eighteenth century.[98] Our imagined host, instead of going to Savannah to dispose of his deerskins, would go to Boatswain's plantation. There he would purchase powder and shot, cloth, and perhaps some sugar. Likely, he would be in debt to the mestizo merchant.

The important influence of mestizo men in the slave trade was duplicated by Creek women married to whites. They facilitated the profiteering of their husbands by giving them important connections to the hunters in their clans. Arturo O'Neill, the commandant of Spanish Pensacola, observed that Indians who participated in the smuggling "were Commissioned by some white men married to Indians and resident in the Nation."[99] One such man was Andrew Briset, who appeared in Pensacola on 6 February 1783, dressed and painted as a Creek and accompanied by his Indian wife. After purchasing some sugar, coffee, and biscuits, they drank themselves to sleep with rum supplied by an indigent Englishwoman. Briset later explained to a suspicious Arturo O'Neill that he had worked as a muleteer for the deerskin traders when the British were in possession of Pensacola. (This town was under British rule between 1763 and 1781.) Presently, he said, he was married to the Indian woman and lived in the Creek town of Fusache. They had traveled to Pensacola to sell two slaves, but after becoming drunk had been unable to carry on their business. Despite the pleas of Briset's wife, who belonged to the powerful Wind clan, O'Neill sent the Englishman to New Orleans. If Briset were to be imprisoned, O'Neill explained to

---

[97] Bartram's account can be found in "Observations," 183.
[98] Benjamin Hawkins reported that Hitchiti's satellite villages had fences by 1799, but that Hitchiti itself still did not. See "A sketch of the Creek Country in the years 1798 and 1799," *LBH*, 1:315.
[99] Arturo O'Neill to Bernardo de Gálvez, 24 March 1783, PC, leg. 36, 556, reel 183, PKY.

his superior, it should be in Europe, for should he ever make his way back to the Creeks, he could incite the relations of his wife against the Spanish. If he were freed, the commandant continued, he should be sent back to Pensacola, for it would satisfy his wife's kin as well as the other Europeans married and settled in Creek country. With two or three children by his Indian wife, Briset had to be handled carefully to avoid alienating the Muskogees.[100] His wife thus facilitated the slave trade by providing Briset with sanctuary among the Creeks and protection in the colonial settlements.

The slave trade that developed during the American Revolution led to an unusual cooperation between traditional hunters and war profiteers. Most Creeks, as Arturo O'Neill observed, were "commissioned" by whites, but others were mestizos who acted in their own interest.[101] Throughout the war, the trade reflected this dual character, with Creeks sometimes behaving like profiteers and at other times like hunters of deer.[102] When Governor James Wright of Georgia inquired into the provenance of "thousands" of refugee slaves in Savannah in 1779, for example, he found that "the Indians had Captur'd in Carolina & brought here upwards of 140."[103] Wright called on the Creeks to sell them, but "could not prevail on them to part" with the captives. He explained, "They said they were told by the General before they went into Carolina, that whatever plunder they got should be their own property and that they saw the Kings Army Seize upon all the Negroes they could get – upon which they did the same, and intend to carry them to the Nation."[104] Other Indians teamed up with whites to steal slaves. In the first two weeks of October 1781, a group of Englishmen stole seven slaves in Spanish-controlled Pensacola and fled for Creek country. One of the captives, a sailor, returned shortly afterward and reported that he had escaped from the Indians. Seven other slaves had in fact fled or been carried to the

---

[100] See Arturo O'Neill to Luis Unzaga, 16 February 1783, PC, leg. 36, 567, reel 183, PKY; Arturo O'Neill to Unzaga, 20 May 1783, PC, leg. 1336, 159, reel 361, PKY; Unzaga to Arturo O'Neill, 10 July 1783, PC, leg. 105, 105, reel 205, PKY; and Arturo O'Neill to Unzaga, 21 August 1783, PC, leg. 1336, 179, reel 361, PKY.

[101] Arturo O'Neill to Bernardo de Gálvez, 24 March 1783, PC, leg. 36, 556, reel 183, PKY.

[102] In 1776, for example, a party of Creeks, employed by Georgia rebels, participated in brutal attacks on African Americans who had fled to Tybee Island (at the mouth of the Savannah River) to seek their freedom with British Loyalists. Peter H. Wood, "'The Facts Speak Loudly Enough': Exploring Early Southern Black History," in *The Devil's Lane*, ed. Clinton and Gillespie, 10–11.

[103] James Wright to George Germain, 31 July 1779, *Collections of the Georgia Historical Society*, 3:256.

[104] At a Council held in the Council Chamber at Savannah, 26 July 1779, CRG, vol. 38, 2:186–187, GDAH.

Creeks from Pensacola shortly before.[105] By the end of the month, an exasperated Arturo O'Neill reported of the English that "many of them are known by the Talapusa Indians who come here and to whom without a doubt they report everything that happens, several of them having deserted to the nations with said Indians, bringing with them horses and slaves."[106] A significant number of the English profiteers were former packhorse men who had befriended the Creeks in the 1760s.[107]

By 1783, there was a thriving slave trade in Pensacola.[108] Just before the beginning of the year, the governor of Georgia received a report that "the Indians and white people is constantly carrying droves of negroes" to Pensacola:

> The Spanish Governor buys the chief of them and encourages them to fetch the rest and tell them they shall receive the cash for all they fetch there and likewise horses. The chief of which negroes and horses belongs to good men in South Carolina and Georgia he sends a great many to the Havanah.[109]

In March of 1783, some Upper Creeks who were carrying slaves to Pensacola for sale suggested to Arturo O'Neill that the trade become regular. He accepted the offer with the rationale that the trade would siphon off those slaves whom the English were moving from Savannah to the Mosquito River in Florida. English traders, he reported, steal the slaves and then sell them to Indians or commission the Indians to sell them in Pensacola. "Also," he noted, "the negros run away on their own accord, and six have arrived here whom I consequently consider free."[110] The commandant later reported that most of the slaves brought into Pensacola by Indians claimed to have belonged to the Americans "from whom, they declare, they have been plundered during the course of the recent war, or taken by force of arms by the Indians and English partisans."[111]

---

[105] Arturo O'Neill to Bernardo de Gálvez, 15 October 1781, PC, leg. 36, 249, reel 183, PKY.
[106] Arturo O'Neill to Bernardo de Gálvez, 31 October 1781, PC, leg. 36, 300, reel 183, PKY.
[107] Arturo O'Neill to Bernardo de Gálvez, 20 November 1781, PC, leg. 36, 317, reel 183, PKY.
[108] Arturo O'Neill makes several references to Indians in town to sell slaves. See Arturo O'Neill to Bernardo de Gálvez, 1 February 1783, PC, leg. 36, 514, reel 183, PKY; Arturo O'Neill to Unzaga, 15 February 1783, PC, leg. 1336, 94, reel 361, PKY; and Arturo O'Neill to Luis Unzaga, 16 February 1783, PC, leg. 36, 567, reel 183, PKY.
[109] Patrick Carr to John Martin, 13 December 1782, CIL 1:40–41, GDAH.
[110] Arturo O'Neill to Bernardo de Gálvez, 24 March 1783, PC, leg. 36, 556, reel 183, PKY.
[111] Arturo O'Neill to Josef de Ezpeleta, 31 July 1783, PC, leg. 36, 1244, reel 185, PKY.

The continued flight of slaves into Creek country illustrates that they still found relative safety there, despite the influence of people such as Boatswain. In 1777, the Spanish governor of Louisiana, Luis de Unzaga, for example, reported to his British counterpart in Pensacola on the ease with which slaves from the vicinity of New Orleans crossed over Lake Pontchartrain to British territory where they found refuge among the Indians. Something had to be done, he stated, because the problem was becoming worse with every passing day.[112] The British governor needed no such notice. For slaves were also running from Pensacola. In 1778, Wexford, a carpenter, Harry, a tailor, and Greenwich, a cooper, ran off to Indian country or to New Orleans.[113] When fugitives did not receive the treatment they expected from Muskogees, they took other measures. In 1781, four slaves from the British colonies, who had lived with the Creeks for "a long time," arrived in Spanish Pensacola to secure their freedom, presumably as Catholic refugees. One of them traveled on to New Orleans to see Governor Bernardo de Gálvez about the matter.[114]

Near the end of the Revolution, Georgia officials began pressing claims in Creek country for the return of stolen property, especially slaves. In July 1782, Governor John Martin of Georgia told Hoboithle Micco and other Creek leaders that the Americans had taken Savannah and would soon overrun Charleston and the Spanish lands. Unless the Creeks

---

[112] Luis de Unzaga y Amezaga to Peter Chester, 7 March 1777, PC, leg. 190, 478, reel 261, PKY. Daniel H. Usner discusses slave fugitivism between Spanish Louisiana and British West Florida in his work *Indians, Settlers, and Slaves*, 137–141. On blacks in West Florida, see Roland C. McConnell, "Black Life and Activities in West Florida and the Gulf Coast, 1762–1803," in *Eighteenth-Century Florida: Life on the Frontier*, ed. Samuel Proctor (Gainesville: University of Florida, 1976), 75–90.

[113] [Peter Chester] to Bernardo de Gálvez, 1778, PC, leg. 204, 719, reel 283, PKY.

[114] These fugitives may have been the four former British slaves mentioned by Arturo O'Neill in his letter to Josef de Ezpeleta, 31 July 1783, PC, leg. 36, 1244, reel 185, PKY. See also Arturo O'Neill to Bernardo de Gálvez, 11 December 1781, PC, leg. 36, 373, reel 183, PKY; and Martín Navarro to Arturo O'Neill, 22 May 1782, PC, leg. 83A, 832, reel 442, PKY. Flight into Creek country was of enough concern that Spanish officials thought it necessary to include a specific article addressing the problem in their treaty with the Creeks in Pensacola in 1784. Article eight read:

> We will not admit deserters, nor negro nor mulatto slaves, fugitives of the provinces of Louisiana and Florida, into our establishments; and those who shall present themselves within them, shall be immediately apprehended by us, at the orders of the Governor, satisfaction being made us, for the apprehension by the corps, if the person apprehended be a soldier, or by the master to whom he belongs, if he be a slave.

American State Papers, Class I: Foreign Relations (Washington, 1833–1859), 1:279 (hereafter cited as *ASPFR*).

turned over the British "commissaries and traders, likewise all our negroes, horses, and cattle that are among you," he informed them, they would suffer the fate of those Creeks who had supported the British: The Americans had killed them and had left their bodies "to the ravenous wolves, and the birds of the air, and [their] bones now lay white upon the ground. Their women are now widows, and their children fatherless, and are now left to mourn the unhappy event."[115] In the debates that followed in Creek towns, Thomas Brown, the British agent among the Creeks during the war, urged his Indian allies to ignore the American threats, while the pro-American Creeks endorsed Martin's request.[116] By the middle of December 1782, white traders were quitting Creek country for fear that they would be caught between the two Muskogee factions.[117] According to one trader, most of the Creek leaders were in fact disposed to honor the Americans' request, except for "some roguish disposed Indians, Boatswain by name being one who has carried numbers to Pensacola and sold them to the Spaniards who immediately ship them for the Havana."[118]

Though the factionalism apparently separated American and British supporters in Creek country, a more important schism was emerging.[119] Those who resisted returning the slaves were in many cases whites and Scots Indians who had some use for them, men such as Boatswain. Most Creeks, however, had no need for slaves, and in the face of the threats made by Georgia were willing to turn over those who had been captured during the war. The morality of slavery was not the issue, though perhaps the internal dissension reflected the incipience of race consciousness among a small number of Creeks; in any event, the division that emerged over African Americans would become deeper in the postwar years, and its eventual closure by force of arms would shape the way Creeks and Seminoles thought about property, African Americans, race, and slavery.

The distinction between wealthy Scots Indians and other Creeks was

---

[115] Governor Martin to Tallassee King, 19 July 1782, ST, bnd. 6677, PC leg. 121/40, PKY.
[116] Daniel McMurphy to John Martin, 22 September 1782, CIL, 1:30–2, GDAH; and Richard Henderson to John Martin, 23 September 1782, CIL, 1:33, GDAH.
[117] Patrick Carr to John Martin, 13 December 1782, CIL, 1:40–41, GDAH.
[118] Richard Henderson to John Martin, 23 December 1782, CIL, 1:42–44, GDAH.
[119] Caleb Swan implied that the struggle was a factional struggle for political power in Creek country. The old Tallassee king and his clan, wrote Caleb, "pronounced M'Gillivray a boy and an usurper" after Alexander McGillivray moved to assume control of the nation. Swan, however, drew nearly all of his information from McGillivray himself. In his account, the old Tallassee King thus appeared a hindrance to the enlightened leadership of McGillivray. Swan, "Position and State of Manners," 281.

marked on the land in the closing months of 1783. In May of that year, Arturo O'Neill, the Spanish commandant in Pensacola, reported that "Alexander McGillivray, an English and Indian mestizo, along with several others of this caste, some English traders who lived in the nations, and other Englishmen who are married to Indians, express the desire to live in" Spanish West Florida.[120] They likely wanted to profit from a close relationship with the settlements of Pensacola and Mobile. Six Scots Indian families settled on the Escambia River, eighteen leagues (some fifty miles) above Pensacola. From there they could easily ship their crops downriver to the Spanish settlement and could readily drive their cattle to market as well. "They are among the richest families in the Creek nation," O'Neill explained, "and they have brought with them about 400 head of cattle, many hogs, and some of them up to 40 slaves."[121] This enclave represented the growing schism in Creek country. Its geographic isolation serves to underline a deep social and economic divide.

By the end of the Revolution, Alexander McGillivray, the son of a Scots trader and a Creek woman of the Wind clan, was on the verge of declaring himself the head of a Creek nation, and a division was rapidly widening between those who were oriented toward the market and those who were not. The emergence of a wealthy mestizo elite during the Revolution brought home the Creeks' long-standing fear of the authoritarian power and dramatic material distinctions between ruler and ruled that they observed in Charleston, Savannah, St. Augustine, and other colonial settlements lying on the borders of Creek country. Mestizo Creeks, more attuned not only to the colonial market but also to the colonial hierarchy, harbored fewer suspicions about power and property than did many of their relatives in the Deep South. In the coming years, slaves would continue to find themselves in the middle of the widening schism. Hoboithle Micco drew the division starkly: "[T]here is not white people in his land that strives to spoil the Virginia talks but Jo. Cornel and Alexr. McGillivray," he explained, referring to recent agreements with the United States, "and it is easy to see what they do it for *Because they have a great number of stolen Negroes which*

---

[120]   Arturo O'Neill to Governor Miró, 11 May 1783, PC, leg. 2351, 10, reel 436, PKY.

[121]   Arturo O'Neill to Josef de Ezpeleta, 19 October 1783, no. 2, in *McGillivray of the Creeks*, ed. John Walton Caughey (Norman: University of Oklahoma, 1938); Arturo O'Neill to Conde de Gálvez, 4 December 1783, PC, leg. 36, 684, reel 183, PKY. Periodically in the late eighteenth and early nineteenth century, cattle were shipped from Mobile to New Orleans. It is possible that the mestizo community established northeast of Mobile took advantage of this market. Clark and Guice, *Frontiers in Conflict*, 106.

they have sent and settled near Mobile." He and most other Creeks, in contrast, had "nothing now but their naked bodies and are now ready to run themselves when they hear of danger."[122] Hoboithle Micco, who rose to power as a great speaker and as the son of the Old Tallassee King, disapproved of these latecomers whose status depended on wealth. The division between prosperous Scots Creeks and those Indians like Hoboithle Micco was perhaps the greatest legacy of the American Revolution in Creek country.[123]

In the 1770s, William Bartram had observed the conspicuous generosity of Creeks. But over the course of the next thirty years, Muskogees in ever greater numbers would begin to secure their growing possessions with locks, whip those who stole their belongings, and execute the recalcitrant. More dramatically, during times of scarcity, some Creeks would starve while their neighbors fared well. How did such a striking transformation occur? The remaining chapters will seek to answer this question.

---

[122] Memorial of the King's proposals and complaints, 1783, "Indian Treaties: Cessions of Land in Georgia, 1705–1837," 117, GDAH.

[123] Regarding the effect of the Revolution on the Creeks, historian Martha Searcy concludes, "The war increased the disparity in wealth of individuals. Some warriors were more successful than others in acquiring plunder, including livestock and slaves." Searcy, *The Georgia-Florida Contest*, 179.

PART II

The new order emerges, 1784–1796

3

Alexander McGillivray: Mestizo yet Indian

Alexander McGillivray, the wealthy Scots Indian who promoted himself as the head of the Creeks in the 1780s, has long dominated the recounting of Muskogee history in the decade following the American Revolution. Born in Creek country in 1750, McGillivray spent the first six years of his life among his mother's people and then moved to Augusta to live on the plantation of his father, Lachlan. A year later, he began his education in Charleston under the tutelage of a Scottish relative.[1] By the time Alexander was twelve, his father was one of the largest landholders in the colony, with over 10,000 acres, and was a business partner in a profitable mercantile firm that dealt in slaves, among other commodities.[2] Alexander, perhaps intending to follow in his father's footsteps, apprenticed in two trading companies, one of which was the second largest importer of slaves in Georgia, but the Revolution intervened, forcing Lachlan to retire to Scotland and Alexander to return to his mother's country.[3] Twenty-five years old, literate, and familiar with the intricacies of plantation management and Atlantic commerce, he modeled himself as best he could after the planters he had known in Augusta and Savannah.[4]

In recounting Creek history of the 1780s and early 1790s, most scholars have focused on McGillivray's role as a great diplomat – the "Talleyrand of the Creeks," as one early historian put it[5] – who ingeniously exploited the rivalry between Spain and the United States in favor of his

---

[1] Edward J. Cashin, *Lachlan McGillivray, Indian Trader: The Shaping of the Southern Colonial Frontier* (Athens: University of Georgia, 1992), 263.

[2] Ibid., 210, 252, 258–259.

[3] Ibid., 258, 263.

[4] Ibid., 209, 257, 289.

[5] Albert James Pickett, *History of Alabama and Incidentally of Georgia and Mississippi, from the Earliest Period* (Sheffield, AL: R. C. Randolph, 1896), 432.

people.[6] Indeed, McGillivray has proven to be an appealing subject because of his status as an educated mestizo Indian who shared many of the values of his white antagonists and because of the abundance of letters he left behind. Despite the obvious incongruity of a wealthy, literate Scots Indian characterizing Creek history, it is easy to see how this historical misconception arose.[7] Historians have unavoidably depended on the written word in interpreting the Muskogee past, and especially on McGillivray's voluminous correspondence, today preserved in the government archives of Spain and the United States. In 1938, many of his letters were collected and published, further securing McGillivray's prominence in accounts of Creek history.[8]

McGillivray's writings contain biases that most historians have failed to recognize. In his letters, McGillivray presented himself as the leader of a Creek nation, and American and Spanish officials, anxious to influence a people who had consistently eluded their control, gladly confirmed his pretensions.[9] Creeks, however, scarcely believed they were a nation and certainly did not agree that he was its leader. McGillivray also practiced a type of diplomacy peculiar to literate peoples, one obsessed with land titles and legal sovereignty, and with the interpreta-

---

[6] See, for example: Caughey, *McGillivray of the Creeks*; Randolph C. Downes, "Creek-American Relations, 1790–1795," *Journal of Southern History* 8 (1942): 350–373; and Downes, "Creek-American Relations, 1782–1790," *Georgia Historical Quarterly* 21 (1937): 142–184; Michael D. Green, "Alexander McGillivray," in *American Indian Leaders: Studies in Diversity*, ed. R. David Edmunds (Lincoln: University of Nebraska, 1980), 41–63; Lawrence Kinnaird, "International Rivalry in the Creek Country, Part I, The Ascendancy of Alexander McGillivray," *Florida Historical Quarterly* 10 (1931): 59–85; J. M. O'Donnell, "Alexander McGillivray: Training for Leadership, 1777–1783," *Georgia Historical Quarterly* 49 (1965): 172–183; Helen Hornbeck Tanner, "Pipesmoke and Muskets: Florida Indian Intrigues of the Revolutionary Era," in *Eighteenth-Century Florida and Its Borderlands*, ed. Samuel Proctor (Gainesville: University of Florida, 1975), 13–39; Thomas D. Watson, "Strivings for Sovereignty: Alexander McGillivray, Creek Warfare, and Diplomacy, 1783–1790," *Florida Historical Quarterly* 58 (1980): 400–414; Arthur P. Whitaker, "Alexander McGillivray, 1783–1789," *North Carolina Historical Review* 5 (1928): 181–203, and "Alexander McGillivray, 1789–1793," *North Carolina Historical Review* 5 (1928): 289–309; J. Leitch Wright, "Creek-American Treaty of 1790: Alexander McGillivray and the Diplomacy of the Old Southwest," *Georgia Historical Quarterly* 51 (1967): 379–400. Arthur Preston Whitaker, in his article on McGillivray, concludes, "As fur trader, stock raiser and planter, he suggests the transition period in which he lived, for the fur trade of the Old Southwest was declining noticeably, and a new economy was taking its place as game disappeared and the pioneer farmer crowded out the hunter and trapper." Whitaker did not develop this insight, however. Whitaker, "Alexander McGillivray, 1789–1793," 309.

[7] The anthropologist William C. Sturtevant noted in a conference in 1976 that the prestige, power, and income of Creek mestizos who lived in colonial and Creek worlds "depended on some degree on fooling both sides." He pointedly commented, "One wonders whether they have not also succeeded in fooling some of the historians who have examined the documents they generated." Sturtevant, "Commentary," in *Eighteenth-Century Florida and Its Borderlands*, ed. Samuel Proctor (Gainesville: University of Florida, 1975), 44.

[8] The collection of letters is Caughey, *McGillivray of the Creeks*.

[9] A similar process occurred among the Cherokees. See Hatley, *The Dividing Paths*, 92–93.

tion of words recorded long ago. Creeks, of course, wanted to hold on to their land and retain their political autonomy as much as any people, but they concerned themselves with actions, promises, and memory rather than with the meaning of written words. They cared little, for example, about the legal ramifications of the Treaty of Paris, signed by European powers in 1783 to end the American Revolution. No matter what the document said, Creeks knew that they were masters of their land. McGillivray and his Spanish and American correspondents, in contrast, obsessed over its failure to address tribal titles. Historians, relying on the documents they produced, followed suit.[10]

A critical examination of McGillivray's writings, and of lesser-known Spanish- and English-language documents, suggests that we should question the conclusion of the Scots Indian's biographer that "he was definitely of the Creeks."[11] In one sense, McGillivray, as the son of a Muskogee woman, was undeniably Creek, not because of his "racial" make-up, but because his maternal line gave him membership in the Wind clan. Were he not Creek, Muskogees easily could have dismissed him as an interloper. Yet, at the same time, McGillivray was deeply alienated from most Creek traditions and from the vast majority of the Creek people. This contradiction placed him at the center of a growing fissure.[12] His rise to prominence in Creek country signaled the beginning of thirty years of dramatic change for Muskogees. Rich in land, live-

---

[10] Witness the following excerpt from Caughey's *McGillivray of the Creeks*:

> The Creeks faced a double predicament. England had abandoned her erstwhile allies without making any provision for the trade that was so essential to them. She had also signed away the Indian territory with no regard for tribal titles. With one or the other of their recent adversaries the Creeks must arrange for a satisfactory trade and recognition of Creek sovereignty. In tribal history so serious a problem was unprecedented. (21–22)

Yet, for the Creeks, the question of legal sovereignty was not a problem at all. Rather, the problem was that the United States wanted their land and legitimized its appropriations with legal chicanery.

[11] Ibid., 57. Michael D. Green, in an excellent, succinct account of McGillivray's life, similarly remarks that "it is quite clear that by 1783 his self-identity was Creek, his loyalties were to the Creeks, and his future was inextricably tied to the Nation." Green, "Alexander McGillivray," 45.

[12] A volume of essays, *Between Indian and White Worlds: The Cultural Broker* (Oklahoma: University of Oklahoma, 1994), edited by Margaret Connell Szasz, discusses various nonnative and Native Americans who bridged the gap between Indian and Anglo cultures. See, in particular, Nancy L. Hagedorn's fascinating essay, "'Faithful, Knowing, and Prudent': Andrew Montour as Interpreter and Cultural Broker," for a contrasting approach to the one I take with McGillivray. See also Karl Kroeber's introduction to the volume *American Indian Persistence and Resurgence* (Durham: Duke University, 1994), and in the same volume, Elaine A. Jahner, "Transitional Narratives and Cultural Continuity." One of the best and most insightful works on "culture brokers" is Alan Taylor, "Captain Hendrick Aupaumut: The Dilemmas of an Intercultural Broker," *Ethnohistory* 43 (1996): 431–458. In addition to these works, see Isabel Thompson Kelsay's

stock, and slaves, McGillivray represented the emergence of a new and controversial political and economic order.

McGillivray's life in the Deep South scarcely resembled those of the vast majority of Creeks. Near the colonial settlement of Tensaw, just above Mobile, McGillivray established a slave plantation on the Little River where, according to one nineteenth-century historian, there "lived many intelligent and wealthy people, whose blood was a mixture of white and Indian."[13] In the winter, when most Creek men were out hunting, McGillivray retired to "the sea-coast among the Spaniards," according to one visitor, "leaving his wife, servants, and horses" at the Little River plantation.[14] During the summer, McGillivray stayed at his second residence, a site called Little Tallassee about five miles up the Coosa River from its junction with the Tallapoosa, just above present-day Montgomery, Alabama. Little Tallassee had "the appearance of a small village" due to the cabins of McGillivray's sixty slaves.[15] Here McGillivray planted a small orchard of ten apple trees. Half a mile further upriver, McGillivray had his "upper plantation" where he had ten more apple trees, these planted by his father. "This place is improved by M'Gillivray," noted one visitor.[16] Across the Coosa, the Scots Indian kept his cowpen. McGillivray, who reportedly had "large Stocks of Horses, Hogs, and horned Cattle," retained two or three white men to "superintend their respective Ranges, and now and then collect them together in Order to brand, mark, &c."[17] In addition to ranchers,

admiring biography, *Joseph Brant, 1743–1807: Man of Two Worlds* (Syracuse: Syracuse University, 1984); and Timothy J. Shannon's exploration of cross-cultural dressing, "Dressing for Success on the Mohawk Frontier: Hendrick, William Johnson, and the Indian Fashion," *William and Mary Quarterly* 53 (1996): 13–42. For a provocative essay that sheds some light on the historiographical treatment of assimilated Indians like McGillivray, see James A. Clifton, "Alternate Identities and Cultural Frontiers," in *Being and Becoming Indian: Biographical Studies of North American Frontiers*, ed. James A. Clifton (Prospect Heights, IL: Waveland Press, 1989), 1–37. In the same volume of essays, see also Gary Clayton Anderson's essay, "Joseph Renville and the Ethos of Biculturalism," and James M. McClurken's "Augustin Hamlin, Jr.: Ottawa Identity and the Politics of Persistence."

[13] Alexander McGillivray to John Linder, 28 December 1788, PC, leg. 201, 1088, reel 279, PKY; Swan, "Position and State of Manners," 252; Arturo O'Neill to Estevan Miró, 16 December 1791, PC, leg. 2352, 8, reel 436, PKY; Declaration of James Leonard, 24 July 1792, *American State Papers, Class II: Indian Affairs* (Washington, 1832), 1:307–308 (hereafter cited as *ASPIA*); and Arturo O'Neill to Barón de Carondelet, 30 January 1793, PC, leg. 39, 1414, reel 162, PKY; Pickett, *History of Alabama*, 418.

[14] Swan, "Position and State of Manners," 252.

[15] Milfort, *Memoir*, 29.

[16] Willett, *A Narrative of the Military Actions of Colonel Marinus Willett* (New York: G. & C. & H. Carvill, 1831), 104.

[17] Pope, *A tour through the southern and western territories*, 46–49.

McGillivray employed a white overseer, William Walker, to supervise his slaves at his plantation on the Little River.[18] McGillivray referred to Walker as his "servant."[19]

Though most Muskogees moved short distances to new, fertile plots of land every decade or so, McGillivray's extensive "improvements" such as orchards and cowpens induced him to build a permanent residence. In early June 1791, visitor John Pope found the wealthy Scots Indian at his upper plantation "superintending some workmen in the erection of a log house embellished with dormer windows" and a stone chimney, a dwelling resembling few other habitations in Creek country.[20] No further details about the residence exist, but it likely shared many of the features of a house built a year earlier in 1790 by McGillivray's friend and in-law, George Colbert, a Chickasaw mestizo.[21] Constructed of thirty-inch hewn logs, Colbert's house was sixteen by twenty feet, two stories tall, and featured a veranda. According to contemporaries, it was "covered with rough Clapboards well shingled & sealed inside with pine Boards" (see Fig. 3). Colbert claimed that the construction of the house, including laying the floor, casing the windows, making the doors, and purchasing the hinges and nails, cost him $650, the equivalent value of almost 850 deerskins, what a Creek hunter might have harvested over a period of twenty-eight years but well within Alexander McGillivray's

---

[18] Alexander McGillivray to John Linder, 28 December 1788, PC, leg. 201, 1088, reel 279, PKY. There is evidence that other Muskogees resented the presence of Walker in Creek country. According to Caleb Swan, one Creek "demanded of Walker, that he should mend his gun without receiving pay for it, alleging that he and his children lived upon the milk of the beloved man's cows, and were indulged to stay in the country without trading, which was pay enough, and more too." Swan, "State of Arts and Manufactures, with the Creek Indians, in 1791," in *Information Respecting the History, Condition and Prospects of the Indian Tribes of the United States*, ed. Henry Rowe Schoolcraft (New York: Paladin Press, 1855), 5:692.

[19] Alexander McGillivray to William Panton, 20 September 1988, printed in Albert James Pickett, "McGillivray and the Creeks," *The Alabama Historical Quarterly* 1, no. 2 (Summer 1930): 138.

[20] Pope, *A tour through the southern and western territories*, 46–49; Swan, "Position and State of Manners," 255; and Benjamin Hawkins, "A sketch of the Creek Country in the years 1798 and 1799," *LBH*, 1:298–9. John R. Swanton includes in *The Indians of the Southeastern United States* a drawing of a Creek log house in the 1790s (plate 58). According to geologist Alan K. Craig and archaeologist Christopher S. Peebles, the house pictured in Swanton's book "can hardly be considered typical of most Indian dwellings from that period. The clay-plastered crib chimney, tall doorway, and window are entirely foreign to the Creeks." Alan K. Craig and Christopher Peebles, "Ethnoecological Change among the Seminoles, 1740–1840," *Geoscience and Man* 5 (1974): 90. In fact, the drawing was executed by one John Caldwell Tidball (1825–1906), who created this fanciful representation from written accounts of the Creeks in the eighteenth century and from his own travels in Indian Territory in the 1850s. Emma Lila Fundaburk, ed., *Southeastern Indians: Life Portraits, A Catalog of Pictures, 1564–1957* (Luverne, AL: Birmingham Printing Company, 1958), plate 131.

[21] McGillivray arranged for a sister of his wife to marry one of the Colbert brothers. Arturo O'Neill to Estevan Miró, 29 December 1788, PC, leg. 38, 675, reel 191, PKY.

Figure 3. House of Chickasaw leader George Colbert, built in 1790 and photographed in 1910. From King, "George Colbert," 57.

budget.[22] McGillivray, who had a "taste for natural history," incurred the additional expense of constructing bookshelves for his substantial library, which he had been collecting for some time.[23]

Contrast such a dwelling with the common Upper Creek residence described by Caleb Swan, an American officer who visited Creek country in 1791. It measured from twelve to twenty feet on one side and from ten to fifteen feet on the other. The floor was of earth and the walls six to eight feet high constructed of canes tied to poles driven into the ground. Over this wattle, clay was daubed to fill in holes. These walls were less permanent than those of McGillivray's log house and they demanded less labor. The pitched roof, supported by rafters and a

[22] F. R. King, "George Colbert – Chief of the Chickasaw Nation," *Arrow Points* 7 (1923): 57; James Robertson and R. Meigs to the Secretary of War, 30 June 1806; George and Levi Colbert to James Robertson and R. Meigs, 24 June 1806, "Colbert Letters," *Arrow Points* 16 (1930): 67–72. McGillivray's residence may also have resembled the plantation houses he had seen in Pensacola. The house of James Bruce, a well-to-do planter in the Pensacola area during the British period, was one room, sixteen feet on each side, with planked floors and weatherboarded walls. It had a fireplace and a shingled roof. Most such plantation houses also had a loft. Fabel, *The Economy of British West Florida*, 110. By comparison, see Clemens de Baillou, "Notes on Cherokee Architecture," *Southern Indian Studies* 19 (1967): 25–34.

[23] Benjamin Hawkins to Thomas Jefferson, 14 June 1786, in Elizabeth Gregory McPherson, "Unpublished Letters from North Carolinians to Jefferson," *North Carolina Historical Review* 12 (1935): 252–254; Pope, *A tour through the southern and western territories*, 51.

central ridge pole, was covered by four to five layers of shingles, and all
joints were fastened with withes rather than nails. The chimney might
have been a simple smokehole, or perhaps a pole and clay flue resting
against an outside wall. Inside the residence, small cane racks covered
with skins might have served as beds, though many Creeks chose to sleep
on the floor rather than construct these platforms.[24] It is certain that,
unlike McGillivray, no other Creek kept a collection of works on natural
history.[25]

The area around the confluence of the Coosa and Tallapoosa rivers
reflected the substantial differences between McGillivray and most of
the Upper Creeks (see Fig. 4). A few log houses built in the style of European colonists stood out among the more common wattle-and-daub constructions of other Native Americans. Though some Creeks had fenced
their outlying fields and small garden plots, these fences were not enclosures meant to define property lines. Rather, they prevented the hogs
and cattle belonging to McGillivray and a few others from destroying
crops. They were built to keep livestock out; McGillivray's cowpen on
the west side of the Coosa, in contrast, was meant to keep them in.[26]
There, after grazing in open fields, his cattle would be collected and
branded, an unmistakable sign to others that these animals, unlike the
deer of the forest, were privately owned.[27]

Another form of chattel, slaves, also distinguished McGillivray and his
relatives from most of their neighbors. The race slavery practiced by these
wealthy residents in fact gave the locality one of the highest densities of
African Americans anywhere among the Creeks.[28] With few exceptions,
these slaves labored to produce surplus crops for market sale. Their clustered residences, as large as some Native American villages, prefigured a
new kind of economic and social organization in the Deep South.

[24] Swan, "State of Arts and Manufactures," 692–3; Gregory A. Waselkov, "Intensive Subsurface
Archaeological Investigations at the I-85 Shorter-Milstead Interchange, Alabama" (report submitted to the Environmental Technical Section of the State of Alabama Highway Department,
15 May 1984), 14–15. William Bartram, who visited several Creek and Seminole towns some
fifteen years before Swan, found much the same kind of construction. Bartram, Travels, 168,
312, and 318.

[25] One archaeologist has investigated how housing reflected growing stratification among the
Mohawks in the late eighteenth century. Comparable work on the Creeks would be enlighten-
ing. Guldenzopf, "The Colonial Transformation of Mohawk Iroquois Society," 87–130.

[26] See the map in Swan, "Position and State of Manners," 255.

[27] Pope, A tour through the southern and western territories, 49. Most Creeks, in contrast, still held
that animals became personal property only after being killed in the hunt. For a comparable distinction between colonists and New England Indians, see Cronon, Changes in the Land, 130.

[28] Journal of Benjamin Hawkins, 25 December 1796, LBH, 1:29. See Chapter 5 for a discussion of
African Americans in the area.

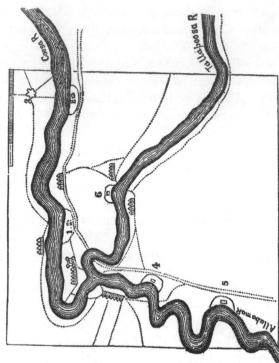

SKETCH OF LITTLE TALLASSIE, OR THE HICKORY GROUND.

Scale three miles to an inch.

Coosa R.

Tallapoosa R.

Alleboma R

Indian towns.
Old French fort Alabama.
Indian paths.

☐ 1. McGillivray's plantation.
☐ 2. McGillivray's apple-grove.
3. McGillivray's cow-pen.

4. Chs. Weatherford's place.
5. McGillivray's sister's place.
6. Melford's place.

Figure 4. Caleb Swan's sketch of the junction of the Coosa and Tallapoosa rivers from his visit in 1791 highlights the contrast and distance between Creek towns and the outlying settlements of Alexander McGillivray and his relatives. Charles Weatherford was a Scotsman married to McGillivray's half-sister, Sehoy. Melford, or Milfort, was a Frenchman who had married Jeanette, another of McGillivray's sisters. From Swan, "Position and State of Manners," 255.

The difference between McGillivray and other Creeks was inscribed on their bodies as well as on the land. William Bartram described the beautiful tattoos of Creek warriors, marked in "bluish, lead or indigo colour." A warrior's chest, according to Bartram, displayed the sun, moon, and planets, while his lower torso and limbs featured zones, belts, and "fanciful scroles," dividing the body into sections illustrated with chase and battle scenes.[29] McGillivray, in contrast, likely had no such markings. He did not participate in the chase, nor did he ever earn distinction as a warrior. Abigail Adams, who as the wife of the vice president met McGillivray in New York, wrote that he "dresses in our own fashion speaks English like a Native, & I should never suspect him to be of that Nation, as he is not very dark."[30]

McGillivray's rise as "most beloved man," a title bestowed on wise and beneficent leaders, depended on the very same forces that separated him from the majority of the people he claimed to represent. Though he relied on his clan for support (the traditional basis of power for Creek leaders), during the Revolution he also used his status as a British deputy to the Upper Creeks to gather dependents, distributing the king's gifts and provisions to the Creeks.[31] Such generosity at the expense of the British government allowed him to parlay his position as commissary into that of "most beloved man."[32] After Britain ceded Florida at the end of the American Revolution, McGillivray turned to Spain, offering his services "as an agent for Indian affairs on the part of his most Catholic majesty."[33] In the summer of 1784, when McGillivray negotiated a treaty officially reestablishing relations between the Creeks and Spain, he also signed a document listing his duties as Spanish commissary in the Tallapoosa nation, the first of which was to keep the Creeks subordinated to Spain.[34]

---

[29] William Bartram, "Observations," 144.

[30] Abigail Adams to Mary Adams, 8 August 1790, *Proceedings of the American Antiquarian Society* 55 (1945):168–9.

[31] O'Donnell, "Alexander McGillivray," 178.

[32] On 12 March 1780, for example, McGillivray handed out eleven yards of strouds, eight white ruffled shirts, fourteen trading shirts, three dozen knives, and one large brass kettle. Five days later, he distributed two days' worth of provisions to 420 Indians at Little Tallassee. Receipt to Alexander McGillivray, 30 June 1780, Sir Guy Carleton Papers, doc. 2861, reel 58A-10, PKY.

[33] Alexander McGillivray to Arturo O'Neill, 1 January 1784, PC, leg. 36, 1357, reel 185, PKY. His position as Spanish commissary to the Tallapoosa nation was made official on 7 June 1784 by the governor of Louisiana. Miró to McGillivray, 7 June 1784, no. 14, *McGillivray of the Creeks*. The following year the captain general of Cuba confirmed his position and salary of $50 per month. Estevan Miró to Alexander McGillivray, 14 June 1785, PC, leg. 3B, 747, reel 154, PKY.

[34] Martín Navarro to Josef de Gálvez, 27 July 1784, PC, leg. 2351, 15, reel 436, PKY. As anthropologist Charles Fairbanks points out, of the Creeks, only McGillivray signed the treaty, a depar-

As Spanish commissary, McGillivray gained the power to distribute gifts destined for the Creeks. In August 1786, for example, he sent the chief warrior of Cluwally, who was one of his relatives, to Arturo O'Neill in Pensacola with a note requesting that the bearer be given 300 pounds of gunpowder, 600 pounds of shot, and 200 flints.[35] A month later at McGillivray's request, Governor Zéspedes of St. Augustine also distributed powder, shot, and flints to the chiefs of Chiaja and Usiche.[36] "You may rest assured," the governor wrote to McGillivray, "that I will continue attentively giving powder and balls and other presents . . . for the Indians as formerly for their hunting, and an even larger quantity of ammunition to whoever gives me a letter from you for the purpose."[37] Clearly, McGillivray had positioned himself in such a manner that whenever Spain determined to distribute arms and ammunition to the Creeks, he was the respected intermediary.[38]

As Spanish commissary, McGillivray also had the power to regulate trade in Creek country.[39] In addition, he worked as a secret partner for the trading firm of Panton, Leslie and Company, one of his "principal sources of . . . power," observed Thomas Jefferson after meeting the Creek leader in 1790.[40] Consequently, Panton, Leslie and Company was

ture from prior custom when scores of Creek leaders marked treaties. Charles H. Fairbanks, *Florida Indians III: Ethnohistorical Report on the Florida Indians* (New York: Garland, 1974), 188. In the late eighteenth century, Spain similarly promoted a leader named Clermont among the Osage west of the Mississippi. Like McGillivray, Clermont used his power to control trade to expand his power. Rollings, *The Osage*, 159–163, 199–201.

[35] Alexander McGillivray to Arturo O'Neill, 26 August 1786, PC, leg. 37, bnd. 2, doc. 117, reel 169, PKY.

[36] Governor of Florida to Conde de Gálvez, 29 September 1786, EF, bnd. 42C4, doc. 10, 58, reel 16, PKY.

[37] Quoted in James F. Doster, *Creek Indians: The Creek Indians and Their Florida Lands, 1740–1823* (New York: Garland, 1974), 1:61.

[38] For a series of notes written by McGillivray that Creeks carried to Pensacola for presents, see PC, leg. 122A, 706–746, reel 395, PKY. In the 1990s, the Huaorani in the Ecuadorian Amazon recognized, like the Creeks some 200 years earlier, that letters requesting gifts carry special weight with literate bureaucracies. See Joe Kane, *Savages* (New York: Alfred A. Knopf, 1995), 140.

[39] McGillivray was officially granted these powers at the treaty of 1784. Martín Navarro to Josef de Gálvez, 27 July 1784, PC, leg. 2351, 15, reel 436, PKY. The powers existed in practice as well as in theory. See Daniel McMurphy to Arturo O'Neill, 11 July 1786, PC, leg. 37, bnd. 4, doc. 112–1, reel 169, PKY, in which McMurphy stated that all traders among the Creeks had their licenses from McGillivray. For an example of a license, see McGillivray to Victor Muhlberger, 15 May 1791, PC, leg. 204, 745, reel 283, PKY.

[40] Panton apparently offered McGillivray a 20 percent share of profits. Watson, "Strivings for Sovereignty," 403. Quote from Thomas Jefferson on 412. Panton later maintained that McGillivray formally renounced his share in the company in 1788, yet in 1810, McGillivray's heirs sold their interest in Panton, Leslie and Company (then Forbes and Company) for $18,000. Whether he held a formal share or not, McGillivray continued to profit from his association with Panton. Alexander McGillivray to William Panton, 20 September 1988, in Pickett, "McGillivray and the Creeks," 139–140; McGillivray to Panton, 10 August 1789, in ibid., 143–144; and Panton

able to use the threat of Indian unrest to secure a monopoly on the Creek trade in Spanish territory.[41] In March 1784, for example, when Spain moved to expel trader Charles McLatchy, who operated a Panton, Leslie store in Apalache some twenty miles below present-day Tallahassee, McLatchy notified the Spanish governor, "Mr. McGillivray has a partial interest with us in the Indian trade. I have communicated to him the contents of your letter on this matter."[42] McGillivray responded with an ominous warning to the governor that the Indians would take up arms to save McLatchy's store.[43] Soon after, in the treaty of 1784 between the Creeks and Spain, McGillivray subtly threatened that unless concessions were granted to Panton, Leslie and Company, Spain could not count on the friendship of the Creeks. The Spanish "were informed of the conditions on which they could or could not conciliate and maintain our friendship," McGillivray wrote to his business partner McLatchy, and "they had too much concern for the peace and well-being of the Floridas not to guard carefully against making us their enemy."[44] With such threats, McGillivray successfully secured Panton, Leslie's position in Apalache and eventually in Pensacola as well.[45] Years later, a Creek Indian named Tustanagee Thlucco (Big Warrior) would recall that Panton and McGillivray "were always giving out such talks, to keep the trade in their hands."[46]

Once Panton, Leslie and Company secured its monopoly, McGillivray

to Lachlan McGillivray, 10 April 1794, in ibid., 143–148; William S. Coker and Thomas D. Watson, *Indian Traders of the Southeastern Spanish Borderlands: Panton, Leslie and Company and John Forbes and Company, 1783–1847* (Pensacola: University of West Florida, 1986), 113.

[41] Whitaker, "Alexander McGillivray, 1783–1789," 190–192. Whitaker claims that McGillivray was not a member of Panton, Leslie and Company.

[42] Charles McLatchy to [Manuel Vicente de Zéspedes], 4 March 1784, EF, bnd. 114J9, reel 43, PKY. In fact, McGillivray had been offered a share in the company as early as 3 January 1784. McGillivray to O'Neill, 3 January 1784, no. 5, *McGillivray of the Creeks*.

[43] Alexander McGillivray to [Manuel Vicente de Zéspedes], 26 March 1784, EF, bnd. 114J9, reel 43, PKY. See also the similar letter to Arturo O'Neill, 26 March 1784, PC, leg. 197, 746, reel 273, PKY; and Alexander McGillivray to Gov. Miró, 24 March 1784, in D. C. Corbitt, "Papers Relating to the Georgia-Florida Frontier, 1784–1800. Part I," *Georgia Historical Quarterly* 20 (1936): 356–65. William S. Coker and Thomas D. Watson cover the side of the story in relation to the history of Panton, Leslie and Company. Coker and Watson, *Indian Traders*, esp. 56–58, and 68–70.

[44] Alexander McGillivray to Charles McLatchy, 25 December 1784, no. 21, *McGillivray of the Creeks*. McGillivray had earlier used veiled threats to ask that duties be removed on the trade. Alexander McGillivray to Arturo O'Neill, 24 July 1785, PC, leg. 198B, 1190, reel 275, PKY.

[45] For details on the establishment of Panton, Leslie and Company in Spanish Florida during this period, see Coker and Watson, *Indian Traders*, chap. 3.

[46] Copy of talk from Big Warrior to General Twiggs, 20 April 1793, "Unpublished Letters of Timothy Barnard, 1784–1820," ed. Louise F. Hays (hereafter cited as LTB), 160, GDAH, also in *ASPIA*, 1:401.

used violent means to protect it. In 1787, for example, he encouraged 500 Creek warriors to fall on American settlements at Cumberland to prevent the establishment of a rival trading post there. That same year, he arranged to take the scalp of William Davenport, a Georgian who was working to regain the Chickasaw trade for Augusta merchants.[47] In so acting, McGillivray exploited his power among the Creeks, using warriors almost as the personal retainers of Panton, Leslie and Company.

In the hierarchy of the deerskin trade, McGillivray and his Creek brethren occupied separate – even opposing – positions. Though Muskogees depended on and benefited from a regular commerce, McGillivray often had his own interests in mind when he lobbied for Panton, Leslie and Company. Soon after the firm secured rights to trade out of Pensacola in 1784, McGillivray wrote McLatchy, "The establishment of the new house if well supported will not fail to be lucrative, and since the matter is such as it is presently certain, I would be glad to see your offers regarding my share."[48] At the same time, much to the chagrin of William Panton and his associates, McGillivray accepted a partnership in the short-lived company of Mather and Strother which intended to trade with the Chickasaws and Choctaws out of Mobile.[49] "Its permit," he explained, "is due to my actions with a view to placating the Indians."[50] As Panton, Leslie and Company gained ascendancy in the trade, however, McGillivray turned against the "house of villains," as he later called Mather and Strother.[51]

McGillivray profited from his association with the governments of Spain and the United States, as well. In 1784, Spain began paying him $600 per year for his services, what a Creek hunter might have grossed over a quarter of a century; yet McGillivray renounced the salary in 1788 because he considered the "pittance of a common interpreter . . . disgraceful to my station."[52] Two years later, a secret article in a treaty between Creeks and the United States granted McGillivray the title of

[47] Whitaker, "Alexander McGillivray, 1783–1789," 197–8; Jack D. L. Holmes, "Juan de la Villebeuvre and Spanish Indian Policy in West Florida, 1784–1797," *Florida Historical Quarterly* 58 (1980): 396. Arturo O'Neill suggested that Davenport was murdered as satisfaction for the deaths of five or six Kasihtas at the hands of Georgians. Arturo O'Neill to Estevan Miró, 3 August 1787, PC, leg. 37, bnd. 7, doc. 244, reel 169, PKY.
[48] Alexander McGillivray to Charles McLatchy, 18 September 1784, EF, bnd. 116L9, reel 44, PKY.
[49] Coker and Watson, *Indian Traders*, 61–8.
[50] Alexander McGillivray to Charles McLatchy, 25 December 1784, EF, bnd. 116L9, reel 44, PKY.
[51] Alexander McGillivray to Manuel Vicente de Zéspedes, 22 May 1785, EF, bnd. 114J9, reel 43, PKY.
[52] [Estevan Miró] to Alexander McGillivray, 14 June 1785, PC, leg. 3B, 747, reel 154, PKY; Alexander McGillivray to Estevan Miró, 28 August 1788, enclosed in Miró to Ezpeleta, 17 September 1788, LOC, AGI, PC, leg. 1394, PKY; Alexander McGillivray to William Panton, 10 August 1789, PC, leg. 203, 1022, reel 282A, PKY.

brigadier general along with a salary of $1,200 per year.[53] This was a substantial sum, especially when added to the $2,000 Spain began paying McGillivray in 1791. A year later, Spain raised his annual stipend to $3,500. McGillivray thus received $4,700 in 1792 from his two salaries, the equivalent value of more than 6,000 deerskins or 200 times what the average Creek hunter might harvest in a year.[54] Moreover, McGillivray's salary was net profit, while a hunter's harvest usually went to pay debts.

McGillivray operated with conflicting interests. As a silent partner in Panton, Leslie and Company, he was expected to secure the most advantageous position for the merchant house, while as the leader of the Creeks, he was supposed to negotiate the best trading terms for his people. Similarly, his status as an agent for Spain and the United States placed him in a compromised position. He had access to power beyond the reach of other Creeks, but that very power, linked to mercantile houses and colonial governments, separated him from the majority of the people he claimed to represent.[55]

Many Creeks objected to McGillivray's authority, and instead turned to Hoboithle Micco for leadership. Also known as the Tame, Tallassee, or Good Child King, Hoboithle Micco continually challenged McGillivray until the Scots Indian's death in 1793 at age forty-three. Their confrontations seemingly revolved around a series of land cessions that Hoboithle Micco made to Georgia in the 1780s. Near the end of 1783, he and Neha Micco (the Fat King) led a small number of Indians to Augusta where they and twelve others ceded land bordering the Oconee

---

[53] On the treaty and its secret articles, see Wright, *Creeks and Seminoles*, 138–40. Benjamin Hawkins, at the time a U.S. Senator, had written McGillivray before the latter's arrival in New York that "the U States have the means of estimating properly the value of your character." Quoted in Whitaker, "Alexander McGillivray, 1789–1793," 296.

[54] Barón de Carondelet to Alexander McGillivray, 6 July 1792, no. 189, *McGillivray of the Creeks*; Alexander McGillivray to Barón de Carondelet, 22 July 1792, PC, leg. 177, bnd. 54, 2, reel 16, PKY; Whitaker, "Alexander McGillivray, 1789–1793," 300. After the raise, McGillivray told Carondelet that he would renounce any monetary gift from Congress, but there is no confirmation that he ever did so.

[55] McGillivray even considered accepting a share in the South Carolina Yazoo Company. In most documents he stated his outright rejection of the project, but in one letter to John Leslie he revealed that he would accept the offer of a 1/20 share if the land speculators could obtain the sanction of the Spanish king. Alexander McGillivray to John Leslie, 20 May 1790, EF, bnd. 114J9, reel 43, PKY; Whitaker, "Alexander McGillivray, 1789–1793," 295–6; A. Moultrie to Alexander McGillivray, 19 February 1790, PC, leg. 203, 1039, reel 282A, PKY; Alexander McGillivray to William Panton, 8 May 1790, PC, leg. 203, 1047, reel 282A, PKY. The grant to the South Carolina Yazoo Company covered 10 million acres between the Mississippi and Tombigbee rivers, land belonging to the Choctaws. George R. Lamplugh, *Politics on the Periphery: Factions and Parties in Georgia, 1783–1806* (Newark, Del.: University of Delaware, 1986), 67–68.

and Apalachee rivers on one side, and the Ogeechee River on the other. In 1785, seventeen Creek Indians, including Hoboithle Micco and Neha Micco, confirmed this cession to Georgia in the Treaty of Galphinton, and in addition ceded land east of a line drawn from the fork of the Ocmulgee and Oconee rivers to the source of the St. Marys River. A year later, at the Treaty of Shoulderbone Creek, Georgia used strong-arm tactics to intimidate and coerce several Creek leaders, once again led by Hoboithle Micco and Neha Micco, into confirming the prior cessions and promising satisfaction for thefts and murders committed since those treaties.[56]

McGillivray actively opposed these land cessions. In 1790, he led a delegation to New York, then the seat of the new federal government, to resolve the controversy over the disputed lands. The delegation settled a treaty that confirmed the cession along the Oconee originally made in 1783 at Augusta but retained for the Creeks the additional lands ceded in 1785 at Galphinton.[57] The treaty also transferred the remaining Creek territory claimed by Georgia from state to federal jurisdiction. McGillivray and others believed that the federal government would be less aggressive than Georgia in its efforts to take possession of Creek lands.[58]

McGillivray, who described Hoboithle Micco as "a roving beggar, going wherever he thinks he can get presents," suggested that the challenge to his leadership came from weak and corrupt men.[59] Hoboithle Micco's three treaties with Georgia were indeed ill-advised, but McGillivray clearly presented a partisan view.[60] From another perspective, the Treaty of New York appears equally ill-advised. A secret article making McGillivray a brigadier general compromised Creek leadership. Moreover, Article 12 of the treaty stipulated that the United States would periodically furnish Creeks with domestic animals and implements of husbandry, thereby turning Muskogees into yeoman farmers.[61] Though many Creeks might have welcomed the aid, minutes of the

---

[56] These negotiations can be followed in Randolph C. Downes, "Creek-American Relations, 1782–1790."

[57] Treaty of New York, *ASPIA*, 1:81–2. The Treaty of New York did not include the cession made at Rock Landing from the confluence of the Oconee and Ocmulgee rivers to the source of the St. Marys. The best account of the treaty is found in J. Leitch Wright, "Creek-American Treaty of 1790."

[58] Alexander McGillivray to Estevan Miró, 26 February 1791, PC, leg. 204, 733, PKY.

[59] Alexander McGillivray to Arturo O'Neill, 10 February 1786, no. 33, *McGillivray of the Creeks*.

[60] Hoboithle Micco apparently recognized that he had been coerced and cajoled into signing the treaties. Questions to the Tallisee King, 6 August 1790, vol. 26, p. 120, Henry Knox Papers, Gilder Lehrman Collection, Pierpont Morgan Library, New York.

[61] Treaty of New York, *ASPIA*, 1:81–82.

treaty negotiations reveal that McGillivray professed the desire to "civ-
ilize" the Creeks by making them "cultivators and herdsmen instead of
Hunters," news that would have disturbed, but perhaps not surprised,
many Muskogees. Henry Knox, the secretary of war, noted that the
United States would "chearfully concur in so laudable a design."[62]

The treaties with Georgia and the United States frame but do not
fully explain the conflict between Hoboithle Micco and Alexander
McGillivray. If we dig beneath the surface disturbance occasioned by
these agreements, other significant features appear. Some historians have
suggested that long-established linguistic or ethnic divisions account for
the opposition to McGillivray's leadership.[63] As practitioners of "new
Indian history," they use the tools of anthropology to understand the
motivations of Native Americans, but in so doing, they sometimes fail
to avoid the pitfalls.[64] The language of anthropology – clans, phratries,
and moieties – provides rules of behavior but does not describe practice;
in fact, practice fluctuated over time and place.[65] Clan divisions, for
example, cannot in themselves explain why some Creeks supported
McGillivray and others did not. Clan identity did not necessarily deter-
mine political affiliation. Take the case of Emistesigo and Hoboithle
Micco, both members of the Tiger (Panther) clan who fought on

---

[62] Minutes for Creek Treaty, August 1790, vol. 27, p. 70, Henry Knox Papers, Gilder Lehrman
Collection, Pierpont Morgan Library, New York.

[63] Different interpretations of the opposition to McGillivray can be found in Green, *The Politics
of Indian Removal* and "Alexander McGillivray"; Gregory Evans Dowd, *A Spirited Resistance:
The North American Indian Struggle for Unity, 1745–1815* (Baltimore: Johns Hopkins, 1992);
Wright, *Creeks and Seminoles*; and Corkran, *The Creek Frontier, 1540–1783*.

[64] Scholars have long attempted to bridge the gap between history and anthropology or between
event and structure. While anthropologists are generally aware of the difficulty of defining
culture, some historians use the term indiscriminately without specifying what it is. For an introduction to the problem of writing ethnohistory, see John K. Chance's address to the American
Society for Ethnohistory in 1995. John K. Chance, "Mesoamerica's Ethnographic Past," *Ethnohistory* 43 (1996): 379–403. For a sustained attack on the concept of culture, see Christopher
Herbert, *Culture and Anomie* (Chicago: University of Chicago, 1991).

[65] Swanton, *Social Organization*, 107–170. See, particularly, his discussion of phratries. See also
Mary R. Haas, "Creek Inter-town Relations," *American Anthropologist* 42 (1940): 479–489.
Bronislaw Malinowski, in his classic work on law in stateless societies, noted:

> The clan is neither a mere fairy tale, invented by Anthropology, nor yet
> the one and only real principle of savage law, the key to all its riddles and
> difficulties. . . . The unity of the clan is a legal fiction in that it demands
> – in all native doctrine, that is in all their professions, and statements,
> sayings, overt rules and patterns of conduct – an absolute subordination
> of all other interests and ties to the claims of clan solidarity, while, in fact,
> this solidarity is almost constantly sinned against and practically non-
> existent in the daily run of ordinary life.

Bronislaw Malinowski, *Crime and Custom in Savage Society* (1926; reprint, Westport, CT: Greenwood Press, 1984), 119.

opposite sides during the Revolution.[66] More to the point, near the end of McGillivray's life, the Scots Indian was losing support even among his own clan.[67] Unless placed in specific historical context, categories of language, kinship, and ethnicity cannot explain behavior without making Creek history static and unchanging.

Rather than arising from ancient divisions, the tensions between Creeks in the decade after the Revolution revolved around the future shape of power and property in the Deep South. Many Creeks resented McGillivray's propensity to concentrate power in his own hands. Hoboithle Micco saw the Scots Indian as a white man and a "boy and an usurper."[68] In 1784, he and his ally Neha Micco were reportedly "very angry with McGillivray for attempting to send down talks without their knowledge."[69] Similarly, in May 1786, Indians from Kasihta and its village Buzzard's Roost complained that McGillivray was keeping his orders secret from them. Referring to a recent raid on the Georgia frontier, they stated, "The Indians does not do these things of there own accord but by the orders of their Beloved man who is employed by the Spaniards."[70]

By 1786 when McGillivray's opponents signed the Treaty of Shoulderbone Creek with Georgia, Hoboithle Micco and other Lower Creeks seemed exasperated with the Scots Indian. Their talk, despite being given amidst a large contingent of Georgia militia sent to intimidate them, seems sincere, for they asserted themselves and ultimately rejected a proposal by Georgia commissioners to kill McGillivray.[71] "The principal person against you is Alexander McGillivray," the Creeks began:

[66] In 1768, Emistesigo assured the governor of Georgia that "all of the Tyger Family are of royal Descent: of which Family he is." Emisteseegoe to James Wright, 5 September 1768, *CRG*, 10:580–582; Arturo O'Neill to Estevan Miró, 21 July 1788, PC, leg. 38, 217, reel 191, PKY. Escuchabe, also of the Tiger Clan, fought against the British, too. Braund, *Deerskins and Duffels*, 166. In 1778, Hoboithle Micco even offered to kill Emistesigo for the rebels. Searcy, *The Georgia–Florida Contest*, 156.

[67] Mr. Middleton to Alexander McGillivray, 24 December 1791, PC, leg. 1436, 4973, reel 156, PKY; and Arturo O'Neill to Estevan Miró, 16 December 1791, PC, leg. 2352, 8, reel 436, PKY. These sources are discussed in detail below.

[68] Swan, "Position and State of Manners," 281; Memorial of the King's proposals and complaints, 1783, "Indian Treaties: Cessions of Land in Georgia, 1705–1837," 117, GDAH.

[69] P. Carr to John Houston, 22 August 1784, CIL, 1:63–4, GDAH.

[70] A Talk from the headmen of the Cussetaws and Buzzard Roost Indians to his honnour the Governour of Georgia, 2 May 1786, LTB, 51, GDAH. A few weeks later, Timothy Barnard reported, "The whole nation I hear seems to be offended with Mr. McGillivray for what he has done which I immagine was entirely by instructions of the Spaniards. The Indians that give out their talks that come from the upper Creeks says his own brother has order'd him to leave the nation on account of it." Timothy Barnard to Edward Telfair, 27 May 1786, LTB, 55, GDAH.

[71] Alexander McGillivray to Estevan Miró, 26 January 1787, PC, leg. 200, 939, reel 277, PKY. Another letter by McGillivray further attests that Hoboithle Micco spoke his mind. McGillivray

He is from a large family, for which reason we will give him
free passage to leave in peace. But we must get rid of him. If
he wishes to live with the Spanish, he can go to them, or else
he must die. It is not our desire to trick you, as up to now he
has done. The talks and letters that McGillivray has sent you
as the voice of the nation are not. They are of his own fab-
rication to serve his private ends and to make our nation
poor.[72]

To differentiate themselves and assert their own authority, these Indians
then added, "We who are here are the chiefs of the Lower Creeks." Two
years later, several Upper and Lower Creeks reportedly agreed that in
the future they would "receive the word of the Spaniards through a
white man and not through McGillivray, who they say is a mestizo
Indian who up to now wished to govern and manage the affairs of the
Creek Nations without consulting with the most respectable chiefs of
these Nations."[73] McGillivray, by attempting to centralize authority, had
begun a process that would culminate in the Redstick War.

As a British, then Spanish and American agent, as a partner in Panton,
Leslie and Company, and as a Creek leader, McGillivray occupied an
ambiguous position in the Deep South. This Scots Indian, who may not
have even had a Muskogee name, was himself ambivalent about his identity.[74] He used an interpreter when addressing his fellow Creeks, perhaps
because he did not have fluent command of the language.[75] He spoke "the

related that Hoboithle Micco, on learning that the Georgians intended to keep him hostage to
ensure that the treaty would be implemented, "thundered out a furious talk and frightened the
Georgians from their purpose of keeping them." Alexander McGillivray to Arturo O'Neill, 3
December 1786, PC, leg. 2352, 35, reel 436, PKY.

[72] "Contextacion que al otro dia 22 hicieron los Reyes, Hombres Principales, y guerreros de la
nacion crique," 22 October 1786, EF, bnd. 114J9, reel 43, PKY.

[73] Arturo O'Neill to Estevan Miró, 10 September 1788, PC, leg. 38, 388, reel 191, PKY.

[74] Sturtevant, "Commentary," 45. On the subject of McGillivray's identity, Arthur Whitaker concludes, "Without attempting to penetrate the mysteries of racial inheritance, we are on reasonably
safe ground when we recognize the disturbing effect of his dual cultural inheritance. . . . Both his
letters and his actions reflect this psychic dualism, of which he seems to have been at times dimly
conscious." Whitaker, "Alexander McGillivray, 1789–1793," 308. Thomas Hatley, writing about
the Cherokees, identifies what he calls "psychological stress" endured by mestizo Indians. He suggests that among the Cherokees, a "métis appearance could be a fatal liability, and the violence
directed at these men was felt by both the children and their kin." Hatley, The Dividing Paths,
61–62. There does not appear to have been a similar Creek hostility toward métis appearance. The
biological diversity of Creeks and Seminoles would have precluded such distinctions.

[75] See, for example, Receipt to Alexander McGillivray, 30 June 1780, Sir Guy Carleton Papers, doc.
2861, reel 58A-10, PKY; Alexander McGillivray to [Arturo O'Neill?], 21 February 1786, PC,
leg. 199, 770, reel 383, PKY; Alexander McGillivray to Estevan Miró, 26 January 1787, PC, leg.
200, 939, reel 277, PKY; Alexander McGillivray to William Panton, 10 August 1789, PC, leg.
203, 1022, reel 282A, PKY.

savage tongue very little," recalled Luis Milfort, a close friend of
McGillivray's for many years.[76] McGillivray also preferred using the
Christian rather than Creek calendar. When addressing colonial officials,
he marked time not by the *Poskita* or busk, but by Christmas.[77] To give
more precise dates, he used both Western and Creek methods of telling
time. In a letter to the Hallooing King, for example, he explained that
"there is this day 10 Broken days" until Creek warriors attacked the
frontier. Then, to confirm the date, perhaps to himself more than to
anyone else, he added redundantly, "The 23 of the month is the time to
set off."[78] More broadly, he understood events in historical rather than
mythic time. In 1790, Henry Knox recorded McGillivray's history of the
Creeks. Instead of telling about white paths and red arrows, McGillivray
recounted a series of rational, chronological events. "About this time,"
he stated, for example, "the French arrived and infected the Taensahs
with the small pox."[79] His mundane history suggests that he did not share
the mythic and religious beliefs of other Muskogees.

In several different letters, McGillivray insisted that he was Creek –
"we Indian country folks," he wrote to his trading partner William
Panton in 1788.[80] In a note to Georgia treaty commissioners that same
year, McGillivray warned against the "extirpation of the first inhabitants
of this Country," depriving "us of Lands which have been ours from the
beginning of time – the possession of which is absolutely necessary to
our Subsistence."[81] The following year, he condemned Americans for
believing that "we being Indians are only fit to be subdued and our
country divided among a people who are white."[82] In other statements,
McGillivray identified himself more explicitly. "It is necessary for one
to inform you that I am a native of this nation and of rank in it," he
informed the governor of Louisiana in 1784.[83] Two years later, at a time
when U.S. commissioners did not need such an introduction, he

---

[76] Milfort, *Memoir*, 28. Historian Edward J. Cashin suggests that McGillivray was not fluent in
Muskogee. Cashin, *Lachlan McGillivray*, 75–76.

[77] Alexander McGillivray to Arturo O'Neill, 26 October 1785, PC, leg. 198B, 1214, reel 275, PKY;
and McGillivray to O'Neill, 10 July 1787, PC, leg. 200, 956, reel 277, PKY.

[78] Alexander McGillivray to Hallooing King, 14 April 1786, PC, leg. 37, bnd. 2, doc. 112–2A, reel
169, PKY.

[79] Minutes taken from Gen. McGillivray respecting the Creeks, August 1790, vol. 26, p. 165, Henry
Knox Papers, Gilder Lehrman Collection, Pierpont Morgan Library, New York.

[80] Alexander McGillivray to William Panton, 20 September 1788, in Pickett, "McGillivray and the
Creeks," 140.

[81] Alexander McGillivray to Generals Pickins and Mathews, 4 June 1788, PC, leg. 201, 1045, reel
279, PKY.

[82] Alexander McGillivray to Thomas Pinckney, 26 January 1789, PC, leg. 202, 657, reel 281, PKY.

[83] Alexander McGillivray to [Maxent], 28 March 1784, PC, leg. 197, 750, reel 273, PKY.

described himself as "a native and ruling chief . . . very deeply interested in the fate of my country," meaning the land of the Creeks.[84]

These declarations have the tone of a man who protests too much, and other statements belie his confidence and certainty. In a letter he wrote in 1784 to Arturo O'Neill, the Spanish commandant of Pensacola, on behalf of several loyalists who wished to settle on the Alabama River, north of present-day Mobile, McGillivray explained that he had informed these refugees of the potential benefits of living in Spanish territory. He added, "I flatter myself that these families will be accepted of to add to the making [of your province] a well cultivated one."[85] It was a curious choice of words for the self-proclaimed representative of the Creeks. Few if any other Muskogees would have spoken of the land in terms of cultivation. Cultivation introduced expansive cleared fields, fences, and plantations where there had once been cane brakes and forests that sheltered bear and deer and yielded important medicinal plants.[86] In another letter, McGillivray noted dismissively that hunting grounds were "the greatest dominion of which an Indian can form an idea," clearly excluding himself from this generalization.[87] It was the odd Creek indeed who cautioned as did McGillivray, "Indian information in general ought to be suspected as they carry tales to ensure a good reception and to obtain presents."[88]

The weight of his double identity is apparent in a 1789 letter to his trading partner William Panton recounting how he successfully blocked a treaty with the United States:

> In this do you not see my cause of triumph in bringing these conquerors of the old & masters of the new world as they called themselves, to bend & supplicate for peace at the feet of a people whom shortly before they despised and marked out for distruction.[89]

[84] Alexander McGillivray to John Habersham, 18 September 1786, PC, leg. 199, reel 383, frame 787, PKY.

[85] Alexander McGillivray to Arturo O'Neill, 5 February 1784, PC, leg. 197, 742l, reel 273, PKY. One early historian of Alabama writes that John Linder, a settler on Lake Tensaw, had become acquainted with McGillivray in Charleston. During the Revolution, the Creek leader assisted in bringing Linder's "family and large negro property" to the Tensaw. Pickett, *History of Alabama*, 417.

[86] Creeks complained in 1796 that cattle destroyed cane swamps where they went to hunt bear. Report of Commissioners to the Secretary of War, June 1796, *ASPIA* 1:597–616. Oak forests attracted deer when acorns dropped in the fall. When game was scarce in 1801, Efau Hadjo asked, "When the Acorns fall deer are usually about, but where now are the deer?" Talk from Efau Haujo to John Forbes, 31 May 1801, Greenslade Papers, PKY.

[87] Alexander McGillivray to Arturo O'Neill, 24 July 1785, PC, leg. 198B, 1190, reel 275, PKY.

[88] Alexander McGillivray to [?], 24 June 1789, PC, leg. 202, 694, reel 281, PKY.

[89] Alexander McGillivray to William Panton, 10 August 1789, PC, leg. 203, 1022, reel 282A, PKY.

The triumph seems personal, a measure of satisfaction for his rejection from the Georgia aristocracy. His diplomatic success at the time promised reconciliation with those who had tried to destroy him. Georgia offered to return to McGillivray the estate left by his father, valued at more than $100,000.[90]

McGillivray's ambiguous position relative to his fellow Creeks explains in part why the Scots Indian found it difficult to rally Creek support against William Augustus Bowles, an adventurer who worked to secure the Indian trade on behalf of a commercial firm in the Bahamas. Bowles first arrived in Florida in 1788 where he began an irregular and sporadic trade with the Creeks and Seminoles. After escorting eight Cherokee and Creek chiefs to England to gather support for his plan to wrest Florida away from Spain, Bowles returned in 1791. The following year, he and his Muskogee allies sacked the Panton, Leslie store in Apalache. Taken prisoner by Spain, he managed to escape and again return to Creek country in 1799, overrunning the Spanish fort in Apalache in 1800. In 1803, Creek leaders and Spanish and American officials successfully plotted his capture and imprisonment in a Havana jail, where he died in 1805.[91] Though Bowles was born in Maryland of Anglo parents, he at times did a better job than McGillivray in shedding his European American heritage and adopting the dress and lifeways of the Creeks. Whites who met him, for instance, nearly unanimously commented on his Indian comportment and "rather ridiculous clothes," a sharp contrast to Abigail Adams's description of McGillivray's fashionable appearance in New York.[92] A hunter and warrior, Bowles outwardly differed markedly from McGillivray, the statesman and plantation owner. In addition, Bowles promised a restoration of the economy that had existed during British rule, while McGillivray represented the very forces that were undermining that economy.

Bowles's activities in 1791 brought on a crisis in McGillivray's life. Arturo O'Neill reported in December of that year that Bowles had won over the Creeks by suggesting that McGillivray had ceded their lands to

---

[90] Ibid.

[91] On Bowles's activities in Florida, see J. Leitch Wright, *William Augustus Bowles, Director General of the Creek Nation* (Athens: University of Georgia, 1967).

[92] Quote is from the testimony of Richard Walker. Of the testimony of seven deserters from Bowles's party, all but one mentioned their leader's dress. See the testimonies taken by Enrique White, 24 October 1799, PC, leg. 2355, 331, reel 382, PKY. An American commissioner who described McGillivray in 1789 disagreed with Abigail Adams: "He dresses altogether in the Indian fashion and is rather slovenly than otherwise." Quoted in Whitaker, "Alexander McGillivray, 1789–1793," 291.

enrich himself. When McGillivray sent a party of Creeks to murder the interloper, Bowles succeeded in befriending the assassins, even winning over members of McGillivray's own clan.[93] At the same time, McGillivray wrote to William Panton from his residence on the Coosa, "I am firmly resolved to move myself, family, and negroes down this River to Little River. I am absolutely worn down with the life I have lived for ten years past."[94]

Christmas Eve of 1791 found McGillivray ill and depressed. On learning that his antagonist Bowles had successfully recruited some Upper Creeks, the would-be leader – according to a Creek messenger – lamented that the Creeks had "thrown his talks away" and "made him ashamed in his own country." From then on, the Creeks "could look for someone else to compose their talks and write their letters," he stated. He would leave the nation, and "next spring he expected to see them all dead or thrown out of the country and that then they would be glad to hear his talks."[95] In January of the new year, McGillivray moved all of his property and slaves out of Creek country to the mouth of the Little River, within Spanish territory, and only a last-minute appeal by a Spanish agent kept him from burning his house on the Coosa.[96] He reportedly complained that "the Indians were altogether regardless of his advice; that he was determined to quit them."[97]

His power further eroded over the course of the year. In March 1792, American commissary Edward White wrote to McGillivray at his plantation to tell him that the president was determined to bring about the restoration of his "former influence, & Authority."[98] Hoboithle Micco and other Creeks, including even his old ally Efau Hadjo, however, prevented him from reestablishing peace with the United States. American Indian agent James Seagrove wrote to McGillivray that he had learned that "the confusion in the towns was so great, that many of your people were oppenly opposed to your going any where until there could be a general meeting of the nation."[99] In June, Upper Creek war parties went out against American settlements at the same time as others went to negotiate peace, leading the Spanish commandant at Mobile to comment

[93] Arturo O'Neill to Estevan Miró, 16 December 1791, PC, leg. 2352, 8, reel 436, PKY.
[94] Alexander McGillivray to William Panton, 28 October 1791, PC, leg. 39, 692, reel 162, PKY.
[95] Mr. Middleton to Alexander McGillivray, 24 December 1791, PC, leg. 1436, 4973, reel 156, PKY.
[96] Arturo O'Neill to Estevan Miró, 16 December 1791, PC, leg. 2352, 8, reel 436, PKY; Declaration of James Leonard, 24 July 1792, ASPIA, 1:307–308.
[97] Testimony of John Ormsbay, 11 May 1792, ASPIA, 1:297–298.
[98] Edward White to Alexander McGillivray, 5 March 1792, no. 174, McGillivray of the Creeks.
[99] James Seagrove to Alexander McGillivray, 21 May 1792, ASPIA, 1:298–299; Testimony of John Ormsbay, 11 May 1792, ASPIA, 1:297–298; John Forrester to the Governor of Florida, 21 May 1792, EF, bnd. 122E10, doc. 1792–192, reel 47, PKY.

that these events and others demonstrated conclusively "that Mr. McGillivray in his nation has a limited power."[100] Seagrove felt the situation serious enough to offer McGillivray asylum if the latter thought it necessary,[101] but McGillivray apparently decided to head to New Orleans instead. "I doubt whether he returns," Seagrove noted.[102] By August, however, McGillivray had gone back to Little Tallassee by way of Mobile and Pensacola.[103]

As his power waned, many Creeks grew suspicious of McGillivray's intentions, especially in relation to Bowles, who was still in Florida promising trade goods from Nassau. In October, Arturo O'Neill received a letter on behalf of the Lower Creeks inquiring into McGillivray's actions with the Spanish. "You must be sensible," the letter read, "Mr. McGillivray has no right to sell any of our lands and we should be glad to know if he says he has when he comes amongst you. In short, his behavior is so misterious that we would be happy you would clear it up if in your power."[104]

At the end of 1792, McGillivray withdrew even further from the Creeks, moving his cattle and slaves off the Little River and deeper into Spanish territory.[105] McGillivray lived only a few months longer, dying in Pensacola on the night of 17 February 1793. William Panton wrote to McGillivray's father in Scotland that his son had "died possessed of sixty negroes, three hundred head of cattle, with a large stock of horses," reminders of what separated him from other Creeks.[106] Just as his settling on the Tensaw in 1783 had marked the beginnings of a social and economic schism in Creek country, McGillivray's retreat into Spanish territory at the end of his life gave notice that this schism was widening.

Should there be any doubt as to the ambiguous position of McGillivray among the Creeks, we can turn to the night of his death. Arturo O'Neill described McGillivray's last moments:

[100] Manuel de Lanzos to Barón de Carondelet, 8 June 1792, no. 7, in letterbook, PC, leg. 225A, reel 24K-4, PKY.

[101] James Seagrove to Alexander McGillivray, 21 May 1792, *ASPIA*, 1:298–299.

[102] James Seagrove to the President, 5 July 1792, *ASPIA*, 1:304–305. See also Juan Nepomuceno de Quesada to Luis de las Casas, 15 July 1792, EF, bnd. 23J2, 188, reel 9, PKY; Alexander McGillivray to Arturo O'Neill, 16 July 1792, PC, leg. 39, 879, reel 162, PKY.

[103] Alexander McGillivray to James Seagrove, 9 October 1792, *ASPIA*, 1:321–322.

[104] Ockillissa Chopka to Arturo O'Neill, 23 October 1792, PC, leg. 39, 1194, reel 162, PKY.

[105] Manuel de Lanzos to Barón de Carondelet, 14 December 1792, no. 245, in letterbook, PC, leg. 225A, reel 24K-4, PKY; and Arturo O'Neill to Barón de Carondelet, 30 January 1793, PC, leg. 39, 1414, reel 162, PKY.

[106] William Panton to Lachlan McGillivray, 10 April 1794, no. 214, *McGillivray of the Creeks*.

He was asked to make his will. I was led to understand that he was Indian and thus did not wish to do so, although Panton demanded to whom he was leaving his goods. He told me then that he was leaving his goods to his sons in equal parts and something to his wives, though he repeated that they be given only a little.[107]

By refusing to make a will, he initially asserted his Indian identity. According to Creek custom, his belongings would have gone to his sisters. Just before his death, however, the Scots Indian embraced the European side of his ancestry by leaving most of his goods to his sons.[108] His body, unaccompanied by the "pipe, ornaments and warlike appendages" buried with other Creek men, was interred in William Panton's garden in Pensacola.[109]

McGillivray's rise to power challenged many of the long-held beliefs of Creeks about property and power. Though an extraordinary figure in Creek country, McGillivray nevertheless marked the entrance of other mestizos, albeit less powerful and less visible than the Scots Indian, into leadership positions in the region. They would continue to disrupt Muskogee communities in the Deep South in the coming years. The Creeks themselves best summed up the challenges presented by these people. They could be neither rejected categorically as outsiders, nor fully embraced as natives. McGillivray, Creeks reportedly said in an assembly in 1788, "was a mestizo and yet at the same time Indian like them."[110]

[107] Arturo O'Neill to Barón de Carondelet, 17 February 1793, PC, leg. 39, 1424, reel 162, PKY.
[108] Initially, McGillivray's wishes were fulfilled, but his sisters eventually asserted their customary privilege, as Hawkins explained:

> According to the custom of this nation a man's children have no claim to his property, it belongs to his relations on the maternal line, and they seize upon it, as was the case in this instance. Mrs. Durand and Mrs. Weatherford, the first a sister and the other a maternal sister only, took possession of the greatest part of the property and have destroyed the stock of horses and cattle. The former or her sons have made way with all the negros they possessed themselves of. Mr. David Tate, a son of the maternal sister, has possession of most of the property which was in possession of his mother.

Benjamin Hawkins to William Eustis, 27 August 1809, *LBH*, 2:556; Whitaker, "Alexander McGillivray, 1789–1793," 307–308.
[109] Martin, *Sacred Revolt*, 106–107.
[110] Arturo O'Neill to Estevan Miró, 10 September 1788, PC, leg. 38, 388, reel 191, PKY.

4

Forging a social compact

Caleb Swan, who visited the Deep South in 1791, wrote of the Creeks:

> Every individual has so high an opinion of his own impor-
> tance and independency, that it would be difficult, if not
> impossible, to impress on the community at large the neces-
> sity of any social compact, that should be binding upon it
> longer than common danger threatened them with the loss of
> their lands and hunting ranges.[1]

Like earlier observers, Swan was struck by the difference between
Muskogee and European political organization. Creek leaders, as Chigellie and Antioche had explained to Georgians in the 1730s, relied solely
on persuasion to command their people. By contrast, the governments
familiar to Swan often resorted to coercion, a power ostensibly granted
in the social contract between ruler and ruled. Swan keenly observed
that Muskogees had no similar binding contract. In fact, they did
not even think in such terms. Yet, in the 1780s and 1790s, a few mestizos and other Creeks began forging a social compact, forcing it on the
mostly unwilling inhabitants of the region. In the language of European
political theory, promoters of the compact violated natural rights; in
the language of the Creeks, they supplanted fair persuasions with the
tomahawk.

The emerging compact dictated that the Creeks turn over judicial
and political authority, which had traditionally resided in the clans, to a
small number of "national leaders" who would act for the good of the
"nation." Creeks objected to the compact on two grounds. First, they
did not wish to compromise their autonomy by granting power to a small

---

[1] Swan, "Position and State of Manners," 279.

circle of men, and second, even if they had granted such power, they did not agree they were a nation with a single good. Promoters of the compact, in contrast, saw the situation differently. They argued that certain acts should be considered crimes against a Creek people, and they insisted that the punishment of these transgressors would benefit everyone. At stake in this debate was the future shape of the Creek peoples: Would they retain the dispersed power structure of their parents and grandparents, or would they embrace a new order built on hierarchy and coercion?

Traditional Creek justice revolved around the clan and worked on the principle of exchange, a life for a life, to "placate the soul of the departed" which remained in turmoil until satisfaction.[2] "It lies with the family injured to revenge their own quarrel," Thomas Campbell, a visitor to the Creeks in 1767, explained; "If a man is killed, his family will revenge it upon him who committed the murder, but if he escaped they will kill one of his family, and none of the rest of the tribes will offer to interfere."[3] Sometimes a single person embroiled his or her clan in a costly exchange of justice, for multiple victims demanded multiple executions, even when the culprit had acted alone. Creek justice also differed markedly from its European counterparts in its disregard of intent or motive. Muskogees exacted the same punishment on those who caused accidental death (we would say manslaughter) as they did on those who intentionally took a life.[4]

---

[2] Swanton, *Social Organization*, 339. See also his following discussion on crime and punishment. John Phillip Reid has an illuminating discussion of Cherokee justice in chapter 1 of *A Better Kind of Hatchet: Law, Trade, and Diplomacy in the Cherokee Nation During the Early Years of European Contact* (University Park: Pennsylvania State University, 1976). See also Reid's more in-depth treatment of the subject in *A Law of Blood. The Primitive Law of the Cherokee Nation* (New York: New York University Press, 1970).

[3] Fabel and Rea, "Lieutenant Campbell's Sojourn Among the Creeks," 109. James Oglethorpe made a similar observation in 1733:

> In the case of murder, the next of blood is obligded to kill the murderer, or else he is looked on as infamous in the nation where he lives; and the weakness of the executive is such, that there is no other way of punishment but by the revenger of blood, as the scripture calls it; for there is no coercive power in any of their nations; their kings can do no more than to persuade. All the power they had is no more than to call their old men and captains together, and to propound to them the measures they think proper; and after they have done speaking, all the others have liberty to give their opinions also; and they reason together with great temper and modesty till they have brought each other into some unanimous resolution.

Quoted in Jones, *Historical Sketch*, 45.

[4] James Adair related how "If an unruly horse belonging to a white man, should chance to be tied at a trading house and kill one of the Indians, either the owner of the house, or the person who tied the beast there, is responsible for it, by their lex talionis." Adair, *Adair's History*, 156. See

Because of the dominance of the family in determining crime and meting out punishment, when a Creek killed an outsider, no clan but the murderer's could rightfully execute the perpetrator.[5] In 1797, Indian agent Benjamin Hawkins reported, "There is here and there a solitary instance where the Chiefs of a town have interposed all their authority, which could only prevail on the weldisposed of the relations to put their offending brethern to death."[6] Justice was a national issue only in the sense that individual clans extended throughout the towns of the Deep South.[7] After white settlers killed eleven people from Kasihta in 1787, for instance, residents of that town "for some time appeared enraged and threatened to take a severe revenge of the Georgians, yet they did not

---

also "A historical narration of the genealogy, traditions, and downfall of the Ispocoga or Creek tribe of Indians," PKY.

[5] For a discussion of the laws of "international homicide" among southeastern Indians, see Reid, *A Law of Blood*, 155–157, and Reid, "A Perilous Rule: The Law of International Homicide," in *The Cherokee Indian Nation: A Troubled History*, ed. Duane H. King (Knoxville: University of Tennessee Press, 1979), 33–45. Reid notes that the southeastern Indians held nations collectively liable in cases of intertribal homicide and that consequently entire towns rather than clans took action in such cases. Indian agent Benjamin Hawkins wrote in 1798 that war was determined by the great warrior of the injured town. The great warrior's determination could be reversed by the town miccos, but if he persisted, warriors could participate as they wished. "It is seldom a town is unanimous," he wrote. The "nation never is; and within the memory of the oldest men among them, it is not recollected that more than one half the nation have been for war at the same time; or taken, as they express it, the war talk." Benjamin Hawkins, "A sketch of the Creek Country in the years 1798 and 1799," *LBH*, 1:320.

[6] Benjamin Hawkins to James McHenry, 6 January 1797, *LBH*, 1:63. Hawkins also stated:

> If murder is committed, the family alone of the deceased have the right of taking satisfaction. They collect, consult, and decide. The rulers of a town or the nation have nothing to do or say in the business. The relations of the deceased person consult first among themselves and if the case is clear and their family are not likely to suffer by their decision, they determine on the case definitively. When the tribe may be effected by it, in a doubtful case, or an old claim for satisfaction, the family consult them; and when they have resolved on satisfaction, they take the guilty on, if to be come at.

Benjamin Hawkins, "A sketch of the Creek Country in the years 1798 and 1799," *LBH*, 1:321–322.

[7] In 1774, Governor James Wright of Georgia worried about obtaining justice from the Creeks after they had murdered fifteen settlers and two black slaves: "so many Murders have been committed and the Murderers have so many Relations and Connections in the Nation that they [Creek leaders] having no coercive Power may find it difficult to give Satisfaction and on which Account they may be drawn in and the whole Nation Involved." Wright, in short, worried that his demands for satisfaction would provoke the implicated clans and force Creek leaders to throw in their lot with those involved. In this way, justice could become a "national" issue. James Wright to the Earl of Dartmouth, 31 January 1774, CRG, vol. 38, 1:169, GDAH; James Wright to the Earl of Dartmouth, 12 March 1774, CRG, vol. 38, 1:188, GDAH. The Creeks eventually agreed to give satisfaction by killing five of the murderers. "At a Congress held at Savannah in the Province of Georgia," 20 October 1774, CRG, vol. 38, 1:336–345, GDAH.

act with a proper spirit on the occasion." Finally, "the family of the murdered Indians who resided in other towns" took satisfaction.[8]

As described by most European observers, satisfaction seems a product of the desire for revenge, but Creeks understood the principle of exchange in moral and religious terms. Satisfaction was sanctioned and demanded by a higher force. William Bartram, who visited the Creeks in the 1770s, explained that they believed it was "the Supreme Being, as the high arbiter of human transactions, who alone claims the right of taking away the life of man."[9] There could be no compromise for the Creeks; satisfaction reflected the very order of the world, from the banks of the Tallapoosa across the Great Water to the king of England. During one case of disputed justice in 1771, members of the Tiger clan, who had observed the lions on the Hanoverian coat of arms, stated:

> We understand that the great King over the Great Water is
> of the Tyger Family so was the [Creek] Man that was murdered he also took up Arms in defence of his Relations   He
> is the first Man which you have killed, and we and all the head
> Men of the Tyger Family, now send to assure you that they
> look upon that matter as taking proper satisfaction.[10]

The emerging social compact threatened to overturn the traditional means of taking proper satisfaction. By denying the right of the Tiger and other clans to satisfy the Giver and Taker of Breath, indeed by challenging the very basis of Creek justice, it dared to replace the supreme being with new arbiters of life and death: national leaders. The emerging social compact consequently engulfed the Creeks in conflict and violence.

Not until after the Revolution did a small number of Creeks begin forging a social compact that would give them unconditional political and judicial authority. In 1775, James Adair noted somewhat romantically that southeastern Indians lacked "the fear of punishment for offences" because the "demon of persecution . . . was never among them – not an individual durst ever presume to infringe on another's

---

[8] Alexander McGillivray to Manuel Vicente de Zéspedes, 6 October 1787, EF, bnd. 114J9, reel 43, PKY.

[9] Bartram, *Travels*, 383.

[10] Head men and warriors of Upper Creeks to James Wright, 1 May 1771, enclosed in Memorial of James Wright to the Lords of Trade, 1771, CRG, vol. 28, 2:808–809, GDAH.

liberties."[11] Colonial officials also noticed the inability of Indians to prosecute guilty individuals, and thus even before the Revolution, they had begun insisting that the Creeks develop a government vested with the authority to turn over or execute warriors who murdered colonists. Muskogees were cautious, however, and evidence reveals that they did not immediately alter their own process of justice to accommodate British demands. In fact, in all cases in which Creeks executed one of their countrymen before the outbreak of the American Revolution, clan members of the executed approved of the action.[12]

In December 1763, for example, seven Creek warriors attacked a British fort at Long Cane, South Carolina, resulting in the deaths of fourteen colonists. The Creek warriors, seen the day of the event with several scalps tied to a pole, had in fact been living with the Cherokees for the previous four or five years, and had committed the murders without the approbation of their families. Because the crime potentially could have had serious repercussions for many Muskogee towns, Creeks held a general meeting to discuss the matter, but the final decision to offer satisfaction rested with the clan directly involved. Accordingly, the White King of Kasihta agreed to satisfy the South Carolina governor by putting to death two of his guilty "sons" when they returned home from hunting.[13] After White King's concession, South Carolina and Georgia officials overlooked the remaining murders to avoid a war with the Creeks.[14]

Several other cases illustrate that throughout the British period, clan-based justice remained the law of the land. In August 1766, for example, some Creeks murdered two British traders, Goodwin and Davies, near the Tensaw River in Alabama. Once again, the colonies were reluctant to force the issue of recompense for fear of starting a war. The Creeks, too, were cautious, denouncing the act, and the perpetrators even black-

---

[11] Adair, *Adair's History*, 406.

[12] In addition to the cases discussed below, see the ones presented in the Journal of Thomas Bosomworth, July–October 1752, *DIASC*, 1:273–292, 310–326; and Jean-Bernard Bossu, *Jean Bernard Bossu's Travels*, 142–143.

[13] Lieutenant Barnard to the Governor of Georgia, 28 December 1763, *CRG*, 9:111–112; Affidavit of Arthur Coody, 28 December 1763, *CRG*, 9:113–114; Tugulkey's talk sent to the Governor and enclosed in Galphin's letter of 8 January 1764, *CRG*, 9:115–116; An Answer from the Wolf and a few of the Head Men of the upper Creek to Captain Stewart's Talk, 14 February 1764, *CRG*, 9:148–149; Talk from the Lower Creeks to the Governor of Georgia, 14 February 1764, *CRG*, 9:150–151. Two of the murderers were said to be the "sons" of the White King, but, in accordance with matrilineal practices, they must have been his nephews. In Creek society, fathers had no responsibility for their biological children.

[14] James Grant to the Board of Trade, 30 August 1766, PRO, CO 5/541, p. 125, in "British Colonial Office Records," 1:256, PKY.

ened their trophy scalps to pass them off as Choctaw hair. Perhaps aware
that Governor George Johnstone of West Florida had resolved to with-
draw all traders, construct five blockhouses, and attack their towns, the
Creeks quickly offered to give satisfaction. The leader of the murderers
was put to death by "a near relation of his own."[15] In another case in
December 1771, a Lower Creek named Sugley, after spending the night
as the guest of a white man, murdered his host. The Georgia governor
demanded justice, and Fullocky and his old brother Cateagea, of the
same family as the murderer, consented to put their relation to death.[16]
Justice remained rooted in the clan.

In giving satisfaction, Creeks were not just responding to pressure
placed on them by colonial officials; rather, they acted out of their
own deeply felt sense of justice. Simpihaphy, Selegee, and Talegee,
three Lower Creek leaders, explained one such case to the governor of
Georgia in 1771. In October of that year, colonists shot dead an innocent Creek at a hunting camp in Georgia. When his companions resolved
to take satisfaction, the victim's uncle intervened. His family "was due
the white people Satisfaction for two white Men killed last Year," he
explained, and "ever since the path had been dark to him." The loss
"might go for an Old debt, which ought to have been paid long ago," he
concluded.[17] On the occasions when family members refused to put murderers to death, it was usually because they believed that their clan
had acted in response to some prior unanswered outrage committed by
colonists.

As some of these cases suggest, the British often sacrificed their own
principles of justice to expediency. A double murder in 1767 illustrates
that the Creeks in fact held the upper hand in determining the shape of
justice. In September, a number of Alachua Indians were caught rustling
horses from white residents on the St. Marys River. The colonists tied
them to trees, whipped, and "pickled" them by rubbing salt into their
wounds. The next day, the Alachuas returned, killed two of their antagonists, and burned down their house. They spared an old man, a woman,

---

[15] James Hendrie to Tayler, 29 August 1766, Haldimand Papers, MG21/B11, BM 21671,
433a/37/38, reel 59C, PKY; John Stuart to Governor Johnstone, 13 December 1766, Haldimand
Papers, MG21/B11, BM 21671, 469/118/143, reel 59C, PKY; John Stuart to Thomas Gage, 19
December 1766, Thomas Gage Papers, American series, reel 140F, PKY; Governor Grant to the
Board of Trade, 8 August 1767, PRO, CO 5/548, p. 445, in "British Colonial Office Records,"
2:687, PKY.

[16] Governor of Georgia to headmen of Creek Nation, 9 December 1771, *CRG*, 12:152–154;
Salegee, Tallegee, Fullokey, and Catagee to James Wright, 17 March 1772, *CRG*, 12:316–317.

[17] Talk given by Simpihaphy, Selegee, and Talegee, 2 November 1771, *CRG*, 12:148–150.

and some children, however, and did not take any scalps. Their behavior led Governor Grant of East Florida to conclude correctly that the matter was a personal one. Nevertheless, he decided to demand satisfaction and tried to involve Creek chiefs by offering cattle in exchange for the perpetrators.[18] As in other conflicts with colonists, the Creeks feared trade sanctions and violent retaliation. Emistesigo, a Muskogee warrior from Little Tallassee, tried to preempt the danger to his own locale by suggesting that Britain embargo trade goods to the "Lower Creeks," referring to those Indians living in Florida who later became known as Seminoles.[19] His suggestion reveals that the Upper Creeks had neither the will nor power to give satisfaction for a murder committed by an Alachua Indian.

The Seminoles eventually did offer satisfaction, putting one person to death in April 1768, but he apparently was not guilty according to European understandings.[20] A Seminole named Bonaichee initially acquiesced to the execution of two of the murderers, his nephews. On learning of their condemnation, however, these "two young fellows of some note" promptly killed their uncle. By European standards, Bonaichee's murder did little to set matters aright, but Creeks viewed the affair differently. Bonaichee's execution, they believed, had properly atoned for the death of one of the colonists.

Governor Grant demurred. He resolved "if possible to get one of the guilty Indians put to death, in the presence of some of His Majesty's Subjects," and he even secured such a promise. Grant explained, "Indians have no idea of any other Rule or Law in such cases, but giving or receiving blood for blood. They flattered themselves that I would be satisfied, as an Indian had died in consequence of the murtheres."[21] His self-congratulatory tone soon gave way to embarrassment, however. Nearly a year later, it was Grant who was administering justice for the Creeks and accommodating the injured clan. "One of our Crackers," he wrote (using the new terminology of the Georgia frontier), murdered an Indian on the St. Johns and consequently was put to death "in the pres-

[18] James Grant to the Board of Trade, 31 October 1767, PRO, CO 5/549, p. 13, in "British Colonial Office Records," 2:706, PKY; John Stuart to Thomas Gage, 27 November 1767, Thomas Gage Papers, American series, reel 140H, PKY.

[19] John Stuart to Thomas Gage, 2 October 1767, Thomas Gage Papers, American series, reel 140H, PKY.

[20] Roderick McIntosh to John Stuart, 18 April 1768, enclosed in Stuart to Gage, 2 July 1768, Thomas Gage Papers, American series, reel 140H, PKY.

[21] James Grant to the Board of Trade, 20 June 1768, PRO, CO 5/549, p. 105, in "British Colonial Office Records," 2:747, and enclosure, PKY.

ence of the murdered Indian's father and a number of other Indians." The murder "might have ruined the colony if the bad consequences which must have attended that affair had not been prevented by giving blood for blood according to their idea of law," Grant explained. He feebly concluded, "I have an account to settle with them of the same kind and they promised satisfaction." Already a year and a half had passed since Bonaichee's nephews had murdered two colonists on the St. Marys, however, and the governor was still waiting.[22] In fact, Creeks would not begin to adopt notions of justice based on a social compact until after the Revolution.

In the 1780s, Creeks faced two threats to their traditional practice of clan justice. First, when warriors and horse rustlers raided colonists, reprisals by a new and powerful United States now threatened the welfare of the entire Muskogee population, thereby compelling the Creeks to create a centralized executive power to control individuals. In the past, by contrast, British officials had been ready to sacrifice white "crackers" to the wider interests of the empire. Second, a growing number of mestizo Creeks wanted to protect private property and trade relations.[23] They were more interested in the balance of their account books than in the balance of justice demanded by the Giver and Taker of Breath.[24] From both of these sources, Creeks felt pressure to become a nation and to punish those who transgressed its laws.

Alexander McGillivray played a significant role in the early stages of the compact. In one failed attempt to reshape Muskogees, he reportedly introduced a law against horse rustling. Rustlers had to return stolen animals and pay a fine of thirty chalks (the accounting marks used in the deerskin trade) or fifteen dollars. Those unable to pay were "tied and whipped thirty lashes by the injured party." Creeks never enforced this law with any regularity. Caleb Swan concluded that the innovation, "although sometimes observed, is oftener dispensed with."[25]

---

[22] James Grant to Thomas Gage, 5 March 1769, Thomas Gage Papers, American series, reel 140H, PKY. I have not found any evidence that the governor ever received his satisfaction.

[23] Peter Linebaugh explores the relationship between the social contract and private property in *The London Hanged*. See especially chapter 2. He argues that the social contract, which legitimated state violence, was based on the need to protect private property. See also E. P. Thompson, *Whigs and Hunters: The Origin of the Black Act* (Harmondsworth, Middlesex, 1975). Thompson shows how ambitious landholders used law and violence to encroach on the customary rights of people to forest resources.

[24] Richard White shows that Choctaw mestizos similarly played an important role in introducing the market economy among their people. White, *The Roots of Dependency*, 97–146.

[25] Swan, "Position and State of Manners," 281–282.

McGillivray nevertheless tried to force the compact on the Creeks.[26] According to Swan, the Scots Indian called on his kin to act as "constables" to "pursue, take up, and punish, such characters as he may direct," and on some occasions, to act as "executioners."[27] He had limited success. In February 1789, for example, he was daily sending out letters instructing Creeks not to raid the Georgia border. Timothy Barnard, a trader and U.S. Indian agent, reported:

> What horses has been stole since I have been up has been
> done by two or thre poor rascals goeing over at a time quite
> against the orderes of the whole nation tho they have been
> told repeatedly by the head men that if any of them gits killed
> that there friends need not expect to goe oute to take sattis-
> faction for them as there shall neaver be none required.[28]

Despite Barnard's dismissal of these "poor rascals," horse rustling was a political act, especially in the context of McGillivray's attempts to punish its practitioners. Raids on white settlements by young warriors sustained the traditional political tension in Creek country by counter-balancing the moderation of older Muskogees. The raids also reaffirmed the economy of hunting and warring in the face of McGillivray's efforts to turn Creek men into "cultivators and herdsmen."[29]

Other promoters of the social compact varied in background and motivation, but generally they were mestizos such as McGillivray who had direct interests in maintaining order. After the Scots Indian's

---

[26] McGillivray's efforts to nationalize justice may have had a basis in his literacy. His law was not written, but clearly derived from the legal system that he had observed and participated in during his residence in Augusta, Savannah, and Charleston. Anthropologist Jack Goody writes, "In written codes there is a tendency to present a single 'abstract' formula which overlays, and to some extent replaces, the more contextualized norms of oral societies. . . . State systems inevitably tend to apply state-wide norms, at least in critical spheres such as the control of force." Jack Goody, *The Logic of Writing and the Organization of Society* (Cambridge: Cambridge University, 1986), 12.

[27] Swan, "Position and State of Manners," 281–282.

[28] Timothy Barnard to George Hanley, 22 February 1789, LTB, 89, GDAH.

[29] The political motivations of young Creek warriors is evident in an event of February 1793. In that month, a warrior dramatized Creek dissatisfaction with encroachments over the Oconee River. Entering Kasihta with a settler's scalp, he "went to the house of the deputy superinten-dent Holmes . . . and threw the scalp down at his feet, and said he had caught that man over the line at the Oconee where he had no business to be." John Forrester to Juan Nepomuceno de Quesada, 18 February 1793, EF, bnd. 123F10, doc. 1793-25, reel 48, PKY. Kathryn Braund shows that another facet of frontier violence committed by young warriors was the erosion of "respect for traditional authority and the virtues of restraint." She writes, "Young warriors drank themselves senseless and committed outrages against their own people and their white neigh-bors." Braund, *Deerskins and Duffels*, 131.

death in 1793, Charles Weatherford, White Lieutenant, and Alexander Cornels, all wealthy men who valued the power and order legitimated by the social compact, became active in its enforcement. Weatherford, who lived just below the junction of the Coosa and Tallapoosa rivers, was a Scotsman married to McGillivray's half-sister.[30] White Lieutenant was half Native American by birth and a war leader from Okfuskee.[31] In 1795, he moved to Nuyaka, a small town fifteen or twenty miles above Okfuskee on the Tallapoosa, perhaps to pursue cattle ranching away from his densely settled hometown.[32] Alexander Cornels was the son of a Creek woman and the Englishman George Cornels whose brother Joseph had been McGillivray's interpreter. Alexander was closely attached to the United States and later would become an assistant to Indian agent Benjamin Hawkins. By the end of the decade, Cornels would have a "farm well fenced and cultivated with the plough," two acres of which were planted with cotton, and nine slaves "under good government."[33] All of these men occupied privileged positions in Creek country, leading them to promote a social compact that protected private property and secured power in their hands.

Some Creeks supported the social compact only with the encouragement and threats of the United States. Efau Hadjo, for example, had been a close associate of McGillivray's but was not as wealthy or familiar with European American ways as the Scots Indian. When he became the Creeks' chief representative to the United States after McGillivray's death, his commitment to the social compact had to be periodically renewed by violent encounters with U.S. troops. In September 1793, for instance, when Creek warriors were raiding the Georgia frontier, a party of Georgia light horsemen took revenge on the settlement of Hothlitaiga (Little Okfuskee), situated forty-five miles above Coweta on the Chattahoochee River. Razing the ten houses of the village, the cavalry killed and scalped six men and took three women and five girls prisoners. The violence must have especially frightened Creeks, considering that

---

[30] Alexander Beaufort Meek, *Romantic Passages in Southwestern History*, 263–266.
[31] Timothy Barnard to James Seagrove, 2 July 1793, LTB, 188, GDAH, also in *ASPIA*, 1:400; Swan, "Position and State of Manners," 255n1.
[32] Enrique White to Barón de Carondelet, 27 September 1795, PC, leg. 32, 1080, reel 386, PKY. White Lieutenant died in 1799 with 26 cattle on hand. Daniel McGillivray to William Panton, 5 June 1799, Greenslade Papers, PKY.
[33] Benjamin Hawkins, "A sketch of the Creek Country in the years 1798 and 1799," *LBH*, 1:291–3; II. S. Halbert and T. H. Ball, *The Creek War of 1813 and 1814* (Montgomery, AL: White, Woodruff, and Fowler, 1895), 165–166.

Hothlitaiga had not taken part in the frontier raids and was home to White Lieutenant, an important and staunch ally of the United States.[34] The following year, Efau Hadjo himself was injured on the Oconee River when Georgia militia began shooting at a camp of friendly Creeks returning from a meeting with Indian agent James Seagrove in Augusta.[35] Often unpredictable and senseless, the actions of American troops nevertheless induced many national leaders to try to appease the United States by punishing Creek warriors who raided the frontier. Expediency proved more compelling than justice.

Young warriors actively opposed the enforcement of the social compact because they depended on warfare and rustling to secure honor and respect. Moreover, they pursued their livelihood through hunting and consequently had a vested interest in clearing the frontier of newly settled families. Men such as Alexander Cornels, in contrast, were already wealthy and powerful, and they depended not on hunting but on ranching and farming. "For among the Indians," McGillivray had explained in 1792, "all rank and condition depend for subsistence on hunting in the woods except they have property."[36] Several years later, Creek headmen noted that white settlements south of the Oconee caused "much distress and displeasure among our young warriors" because of the destruction of hunting grounds.[37]

A few wealthy mestizos also opposed the social compact. The son of James Burgess, a white trader who had settled among the Lower Creeks, participated in raids on the St. Marys River, for example, as did John Galphin, the son of trader George Galphin and Metawney, a Creek woman. John had inherited sixteen adult slaves and their children from his father in 1782.[38] He had "learning," one mestizo noted disapprovingly, yet had spent all his property and now lived by plundering.[39]

[34] Halooing King to Henry White, 24 September 1793, PC, leg. 208A, 559, reel 286, PKY; James Durouzeaux to Henry White, 24 September 1793, PC, leg. 208A, 560, reel 286, PKY; James Seagrove to the Secretary of War, 9 October 1793, *ASPIA*, 1:411–412.

[35] "News from the Newspaper of Georgia," 10 May 1794, EF, bnd. 114J9, reel 43, PKY; Constant Freeman to the Governor of Georgia, 10 May 1794, CIL, 2:378, GDAH; Constant Freeman, Jr., to the Secretary of War, 10 May 1794, LTB, 234, GDAH, also in *ASPIA*, 1:483; Report of Dr. Frederick Dalcho, Surgeon's Mate to the troops of the United States in Georgia, 10 May 1794, LTB, 236, GDAH, also in *ASPIA*, 1:484. The militia were responding to the earlier murder of an officer, but the perpetrators remained unknown. Constant Freeman to the Governor of Georgia, 9 May 1794, CIL, 2:375–377, GDAH.

[36] Alexander McGillivray to Estevan Miró, 10 April 1792, PC, leg. 204, 741, reel 283, PKY.

[37] Rey Buen Hijo, Rey Mas Distante, Perro Ravioso to Juan Nepomuceno de Quesada, 8 January 1795, PC, leg. 1438, doc. 680, frame 1052, reel 26, PKY.

[38] George Galphin's will, dated 1778, CIL, 1:8–15, GDAH.

[39] John Cannard to Juan Nepomuceno de Quesada, 25 May 1793, EF, bnd. 114J9, reel 43, PKY.

Burgess and Galphin, in contrast to Cornels, Weatherford, and White Lieutenant, accumulated their wealth through pillaging and robbery, while the former acquired it under the guise of legality, by force during the Revolution or by trade and deceit thereafter. For many young Creek warriors, a crucial difference existed between the two means of obtaining property. Cornels's practice of using the labor of enslaved African Americans to ranch and farm excluded young men and left no means for them to earn honor or wealth, whereas Burgess's and Galphin's frontier raids provided them with opportunities to become respected warriors. Robbery and pillaging took the place of war as a means of displaying bravery.[40] Despite their own personal wealth, Burgess and Galphin appeared to oppose the encroachment of "civilization" and the social compact that went along with it.

The social compact introduced more than a new procedure for identifying and punishing crimes. It also advanced a novel way of understanding justice, what Muskogees called the "doctrine of guilt and innocence."[41] Creeks already had a deeply felt sense of responsibility for their actions, but they did not believe in guilt or innocence in the English sense of the words. In fact, the Muskogee language did not even have terms to convey these concepts. When Creeks translated the English word "guilty," they said "*emmu'tte*," or "his fault." In the eighteenth century, "*mu'tte*," or "fault," perhaps more accurately meant "cause" because Creeks did not have the sense of sin that "fault" implies. A warrior threatened with execution might have rightly insisted, "My clan is not the cause." By contrast, he would not have said, "My clan is not at fault," for this statement implies that the crime was accidental, a matter of irrelevance in Creek country. To express the concept of innocence, Muskogees said "*mu'ttekós*," or "not his fault."[42] In capital offenses, the English definition of the word allows the accused to

---

[40] Choctaw warriors similarly substituted horse rustling for warfare in the late eighteenth century. James Taylor Carson, "Horses and the Economy and Culture of the Choctaw Indians, 1690–1840," *Ethnohistory* 42 (1995): 500.

[41] "Journal of Occurrences at Fort Wilkinson during the Conference and Treaty with the Creek Indians there, by Benjamin Hawkins," *LBH*, 2: 428.

[42] R. M. Loughridge and David M. Hodge, *English and Muskokee Dictionary Collected from Various Sources and Revised* (1890; reprint, Okmulgee, OK: B. Frank Belvin, 1964), 123, 163. John Phillip Reid, a legal scholar who often writes on Indian jurisprudence, notes that circumstances such as accident, self-defense, and intent, were "factors relating to common-law or Christian 'guilt' that were usually not considered when determining 'liability' under Indian law." Reid, "Principles of Vengeance: Fur Trappers, Indians and Retaliation for Homicide in the Transboundary North-American West," *Western Historical Quarterly* 24 (1993): 32n37.

be innocent of premeditated malice yet guilty of manslaughter. "*Mu'ttekós*," however, disallowed such distinctions. The term said nothing about either the motivation or morality of the individual.

With its insistence on moral culpability, the doctrine of guilt and innocence concretely promoted the social compact by stressing the personal responsibility of individuals over the collective responsibility of clans. By considering intent or motive, it freed kin from being held accountable for the actions – now interpreted as "moral" failings – of their relatives. They no longer feared execution for the crime of a fellow clan member. Moreover, when an individual killed several people, justice was now served with the execution of the lone perpetrator. Guilt thus isolated murderers and thieves from their clans, creating a "criminal" class and undermining unified resistance to the enforcement of the social compact.

Guilt and innocence had broader implications as well. By defining dissenting Creeks as criminals, these categories weakened opposition to the economic and social innovations taking hold in the 1780s and 1790s. In addition, by contributing to a general decline in clans, the doctrine of guilt and innocence indirectly furthered these same economic and social reforms. The web of obligations and rights between clan members hindered the market exchange of material possessions because no single person could claim sole and absolute ownership of his or her property. As family connections weakened, therefore, Creeks were allowed greater autonomy to buy and sell goods freely. Creek ranchers and planters in fact often came into conflict with their relatives who, in the tradition of kin-based communities, demanded "customary" rights to their property.[43]

More abstractly, the doctrine of guilt and innocence allowed promoters of the social compact to suggest that individual Creeks were morally responsible to a larger nation. In the past, clans had defined crimes and punished people who injured their members. Under the social compact, by contrast, national leaders defined crimes against an imagined nation and took action against the guilty (just as today the state prosecutes criminal cases). Guilt and innocence provided categories by which to

---

[43] See, for example, the case of Alexander Cornels, discussed in Chapter 6. By comparison, see Martin Chanock, "A Peculiar Sharpness: An Essay on Property in the History of Customary Law in Colonial Africa," *Journal of African History* 32 (1991): 65–88. Chanock shows how the development of Western property rights in Africa depended on the "narrowing of the circles of obligation" to kin.

condemn individuals who, according to older practices, had not committed any crime. A horse rustler in Georgia may not have directly
offended his fellow Muskogees, but according to national leaders he was
nevertheless "guilty."

Like many Creeks, Hoboithle Micco preferred taking satisfaction to
punishing the guilty. In 1784, the governor of Georgia upbraided him
for defending the murder of an "innocent" white woman, killed for satisfaction. The governor explained that he would try to find and execute
the white murderer and insisted:

> The Indians should do the same in regard to those who had
> killed the white woman, for . . . (as the laws of the white
> people [stated]) . . . if Blood was spilt in the land that blood
> ought to wash out by the blood of the murderer and that he
> thought both murders [*sic*] ought to die.

Hoboithle Micco curtly responded that "that was not their rule and that
they being perfectly satisfied on their side, thought the white people
ought to be so too."[44]

Despite his resistance, Hoboithle Micco went on to sign two treaties
that explicitly proscribed punishment of "innocent" men and women.[45]
Yet Creeks continued to practice their traditional form of justice, though
on occasion both whites and Native Americans abandoned their positions when it suited them. In early summer 1787, for example, Georgians killed twelve Kasihtas (Lower Creeks) in retaliation for murders
committed by Creeks from Okchoy, a village of the Upper Creeks. Lower
Creek leaders asked George Mathews for satisfaction, reminding the
Georgia governor, "It was your rule that the innocent should not suffer
for the guilty."[46] Mathews, betraying his own principles, told the Lower

---

[44] Talk delivered by the Governor and Council of Georgia to the Tallassee King, 24 September
1784, "Indian Treaties: Cessions of Land in Georgia, 1705–1837," 164, GDAH.

[45] Treaty at Galphinton with the Creek Indians, 1785, "Indian Treaties: Cessions of Land in
Georgia, 1705–1837," 171, GDAH. Article 3 states, "It shall in no case be understood, that the
punishment of the innocent, under the idea of retaliation shall be practiced on either side." And
Article 4 repeats, "The punishment of innocent persons under the idea of retaliation shall not
be practised on either side." Treaty at Shoulderbone with the Creek Indians, 1786, "Indian
Treaties: Cessions of Land in Georgia, 1705–1837," 183, GDAH. The Spanish too tried to
enforce the European conception of justice on the Creeks and Seminoles. In 1789, Governor
Zéspedes of East Florida explained to Seminole chiefs, "None but the blood of a bad man can
be spilled. The innocent cannot suffer for the guilty. The great god who gives breath to the white
and to the red forbids it." Vicente Manuel de Zéspedes to Seminole Chiefs, 13 October 1789,
EF, bnd. 114J9, reel 43, PKY.

[46] Hallowing King and Fat King to George Mathews, 14 June 1787, *ASPIA*, 1:32.

Creeks to take satisfaction from the Upper Creeks because they had indirectly caused the murders by killing white settlers.[47] At this impasse, the
Creeks responded by falling back on their traditional methods of justice,
demanding a life for a life so that "tears of the relations of the dead will
be dried up, and our hearts not continue hot against you."[48]

Resistance to the social compact exploded in 1793 when Creek warriors,
dissatisfied with the Treaty of New York, fell on the Georgia frontier.
Creeks particularly objected to the large number of cattle frequently
driven across the Oconee and to the intruders who hunted on their land
with "great gangs of dogs."[49] They also disapproved of the surveying of
a new line in Georgia demarcating American from Creek lands.[50] As
Muskogees considered their options, deep divisions emerged between
their towns. Factionalism had characterized Creek politics for over a
century; indeed, it had been a strength of the Muskogee peoples. This
time, however, some Creeks attempted to close the divisions by coercion
rather than persuasion.

The charged political climate of 1793 began forming in February
when a delegation of ten Shawnees traveled through the Deep South
urging Creeks to take up arms against the United States.[51] They
reminded Muskogees of the friendship they had confirmed in Tuckabatche in 1786 when they had agreed to aid and assist one another against
their enemies. By ceding land, the Shawnee delegates now warned, the
Creeks were ruining themselves.[52] As the Shawnee message spread
throughout the Southeast, eleven Creek emissaries returned to Florida
from Nassau, Bahamas, where they had gone to secure an alternative
source of trade. Four hundred Indians awaited their return in the
Apalache area. Under the direction of Bowles's agent, George Wellbank,
they intended to construct a trading post at the mouth of the Ochlock-
onee on the coast of the Florida panhandle. Several successive years of

---

[47] George Mathews to the headmen and warriors of the Lower Creeks, 29 June 1787, *ASPIA*,
    1:32–33.
[48] Fat King to George Mathews, 27 July 1787, *ASPIA*, 1:33.
[49] Timothy Barnard to James Seagrove, 26 March 1793, LTB, 136, GDAH, also in *ASPIA*, 1:381.
    See also John Forrester to Juan Nepomuceno de Quesada, 8 April 1793, EF, bnd. 123F10, doc.
    1793–67, reel 48, PKY.
[50] John Forrester to Juan Nepomuceno de Quesada, 18 February 1793, EF, bnd. 123F10, doc.
    1793–25, reel 48, PKY. This line was actually the old British border as established in the Treaty
    of Picolata in 1765.
[51] Ibid.; Timothy Barnard to Major Henry Gaither, 18 February 1793, LTB, 125, GDAH, also in
    ASPIA, 1:418.
[52] Juan Nepomuceno de Quesada to Luis de Las Casas, 26 April 1793, PC, leg. 1436, 5614, reel
    158, PKY.

poor crops in the area had only aggravated their discontent over the high prices at the Panton, Leslie store in Apalache.[53] The Shawnee message coupled with the possibility of a new source of trade inspired young warriors to take action against the colonists on their land.

National leaders began intervening in early March 1793, first relying on persuasion, then resorting to force. When Efau Hadjo traveled to the Lower Creeks to urge them to reject the Shawnee talks, Kasihta Micco accused the Cowetas of horse rustling along the Oconee. The Americans should restrain themselves, Kasihta Micco told U.S. agent Timothy Barnard, "and not let the innocent suffer for the guilty, especially those who have always been, and are still your friends."[54] We do not know the actual words spoken by Kasihta Micco, for the ones we have today were translated from Muskogee. Subsequent events make clear, however, that his recourse to the doctrine of guilt and innocence had profound implications; it isolated the "guilty" from the "innocent" and gave national leaders a justification for executing those who violated the good of the nation.

Despite Efau Hadjo's plea and the best efforts of Indian agent James Seagrove, who offered a horseload of goods for each Shawnee prisoner and half as much for every scalp, residents in several Upper and Lower towns sent warriors against colonial settlements.[55] In mid-March, thirty Lower Creeks led by mestizo John Galphin attacked a trading store on the St. Marys, killing two men including the storekeeper.[56] Two days later, another party murdered four other whites six miles from the site

---

[53] Extract of a letter from Robert Leslie to John Leslie, 1 March 1793, EF, bnd. 114J9, reel 43, PKY; Francisco Montreuil to Arturo O'Neill, 10 March 1793, ST, PC leg. 123/35, PKY; Francisco Montreuil to Juan Nepomuceno de Quesada, 19 April 1793, EF, bnd. 114J9, reel 43, PKY.

[54] Elijah Clarke to Colonel Elholm, 19 February 1793, CIL, 1:268, GDAH; Timothy Barnard to Henry Gaither, 4 March 1793, LTB, 130, GDAH, also in *ASPIA*, 1:418.

[55] For Seagrove's offer for scalps, see James Seagrove to the chiefs and headmen of the Cussita and Coweta towns, 20 February 1793, *ASPIA*, 1:375. Regarding the towns that took Shawnee talks, see John Cannard to John Leslie, 12 March 1793, EF, bnd. 114J9, reel 43, PKY; Timothy Barnard to James Seagrove, 26 March 1793, LTB, 136, GDAH, also in *ASPIA*, 1:381; Talk from the headmen of the Chehaws and Telluiana, 29 March 1793, *ASPIA*, 1:383; Timothy Barnard to [James Seagrove], 9 April 1793, LOC, PKY; Alexander Cornell in behalf of himself and the Upper Creeks to James Seagrove, 15 April 1793, *ASPIA*, 1:384; Timothy Barnard to James Seagrove, 12 May 1793, LTB, 165, GDAH, also in *ASPIA*, 1:391.

[56] In addition to the Shawnees and George Wellbank, William Panton may have been partially responsible for these raids and, in particular, for ordering the theft of Robert Seagrove's account books. Timothy Barnard wrote to Seagrove that "Panton would rather see the whole State of Georgia in flames and women and children massacred by the savages than lose a hundred deer skins." Timothy Barnard to James Seagrove, 2 July 1793, LTB, 188, GDAH, also in *ASPIA*, 1:400; Governor of Florida to Marqués del Campo, 9 April 1793, EF, bnd. 46G4, 128, reel 18, PKY; James Seagrove to the Secretary of War, 19 April 1793, *ASPIA*, 1:378–789; James Seagrove to the Secretary of War, 31 July 1793, *ASPIA*, 1:399–400.

of the first raid.[57] Thereafter, the area remained quiet until 17 April when Creeks, once again led by John Galphin, raided plantations in East Florida, stealing slaves, cattle, horses, and household belongings and burning down buildings.[58]

The aftermath of these raids pitted the social compact against the traditionally diffuse power of Creek clans. James Jackson, a major general in Georgia's militia, demanded man-for-man satisfaction and the return of all stolen property, a request that in the past would have fallen on deaf ears considering the number of different clans involved in the raids. But warriors found that their towns refused to accept the American scalps they had taken on the St. Marys. Other towns not only refused to condone their actions but also demanded that the people of Chiaja, Coweta, Usiche, and Broken Arrow execute the participants. The cause of this unusual behavior was U.S. agent Timothy Barnard and mestizo Jack Cannard. By eliciting such actions, Barnard and Cannard were promoting the nation – the good of the Creek people, as they interpreted it – over the clans. To James Jackson's demand, then, the concerned clans responded by threatening the lives of Barnard and Cannard.[59]

At a meeting in Kasihta following the raids, a group of Upper and Lower Creeks resolved to enforce their will on the offending towns. They offered to turn over to Seagrove five warriors plus John Galphin and a white man named Upton. Alexander Cornels wrote on behalf of the Upper Creeks, "This will be a warning to the young people; then they will mind what their head-men say to them, and not before."[60] Only five days after Cornels's triumphant declaration, however, Timothy Barnard reported that there were too many towns involved in the raid to demand satisfaction.[61] In fact, Hoboithle Micco, on learning of the

[57] James Seagrove to Edward Telfair, 17 March 1793, CIL, 1:272–274, GDAH; Timothy Barnard to Henry Gaither, 10 April 1793, LTB, 145, GDAH, also in *ASPIA*, 1:419; James Seagrove to the Secretary of War, 19 April 1793, *ASPIA*, 1:378–379. Seagrove accuses Panton again in his letter to the secretary of war, 31 July 1793, *ASPIA*, 1:399–400. Galphin began threatening raids as early as October 1792. John Forrester to Juan Nepomuceno de Quesada, 1 October 1792, PC, leg. 1439, 1495, reel 30, PKY.

[58] Richard Lang to the Governor of Florida, 19 April 1793, EF, bnd. 123F10, doc. 1793–79, reel 48, PKY; James Seagrove to the Secretary of War, 19 April 1793, *ASPIA*, 1:378–9; John Forrester to the Governor of Florida, 20 April 1793, EF, bnd. 123F10, doc. 1793–84, reel 48, PKY.

[59] John Forrester to Juan Nepomuceno de Quesada, 8 April 1793, EF, bnd. 123F10, doc. 1793–67, reel 48, PKY; Timothy Barnard to James Jackson, 9 April 1793, LTB, 142, GDAH, also in *ASPIA*, 1:390.

[60] Alexander Cornell in behalf of himself and the Upper Creeks to James Seagrove, 15 April 1793, *ASPIA*, 1:384.

[61] Timothy Barnard to Henry Gaither, 20 April 1793, LTB, 157, GDAH, also in *ASPIA*, 1:421.

results of the meeting in Kasihta, had sent out warriors to commit further hostilities, involving the implicated clans ever more deeply. The Chiajas also organized new war parties so that "the heads see that its out of their power to kill man for man."[62] Faced with overwhelming opposition, the forgers of the social compact backed down. Kasihta Micco, Efau Hadjo, White Lieutenant, and Cannard wrote Seagrove, "The heads of your friend towns were determined to give satisfaction; but, after there were so many of your people killed, it was out of our power to do any more with them."[63] These Creeks still did not wield enough power to enforce the social compact.[64]

Despite their intentions, national leaders had no institutions to support a centralized judicial and penal system. Tustanagee Thlucco of Kasihta (not to be confused with Tustanagee Thlucco of Tuckabatche) explained that "the red people, have no laws to restrain their people from doing mischief, neither is it in their power to command each other to take up arms to suppress such conduct."[65] Not only did they lack centralized judicial and penal institutions, but there was no consensus about what was a crime. A trader who had been present at the meeting in Kasihta reported, "They consider it hard to demand men for the robbery, which, they say, was never done before; but satisfaction for the murder they think just on every principle."[66]

Frustrated in their attempts to enforce the social compact, Kasihta Micco, Efau Hadjo, White Lieutenant, and Cannard called on the United States to do so. In May 1793, they reported to Seagrove, "the only plan we have concluded on, is, to send your people up, and give them one drubbing, and burn their towns, and drive what property they have out of the land, and without this is done, you may depend you never will get

---

[62] Timothy Barnard to James Seagrove, 12 May 1793, LTB, 165, GDAH, also in *ASPIA*, 1:391.

[63] The Cussetah King, the Mad Dog of Tuckabatchee, the White Lieutenant, and Kinnard to James Seagrove, 16 May 1793, *ASPIA*, 1:388–9.

[64] In past times, Creeks had forced wars against their neighbors when demands for satisfaction were too great to be honored. The *South Carolina Gazette* wrote of the Creeks in 1762:

> Their young men, and some others, have been too frequently heard to say, that the only way they had to quash all demands for satisfaction for past outrages in their nation, is, to kill more white people, and bring on a war; that 'till then there will be no forgivenness for them, while they don't choose to deliver up or punish any offenders.

In 1793, young warriors confronted not only their American enemies but also Creek leaders, asking forgiveness from both groups. The Creeks had become divided against themselves. *SCG* (Supplement), 24 July 1762.

[65] Copy of talk from Big Warrior to General Twiggs, 20 April 1793, LTB, 160, GDAH, also in *ASPIA*, 1:401.

[66] James M. Holmes to James Seagrove, 20 April 1793, *ASPIA*, 1:386.

satisfaction."[67] Two weeks later, however, they reaffirmed their decision to "kill six of the ringleaders in the late mischief." "We all mean to give up, to be punished, the people you required," Efau Hadjo, White Lieutenant, Alexander Cornels, and Charles Weatherford stated, "but it is a thing that cannot be done at once, for it must be kept a secret; for Indians are not like white men, that can do a thing directly."[68]

Newly resolved to enforce their will, Creek chiefs dispatched warriors to murder five Lower Creeks and John Galphin. They failed once again and called on the United States for assistance.[69] "No other step can be taken to bring them to their sense, but for you to come amongst them and subdue them," Tustanagee Thlucco told General John Twiggs. He supplied the officer with detailed directions to Coweta, Chiaja, and Usiche, and concluded by asking that the Kasihtas be notified before the troops arrived, promising to keep the information secret from the hostile towns.[70]

At the same time, Creek leaders took another step toward centralized judicial and penal systems. To "prevent our young men from stealing," White Lieutenant reported, "we have come to a resolution to punish them by whipping." They perhaps were inspired by McGillivray's earlier effort in 1790 to punish horse rustling in the same manner. In addition, the headmen decided to put to death people guilty of murder. Creek clans, of course, had traditionally traded a life for a life, but here, a small group composed mostly of mestizos assumed responsibility both for determining when to take satisfaction and for administering punishment.

White Lieutenant next addressed the issue of guilt and innocence. Creek leaders, he told Seagrove, needed time to catch the guilty, for it

---

[67] The Cussetah King, the Mad Dog of Tuckaubatchee, the White Lieutenant, and Kinnard to James Seagrove, 16 May 1793, *ASPIA*, 1:388–389. The hostile towns, they said, were Coweta, Broken Arrow, Yuchi, Usiche, and Tallassee.

[68] For accounts of the meeting see Upper and Lower Creeks to James Burges and the headmen of the Seminoles, 9 June 1793, EF, bnd. 114J9, reel 43, PKY; Charles Weatherford to James Seagrove, 11 June 1793, *ASPIA*, 1:395–396. For quote, see Mad Dog, White Lieutenant, Alexander Cornell, and Charles Weatherford to James Seagrove, 14 June 1793, *ASPIA*, 1:396. Creek leaders had made much the same distinction between secrecy and directness in 1772 when they asked Indian agent David Taitt "not to demand Satisfaction publickley, but promised to give it as soon as they Could get an Opportunity to do it, as they Could not Kill any person publickley." Taitt, "David Taitt's Journal," 520.

[69] Timothy Barnard to [James Seagrove], 20 June 1793, LOC, PKY. Much the same information is contained in Timothy Barnard to James Jackson, 20 June 1793, LTB, 171, GDAH, also in *ASPIA*, 2:395; and Timothy Barnard to Henry Gaither, 21 June 1793, *ASPIA*, 1:422–423.

[70] Copy of talk from Big Warrior to General Twiggs, 1793, LTB, 160, GDAH, also in *ASPIA*, 1:401.

was unreasonable "to suppose [satisfaction] can be taken on the innocent." "I . . . understand by your laws," he continued, "that the innocent cannot suffer for the guilty; therefore, as eldest brother, hope you
will not so much unman yourselves, as to deviate from your own laws,
and copy ours." Renegade whites "have learned our young men their bad
ways," White Lieutenant concluded, "and, on account of our not having
laws to punish, we, by bad precedents, are become miserable."[71]

Fear clearly shaped much of White Lieutenant's posturing. By
appealing to the doctrine of guilt and innocence, he desperately tried to
buy time for Creek leaders and forestall an indiscriminate attack on
Muskogee towns. (He ultimately failed. Troops burned down Hothlitaiga in September 1793.) Yet, regardless of White Lieutenant's
resourceful strategy, the social compact indeed appeared to offer a solution to his misery. That solution, however, had enormous political and
social implications, and few Creeks were willing to embrace it.

In December 1794, Efau Hadjo again made a concerted effort to direct
the affairs of Creek towns, this time by returning stolen property to the
United States.[72] He sent out runners to call Lower Creek leaders into
their villages "for the purpose of collecting the prisoners and property,
horses, negroes, &c." Those who did not "give up the property by fair
means," he said, "shall by foul." A party of Kasihtas volunteered to
accompany Efau Hadjo to seize stolen slaves.[73] But these efforts failed.
It was the second time in two years that national leaders had tried to
impose their will on Creek towns. Most Muskogees simply did not share
Efau Hadjo's definition of the social good, nor did they approve of the
convergence of power in the hands of a few men, but that would become
clearer in the coming years.

John Cannard recognized that an irreconcilable division was emerging between Creeks.[74] In the beginning of 1795, he moved his slaves to
the Wakulla River near San Marcos de Apalache to avoid losing his property to reprisals by the Georgia militia. He explained:

---

[71] The White Lieutenant to James Seagrove, 23 June 1793, *ASPIA*, 1:401.

[72] Translation of talk of Mad Dog to the Governor of Georgia, from the Charleston Newspaper
of 7 February 1795, EF, bnd. 115K9, reel 43, PKY.

[73] Extract of a letter from Timothy Barnard to James Seagrove, 18 December 1794, LTB, 241,
GDAH, also in *ASPIA*, 1:559; A talk from the headmen of the Cussetas and Cowetas to the Mad
Dog and the Head Warrior and Aleck Cornell of Tuckabatchies and the Tuckabatchie King, 27
June 1794, in D. C. Corbitt, "Papers Relating to the Georgia-Florida Frontier, 1784–1800. Part
XV," *Georgia Historical Quarterly* 24 (1940): 155.

[74] Tom Hatley similarly finds a division between hunters and nonhunters, young and old men,
among the Cherokees. *The Dividing Paths*, 214–215, 217–218, 223.

> Whenever the claims made by the [U.S.] President . . . have
> been put forward in their assemblies, they had been sup-
> ported by the wealthy and aged of experience and good judg-
> ment, but rejected by the young people and bandits.[75]

Cannard had recently refused to attend a congress at Coweta, despite an invitation by Efau Hadjo. "It was useless," he claimed, "since for every one of these [wealthy and elderly men] there were a hundred of the opposite party of mad young men, as he had seen in the past assemblies."[76] As pressure mounted to return pilfered goods, Cannard wrote to Juan Nepomuceno de Quesada, the Spanish governor at St. Augustine in May 1795, to tell him that the entire nation was busy collecting the stolen property. He corrected himself: "When I say we have collected all, I say wrong as some of [the] young people have run off with some of it, but we mean to return all as soon as possible that we may have peace and enjoy what little land we have left."[77]

Creeks had long tolerated and even relied upon conflict between young and old, but by describing the participants in terms of wealth and banditry, Cannard revealed that a more serious breach had opened. Alert to the threat that this schism represented to their interests, wealthy mestizos readily promoted coercive measures to punish "bandits." Other Creeks, witnesses to the powerful and indiscriminate retaliations by U.S. troops, decided to follow their lead, choosing an imperfect solution to a terrible problem. The social compact forced Creeks to deviate from the white path, but few were pleased with the new direction.

[75] Diego de Vegas to Enrique White, 29 January 1795, PC, leg. 2354, 6, reel 380, PKY.
[76] Ibid.
[77] John Cannard to Juan Nepomuceno de Quesada, 2 May 1795, EF, bnd. 115K9, reel 43, PKY.

5

Blacks in Creek country

Throughout the widely scattered towns of Creek country, the status of African Americans varied according to the uneven expansion across the land of private property and centralized power. At one extreme, Creeks used African Americans as slaves, particularly at the confluence of the Coosa and Tallapoosa where the loamy riverbanks permitted wealthy mestizos to establish plantations. At the other extreme, some Creeks adopted blacks into their clans and gave them all the rights and obligations of other kin. This contrasting pattern also had a specific location, for it focused around a number of Creek towns on the lower Chattahoochee and in north-central Florida. Here, despite the threats issued by self-proclaimed "national leaders," Creeks welcomed African American fugitives as full-fledged participants in community life. The significance of this geographic and social distinction is greater than the small numbers of blacks in Creek country in the 1780s and 1790s would seem to indicate. African Americans, as slaves on the one hand and as equal members of society on the other, became central to the struggle for and against the new order emerging in the region. They played key roles in shaping how private property and centralized power expanded across the Deep South.

Unlike the neighboring colonists who divided people according to religion and skin color, Creeks had their own ways of categorizing the Africans and Europeans who invaded their land.[1] To be sure, they

[1] The question of racism among Native Americans has drawn a substantial amount of attention from historians and anthropologists. William S. Willis opened the discussion with his article "Divide and Rule: Red, White, and Black in the Southeast," *Journal of Negro History* 48 (1963): 157–76. See also William G. McLoughlin, "Red Indians, Black Slavery and White Racism: America's Slaveholding Indians," *American Quarterly* 26 (1974): 366–383; James H. Merrell, "The Racial Education of the Catawba Indians," *Journal of Southern History* 50 (1984): 363–384; Perdue, *Slavery and the Evolution of Cherokee Society, 1540–1866*; and Kathryn E. Holland

noticed the most striking physical difference between themselves and the newcomers: The latter had "hair all over their bodies."[2] Creeks categorized according to other differences, too. Like most southeastern Indians, they often believed that outsiders, whether European, African, or Native American, were the equivalent of "dunghill fowl," and that they could "equally knock off the head of one animal as of the other, with impunity."[3]

Color symbolism also helped the Creeks distinguish themselves from newcomers. In the early eighteenth century, a few Muskogees began referring to themselves as red people. Creeks had long divided the world into binary categories, and they considered red and white, as Europeans sometimes described themselves, to be natural opposites.[4] Though "red people" appears occasionally in French and English documents as early as the mid-1720s, it did not become common until the 1760s.[5] The Spanish did not record the term "*hombres colorados*" until the 1770s.[6] Its growing frequency was probably due to the departure of the French and Spanish from the Southeast in 1763. With only one European power remaining east of the Mississippi, the binary categories of red and white had greater relevance to the political situation in the Deep South. Moreover, the British insisted more consistently than other Europeans that they were white. The Spanish, in contrast, just as often divided the world between Christians and infidels, and the French usually referred to themselves by nationality.[7]

Braund, "The Creek Indians, Blacks, and Slavery." For an important contribution to the literature, see Nancy Shoemaker, "How Indians Got to Be Red," *American Historical Review* 102 (1997): 625–644.

[2] Creek leader Alexander McGillivray reportedly learned "upon the best traditional authority" that the Creeks had identified De Soto and his party by the "hair over their bodies." Pickett, *History of Alabama*, 75.

[3] George Johnstone to Henry Seymour Connay, 23 June 1766, PRO 5/583, p. 609, reel 66Q, PKY. Also see *SCG*, 19 July 1760; Adair, *Adair's History*, 2; and James Adair to Governor Johnston, September 16 1766, Haldimand Papers, MG21/B11, BM 21671, 441/53/55, reel 59C, PKY. For the attitudes of the Catawbas, see Merrell, "The Racial Education of the Catawba Indians," 365. For the Cherokees, see Hatley, *The Dividing Paths*, 162–163. Many Native American groups identified outsiders as nonhumans. Among the Kato Indians of northern California, for example, the phrase *na nesh* originally meant "human, not animal." Later, it came to distinguish Indians (*na nesh*) from Europeans. Karl Kroeber, "An Introduction to the Art of Traditional American Indian Narration," in *Traditional Literatures of the American Indian*, ed. Karl Kroeber (Lincoln: University of Nebraska, 1981), 7.

[4] Shoemaker, "How Indians Got to Be Red," 629–630.

[5] Ibid., 627–629.

[6] See, for example, Bernardo de Gálvez to Joseph de Gálvez, 13 October 1777, ST, bnd. 6614-A, 87-1-6/63, SD 2596, PKY.

[7] Shoemaker, "How Indians Got to Be Red," 631–633. The classic work on the caste system in the Spanish empire is Magnus Mörner, *Race Mixture in the History of Latin America* (Boston: Little, Brown and Co., 1967). For a fascinating account of the arbitrariness of racial categorization – and

The categories of red and white people appear to be joint Native American and English creations. The English influence is evident in the evolving meaning of "white people" in the Muskogee language. In the 1730s, Creeks called all Europeans whites. One observer noted in 1735 that "white man" was "the name they give to any European."[8] A decade later, a Creek leader named Chicate described how his people were surrounded by "three nations of whites, who were the Spanish, French, and English."[9] By the 1760s, however, they were labeling only the English as such, to the exclusion of the French, Spanish, and other Europeans, suggesting that the insistence of the English on their whiteness affected the way Creeks used the word. In 1761, for example, the *South Carolina Gazette* reported that the Upper Creeks used "white people" to "distinguish the English from all other nations."[10] A year later, some Seminoles were seen carrying the colors of two Dutch vessels whose crews they had put to death on the Florida Keys. "They were resolved," the Indians explained to a British storekeeper, "to take every vessel that put in there, of all nations, except the white people's," apparently referring to the British.[11] Similarly, in 1766, Governor James Grant of East Florida wrote that some Creeks had murdered a group of Frenchmen, but that finding "upon inquiry that there were not white men killed (so they call the English) they thought there was no great harm done."[12] In 1784, Hoboithle Micco identified Americans as the sole white representatives in the Southeast, to the exclusion of the Spaniards and remaining French colonists.[13]

For most of the eighteenth century, Creeks only weakly associated red

---

Creeks surely knew just how arbitrary it was – see Virginia R. Dominguez, *White by Definition: Social Classification in Creole Louisiana* (New Brunswick: Rutgers University, 1986).

[8] Patrick Mackay to the Trustees, 23 March 1734/5, *CRG*, 20:278–281.

[9] Governor of Florida to the King, 17 February 1745, ST, bnd. 6151, 58-2-13/17, SD 862, PKY.

[10] *SCG*, 16 May 1761. A French naval officer who visited Fort Toulouse in 1759 reported that the Indians there "call the English 'blond men' to distinguish them from the French and Spanish." Bossu, *Jean Bernard Bossu's Travels*, 138.

[11] *SCG*, 22 May to 29 May 1762.

[12] James Grant to the Board of Trade, 5 August 1766, PRO, CO 5/541, p. 113, in "British Colonial Office Records," 1:249, PKY. Two years later, Creeks again referred to the English as whites to the exclusion of the French and Spanish. Sempoyaffe noted that "in future he should look upon [illegal traders] as French or Spaniards, and not white Men, and treat them accordingly." Emisteseegoe to James Wright, 5 September 1768, *CRG*, 10:580–582. For another example, see *SCG*, 29 May 1762.

[13] In 1784, Hoboithle Micco told the governor of Georgia, "The French and Spaniards are at Pensacola and Mobile and that as they deal for money, that the Indians can't deal with them, but choose to trade with the white people." Talk delivered by the Tallassee King to the Governor and Council of Georgia, 22 September 1784, "Indian Treaties: Cessions of Land in Georgia, 1705–1837," 161, GDAH.

and white with complexion, but the influence of whites and mestizos, familiar with European racial categories, eventually induced change. In the 1770s, some Creeks were calling African Americans "*Esta Uste*," literally "black men," and Spanish "*Esta Cane*," or "yellow men," terms that probably included an indeterminate mix of what the Creeks imagined to be physical description and abstract symbolism.[14] By 1795, the mix was richer in physical description. A Chickasaw Indian described his relationship with whites to a Creek leader: "I loved you as well as them which although their flesh is whiter then mine we are as brothers and I thought to be so with all red people like myself."[15] Nevertheless, as late as 1810, some Creeks were still referring to Spaniards as Christians rather than whites.[16]

Despite the growing color-consciousness of Creeks, the complex relations among Africans, Europeans, and Native Americans in the Southeast prevented Muskogees from drawing any definite conclusions about the connection between complexion and identity. In 1752, the Florida governor explained that there existed a large population of "free people of color" in the Spanish empire, including "negros, chinos y Indios [Negroes, half-breeds, and Indians]."[17] Racial assumptions that worked in South Carolina did not necessarily pertain to Spanish Florida. In 1724, for example, a Yamasee Indian named Mad Dog traveled to Florida to sell ten fugitive slaves from South Carolina. When the Spanish governor reprimanded him for selling Christian refugees, Mad Dog pleaded ignorance: "[H]e did not know who could be sold and who could not because he was an infidel Indian who had just come to know the Christians."[18] Moreover, the Creek practice of tracing descent through the

---

[14] William Bartram, "Observations," 139; Pope, *A tour through the southern and western territories*, 65–66. See also Shoemaker, "How Indians Got to Be Red," 639.

[15] Opaymingo to James Seagrove, 1 September 1795, ST, PC leg. 203/49, PKY.

[16] See, for example, Hoboheithle Micco to [Francisco Maximiliano de San Maxent], 6 February 1810, PC, leg. 1568A, doc. 890, frame 469, reel 73, PKY.

[17] Fulgencio García de Solis to Marqués de la Ensenada, 25 August 1752, SD, leg. 846, 81, reel 17, PKY. On race in Spanish Florida, see Kathleen A. Deagan, *Spanish St. Augustine: The Archaeology of a Colonial Creole Community* (New York: Academic Press, 1983); Deagan, "Sex, Status, and Role in the *Mestizaje* of Spanish Colonial Florida" (Ph.D. diss., University of Florida, 1974); Jane Landers, "Black Society in Spanish St. Augustine, 1784–1821" (Ph.D. diss., University of Florida, 1988); Landers, "Traditions of African American Freedom and Community in Spanish Colonial Florida," in *The African American Heritage of Florida*, ed. David R. Colburn and Jane L. Landers (Gainesville: University Press of Florida, 1995), 17–41; Landers, "Black-Indian Interaction in Spanish Florida," *Colonial Latin American Historical Review* 2 (1993): 141–162; Landers, "Spanish Sanctuary: Fugitives in Florida, 1687–1790," *Florida Historical Quarterly* 62 (1984): 296–313; and Landers, "Gracia Real de Santa Teresa de Mose: A Free Black Town in Spanish Colonial Florida," *American Historical Review* 95 (1990): 9–30.

[18] Manuel de Montiano to the King, 31 May 1738, SD, leg. 844, 521, reel 15, PKY.

female line often came into conflict with racial hierarchy. In Spanish Florida, for example, the child of a white man and Creek woman was mestizo; in Creek country, the same child was Muskogee.

Creeks also used language to discriminate among individuals. Muskogee speakers, for example, used the word "*Chelokculga*," meaning "people who use an imperfect or mixed language," to describe Creeks who spoke Alabama, and they distinguished the Hitchiti speakers among them, as well.[19] But in the context of the French, Spanish, and British colonies of the eighteenth century, language proved just as unreliable as physical appearance. In 1768, the governor of British East Florida expressed concern about establishing a colony near St. Augustine of southern Europeans who resembled the Spanish in language and complexion.[20] He explained to the Creeks that the colonists "were not White People (English) but that they were subjects to the Great King."[21] Some seventy Indians later threatened the settlement under the mistaken impression that some of its occupants were Spanish.[22] Nine years later, Creek warriors attacked French-speaking settlers near British Mobile. When the English Indian agent reprimanded them, they claimed that they had mistaken the French language for Spanish.[23]

Behavior, rather than physical characteristics or language, proved the most important factor to Creeks in distinguishing outsiders. In the parlance of Creeks, for example, "Virginian" referred to any nonnative settler who encroached on their land. In 1765, Sempoyaffe, the head of the Cowetas, explained that "the white people in Georgia had passed the Line and were settled near Okonie, and that these white people were Virginians."[24] During the Revolution, the rebellious colonists received

[19] "A historical narration of the genealogy, traditions, and downfall of the Ispocoga or Creek tribe of Indians," PKY.

[20] On the history of this settlement, known as New Smyrna, see E. P. Panagopoulos, *New Smyrna: An Eighteenth Century Greek Odyssey* (Gainesville: University of Florida, 1966); and Bernard Bailyn, *Voyagers to the West: A Passage in the Peopling of America on the Eve of the Revolution* (New York: Vintage Books, 1986), 451–461.

[21] James Grant to the Board of Trade, 29 August 1768, PRO, CO 5/549, p. 282, in "British Colonial Office Records," 2:768, PKY.

[22] John Moultrie to the Board of Trade, 23 May 1771, PRO 5/552, reel 66B, PKY.

[23] Kathryn Holland, "The Anglo-Spanish Contest for the Gulf Coast as Viewed from the Townsquare," in *Anglo-Spanish Confrontation on the Gulf Coast During the American Revolution*, vol. 9, *Proceedings of the Gulf Coast History and Humanities Conference* (Pensacola: Perdido Press, 1982), 96.

[24] "At a Congress held at the Fort of Picolata in the Province of East Florida . . . ," 9 December 1765, PRO, CO 5/548, p. 113, in "British Colonial Office Records," 2:574, PKY; Copy of letter from William McIntosh to Thomas Brown, 14 April 1783, Sir Guy Carleton Papers, doc. 10091, reel 58A-28, PKY; Thomas Brown to Carleton, 28 April 1783, Sir Guy Carleton Papers, doc. 7572, reel 58A-21, PKY; "Substance of talks delivered at a conference by the Indians, to his

the appellation "Virginians," not because of their geographic location, but because they encroached on Creek lands. The British king, in contrast, as presented by his agents, protected these lands.[25] "Virginian" continued to refer to encroaching nonnatives through the eighteenth and early nineteenth century.[26] People of African as well as European descent fell under this rubric. As late as 1812, Seminoles would identify a black mail carrier in southern Georgia as a Virginian.[27] Creeks cared little whether strangers were black or white.[28]

When the Shawnee delegation visited Creek country in 1793, whites reported that it was composed of nine Indians and one white man.[29] But in fact all ten were Shawnee. U.S. agent Timothy Barnard met two of the delegates and noted to his surprise that "one of them is as white a man as me, and speaks nearly as good English."[30] To European Americans, the skin color of this Shawnee indicated he was a white man. To the Creeks and Shawnees, however, he was Indian. Racial stereotyping, which already pervaded the United States, was still uncommon in Creek country. Nevertheless, in the 1780s and 1790s, two opposing groups were forming among the Creeks, one distinguished by prominent members who enslaved blacks, the other by prominent members who themselves were black.

The first of these groups was centered at the confluence of the Coosa and Tallapoosa rivers. In all, a minimum of 300 black slaves lived in the area in the 1790s, most of them on plantations owned by white traders

Excellency Governor Tonyn, Brigadier General McArthur, and the Superintendent," 15 May 1783, LOC, PRO, CO 5/110, PKY; Thomas Brown to Guy Carleton, 1 June 1783, Sir Guy Carleton Papers, doc. 10116, reel 58A-28, PKY. The British in fact encouraged the association between patriots and Virginians. See, for example, Thomas Brown to Guy Carleton, 12 January 1783, Sir Guy Carleton Papers, doc. 6742, reel 58A-19, PKY; Louis De Vorsey, *The Indian Boundary in the Southern Colonies, 1763–1775* (Chapel Hill: University of North Carolina, 1966), 160–161.

25 Patrick Tonyn to the Earl of Dartmouth, 15 September 1775, PRO 5/555, p. 341, reel 66B, PKY.

26 See, for example, Richard Lang to the Governor of Florida, 13 July 1789, EF, bnd. 120C10, doc. 1789–145, reel 46, PKY; Testimony of John Ormsbay, 11 May 1792, *ASPIA*, 1:297–298; Diary of John Hambly, 1794, LOC, New York Historical Society, B. Smith Papers, PKY; John Galphin to Tallessa King, 1 January 1800, PC, leg. 216B, 336, reel 300, PKY.

27 Thomas Perryman to the Governor of Pensacola, 20 August 1812, PC, leg. 2356, 125, reel 172, PKY; Benjamin Hawkins to the Governor of Georgia, 24 August 1812, LOC, PKY; Benjamin Hawkins to William Eustis, 24 August 1812, *LBH*, 2:615.

28 In contrast to the relative disinterest that Creeks showed toward complexion, note the slave code of West Florida. Drafted in 1767, it stated that dark skin was the "badge of slavery." Fabel, *The Economy of British West Florida*, 24.

29 John Forrester to Juan Nepomuceno de Quesada, 18 February 1793, EF, bnd. 123F10, doc. 1793–25, reel 48, PKY.

30 Timothy Barnard to James Seagrove, 26 March 1793, LTB, 136, GDAH, also in *ASPIA*, 1:381.

and wealthy mestizos.[31] These slaveholders had accumulated human
property during the Revolution or in border raids thereafter. By one
account, when Britain evacuated East Florida in 1783 and 1784, some
4,745 blacks, or 42 percent of the African American population of the
colony, were missing. Many of them must have ended up in Creek
country.[32] Moreover, between 1787 and September 1789, Creeks were
said to have stolen 110 slaves and killed 10 others in attacks on the
Georgia border, while during the same period, they allegedly killed 72
whites and wounded 29, taking only 30 as prisoners.[33] Clearly, some
Muskogees had singled out blacks as war booty. Many black prisoners
were later sold in Pensacola, but others remained in Creek country.[34] In
addition, some Muskogee planters occasionally bought slaves in colonial
settlements and transported them inland. McGillivray even purchased
and shipped slaves from Jamaica: A "Very Small Vessell will answer the
purpose," he wrote regarding their transport.[35]

Wealthy Creeks along the Coosa and Tallapoosa rivers acted as agents
of racial segregation. McGillivray and others worked with Spanish
authorities to limit the freedom of Africans and their descendants, and

---

[31] It is impossible to arrive at an exact number of slaves in the region. We can be sure of the following: McGillivray died with sixty slaves, some but not all of whom would have worked at his
residence at Hickory Ground; Robert Grierson, a Scotch trader who lived at Hilabee on the Tallapoosa, owned forty slaves; McGillivray's sister Sophia at one time owned eighty slaves, many
of whom would have worked at her residence near the fork; Sehoy, another of McGillivray's
sisters, owned thirty slaves. Richard Bailey, who lived in Atasi, owned seven slaves. In addition
to these people, there surely were other large slaveholders in the area. Milfort likely owned a
number of slaves, and almost every trader owned one or two. See, respectively, the following
documents. William Panton to Lachlan McGillivray, 10 April 1794, no. 214, *McGillivray of the
Creeks*; Journal of Benjamin Hawkins, 11 December 1796, in *Letters of Benjamin Hawkins,
1796–1806: Collections of the Georgia Historical Society* (Savannah: Georgia Historical Society,
1916), 9:31; Journal of Benjamin Hawkins, 24 December 1796, *LBH*, 1:24; Benjamin Hawkins,
"A sketch of the Creek Country in the years 1798 and 1799," *LBH*, 1:298–299, Journal of
Benjamin Hawkins, 18 December 1796, *Letters of Benjamin Hawkins, 1796–1806*, 39–41. More
difficult to deduce are the number of slaves held in small numbers by other mestizos and Creeks.
Efau Hadjo, we know, owned five black slaves and Alexander Cornell owned nine. Hawkins
reported that in Eufala "several of the Indians have negros taken during the revolution war."
Benjamin Hawkins, "A sketch of the Creek Country in the years 1798 and 1799," *LBH*,
1:292–293 and 316. It seems then that 300 would be a conservative estimate of the number of
slaves along the Coosa and Tallapoosa rivers.
[32] Riordan, "Seminole Genesis," 250–252.
[33] Return of depredations committed by the Creek Indians since the commencement of hostilities
in the State of Georgia, 5 October 1789, *ASPIA*, 1:77.
[34] In one such case, McGillivray himself sold three stolen slaves in Pensacola, claiming all the while
that other Creeks had sold them. Affidavit of John McKenzie, 22 January 1822, "Indian Depredations, 1787–1825," ed. Louise F. Hays, 2, pt. 2:391b, GDAH.
[35] Alexander McGillivray to the Intendant-General Martín Navarro, 7 November 1785, in D. C.
Corbitt, "Papers Relating to the Georgia-Florida Frontier, 1784–1800. Part II," *Georgia Historical Quarterly* 21 (1937): 75.

by establishing slave plantations, they linked physical appearance with division of labor. Two days after offering his services to the Spanish crown, for example, McGillivray had written Commandant O'Neill of Pensacola, "The nation is now pretty well drained of Negroes what few there is, don't answer the description you wish."[36] In fact, McGillivray's correspondence is full of instances in which he secured the return of fugitive slaves to colonial settlements.

Native Americans in the Southeast had served as slave catchers for a century, but McGillivray allowed Spanish authorities to exercise a control over blacks in the Deep South that was significantly greater than in the past. Because McGillivray was literate, Spanish officials could send letters directly into Creek country describing the appearance of fugitive slaves. In November 1785, for example, O'Neill informed McGillivray to keep an eye out for Louis McCarty's slave Ciro, who had run away from New Orleans. Ciro was a creole from Illinois, twenty-two years old, and five feet, three fists high. A few months later, McGillivray captured the fugitive, who had been "roving about the country."[37] McGillivray's literacy also allowed Spanish officials to send lists of fugitive slaves, and the Scots Indian could keep these lists for an unlimited time. Memory, in contrast, was transitory.[38] In 1786, he examined a list of runaway slaves and noted his regret at finding some belonging to Martin Paloa. "I will preserve the negro list," he assured O'Neill, "and if chance should direct any to these parts you may be assured of them."[39] Almost eight months later, McGillivray secured their return.[40] By facilitating communication over long distances and by permitting permanent lists and descriptions, literacy allowed a greater degree of control over the movements and actions of blacks in Creek country.

Not only did McGillivray and other mestizos try to enforce a racial order, but their plantations served as models for its organization. Contact with the racial hierarchy of plantations had a concrete effect on Upper

[36] Alexander McGillivray to Arturo O'Neill, 3 January 1784, PC, leg. 197, 738, reel 273, PKY.
[37] [Estevan Miró] to Arturo O'Neill, 15 October 1785, PC, leg. 40, 48, reel 193, PKY; Arturo O'Neill to Estevan Miró, 7 November 1785, PC, leg. 37, bnd. 1, doc. 43, reel 169, PKY; Alexander McGillivray to [Arturo O'Neill], 21 February 1786, PC, leg. 199, 770, reel 383, PKY; Arturo O'Neill to Estevan Miró, 12 March 1786, PC, leg. 37, bnd. 2, doc. 67, reel 169, PKY; Estevan Miró to Arturo O'Neill, 25 April 1786, PC, leg. 37, bnd. 8, doc. 304, reel 169, PKY.
[38] Jack Goody, *The Domestication of the Savage Mind* (Cambridge: Cambridge University, 1977), chap. 5. See also Goody, *The Interface between the Written and the Oral* (Cambridge: Cambridge University, 1987), chap. 8.
[39] Alexander McGillivray to [Arturo O'Neill], 10 February 1786, PC, leg. 199, 767, reel 383, PKY.
[40] Alexander McGillivray to Arturo O'Neill, 5 October 1786, PC, leg. 199, 791, reel 383, PKY.

Creeks.[41] In 1783, for example, five Alabama Indians, who lived closer than other Creeks to the plantations of the Tensaw settlement, murdered two black slaves and stole three others. Arturo O'Neill reported a month after the murders that he had settled matters with the Alabamas, arranging for appropriate satisfaction. "They acquiesced to everything," he reported, "except taking the lives of two Indians in place of the two dead negroes, alleging that these were not equivalent to the Indians."[42] Similarly, in 1792, two Pensacola convicts, Josef Antonio Beltrán, of Spanish descent, and Leonardo de la Trinidad Poveda, of African descent, murdered a Creek Indian named Esnite. According to Arturo O'Neill, Beltrán was sentenced to death "as much for being the most guilty as for it being understood that the Indians would not be satisfied with the death of Leonardo de la Trinidad because, being a Negro, they look on him with the greatest contempt."[43] The governor of Louisiana, following the proceedings from New Orleans, shared O'Neill's concern. He insisted that the Indians be told that Trinidad was killed because he committed a crime, "not to satisfy the death of the Indian Esnite because that was done with the execution of the white man Beltrán."[44] The governor and O'Neill's anxiety was fueled by their own racist understandings, but it was also fed by years of experience with Native Americans in the region.

Despite the efforts of men like McGillivray, slaveholders in Creek country could not recreate the conditions in European American settlements that allowed for plantation slavery. The landscape and diffuse political geography were not conducive to an extensive system of social control. Easily accessible and unpatrolled forests offered slaves a quick escape. Moreover, the tools of control had to be imported.[45] In 1799,

[41] James Merrell finds that the Catawbas similarly began assuming the racial ideology of their white neighbors in the decades following 1800 when plantations began encroaching on their land. Merrell, "The Racial Education of the Catawba Indians." Kathryn Braund argues that the Creeks were racist by the 1730s, citing an Uchee account of the afterlife recorded by a Philip Georg Friedrich von Reck, a German Salzburger. The Uchees that Von Reck interviewed, however, had close relations with the colonists, and were not representative of the majority of Creeks. Braund, "Creek Indians, Blacks, and Slavery," 608; Kristian Hvidt, ed., Von Reck's Voyage: Drawings and Journal of Philip Georg Friedrich von Reck (Savannah: Beehive Press, 1980), 44–45 and 49.

[42] Arturo O'Neill to Henrique Grimarest, 19 March 1783, PC, leg. 36, 1133, reel 184, PKY; Arturo O'Neill to Henrique Grimarest, 28 April 1783, PC, leg. 36, 1143, reel 184, PKY.

[43] Arturo O'Neill to Barón de Carondelet, 5 July 1792, PC, leg. 39, 766, reel 162, PKY.

[44] Barón de Carondelet to Arturo O'Neill, 15 September 1792, PC, leg. 40, 455, reel 193, PKY. The trial of Trinidad and Beltrán can be found in the Papeles Procedentes de Cuba. See the proceedings on 11 March 1792, PC, leg. 122A, 487, reel 395, PKY.

[45] In 1730, the Cherokees, objecting to a treaty article that stipulated the return of fugitive slaves, stated, "This small rope we shew you is all we have to bind our slaves with, and may be broken, but you have Iron Chains for yours." Quoted in Hatley, The Dividing Paths, 104, and Wood, Black Majority, 262n85.

when one Georgian volunteered to travel to Creek country to recover stolen slaves, he explained, "I have in my employ a very good blacksmith which I would take on with me and place in the most central part of the nation where he could take care of negroes as we would collect them, and place irons on them to prevent their escape."[46] McGillivray acknowledged the difficulty of disciplining slaves in this environment by expressing his regret that he "could not use them in this country."[47]

For McGillivray and others, the impediment to the development of plantation agriculture was external; the political and economic geography of Creek country prevented them from working their slaves. For Sophia Durant, McGillivray's sister, it appeared to be internal as well. She, like many other Creeks, had little desire to produce a substantial agricultural surplus. U.S. Indian agent Benjamin Hawkins noted that Sophia's slaves were a "burthen" to her because "they are all idle."[48] "The black people here are an expense to their owners," Hawkins complained. "They do nothing the whole winter but get a little wood, and in the summer they cultivate a scanty crop of corn barely sufficient for bread."[49]

Hawkins saw Sophia's relationship with her enslaved African Americans solely in terms of economy, but evidence suggests that she developed close personal, perhaps kinship, ties with her slaves. One of her bondsmen, for example, married a Creek woman who may have been of Sophia's Wind clan. According to Alexander McGillivray, this particular slave, a well-known horse rustler, was "of no service." Yet Sophia, despite heavy debts and advice to sell the slave, refused to part with him.[50] A year later, debts had forced her to sell some of her slaves, but she remained "very much concerned" about them and hoped to redeem them as soon as possible.[51]

Sophia in fact allowed her slaves a good deal of autonomy. In 1795, for example, one of them journeyed to Pensacola, perhaps to sell a horse and some cattle that he had stolen or repossessed from Spanish Indian agent Marcos de Villiers. Before leaving Pensacola, Sophia's slave visited William Panton to secure money that Villiers owed him. This slave thus

[46] Murdoch McLeod to James Jackson, 6 May 1799, CIL, 2:558–559, GDAH.
[47] Alexander McGillivray to Charles Mclatchy, 25 December 1784, EF, bnd. 116L9, reel 44, PKY.
[48] Journal of Benjamin Hawkins, 24 December 1796, LBH, 1:24.
[49] Ibid., 25 December 1796, LBH, 1:29.
[50] Alexander McGillivray to Arturo O'Neill, 25 July 1787, PC, leg. 200, 962, reel 277, PKY.
[51] Alexander McGillivray to Arturo O'Neill, 1 March 1788, PC, leg. 201, 1045, reel 279, PKY.

not only traveled to Pensacola for his own purposes, but also owned property substantial enough to lend goods to the Spanish Indian agent.[52] In December 1796, Hawkins reported meeting slaves traveling down the Tallapoosa to a gathering at Durant's. Every Christmas, the slaves stated, they had a "proper frolic of rum drinking and dancing." "The white people and Indians met generally at the same place with them and had the same amusement," they explained.[53]

Sophia perhaps established the closest ties with a "negro preacher" whom she "owned." Alexander McGillivray, whose plantation was next to Sophia's on the Tensaw, complained in 1793 that "his negroes were not working and were going to waste because of a Negro Preacher whom his sister supported." The slave preached "his doctrine to the Negroes in the woods," and Sophia concealed the minister when McGillivray attempted to capture him. This man was in fact only nominally a slave; he was not a commodity. Once "owned" by a Mikasuki Indian, he had been given for free to Luis de Bertucat, the Spanish commandant at Apalache. Bertucat in turn had handed the preacher over to Benjamin Durant, Sophia's husband. No money changed hands.[54]

Sophia's preacher illustrates the distinctive nature of slavery in Creek country. The economy and geography of the region partially shaped the fate of slaves, for there was little means of disciplining a recalcitrant bondsman. But the beliefs of the Creek people also determined how slaves fared. Like Sophia, many Creeks would have been reverent and frightened of a powerful preacher no matter what his or her skin color. In 1798, for example, Indians murdered a black slave working at a forge in Tuckabatche because they suspected him of being "a wizzard."[55] He in fact may have been. In Yoruba culture in West Africa, ironsmithing is associated with the fearsome god Ogún.[56] Educated in Charleston, McGillivray little feared or respected Sophia's preacher, but Sophia, who lived her entire life in Creek country, felt otherwise.

For African Americans in New Orleans, Mobile, and Pensacola, Creek country sometimes offered an inviting alternative to enslavement in these colonial settlements. Luis, for example, apparently fled from Mobile, and

[52] Enrique White to Barón de Carondelet, 22 November 1795, PC, leg. 32, 1149, reel 387, PKY.
[53] Journal of Benjamin Hawkins, 25 December 1796, *LBH*, 1:29.
[54] Arturo O'Neill to Barón de Carondelet, 30 January 1793, PC, leg. 39, 1414, reel 162, PKY.
[55] Journal of Richard Thomas, 2 August 1798, *Letters of Benjamin Hawkins, 1796–1806*, 492–496.
[56] Robert Farris Thompson, *Flash of the Spirit: African and Afro-American Art and Philosophy* (New York: Vintage, 1983), 52–57.

"was long in this Country & no one Claiming him he passed as free & used to go where he pleased."[57] Even if fugitive slaves could not pass as free, their situation would likely have been better in Creek country than in colonial settlements. Most of the Muskogees who owned slaves demanded only a small portion of their labor. Hopoy Micco, a Creek leader from Little Tallassee, had "a Young Negro fellow" who served as a "cow hunter," but work must have been sporadic, especially since Hopoy Micco went hunting for several months every year.[58] Similarly, Efau Hadjo's five slaves must have labored most of the time for themselves, for they "put only forty baskets (about 20 bushels) of corn in the old man's crib" in 1801.[59]

Many slaves ended up working for traders who provided their bondsmen with shelter and agricultural tools in exchange for a portion of their labor. It was an unequal relationship, but were it to become too unbalanced, slaves could run away. Brutus, said to be "roving among the Seminole Indians" after fleeing from Pensacola early in 1786, probably ended up working for a trader. An Englishman offered $150 for the fugitive, and stated that should his master accept, he would go get (recoger) him.[60] This relationship was clearly on the coercive side of the spectrum; Brutus was being sold without his knowledge, but even so, we can imagine that he would have been of little use in Creek country had his new English master not negotiated with him. Perhaps more typical was the relationship between trader Stephen Sullivan and his slaves. In August 1788, Gerald Burns's bondsman fled from Pensacola with two others, only to be captured in Creek country by a Mr. Black. Sullivan spoke to them on the sly and successfully planned their escape with the assistance of his own slaves. He later denied knowing their whereabouts. Two months thereafter, at least two of the original three slaves were reportedly among the Cherokees.[61] The third may have still been with Sullivan.

Slaves who fled to the Muskogees often did so because they had

---

[57] Alexander McGillivray to Captain Folch, 2 March 1790, PC, leg. 52, Elizabeth Howard West Papers, PKY.

[58] Daniel McGillivray to William Panton, 28 September 1799, Greenslade Papers, PKY.

[59] Benjamin Hawkins, "Journal of Occurrences in the Creek Agency from January to the Conclusion of the Conference and Treaty at Fort Wilkinson by the Agent for Indian Affairs," LBH, 2:410.

[60] Alexander McGillivray to [Arturo O'Neill], 10 February 1786, PC, leg. 199, 767, reel 383, PKY; Arturo O'Neill to Estevan Miró, 12 March 1786, PC, leg. 37, bnd. 2, doc. 67, reel 169, PKY; Estevan Miró to Arturo O'Neill, 25 April 1786, PC, leg. 37, bnd. 8, doc. 304, reel 169, PKY.

[61] Martín Palao and Josef Monroy to Arturo O'Neill, 23 November 1788, PC, leg. 38, 600, reel 191, PKY; Gerald Burns to Arturo O'Neill, 3 December 1788, PC, leg. 38, 628, reel 191, PKY; Alexander McGillivray to Arturo O'Neill, 2 February 1789, PC, leg. 202, 663, reel 281, PKY.

firsthand accounts about living in Creek country. When eight slaves ran away from a Spanish official in New Orleans in November 1785, they were probably led by Pitter, who had once belonged to the Spanish commissary and interpreter for the Indians. King, another of the fugitives, knew about Creek country as well. He headed for his former owner, an Englishman, and in May 1786 was reportedly with him in the "Talapusa nation."[62] Slave owners eventually concluded that former black residents of Creek country made undesirable property. In 1794, one Louisiana planter sued William Panton for selling slaves who quickly turned fugitive. Panton wrote, "Pray was it not made known to the purchaser that the negroes were from the Indian Country."[63] In another case in 1798, a Panton slave turned to an Indian named Coosada Emathla for assistance in his escape. The Indian later excused his behavior for honoring the request by explaining that he "was very Drunk and did not Know what he was a doing for the Negroe wanted to run away & was plaugeing of him."[64] In 1802, Vicente Folch, the commandant of Pensacola, concluded that all slaves more than twelve years old believed that Indians, too lazy to oversee and punish their human property, made the best masters. Colonists, he continued, never knowingly purchased slaves who had belonged to Indians for fear of their nearly certain flight back to Creek country.[65]

Though slave life in Creek country surpassed work on a coastal plantation, not all slaves found their situation appealing. Andrew, for example, forced his Indian master to sell him. "I assure you he never will come this way," McGillivray wrote to O'Neill, but suggested Andrew might be found at the Spanish settlement on the Tensaw.[66] Black craftsmen may have found themselves better off in colonial settlements. In 1781, when four Englishmen absconded from Spanish-controlled Pensacola to the Creeks with three slaves, one of the bondsmen, a sailor, escaped and returned to the Spanish port a few days later. His skills were of little use in Creek country.[67]

[62] Estevan Miró to Arturo O'Neill, 29 November 1785, PC, leg. 3B, 1079, reel 155, PKY; Nota de los Negros, 29 November 1785, PC, leg. 3A, 721, reel 154, PKY; Arturo O'Neill to Estevan Miró, 16 December 1785, PC, leg. 37, bnd. 1, doc. 50, reel 169, PKY; [Estevan Miró] to Arturo O'Neill, 26 May 1786, PC, leg. 40, 63, reel 193, PKY.
[63] Quoted in Riordan, "Seminole Genesis," 253.
[64] Daniel McGillivray to William Panton, 24 April 1798, Cruzat Papers, PKY.
[65] David Hart White, *Vicente Folch, Governor in Spanish Florida, 1787–1811* (Washington: University Press of America, 1981), 73.
[66] Alexander McGillivray to [Arturo O'Neill], 10 February 1786, PC, leg. 199, 767, reel 383, PKY.
[67] Arturo O'Neill to Bernardo de Gálvez, 15 October 1781, PC, leg. 36, 249, reel 183, PKY. Of the other two slaves, one was the interpreter of a Mobile resident named Forneret. The other belonged to the treasurer of Mobile, Courville.

The casual labor on farms and ranches along the Coosa and Tallapoosa clearly differed from the backbreaking work on sugar, tobacco, and rice plantations elsewhere, but this marked contrast should not obscure the significant variations within Creek country itself. The lower Chatta-hoochee and north-central Florida formed another extreme on the scale of black–Indian relations in the region. Near the end of 1790, Julian Carballo, an interpreter for the Spanish, wrote a brief note to Arturo O'Neill: In Chiaja, he informed the Pensacola commandant, "free and maroon negroes, from the Americans and a few from Pensacola, are forming a type of palisade. They number more than 110."[68] This settle-ment, unlike anything among the Upper Creeks, points to the autonomy and strength of blacks living in the area.

Before 1790, most African Americans in the southeastern part of Creek country were concentrated in settlements like those along the Coosa and Tallapoosa. John Cannard, "a noted trader, farmer, and herdsmen" who lived between the Flint and Chattahoochee rivers, owned forty black slaves as well as some Indian slaves. Bully, another mestizo who lived on the Apalachicola, reportedly owned sixty-one slaves. Like McGillivray, these men were among the wealthiest in the region.[69] They got their slaves through pillaging, during and after the Revolution.

Unlike their counterparts in Pensacola, Mobile, and New Orleans, slaves who fled from Georgia before 1790 headed not for Creek settle-ments but for St. Augustine (with the exception of the twenty years between 1763 and 1783 when Florida was under British rule). There they could secure their freedom, offered to American slaves who professed a desire to convert to Catholicism. At a deserted hacienda near the St. Johns River in August 1785, for example, Spanish soldiers encountered some maroons who were probably headed for St. Augustine.[70] Three years later, a group of twenty-one slaves from Georgia fled to the Spanish city, at least five of whom a fugitive slave named Primus had "inveigled" from their Georgia plantation, providing a canoe for the escape. They joined thirty-six others in St. Augustine who had fled

[68] Julian Carballo to Arturo O'Neill, [1790?], PC, leg. 39, 1635, reel 162, PKY.
[69] Swan, "Position and State of Manners," 260–261; and Pope, *A tour through the southern and western territories*, 64–65. Boatswain, mentioned in Chapter 2, also owned slaves in the region. Bartram, "Observations," 156.
[70] Domingo Molina to Vicente Manuel de Zéspedes, 8 August 1785, EF, bnd. 118A10, doc. 1785–73, reel 44, PKY; Domingo Molina to Vicente Manuel de Zéspedes, 13 August 1785, EF, bnd. 118A10, doc. 1785–79, reel 44, PKY.

under "the pretext of religion."[71] In so doing, they were following in the steps of their South Carolina forebears who had been fleeing to St. Augustine for a century.[72] Though these fugitives were sent to Havana as free men and women,[73] they were among the last blacks to secure their liberty in Spanish Florida.

In July 1790, as part of a larger policy to halt the spread of revolutionary ideas in the New World, the Spanish government ordered the governor of St. Augustine to desist from freeing fugitive slaves. The decree was to be publicized so that slaves in the United States learned of it.[74] In Florida, the denial of sanctuary had the unintended consequence of driving fugitive slaves into Creek country where, perhaps inspired by their knowledge of Atlantic world uprisings and the "advantage of liberty," they would later become among the staunchest opponents of the new order spreading across the land.[75]

At the end of 1790, when Carballo noted the beginnings of a black settlement at Chiaja, African Americans on the Flint and Chattahoochee rivers were just beginning to attain significant numbers. Slaves who fled Georgia, noted the state's governor about a decade later, "will very probably be concealed by some negro fellows who are in the [Creek] nation and run away some years ago."[76] Spain's new policy denying asylum to

---

[71] Memorial of Alexander Bisset, 1 October 1788, LOC, PKY; Vicente Manuel de Zéspedes to José de Ezpeleta, 3 November 1788, LOC, AGI, PC, leg. 1395, PKY; Josef de Espeleta to Vicente Manuel de Zéspedes, 19 December 1788, EF, bnd. 1B, 318, reel 1, PKY.

[72] The Spanish side of the equation can be studied in Jane Landers's articles, "Spanish Sanctuary: Fugitives in Florida, 1687–1790," and "Gracia Real de Santa Teresa de Mose." See also John J. TePaske, "The Fugitive Slave: Intercolonial Rivalry and Spanish Slave Policy, 1687–1764," in Eighteenth-Century Florida and Its Borderlands, ed. Samuel Proctor (Gainesville: University of Florida, 1975), 1–12. In Black Majority, Peter H. Wood discusses how blacks in South Carolina responded to the lure of sanctuary in Spanish Florida. Landers estimates that at least 251 fugitive slaves gained their freedom in Spanish Florida through religious sanctuary. Jane L. Landers, "Traditions of African American Freedom and Community in Spanish Colonial Florida," 25.

[73] Vicente Manuel de Zéspedes to Domingo Cavello, 17 October 1789, EF, bnd. 22I2, 219, reel 8, PKY.

[74] Luis de la Casas to Juan Nepomuceno de Quesada, 21 July 1790, EF, bnd. 1C, 527, reel 1, PKY. For a discussion of the larger Atlantic-world context of the Spanish decree in 1790, see Julius S. Scott, "The Common Wind: Currents of Afro-American Communication in the Era of the Haitian Revolution" (Ph.D. diss., Duke University, 1986), 102–103, 177–189.

[75] Governor Enrique White of St. Augustine complained in 1796 that fugitive slaves "dedicate themselves to instilling in the minds of the pacific Spanish slaves ideas of the advantage of liberty." Enrique White to Carlos Martínez de Yrujo, 4 October 1796, PC, leg. 1439, 829, reel 29, PKY. On the spread of revolutionary ideology among slaves, see Scott, "The Common Wind," and Peter H. Wood, "'Taking Care of Business' in Revolutionary South Carolina: Republicanism and the Slave Society," in The Southern Experience in the American Revolution, ed. Jeffery J. Crow and Larry E. Tise (Chapel Hill: University of North Carolina, 1978), 268–293.

[76] [Governor of Georgia] to the Chehaw King, 5 March 1799, CIL, 2:551–2, GDAH.

fugitive slaves contributed to the influx of African Americans. So too did a policy granting head rights to whites who immigrated to Florida with slaves, an attempt to repopulate the colony after the exodus of English settlers in 1784. In the first three months after this policy was instituted in 1790, about 300 whites migrated to Florida bringing with them over 1,000 slaves, many of whom probably looked to Creek country for freedom.[77] In addition, the Treaty of New York, though a dead letter after it was signed in August 1790, provided for the return of "white inhabitants or negroes, who are now prisoners,"[78] and blacks in Creek country may have felt it prudent to leave the area around the Coosa and Tallapoosa for the Flint and Chattahoochee because of McGillivray's influence in the former region.

Once the black population began to expand, Creeks took active measures to continue the trend. In February 1793, a group of Indians stole some slaves on the south side of the Altamaha River, and a month later, George Galphin led a raid on the St. Marys, stealing seven slaves along with some horses and cattle.[79] In early May 1793, Creeks raided William Smith's rice plantation in Liberty County, Georgia, and carried off thirteen more slaves, and the same month it was reported that the Chiajas "brought large gangs of cattle and horses in with them with some negroes."[80] Twelve months later, according to a Georgia newspaper, the Usiches and Chiajas again raided the Altamaha frontier with the intention of stealing cattle and slaves, and at the close of the 1794, a party of Hitchitis stole six slaves from Georgia.[81] The palisade Carballo noted at the opening of the decade had become the hub of African and Indian relations in Creek country.

African Americans were more than passive objects in these raids.

[77] Landers, "Traditions of African American Freedom and Community in Spanish Colonial Florida," 20.
[78] Article 3, Treaty of New York, *ASPIA*, 1:81–82.
[79] J. Houston to Edward Telfair, 18 March 1793, CIL, 1:275, GDAH; Richard Lang to the Governor of Florida, 19 April 1793, EF, bnd. 123F10, doc. 1793–79, reel 48, PKY; John Forrester to Juan Nepomuceno de Quesada, 23 April 1793, EF, bnd. 123F10, doc. 1793–87, reel 48, PKY.
[80] Affidavit of William Smith, 4 June 1821, "Indian Depredations, 1787–1825," 2, pt. 2:628, GDAH; James Jackson to Edward Telfair, 9 May 1793, CIL, 1:309–310, GDAH; John Cannard to William Panton, 27 May 1793, PC, leg. 208A, 631, reel 286, PKY.
[81] "News from the Newspaper of Georgia," 10 May 1794, EF, bnd. 114J9, reel 43, PKY. On the Hitchitis, see James Durouzeaux to Henry White, 19 November 1794, PC, leg. 208A, 572, reel 286, PKY; and Enrique White to Barón de Carondelet, 26 December 1794, PC, leg. 30, 750, reel 418, PKY. When Upper Creeks promised to secure the return of slaves stolen from Americans, they pointed to Usiches and Chiajas as the culprits. Extract of a letter from Timothy Barnard to James Seagrove, 18 December 1794, LTB, 241, GDAH, also in *ASPIA*, 1:559; Translation of talk of Mad Dog to the Governor of Georgia, from the Charleston Newspaper of 7 February 1795, 7 February 1795, EF, bnd. 115K9, reel 43, PKY.

In 1793, for example, a "horrid banditti of negroes" fled from South Carolina for the Creeks. (There is no record that they successfully reached their destination.)[82] Another slave from Georgia reportedly "got with the Indians" on his own accord and "made his escape with them to the nation."[83] That same year, when Georgia militia retaliated by marching against Chiaja, "where they expected a large booty in negroes and other property," they were beaten back by sixteen Indians and four blacks.[84]

Slaves were inspired to flee and Indians to welcome them by African Americans who had previously joined the Creeks. In 1795, for example, ten Indians entered the Spanish settlements along the St. Johns River where they were seen "burning forests and pastures and even introducing themselves into the houses of the residents." "They have in their company two negroes stolen in past years from the then Governor of Georgia, Houston," explained Carlos Howard, a Spanish officer. He continued:

> [The two Negroes] already speak Indian, and through them the savages have indicated that the adjacent country belongs to them, and that they will hunt in it as long as they like. Here one should add that the aforementioned negroes are praising to the residents' slaves the good life that people of their color enjoy in the nation where they eat the same as their masters and work only when they wish without fear of punishment.[85]

Howard clearly feared the possibility of widespread flight or insurrection, especially because the group had already visited John McQueen's plantation where nine fugitive slaves, led by one Titus, were being held.[86] The intersection of the fugitive slaves and this band of Indians with

---

[82] [James Jackson?] to [the Governor of Georgia], 21 July 1793, CIL, 1:334–337, GDAH.

[83] Affidavit of Nathan Atkinson, 31 October 1802, "Indian Depredations, 1787–1825," 2, pt. 1:85.

[84] James Seagrove to the Secretary of War, 31 October 1793, ASPIA, 1:468–469; Extract of a letter from Lieutenant Van Allen to Colonel Henry Gaither, 18 October 1793, CIL, 1:338–9, GDAH. Spanish officials had mixed success when they negotiated the return of some of the slaves stolen from East Florida. Juan Nepomuceno de Quesada to Luis de las Casas, 7 September 1793, EF, bnd. 24, 177, reel 9, PKY; Juan Nepomuceno de Quesada to Francisco Montreuil, 14 November 1793, EF, bnd. 114J9, reel 43, PKY; Carlos Howard to Richard Lang, 3 December 1793, EF, bnd. 124G10, doc. 1793, reel 49, PKY; Francisco Montreuil to Juan Nepomuceno de Quesada, 25 February 1794, EF, bnd. 115K9, reel 43, PKY.

[85] Carlos Howard to Juan Nepomuceno de Quesada, 16 April 1795, EF, bnd. 128K10, 1795–218, reel 51, PKY.

[86] These Indians had been in the area for over two months, since the end of January 1795. Carlos Howard to Juan Nepomuceno de Quesada, 3 February 1795, EF, bnd. 128K10, 1795–92, reel 51, PKY; and Carlos Howard to Juan Nepomuceno de Quesada, 27 April 1795, EF, bnd. 128K10, doc. 1795–251, reel 51, PKY.

their black interpreters reflects a larger convergence of interests. The Creeks were led by Cohiti, a "witch" from Hitchiti who had been expelled from his town for making false "exorcisms or predictions."[87] Regardless of the cause of Cohiti's expulsion, his subsequent actions indicate that he was angry about the expansion of plantations on Creek lands. When Howard told him he could not hunt and burn forests and pastures among the plantations, Cohiti, whose rich dress and elaborately painted body and face attested to his position as a powerful shaman, explained through his black translator Peter that the Americans had taken their hunting lands. They had nowhere else to hunt, he stated, and in any case, the Florida lands were theirs. At the same time, Peter was spreading news of the "good life" and "bribing the slaves to flee to the nation." Howard noted with certain anger that Peter met his orders to desist by brazenly laughing in his face.[88] Peter and Cohiti, as well as Titus and his companions, were all responding to the same process, the expansion of white settlers, and of plantation agriculture, in the Southeast.[89]

Howard's fears were warranted, for shortly after Peter had an extended conversation with Titus, Titus and three other slaves escaped.[90] Supplied with venison by Cohiti's band, Titus and the other fugitives were to hide in a swamp until they and the Indians could steal into Creek country, but pressure from Howard forced Cohiti to return them to McQueen's plantation two days later.[91] He and seven other Indians brought the fugitives in unbound and, along with McQueen's astonished field slaves, proceeded to watch, loaded shotguns in hand, as Titus drew a knife and threatened to cut out McQueen's bowels. Titus then fled across a newly cleared field still strewn with timbers, making pursuit on horseback impossible. Cohiti's casual observation of this escape was a not-so-subtle message that he cared little for McQueen and his plantation. Should the message have gone unheeded, Peter responded "with

[87] Carlos Howard to Bartolomé Morales, 25 May 1795, EF, bnd. 128K10, doc. 1795–304, reel 51, PKY; Carlos Howard to Bartolomé Morales, 26 May 1795, EF, bnd. 128K10, doc. 1795–307, reel 51, PKY.

[88] Carlos Howard, Report on Indian relations at San Vicente Ferrer, 26 April 1795, EF, bnd. 128K10, doc. 1795–244, reel 51, PKY.

[89] Both Titus and Cohiti exhibited self-destructive and violent behavior, an indication that oppression breeds not only resistance, but also unproductive anger. Cohiti and his band drank excessively. Titus on more than one occasion beat his wife senseless. Carlos Howard, Report on Indian relations at San Vicente Ferrer, 26 April 1795, EF, bnd. 128K10, doc. 1795–244, reel 51, PKY.

[90] Carlos Howard, Report on Indian relations at San Vicente Ferrer, 26 April 1795, EF, bnd. 128K10, doc. 1795–244, reel 51, PKY.

[91] John McQueen to Carlos Howard, 24 April 1795, EF, bnd. 128K10, doc. 1795–245, reel 51, PKY.

much haughtiness" to McQueen's angry reprimand, stating that "his master and every other Indian there were as good as [McQueen]."[92]

Titus was soon captured and sent on to St. Augustine with two guards,[93] but Cohiti and Peter remained, "daily inconveniencing the settlers by conspiring with their negroes and . . . persuading them to flee."[94] Throughout May, June, and July 1795, they danced with the slaves in the region, and Peter preached the good life to them.[95] It must have given Peter, the former slave of the governor of Georgia, particular satisfaction to accompany Cohiti to St. Augustine to meet the Spanish governor on equal terms. Peter and Cohiti eventually disappeared from the watchful eyes of literate European Americans into Creek country, but there, the relationship between blacks and Indians continued to evolve and expand. It would soon prove to be a point of friction between Seminoles and the promoters of the new order in central towns such as Tuckabatche and Coweta.

Though European Americans wrote less about Seminole settlements than they did about Upper Creek towns, Spanish sources coupled with American documents allow us to catch glimpses of the areas where people like Peter and Cohiti lived. We might best observe these settlements by following Nathan Atkinson's slave, who saw them himself in 1793. "A thick wide set fellow not very high" who was "country born" and spoke "plain English," his companion bore the marks of slavery burned in his cheeks: On one side his owner had branded an N, on the other a W, both letters nearly an inch long and meant to "shew very plain." Nearly thirty years old, this "excellent sawyer, cooper, tanner,

[92] Ibid.

[93] John McQueen to Carlos Howard, 25 April 1795, EF, bnd. 128K10, doc. 1795–246, reel 51, PKY; [Governor of Florida] to Carlos Howard, 29 April 1795, EF, bnd. 128K10, doc. 1795–252, reel 51, PKY; Carlos Howard to Juan Nepomuceno de Quesada, 30 April 1795, EF, bnd. 128K10, doc. 1795–258, reel 51, PKY.

[94] Andrew Atkinson to Carlos Howard, 15 May 1795, EF, bnd. 128K10, doc. 1795–287, reel 51, PKY.

[95] Carlos Howard to Bartolomé Morales, 17 May 1795, EF, bnd. 128K10, doc. 1795–282, reel 51, PKY; Carlos Howard to Bartolomé Morales, 26 June 1795, EF, bnd. 128K10, doc. 1795–355, reel 51, PKY. Cohiti's motions can be traced in the following other sources: [Interim Governor of Florida] to Carlos Howard, 21 May 1795, EF, bnd. 128K10, doc. 1795–300, reel 51, PKY; Carlos Howard to Bartolomé Morales, 25 May 1795, EF, bnd. 128K10, doc. 1795–304, reel 51, PKY; Carlos Howard to Bartolomé Morales, 26 May 1795, EF, bnd. 128K10, doc. 1795–307, reel 51, PKY; [Interim Governor of Florida] to Carlos Howard, 1 June 1795, EF, bnd. 128K10, doc. 1795–317, reel 51, PKY; Carlos Howard to Bartolomé Morales, 5 July 1795, EF, bnd. 129L10, doc. 1795–404, reel 52, PKY; Carlos Howard to Juan Nepomuceno de Quesada, 19 July 1795, EF, bnd. 129L10, doc. 1795–465, reel 52, PKY; Carlos Howard to Juan Nepomuceno de Quesada, 1 November 1795, EF, bnd. 130M10, doc. 1795–893, reel 53, PKY; Nathaniel Hall to Carlos Howard, 4 November 1795, EF, bnd. 130M10, doc. 1795–897, reel 53, PKY.

and plowman" chose to run away from Atkinson's settlement in Camden County, Georgia, sometime at the end of February 1793.

He must have subsisted for about two weeks by stealing from settlements on the St. Marys River, because it was not until 11 March that he left the area in the company of a party of Indians returning from Trader's Hill on the Florida–Georgia border with the scalps of two white settlers. Sometime within the next two or three months, Hoopawne, who lived near the Kinchafoonee Creek, a tributary of the Flint River, purchased Atkinson's slave from another Indian for 600 chalks, the equivalent of about 200 deerskins. We might expect that Hoopawne anticipated a good return on such an outlay, but living among the Lower Creeks, where farming was not linked to export markets, he would never have been able to secure a profit except by reselling his slave. Nor apparently did he demand an excessive amount of labor from his bondsman. Confronted by Atkinson's agent two or three months after his escape, this slave "confessed that he did belong to the said Atkinson but that he would not go back if he could help it."[96]

Atkinson's slave would have had ample opportunity to observe the varied lives of blacks living among Seminoles. Most of the plundered slaves in the 1790s were taken directly to a settlement near the Suwannee River. "A black half breed by the name of the Black Factor," a trader reported, "is the chief of this town, as big a pirate as Galphin." Another report blamed "the half breed negro who lives low down on Flint River."[97] Among the Creeks, the "half breed negro" was known as Ninnywageechee, and he joined the mestizo Galphin and an Indian named Tuscayeppey in leading the raids of 1793.[98] Ninnywageechee was in fact an "Indian and negro mestizo, [a] trader among the Lower Creeks" who was usually in debt to Panton, Leslie and Company.[99] In 1798, for example, he owed Panton's establishment at Apalache a little over $185, and that same year, the storekeeper took some of Ninnywageechee's cattle in partial payment for his debt.[100] Though he constantly owed money, Ninny-

[96] Affidavit of Nathan Atkinson, 31 October 1802, "Indian Depredations, 1787–1825," 2, pt. 1:85, GDAH; Affidavit of Richard Carnes, 18 March 1800, ibid., 87b, GDAH. Apparently, Atkinson never secured the return of his slave. His affidavit was filed in 1802 in an attempt to obtain remuneration.

[97] John Forrester to Juan Nepomuceno de Quesada, 23 April 1793, EF, bnd. 123F10, doc. 1793–87, reel 48, PKY; John Hambly to Carlos Howard, 8 May 1793, EF, bnd. 114J9, reel 43, PKY.

[98] John Cannard to Juan Nepomuceno de Quesada, 25 May 1793, EF, bnd. 114J9, reel 43, PKY; John Cannard to the kings, principals, and chiefs of the Lower Creeks, 25 May 1793, EF, bnd. 114J9, reel 43, PKY.

[99] James Burges to Robert Leslie, 1 July 1793, EF, bnd. 114J9, reel 43, PKY.

[100] List of debts due by traders, half breeds and Indian factors to Panton Leslie and Co. of Appalachy commencing October 1787 and ending September 1792 [with addendum through

wageechee continued to purchase and pay for goods until he disappeared from the sources in 1813. His debt is thus less a sign of poverty than of his high status and ability to command credit at Panton's store.[101] Ninnywageechee also owned a plantation worked by African Americans.[102]

Despite his resemblance to other people of African descent (whites sometimes mistook him for another Afro Creek named Philatouche),[103] Ninnywageechee clearly saw himself as a Muskogee. When he promised in 1793 to return two stolen slaves or when he purchased a "Negro slave" in 1806, he was acting as a Creek, not a black man.[104] He also belonged to a matrilineal family, like other Creeks.[105] Slaves such as Atkinson's nevertheless would have taken note of Ninnywageechee's African fea-

1798], Greenslade Papers, PKY; William Laurence to William Panton, 15 August 1798, Cruzat Papers, PKY.

[101] His debts and payments appear in the following documents: Balance sheet, 30 April 1799, and Balance sheet, 31 August 1799, Forbes-Innerarity Papers, reel 147P, PKY; Appal.a L. purchase for sundry Negroes sent to the Establishment at Prospect Bluff, Negroes purchased there, and other charges incurred in Consequence of that Establishment, 30 September 1804 to 30 November 1814, Greenslade Papers, PKY; Account of Prospect Bluff, March 1813, Greenslade Papers, PKY. His status is further confirmed by a payment of $50 in 1811 from Forbes and Company, Panton, Leslie, and Company's successor, to Ninnywageechee "for accompanying us at the running of the line of this cession." Forbes in effect purchased his cooperation to ensure that other Creeks would not interfere with proceedings. Expenses attending the Cession of a Tract of Land by the Creek Indians to the House of John Forbes and Co. of Pensacola, 4 February 1810 to 31 July 1811, Greenslade Papers, PKY.

[102] In 1810, Forbes and Co. rented a horse from the "Black Factor's plantation" in order to pursue some fugitive slaves. Appal.a L. purchase for sundry Negroes sent to the Establishment at Prospect Bluff, Negroes purchased there, and other charges incurred in Consequence of that Establishment, 30 September 1804 to 30 November 1814, Greenslade Papers, PKY. Also in April 1814, the following expense is listed in the books of John Forbes and Co.: "To this sum paid the Black factors Negroes and an indian for their services for driving Cattle out of the swamp at the forks of the River at different periods during the high Water in the Winter of 1813." Land Purchase Appa.la for sundry Cattle purchased there and Expences attending them to John Forbes and Co., 28 February 1813 to December 1814, Greenslade Papers, PKY.

[103] Richard Lang, working from the descriptions given to him, assumed that the culprit was Philatouche, noting, "Some call him the Black Factor. . . . The said Factor is a half Negro." Richard Lang to the Governor of Florida, 19 April 1793, EF, bnd. 123F10, doc. 1793–79, reel 48, PKY. John Hambly and John Cannard corrected his mistake. John Hambly to Carlos Howard, 8 May 1793, EF, bnd. 114J9, reel 43, PKY; John Cannard to Juan Nepomuceno de Quesada, 25 May 1793, EF, bnd. 114J9, reel 43, PKY; and John Cannard to the kings, principals, and chiefs of the Lower Creeks, 25 May 1793, EF, bnd. 114J9, reel 43, PKY.

[104] For return of slaves, see James Burgess to Robert Leslie, 1 July 1793, EF, bnd. 114J9, reel 43, PKY; and for purchase of slaves see Appal.a L. purchase for sundry Negroes sent to the Establishment at Prospect Bluff, Negroes purchased there, and other charges incurred in Consequence of that Establishment, 30 September 1804 to 30 November 1814, Greenslade Papers, PKY.

[105] Ninnywageechee's matrilineality is suggested by two references to his nephew in the accounting books of Forbes and Co. In Creek families, a father was closer to his nephews than his own children. A List of Outstanding Debts at Prospect Bluff, Appal.a, 31 July 1811, Innerarity-Hulse Papers, reel 147, PKY; and Account of Prospect Bluff, March 1813, Greenslade Papers, PKY. For a different view of the identity of black Seminoles, see Kevin Mulroy, *Freedom on the Border: The Seminole Maroons in Florida, the Indian Territory, Coahuila, and Texas* (Lubbock, TX: Texas Tech University, 1993).

tures and recognized that in Creek country, people of African descent were not automatically relegated to the bottom of the social order.[106]

Atkinson's slave may have also met Creek leader Philatouche, called the "Black Factor."[107] He first appears in the sources in 1777 as a Lower Creek fighting for the British.[108] His status as a leader of Chiaja may explain why this town later became the center of the black population among the Lower Creeks in the 1790s.[109] Philatouche was deeply involved in Bowles's activities, participated in the adventurer's attack on Panton's store in 1792,[110] and in 1793, as one of Bowles's allies, journeyed to Providence in the Bahamas where he received a commission from Lord Dunmore.[111] By 1795, he was wealthy enough to hire a carpenter to build a new house in Creek country.[112]

His complexion may have made him especially sensitive to American encroachments on Creek country. In October 1795, when rumors were swirling that Efau Hadjo had granted a large tract of land to the United States and that France was planning to invade Spanish Florida with U.S. support, Philatouche journeyed to St. Augustine with several other warriors to offer assistance against the French. There, he strongly condemned Efau Hadjo, who was "so much attached to the Americans that he does all that is in his power to draw all the nation over to his way of thinking."[113] "I mean to go out myself" against the American aggres-

[106] Ninnywageechee's descendants include Billy and Samuel Factor, wealthy Seminole slaveowners. Littlefield, *Africans and Creeks*, 192.

[107] Richard Lang to Governor of Florida, 19 April 1793, EF, bnd. 123F10, doc. 1793–79, reel 48, PKY.

[108] Colonel Brown to Patrick Tonyn, 20 February 1777, enclosed in Tonyn to Germain, 2 April 1777, PRO 5/557, p. 345, reel 66C, PKY.

[109] Alexander McGillivray identifies him as such in his letter to Manuel Vicente de Zéspedes, 3 August 1786, EF, bnd. 114J9, reel 43, PKY. He is identified again as the *"gefe muy conocido del pueblo de Chiaja,"* or the very well-known chief of Chiaja, in Bartolomé Benites y Gálvez to the Governor of St. Augustine, 6 April 1790, EF, bnd. 385, doc. 1791–2, reel 173, PKY.

[110] His participation in the attack on Panton's store is noted in List of debts due by traders, half breeds and Indian factors to Panton Leslie and Co. of Appalachy commencing October 1787 and ending September 1792, Greenslade Papers, PKY.

[111] The journey to Providence was reported in Arturo O'Neill to Barón de Carondelet, 30 January 1793, PC, leg. 39, 1414, reel 162, PKY. Also see Extract of a letter from Robert Leslie to John Leslie, 1 March 1793, EF, bnd. 114J9, reel 43, PKY; Francisco Montreuil to Arturo O'Neill, 10 March 1793, ST, PC leg. 123/35, PKY; and Juan Nepomuceno de Quesada to Luis de Las Casas, 26 April 1793, PC, leg. 1436, 5625, reel 158, PKY. At the end of May, Philatouche turned over his commission to the Governor of Florida as proof that he had abandoned Bowles. Juan Nepomuceno de Quesada to Luis de las Casas, 6 June 1793, EF, bnd. 24, 97, reel 9, PKY. The commission itself can be found in the East Florida Papers, 5 February 1793, EF, bnd. 114J9, reel 43, PKY.

[112] Carlos Howard to Juan Nepomuceno de Quesada, 3 February 1795, EF, bnd. 128K10, 1795–92, reel 51, PKY.

[113] James Durouzeaux to Juan Nepomuceno de Quesada, 12 October 1795, EF, bnd. 115K9, reel 43, PKY.

sors, he said. When he repeatedly told the governor, "I expect to be lost shortly," his skin color lent special weight to his words.[114] In addition to Philatouche, Cudjomicco, identified as an Indian chief of Chiaja or Usiche, was also of African descent.[115] Cudjo is a common West African day name meaning Monday, while micco can be roughly translated from Muskogee as "chief."[116]

Though Atkinson's slave might have encountered prominent men such as Ninnywageechee, Philatouche, and Cudjomicco, most African Americans in the region were black servants and slaves. John Cannard, the largest slaveholder in the area, reportedly was "a despot, shoots his negroes when he pleases, and has cut off the ears of one of his favorite wives, with his own hands, in a drunken fit of suspicion."[117] Other evidence paints a more complex picture of Cannard's relationship with his slaves. Caleb Swan noted meeting Cannard's bondsmen on their way to the St. Marys River with a drove of horses for sale, suggesting that Cannard could trust his slaves with a fair amount of independence.[118] Ten years later, a Georgian reported meeting a slave of Cannard's named Sam in the town of Tallassee. Sam had been "seduced and taken away" from Savannah by Muskogees during the Revolution and had apparently decided he preferred living in Creek country.[119] Cannard also had a "negro servant . . . whom he always brings with him, and he serves him as an interpreter to treat with the whites."[120] Cannard especially entrusted his "confidential negro Joe" with significant authority.[121]

At the beginning of 1796, Cannard established a small plantation about twelve miles from the Spanish fort at Apalache, at the head of the Wakulla River.[122] At this establishment slaves worked unsupervised, pro-

---

[114] Philatouche to Juan Nepomuceno de Quesada, 22 October 1795, EF, bnd. 115K9, reel 43, PKY. Philatouche died some time after 1804. His name last appears in "A just balance of accounts and debts due by Indians and others residing among them to the firm and store of Messrs Panton, Leslie, and Co. formerly established on the Saint Johns River in East Florida," 19 June 1804, EF, bnd. 116L9, reel 44, PKY.

[115] Payemicco, Cudgomicco, Pohosimicco, and Tustoncos to [?], 21 October 1791, EF, bnd. 114J9, reel 43, PKY.

[116] On African names, see Wood, *Black Majority*, 181–186.

[117] Swan, "Position and State of Manners," 261.   [118] Ibid., 254.

[119] Affidavit of Patrick Mackelmurray, 14 October 1802, "Indian Depredations, 1787–1825," 2, pt. 3:784, GDAH; Affidavit of Alexander Shaw Newman, 14 October 1802, ibid., 784, GDAH.

[120] Quesada to Las Casas, 7 December 1792, PC, leg. 1436, 5372, reel 158, PKY. John Galphin also had a black interpreter.

[121] Wiley Thompson to the Governor of Florida, 20 April 1803, EF, bnd. 139H11, 1803–63, reel 57, PKY.

[122] John Cannard to Robert Leslie, 21 January 1796, Forbes-Innerarity Papers, 81/13, reel 147P, PKY; Diego de Vegas to Enrique White, 8 February 1796, no. 192, in letterbook Correspondencia de officio con el S.or Governador de Panzacola, PC, leg. 225B, reel 431, PKY.

ducing corn for the nearby Spanish fort and for Mikasuki. Corn demanded little labor compared with export crops such as tobacco, rice, or sugar, and most of the year, especially from November to April, Cannard's slaves probably worked only occasionally for their master. At times Cannard rented them out to work at the Spanish fort.[123]

Kinache, the head of the town of Mikasuki on the lake of the same name, and Payne, the head of the Alachua Seminoles near present-day Gainesville, Florida, practiced a different type of slavery. In Alachua, blacks owned and traded their own property. Spanish agent John Hambly purchased a horse from "Payne's Joe" in January 1794, for example. Later that same year he bought two horses from "Payne's negro Pompey" and paid "Payne's Jose" for a horse he had rented, giving them promissory notes payable by Mrs. Hambly.[124] Payne, who succeeded Cowkeeper as the head of the Alachua Seminoles, probably used his slaves as cowboys. So too did Kinache, who settled his slaves about a mile and a half above the town of Mikasuki.[125]

Though Atkinson's slave may have ended up as a servant, he also may have been adopted directly into a Creek family.[126] The initial step to adoption might be ownership by the clan rather than the individual. Such was the case of Sambo, who in 1788 was owned by the Tiger or Panther clan in Chiaja.[127] Sambo's role as clan property derived from the Creek practice of taking captives in war. Such captives were resold, killed to satisfy a relative's death, or adopted into the clan.[128] They were not

---

[123] Diego de Vegas to Enrique White, 5 March 1796, no. 197, in letterbook Correspondencia de officio con el S.or Governador de Panzacola, PC, leg. 225B, reel 431, PKY; Vegas to Gelabert, 31 May 1796, PC, leg. 122B, 1201, reel 397, PKY. Cannard had another plantation, which he disbanded in 1789, across the bay from Pensacola. A bond of debt from one John Etherington, identified as a former overseer, to Cannard suggests that Etherington may have supervised Cannard's slaves at this establishment. Etherington Bond, 15 February 1788, Cruzat Papers, PKY; and Arturo O'Neill to Estevan Miró, 3 January 1789, PC, leg. 38, 681, reel 191, PKY. Bowles mentioned the sale of corn by Cannard's slaves to Mikasuki and Apalache. William Bowles to [John Cannard], 1 January 1801, PC, leg. 211B, 541, reel 291, PKY.

[124] Diary of John Hambly, 14 January and 29 June 1794, LOC, New York Historical Society, B. Smith Papers, PKY. José and Joe may have been the same person.

[125] Tomás Portell to Vicente Folch, 1 October 1799, PC, leg. 2355, 697, reel 382; Jacobo Dubreuil to Vicente Folch, 28 March 1801, no. 19, in letterbook Correspondencia de officio con el S.or Governador de Panzacola, PC, leg. 225B, reel 431, PKY.

[126] In 1799, for instance, an Indian named Tossicio purchased a slave and adopted him into his family, renaming him Chenapkee. Edward Price to Benjamin Hawkins, 11 January 1799, p. 183, Records of the Creek Trading House, Letter Book, 1795–1816, U.S. Bureau of Indian Affairs, reel 94O, PKY.

[127] Chehaw Tiger King noted that Sambo was "one of his family property" and that though he had received five kegs of rum from Arturo O'Neill in exchange for the slave, "he was not the right owner" and could not sell him. John Millar to Arturo O'Neill, September 1788, LOC, AGI, PC, leg. 121, PKY.

[128] Perdue, *Slavery and the Evolution of Cherokee Society*, 3–15.

valued for their surplus labor. By adopting or owning slaves, clans became larger and hence more powerful. While living among the Creeks, Mary, for instance, stolen in 1793 from Liberty County, Georgia, gave birth to four children whom "the Indians kept because they were born upon their hands."[129] Fanny, stolen in 1796 also from Liberty County, contributed eighteen children and grandchildren to the Creek population in a little more than twenty years.[130]

Though the variety of positions occupied by blacks along the Coosa–Tallapoosa and in north-central Florida overlapped significantly, the African American population in the latter region proved more dynamic. With leaders such as Ninnywageechee and Philatouche, it expanded rapidly, forming close, sometimes indistinguishable ties with the Creek population, but also in places creating semiautonomous settlements. In the coming years, the contrast between black experience along the Coosa and Tallapoosa, on the one hand, and along the lower Chattahoochee and in north-central Florida, on the other, would continue to grow, and more and more African Americans, weighing their options, would flee to the second location. There, they sided heavily against the centralization of power and the expansion of plantation agriculture.

---

[129] Affidavit of William Smith, 4 June 1821, "Indian Depredations, 1787–1825," 2, pt. 2:628, GDAH.
[130] Affidavit of John A. Cuthbert, 8 August 1835, "Indian Depredations, 1787–1825," 2, pt. 1:17, GDAH.

PART III

The "plan of civilization," 1797–1811

6

New roles for women and warriors

In December 1796, Benjamin Hawkins arrived in Creek country to assume his new position as Principal Temporary Agent for Indian Affairs South of the Ohio.[1] A proponent of what later became Jeffersonian Indian policy, Hawkins intended to transform the Creeks gradually and peacefully into respectable members of the new American republic. He explained in 1807:

> The plan I persue is to lead the Indian from hunting to the pastoral life, to agriculture, household manufactures, a knowledge of weights and measures, money and figures, to be honest and true to themselves as well as to their neighbors, to protect innocence, to punish guilt, to fit them to be useful members of the planet they inhabit and lastly, letters.[2]

Behind his inexact reference to "the Indian," Hawkins hid another goal: to reshape gender roles in Creek country. He encouraged men to abandon the chase in favor of ranching and planting, and women to vacate their farms for the production of "household manufactures." In addition, the Indian agent urged men to take control of family property and to assume command over their wives and daughters. Any analysis of the Creek response to the "plan of civilization" must therefore first consider the relationship between men and women before Hawkins's arrival, for when Creeks welcomed or rejected the Indian agent's proposals, they did so in large part because of the quality of this relationship.

---

[1] Florette Henri, *The Southern Indians and Benjamin Hawkins, 1796–1816* (Norman: University of Oklahoma, 1986), 58–59 and 93.
[2] Carl Mauelshagen and Gerald H. Davis, ed., *Partners in the Lord's Work: The Diary of Two Moravian Missionaries in the Creek Indian Country, 1807–1813* (Atlanta: School of Arts and Sciences Research Papers, Georgia State College, 1969), 7.

Balance, harmony, and tradition, so often used to describe Native American gender relations before the incursion of Western patriarchy, fail to describe the dynamic relationship between Creek men and women in the eighteenth century.[3] Deep-seated tensions, rather than static balance, characterized relations between the sexes in the 1700s, and disquiet provoked by the deerskin trade precluded any attachment by Creeks to an obscure and ill-defined "tradition." These tensions shaped how women and men responded to the "plan of civilization."[4] (Other factors include an individual's cultural proximity to American settlers, often determined by family marriages to traders.)

Gender roles, though always defined in opposition to each other, can have acknowledged gray areas inhabited by both men and women. Among Creeks in the eighteenth century, these shared areas were few.[5] Men and women stood in extreme opposition in the real and symbolic worlds. "In ancient times men and women were almost like two distinct peoples," recalled Jackson Lewis in 1911 or 1912, one of anthropologist John Swanton's "oldest and best" Creek "informants."[6] Benjamin Hawkins observed as much first-hand, writing in 1797, "It is not customary anywhere among the Creeks to associate with the women."[7] The separation of men and women began in early childhood. According to Bernard Romans, who worked as an engineer and surveyor for the British in Florida in the late 1760s and early 1770s, "a boy of seven or eight years old is ashamed to be seen in his mother's company."[8] Whether for shame or not, the separation was real, for by the time girls and boys

---

[3] An excellent monograph by Theda Perdue on Cherokee gender relations, for example, heavily emphasizes the balance between men and women and the persistence of tradition. Perdue, *Cherokee Women: Gender and Culture Change, 1700–1835* (Lincoln: University of Nebraska, 1998), esp. chaps. 1 and 3.

[4] In the 1990s, historians began to do justice to the complexity of the response of Indian women to colonization. See, for example, Nancy Shoemaker, "Kateri Tekakwitha's Tortuous Path to Sainthood," in *Negotiators of Change: Historical Perspectives on Native American Women*, ed. Shoemaker (New York: Routledge, 1995), 49–71; Lucy Eldersveld Murphy, "Autonomy and the Economic Roles of Indian Women of the Fox-Wisconsin River Region, 1763–1832," in *Negotiators of Change*, 72–89; Hatley, "Cherokee Women Farmers Hold Their Ground," in *Appalachian Frontiers: Settlement, Society, & Development in the Preindustrial Era*, ed. Robert D. Mitchell (Lexington: University of Kentucky, 1991), 37–51; David Peterson-del Mar, "Intermarriage and Agency: A Chinookan Case Study," *Ethnohistory* 42 (1995): 1–30; and Perdue, "Women, Men and American Indian Policy," in *Negotiators of Change*, 80–114. As Perdue points out, many Cherokee women welcomed the "program of civilization" introduced by Benjamin Hawkins because it appeared to validate their work.

[5] Cherokee men and women also lived and worked in markedly separate spheres. Perdue, *Cherokee Women*, chap. 1.

[6] Swanton, *Social Organization*, 384.

[7] Benjamin Hawkins to Elizabeth House Trist, 25 November 1797, *LBH*, 1:164–165.

[8] Romans, *A Concise Natural History of East and West Florida*, 41.

reached puberty, they spoke different feminine and masculine versions of the Muskogee language. Boys imitated the speech of their uncles by attaching distinct endings to verbs, while girls adopted the speech of their mothers by accenting different syllables.[9] In the first grammar of the Creek language, published by a Baptist missionary in 1860, the author H. F. Buckner concluded that the "old custom of having one dialect for the men, and another for the women," resulted from "the oppression of the females." It "was regarded indelicate and unwomanly for a female to speak to men in the language of men," he wrote. With an obvious Christian bias, Buckner failed to consider the possibility that these separate dialects were emblematic of women's power rather than weakness, but his observations nevertheless suggest that language reflected the opposing identities of women and men.[10]

Raised to speak distinct dialects and to perfect different skills, men and women worked in two different spheres. Women cared for children and the elderly, made clothes, and prepared food, while men hunted and went to war. At times, the two sexes lived apart for weeks on end. In October 1775, for example, one traveler found the Alachua settlement of Seminoles inhabited solely by women and children. The men were away in battle.[11] Nearly twenty years later, another visitor to the Seminoles during a war described a settlement on the Oklawaha in the same condition.[12] On seasonal hunting trips, women sometimes accompanied men but just as often stayed in town to care for the very young and very old. One newspaper reported in 1761 that in the month of February "the *Creek* gunmen are then generally out from home on their hunts, and leave only a few old men with the women and children . . . in their towns."[13]

The separation of men and women extended beyond everyday life

[9] Linguists debate the existence of men's and women's speech forms in Koasati, a Muskogee language, but because present-day speakers no longer use these forms, the dispute is unlikely to be resolved. There seems to be good evidence from the first half of the twentieth century, however, that distinct forms of men's and women's speech did exist in Hitchiti, Muskogee proper, and Koasati. Mary Haas, "Men's and Women's Speech in Koasati"; Geoffrey Kimball, "Men's and Women's Speech in Koasati: A Reappraisal," *International Journal of American Linguistics* 53 (1987): 30–38; Muriel Saville-Troike, "A Note on Men's and Women's Speech in Koasati," *International Journal of American Linguistics* 54 (1988): 241–242; Geoffrey Kimball, "A Further Note on Men's Speech in Koasati," *International Journal of American Linguistics* 55 (1990): 158–161; Geoffrey Kimball to the author, 24 October 1996.
[10] H. F. Buckner, *A Grammar of the Maskwoke, or Creek Language* (Marion, AL: The Domestic and Indian Mission Board of the Southern Baptist Convention, 1860), 9–10.
[11] Testimony of Thomas Gray, 10 October 1775, enclosed in Patrick Tonyn to the Earl of Dartmouth, 25 October 1775, PRO 5/555, p. 483, reel 66B, PKY.
[12] Diary of John Hambly, 9 April 1794, EF, bnd. 196A16, doc. 1794–18, reel 83, PKY.
[13] *SCG*, 7 March 1761. See also William Bartram, "Observations," 152. Women did at times accompany men. See, for example, Daily reports of the two pastors, 9 July 1751, in Jones, *Detailed*

into the ceremonial world.[14] At the *Poskita*, the annual festival of renewal, for example, men and women refrained from touching or even speaking to one another for fear of the harmful consequences.[15] During preparations for battle, as well, men and women avoided each other.[16] Similarly, in the period before menstruation and surrounding childbirth, women withdrew from the rest of the town, but especially from men who were believed to be particularly susceptible to the effects of menstruating or pregnant women.[17] In Koasati and Alabama, two Muskogee languages, the word for menstruation, *hollo*, was associated with dangerous magic and spiritual energy.[18] A woman's retreat from town during menstruation may have reflected a positive choice to sustain her life-giving power, but at the same time, it permitted if not encouraged both women and men to hold fears about the other sex.[19] Even the Creek cosmology was imbued with the opposition between male and female.[20]

Reports on the Salzburger Emigrants who Settled in America, 15:101–102; Abstract of Galphin's letter to the Governor of Georgia, 5 January 1764, *CRG*, 9:114–115; and Timothy Barnard to James Seagrove, 10 October 1793, LTB, 220, GDAH, also in *ASPIA*, 1:416.

[14] Amelia Bell Walker, "The Kasihta Myth."

[15] "A historical narration of the genealogy, traditions, and downfall of the Ispocoga or Creek tribe of Indians, written by one of the tribe," PKY; Adair, *Adair's History*, 115.

[16] Ibid., 171–172; Swan, "Position and State of Manners," 272.

[17] Adair, *Adair's History*, 129–130; Swanton, *Social Organization and Social Usages*, 358–361. Amelia Rector Bell, an anthropologist who works with Creeks in Oklahoma, argues that even today, Creek men see menstruation as a reflection of women's "generativity and unboundedness," forces that Muskogees try to control. Amelia Rector Bell, "Separate People: Speaking of Creek Men and Women," *American Anthropologist* 92 (1990): 332–346. See also the response by J. Anthony Parades, "Some Creeks Stayed: Comments on Amelia Rector Bell's 'Separate People: Speaking of Creek Men and Women,'" *American Anthropologist* 93 (1991): 697–700.

[18] Geoffrey D. Kimball, *Koasati Dictionary* (Lincoln: University of Nebraska, 1994), 69; Cora Sylestine, Heather K. Hardy, and Timothy Montler, *Dictionary of the Alabama Language* (Austin: University of Texas, 1993), 127, 274. In the contemporary Alabama language, the old word for menstruation, *hollo*, has been replaced by *ɬakhaniɬopotli*, literally meaning "to pass blood." In 1981, when anthropologist Amelia R. Bell was doing field work among the Creeks in Oklahoma, she found that Muskogee speakers referred to menstruation as "stink lying down," or, euphemistically, as "sickness." Bell, "Creek Ritual: The Path to Peace" (Ph.D. diss., University of Chicago, 1984), 79n5. Gregory Evans Dowd explores the theme of male and female opposition as manifested in Indian attitudes toward menstruation. See Dowd, "North American Indian Slaveholding and the Colonization of Gender: The Southeast Before Removal," *Critical Matrix* 3 (1987): 11–15.

[19] Historian Martha Harroun Foster points out that in some cultures, men's fears of female pollution may be confirmations of women's strength rather than weakness. Foster, "Of Baggage and Bondage: Gender and Status among Hidatsa and Crow Women," *American Indian Culture and Research Journal* 17 (1993): 142. Similarly, anthropologists Mona Etienne and Eleanor Leacock highlight the scholarly biases surrounding the subject of menstruation, noting "the generalized tendency to see women's menstrual lodges as signifying their inferiority and their own exclusion from society, while men's houses are taken as evidence of superiority and the exclusion of women from society." Etienne and Leacock, introduction to *Women and Colonization*, 4. See also Marla N. Powers, "Menstruation and Reproduction: An Oglala Case," *Signs* 6 (1980): 54–65; and Thomas Buckley, "Menstruation and the Power of Yurok Women: Methods in Cultural Reconstruction," *American Ethnologist* 9 (1982): 47–60.

[20] Walker, "The Kasihta Myth."

An integral part of Creek society, this opposition occasionally produced mutual hostility rather than balance or harmony. Most southeastern Indian men, for example, equated defeat with feminization, an association that might be characterized as misogynist. Bernard Romans wrote of the Chickasaws, whose hunting grounds in western Alabama bordered those of the Creeks, "They are horridly given to sodomy, committing that crime on the dead bodies of their enemies, thereby (as they say) degrading them into women."[21] Romans had perhaps mistaken a figurative expression for a literal statement, but his comment about sodomizing the enemy appears to have a metaphorical truth. The Chickasaws and the Creeks both forced their enemies to "wear the petticoat," as they put it. During a tense meeting with the Cherokees in Augusta in 1773, Creek leaders berated their former enemies for ceding land by calling them "old women, and saying they had long ago obliged them to wear the petticoat." William Bartram, who observed the proceedings, noted that the insult was a "most humiliating and degrading stroke."[22] "No greater disgrace can be thrown on a man than calling him by the odious epithet of Woman," explained Romans.[23] In insulting their traditional Cherokee enemies, Creek warriors might have also been referring disdainfully to the status of Cherokee women, who wielded a substantial amount of power. In his history of the American Indians written in the 1770s, trader James Adair summed up the difference between Cherokee and Creek women by contrasting the "petticoat-government" of the Cherokees with the "patriarchal-like" government of the Creeks.[24]

In the 1760s, changes in the structure of the deerskin trade further polarized relations between Creek women and men and drew resources away

---

[21] Romans, *A Concise Natural History of East and West Florida*, 70.

[22] Bartram, *Travels*, 382.

[23] Romans, *A Concise Natural History of East and West Florida*, 41. In contrast to the interpretation presented here, one historian argues that Native Americans drew on "European concepts of the female gender" when they disparaged warriors as women. Jane T. Merritt, "Metaphor, Meaning, and Misunderstanding: Language and Power on the Pennsylvania Frontier," in *Contact Points: American Frontiers from the Mohawk Valley to the Mississippi, 1750–1830*, ed. Andrew R. L. Cayton and Fredrika J. Teute (Chapel Hill: University of North Carolina, 1998), 77–81.

[24] Adair, *Adair's History*, 153. For a direct comparison of the status of women in Cherokee and Creek societies in the late eighteenth and early nineteenth century, see Richard A. Sattler, "Women's Status among the Muskogee and Cherokee," in *Women and Power in Native North America*, ed. Laura F. Klein and Lillian A. Ackerman (Norman: University of Oklahoma, 1995), 214–229. Sattler shows how Creek women had substantially less power than their Cherokee counterparts. His article must be read carefully, however, because he mixes evidence from the past and present. On the Cherokees specifically, see Hatley, *The Dividing Paths*, 149–150.

from female-controlled households. Before that time, women and men by necessity shared the additional labor of the widened deerskin trade.[25] Men expanded their subsistence hunting to produce excess skins, and women cleaned and cured the hides for export. Beginning in the 1760s, however, the demand for raw deerskins (hides that had undergone only minimal preparation) increased significantly in European markets, and young Creek men found that this change, which eliminated the need for women's labor in the dressing of the skins, allowed them to turn the trade into an exclusively masculine pursuit, as separate from women as the distinct dialect they spoke. Free from the direction of women who had channeled its proceeds into the matrilineal and matrilocal household, the deerskin trade rapidly became the province of young and relatively independent men. By the 1780s, the trade was exclusively in undressed skins due to the mutually reinforcing influence of European demand and Creek supply.[26]

On the Creek side of the exchange, documents suggest that men rather than women were the forces of change. The trade in raw hides initially occurred in the woods between unlicensed traders and hunters who accepted lower prices for their skins in order to purchase rum. These hunters – young, unmarried men who, as Romans noted, little associated with women – looked to consume their earnings immediately.[27] Creek leaders and colonial officials tried to prohibit this trade for two reasons. First, because hoofs, heads, and some flesh remained on undressed hides, raw skins were exchanged by rough estimate of size rather than by weight, allowing traders greater room to swindle hunters. Second, because the trade in raw skins was free from the moderating

---

[25] Carol Devens argues that in New France, the power of Native American women declined as they spent more time preparing furs for the market. Devens, "Separate Confrontations," 472.

[26] Braund, *Deerskins and Duffels*, 68–69; Fabel, *The Economy of British West Florida*, 56; William Panton, 2 June 1787, PC, leg. 200, 914, reel 277, PKY. Panton noted, "Lately it was found necessary to leave off dressing Skins as they Sold badly in Europe & to buy none except in a Raw State." Another impetus to trade in undressed skins perhaps came from colonial traders. In 1763, the Directors of the Indian Trade in South Carolina complained of "the enormous foul Dressing of Deer Skins by the Indians, and their still leaving the same incumbered with Hoofs and Snouts, so detrimental to the Leather." Quoted in M. Thomas Hatley, "The Three Lives of Keowee: Loss and Recovery in Eighteenth-Century Cherokee Villages," in *Powhatan's Mantle*, 236.

[27] Braund writes that women "perceived that it was to their advantage to trade undressed, rather than dressed, hides," suggesting that they played a part in insisting that traders accept raw skins. *Deerskins and Duffels*, 69. It seems equally possible that Creek women were forced out of their niche in the trade by Creek hunters. For a discussion of Cherokee women in the deerskin trade, see Hatley, "The Three Lives of Keowee," 235–239. Hatley observes that Cherokee women were "locked out of the men-only deerskin business." Hatley, *The Dividing Paths*, 161. Those Creek women who lived with traders, it should be noted, sometimes facilitated the exchange of deerskins for rum. Taitt, "David Taitt's Journal," 512.

influence of Creek women, warriors purchased alcohol instead of "other necessaries." After consuming their proceeds, they frequently plundered the necessities they could no longer afford to purchase.[28]

Attempts to control young warriors failed, however. In 1755, for example, a trader named Williams was accused of illegally trading rum for undressed skins in the woods at a place called Honey Mountain.[29] A year later, Creek leaders asked Governor Lyttelton of South Carolina to "stop all Out Stores." The remote trading posts, they complained, kept young warriors from returning to their towns and led to drunken and often fatal brawls.[30] Continued protests by Creek leaders indicate that the problem only worsened. At treaty negotiations in 1763, one Creek chief asked the governors on hand "not to suffer any people to trade in the woods, because the young people there got drunk, and disposed of their skins for that commodity."[31] In spring 1768, Creek warriors, supported by British Indian agent John Stuart, broke up one site of exchange at Buzzard's Roost on the Flint River where traders had established stores to intercept young Creek men returning from the hunt.[32] By 1772, however, despite efforts of Creek leaders and colonial officials, raw skins were becoming the dominant form of exchange.[33]

The preponderance of rum in the deerskin trade – in the late 1760s, about 80 percent of skins brought into Mobile were traded for sugar-cane liquor[34] – attests to its masculine character.[35] Alcohol not only

---

[28] "Regulations for the Better Carrying on the Trade with the Indian Tribes in the Southern District," in Braund, Deerskins and Duffels, 189–192.

[29] James Beamer to Governor Glen, 21 February 1756, DIASC, 2:104–106. During the Cherokee War, when Governor Wright of Georgia revoked a number of trading licenses to the Creeks in order to stem the flow of ammunition to the Cherokees, the South Carolina Gazette reported that "there are nevertheless people who trade in the woods with the Indians, and bring in great quantities of raw skins." SCG, 7 March 1761. Young warriors also began trading stolen horses for rum along the Georgia frontier. John Alden, John Stuart, 296.

[30] Headmen of the Lower Creeks to Governor Lyttelton, 13 October 1756, DIASC, 2:212–213.

[31] Journal of the Congress of the Four Southern Governors . . . with the Five Nations of Indians, at Augusta, 1763, 27.

[32] Emistesiguo to James Wright, 5 September 1768, CRG, 10:580–582; and John Stuart to Thomas Gage, 2 July 1768, and enclosures, Thomas Gage Papers, American series, reel 140H, PKY.

[33] Thus Escuchabe asked John Stuart for "steelyard trade the same as the Cherokees," promising that the Creeks "will give dressed leather." A talk from the Lower Creeks to John Stuart, 19 September 1772, enclosed in Stuart to Gage, 24 November 1772, Thomas Gage Papers, American series, reel 140H, PKY. See also Fabel, The Economy of British West Florida, 56. Fabel notes the case of West Florida merchant John Fitzpatrick, who, because of the demand in Europe, traded almost exclusively in undressed skins.

[34] Alden, John Stuart, 315–316. Kathryn Braund writes that with "easier access to rum, the absence of the French 'menace,' and large numbers of traders competing in a limited market after 1763, the rum traffic exploded. . . ." Braund, Deerskins and Duffels, 105–106.

[35] Other eastern Indians drank for the same reason. Peter C. Mancall, Deadly Medicine: Indians and Alcohol in Early America (Ithaca: Cornell University, 1995), 68–70, 75.

distanced warriors from the household-oriented and feminine trade in clothing, but it also facilitated the bold, daring behavior expected of young men. In the eighteenth century, Creeks appear to have associated drunkenness with madness, the quality of bravery and recklessness that warriors sought, and men consequently consumed rum in greater quantities than did women.[36] A Muskogee–English dictionary from the late nineteenth century glosses the Creek term *hache* as "drunk, crazy, resolute, daring," a word related etymologically to *hadjo*, as in the warrior titles Efau Hadjo, meaning "mad dog" or "drunken dog," and Itcho Hadjo Tassikaya, meaning "mad deer warrior," or, translated another way, "foolish, mad, drunken deer warrior."[37] As Tuckabatche leader Old Bracket recognized in 1752, alcohol deluded young men into believing they were brave warriors: "at Best they were all a Parcell of Madman, that when they were drunk they were all Men and Warriors, and thought they shewed their Manhood in insulting, abusing, and threatning to kill the white People."[38] Drunkenness also helped a warrior maintain the fearless visage that others expected.[39] When Benjamin Hawkins tried to

---

[36] For a different view on the consumption of alcohol, see Braund, *Deerskins and Duffels*, 125–127. She argues that Creeks "did not drink alcohol in a ceremonial context," but rather "to enjoy themselves" (125 and 126). As Braund illustrates, evidence certainly suggests that Creeks drank in part for amusement. William Bartram witnessed a "bacchanalian" drinking scene among the Seminoles at a trading post on the St. Johns River in 1774. Describing the singing, dancing, and "sacrifices to Venus," he noted that "in these frolicks both sexes take such liberties with each other, and act, without constraint or shame." Clearly, Creeks drank as a diversion, but even in the "frolick" that Bartram witnessed, they may have also used alcohol as a transformative drug. After recovering their sobriety, they prepared to depart for war. Bartram, *Travels*, 214–215. Throughout colonial America, it appears that young Indian men consumed greater quantities of alcohol than did Indian women. Historian Peter Mancall suggests that this consumption pattern may have been a result of the active participation of young men in the fur trade. See Peter C. Mancall, "'The Bewitching Tyranny of Custom': The Social Costs of Indian Drinking in Colonial America," *American Indian Culture and Research Journal* 17 (1993): 28.

[37] Loughridge and Hodge, *English and Muskokee Dictionary*, 140–141. See also Gatschet, *A Migration Legend of the Creek Indians*, 161.

[38] Second Journal of Thomas Bosomworth, October–December 1752, *DIASC*, 1:319. One night in February 1758, Keowee Indians in South Carolina dreamed "that they must have a Cagg of Rum before they go to War or they shall have no Success." Quoted in Mancall, *Deadly Medicine*, 64.

[39] There are striking parallels between the drinking patterns of Creeks and of northeastern Indians in the colonial era. A missionary to New France in the 1680s noted that the Indians he encountered "imbibe only to become drunk," so that when only a limited amount of alcohol was available, one Indian would drink to excess while his companions remained sober. There was "only one degree of drunkenness worthwhile," the missionary observed, "the sort which they call 'Gannontiouaratonseri,' complete insobriety. And when they begin to feel the effects of the brandy they rejoice shouting, 'Good, good, my head is reeling.'" Such drinkers were usually young men who were "professedly given to bravado, whose pride urges them to seek notoriety whereby they may receive attention for some deed or other." Closer to home, the Chickasaws also shared Creek ideas about madness and alcohol. In 1725, they stated that "if the Young Men

comfort a Creek who faced imminent execution in 1811, the warrior responded, "I do not fear death, for I am drunk to numb my feeling if they kill me."[40]

Creek attitudes toward drunken behavior further suggest that they associated inebriation and madness. In war, Creek men went through a ceremonial transition, donning black and red paint to symbolize their entry into the world of asocial behavior. On their return, they participated in another ceremony to mark their reentry into the social world of the square ground.[41] This transformation allowed Creek men to scalp and mutilate their enemies yet return home as peaceful, social members of their clan and town. Creeks believed alcohol had similar transformative properties.[42] In his "Report of 1755" on the state of British relations with southeastern Indians, Edmond Atkin noted that Creeks and their neighbors denied responsibility for their drunken behavior. "If complained of, or upbraided for it," he wrote, "they say with great Composure, 'that they are sorry for what hath happened, But that it was not they that did it, 'twas Rum did it.'"[43] Even as late as the 1830s, one observer would describe similar behavior. After drunken brawls, wrote a longtime resident of the Deep South, the Creeks "attribute the whole

were drunk and Mad," they "could not help it." Quoted in Mancall, "'The Bewitching Tyranny of Custom': The Social Costs of Indian Drinking in Colonial America," 20 and 29.

[40] Mauelshagen and Davis, *Partners in the Lord's Work*, 55.

[41] Benjamin Hawkins, "A sketch of the Creek Country in the years 1798 and 1799," *LBH*, 1:324–325; Swanton, *Social Organization*, 436. On the symbolism of colors, see the provocative articles by George R. Hamell, "The Iroquois and the World's Rim: Speculations on Color, Culture, and Contact," *American Indian Quarterly* 16 (1992): 451–469; and Hamell, "Strawberries, Floating Islands, and Rabbit Captains: Mythical Realities and European Contact in the Northeast During the 16th and 17th Centuries," *Journal of Canadian Studies* 21 (1987): 72–94. One trader among the Cherokees reported in the *South Carolina Gazette* that "it was usual for the Cherokee warriors when they had done mischief, to take some kind of drug to ease their minds after it." The use of such drugs by southeastern Indians further delineated the social from the asocial world. *SCG*, 9 February 1760.

[42] The ceremonial aspect of drinking is apparent in an account of Seminole drinking customs in the second decade of the nineteenth century, when both men and women were abusing alcohol. After trading for several kegs of rum, noted an observer, Seminole warriors set aside one cask for the women and then imbibed in one sitting their entire share, "the produce of many months indefatigable labour in the chace." "On the following day," the observer wrote, "the orgies of the women commence, and no interference, or intrusion is offered, or permitted by the men." Such distinctive drinking patterns suggest that for the Seminoles, alcohol was more than a diversion or entertainment. The segregation of the sexes, reminiscent of the separation during the annual Green Corn Ceremony, indicates that drunkenness had specific and distinct cultural meanings for men and women. *Narrative of a Voyage to the Spanish Main, in the Ship "Two Friends"; the occupation of Amelia Island, by M'Gregor, etc. – Sketches of the Province of East Florida; and anecdotes illustrative of the Habits and Manners of the Indians: with an Appendix, containing a Detail of the Seminole War, and the execution of Arbuthnot and Ambrister* (London: John Miller, 1819), 175–177.

[43] Atkin, *The Appalachian Indian Frontier*, 26.

scene to the spirits they have drunk, very truly saying it was not them but the liquor what was in them that fought."[44]

Just as women voiced their opposition to the wanton behavior of warriors, they also objected to the consumption of rum.[45] In 1755, Edmond Atkin wrote that after trading three or four months' harvest of deerskins for alcohol, warriors returned home "without the means of buying the necessary Clothing for themselves or their Families." "Their Domestick and inward Quiet being broke," he stated, "Reflection sours them, and disposes them for Mischief."[46] Though Atkin suggested that reflection changed the minds of some warriors, his description of "Domestick" unrest indicates that women played an important role in such conversions, especially when the madness of their men came at the expense of clothes and other necessities.

Creek men not only consumed much of the profits of the deerskin trade in the form of rum, but they also used a good portion of what remained to purchase goods once made by women. Many of these items had practical advantages and saved women hours of hard work, yet the diminishing value of their labor must have troubled them. William Bartram noted from his observations in the 1770s that women "yet amuse themselves in manufacturing some few things, as Belts & Coronets, for their husbands, feathered cloaks, macasens, &c."[47] But the naturalist seems painfully aware that these "few things" manufactured by women, though still significant, were rapidly becoming less crucial to the domestic economy of the Creek Indians as the deerskin trade dramatically altered their way of life.[48] Instead of garments created from deerskins,

---

[44] "A historical narration of the genealogy, traditions, and downfall of the Ispocoga or Creek tribe of Indians," PKY. Other eastern Indians similarly forgave the excesses of drunken people. Mancall, *Deadly Medicine*, 79–82.

[45] See ibid., 112–114, for a brief discussion of the temperance of Indian women. Anthropologist Amelia R. Bell suggests that today, Creek women struggle to control the male anger and violence unleashed by alcohol. She ties the opposition of male anger and female control to deeply rooted cultural beliefs. Bell, "Creek Ritual," 84–85.

[46] Atkin, *The Appalachian Indian Frontier*, 35. A Creek speech against "the immoderate Use of *Spirituous Liquors*," printed in 1754, has as one of its themes the discord that alcohol caused between men and women. The speech is probably not authentic. *New York Packet*, 10 July 1790; William Smith, *Some Account of the North-America Indians* (London: R. Griffiths, 1754), 9–21; Mancall, *Deadly Medicine*, 121.

[47] William Bartram, "Observations," 29. In his *Travels*, he also added that women "make all their pottery or earthen-ware" (401).

[48] Bartram recalled that by the 1770s, the Creeks "were now entirely ignorant of any of the arts, whereby, to supply themselves with necessary clothing; they had almost forgotten how to make earthen Pott's & not one amongst them knew how to form a Stone axe, or wooden Hough. All their dependance had rested upon the Traders, who supplied them with European Manu-

mulberry-tree bark, and tree moss, Creek clothing was increasingly made of strouding, calico, osnaburg, and other European textiles.[49] Men still used moccasins and occasionally leggings fashioned from deerskins, but most of their clothing now consisted of foreign materials. They dressed in breechcloths and leggings made of strouding, and they wore shirts and mantles fashioned from imported calico, decorated, like their breechcloths and leggings, with European gartering, beads, and bells.[50] Women wore petticoats and, at times, calico waistcoats, also richly decorated, and in the winter they donned wool mantles. Duffel, a woolen cloth, replaced deerskins as blankets.

Trading post inventories, showing large quantities of thread and needles, reflect the amount of labor women still invested in sewing clothes.[51] When Charles McLatchy, a trader operating in Apalache, died in 1787, for example, he had on hand 2,200 sewing needles and 291 pounds of thread. In addition, women continued to produce fingerwoven garters and belts with elaborate bead decorations.[52] But the labor involved in decorating clothes with beads, gartering, and bells represented less work – and less essential work – for women. Most shirts came ready-made, and breechcloths of strouding were easier to fashion than those of deerskins, which demanded the laborious preparation of the hide. More important, all of these goods were purchased by men through the deerskin trade. Men depended on women to finish clothes with beads and gartering, but women themselves had no direct access to the materials.[53]

Men also distanced themselves from women by purchasing foreign-

factures." Bartram, "Some Hints & Observations, concerning the civilization, of the Indians, or Aborigines of America," in *William Bartram on the Southeastern Indians*, ed. Gregory A. Waselkov and Kathryn E. Holland Braund (Lincoln: University of Nebraska, 1995), 195.

[49] Strouding, or strouds as it was called, was a coarse blanketing made of woolen rags. Calico was a plain weave, brightly printed cotton cloth, and osnaburg was a coarse, plain weave cotton fabric usually dyed in checks and solid colors. Braund, *Deerskins and Duffels*, 123, and Isabel B. Wingate, *Fairchild's Dictionary of Textiles* (New York: Fairchild Publications, 1979).

[50] Dorothy Downs, "British Influence on Creek and Seminole Men's Clothing, 1733–1858," *Florida Anthropologist* 33 (1980): 48, 51.

[51] Ibid., 60–62.   [52] Ibid.

[53] On clothing, see Josephine Paterek, *Encyclopedia of American Indian Costume* (Santa Barbara, CA: ABC-CLIO, 1994), 36–37; William Bartram, *Travels*, 393–395; and John Swanton, *Indians of the Southeastern United States*, 456–480. Sources reveal that calico, strouding, gartering, and other textiles, along with finished shirts, were common items in trade and as gifts. See, for example, "An assortment of goods proper for Indian presents for West Florida," enclosed in George Johnstone to the Secretary of the Board of Trade, 29 January 1764, PRO 5/574, p. 11, reel 66K, PKY; Martín Navarro to Josef de Gálvez, 27 July 1784, PC, leg. 2351, 15, reel 436, PKY; Luis de Bertucat to Arturo O'Neill, enclosing inventory of Charles McLatche's goods, 14 October 1787, PC, leg. 37, bnd. 7, doc. 276–2, reel 169, PKY; List of goods suitable for the State of Georgia and the Indian and Spanish Trade, St. Marys, Georgia, 6 April 1805, in box 45, PKY.

manufactured kettles and bowls. Though earthen and wooden containers, the handiwork of women, remained in use in towns, warriors carried the lighter and stronger brass and tin versions when they went hunting or warring.[54] A Creek hunter who was murdered in 1790, for example, had with him three kettles, forty skins, six new shirts, three calico hunting shirts, two rifles, three saddles and a bridle, five blankets, and five pack saddles.[55] Where he once would have depended on women's labor for all of these goods, the kettles, shirts, and undressed skins made him less reliant on his wife and female relatives.[56]

Women farmers still provided the bulk of the foods on which their families depended, but Creeks could not live comfortably without the proceeds of the chase. When men consumed these profits in the form of alcohol, women traded surplus produce "to cover their nakedness." Yet

---

[54] In 1789, Alexander McGillivray thus requested 100 brass kettles by 15 March in order to send Creek warriors against the Americans. Similarly, in 1812, Thomas Perryman requested from the commandant of Pensacola "pots to travel with" so the Seminoles could go to war. In Louisiana in 1745, Governor Vaudreuil also received requests from Indians for lighter brass kettles, illustrating that southeastern Indians valued the portability of these utensils. Alexander McGillivray to Estevan Miró, 1 February 1789, PC, leg. 142, 110, reel 173, PKY; Thomas Perryman to the Governor of Pensacola, 20 August 1812, PC, leg. 2356, 125, reel 172, PKY; and Patricia Dillon Woods, *French-Indian Relations on the Southern Frontier, 1699–1762* (Ann Arbor, MI: UMI Research Press, 1980), 151. Archaeological and documentary evidence reveals that Creek women continued to use earthen pots. Swan, "State of Arts and Manufactures," 692; Vernon J. Knight, *Tukabatchee: Archaeological Investigations at an Historic Creek Town, Elmore County, Alabama* (Office of Archaeological Research, Alabama State Museum of Natural History, University of Alabama, 1985), 121–123, 165–167; Charles H. Fairbanks, "Excavations at Horseshoe Bend, Alabama," *The Florida Anthropologist* 15 (1962): 51–53; Carol I. Mason, "Eighteenth Century Culture Change Among the Lower Creeks," *The Florida Anthropologist* 16 (1963): 68–69. But see also Vernon J. Knight, Jr., and Marvin T. Smith, "Big Tallassee: A Contribution to Upper Creek Site Archaeology," *Early Georgia* 8 (1980): 59–74. Carol I. Mason argues that changes brought on by European trade "centered about male roles in the society and left those of the women basically unaltered" (69). Chattahoochee Brushed, a type of Creek pottery identified by archaeologists, became increasingly common in the eighteenth century, and is found in most Creek town sites from that period. Though its prevalence may be interpreted as an indication of the cultural continuity maintained by Creek women, pottery types can remain consistent through dramatic cultural, social, and economic changes. Creek women continued to make Chattahoochee Brushed pottery after removal, for example, and may have done so into the twentieth century, selling their works to tourists. Federica R. Dimmick and Ian W. Brown, "A Survey of Upper Creek Sites in Central Alabama," *Journal of Alabama Archaeology* 35 (1989): 8–9, 46; Gordon R. Willey and William H. Sears, "The Kasita Site," *Southern Indian Studies* 4 (1952): 6, 11.

[55] A talk from six chiefs of the lower towns to the Governor of Georgia, 17 July 1790, CIL, 1:221b–221c, GDAH.

[56] One archaeological excavation of Creek burial sites has turned up evidence suggesting that sometime between 1715 and 1725, Creeks replaced Indian-manufactured burial goods with trade articles made in Europe. Such evidence suggests that the position of women in the Creek economy had deteriorated significantly as early as 1725. L. Ross Morrell, "The Woods Island Site in Southeastern Acculturation, 1625–1800," *Notes in Anthropology* (1965): 66. A Seminole burial from the mid-eighteenth century similarly illustrates the prevalence of European trade goods at the time. John M. Goggin, "An Historic Indian Burial, Alachua County, Florida," *Florida Anthropologist* 2 (1949): 10–25.

by 1771, according to warrior Emistesigo, plantations in Creek country, recently established by traders, were beginning to push them out of the market.[57] Creek leaders repeatedly complained about this innovation, and in 1772, residents living on the Tallapoosa forbade traders from establishing plantations in the future.[58] The number of such settlements continued to rise, however.

The plight of women may have worsened further in the 1780s and 1790s when American Indian agents and their Creek allies began to curb frontier raids. With fewer opportunities to distinguish themselves in battle, warriors asserted their masculinity by expressing hostility toward women. Women "are universally called wenches," Caleb Swan, a visitor to the Deep South, wrote in 1791. Men "who have seldom been abroad and are not distinguished by war-names," Swan continued, "are styled old women, which is the greatest term of reproach that can be used by them."[59] No man could ignore the threat of Shawnee visitors in 1793 to "twist their ears and noses and take them for old women" if they did not turn out for war.[60]

The animosity evident in such language occasionally manifested itself in rapes and in the mutilation of white women. These events did not directly concern Creek women, but they nevertheless illustrate that warriors expressed their masculinity through violence toward the opposite sex. Part of this hostility may have arisen from the simple fact of population dynamics: As mothers, white women contributed to the growing number of colonists.[61] In 1786, one Creek warrior told the governor of Florida that he wished to murder American women and children because "the former give birth and the latter would grow up to be warriors."[62] Yet, the strategic considerations of warriors and their more general antagonism toward women cannot be separated. The occasional rapes they committed – acts that were at once deliberately political and

---

[57] "At a Congress of the Principal Chiefs and Warriors of the Upper Creek Nation," 29 October 1771, LOC, PRO, CO 5/589, PKY.

[58] David Taitt to John Stuart, 4 May 1772, in Mereness, *Travels in the American Colonies*, 552–554. See also Taitt, "David Taitt's Journal," 501, 510, 535.

[59] Swan, "Position and State of Manners," 272 and 280.

[60] Juan Nepomuceno de Quesada to Luis de Las Casas, 26 April 1793, PC, leg. 1436, 5614, reel 158, PKY. In 1802, the adventurer William Augustus Bowles successfully used a similar tactic, telling Creek warriors that only women would return their white and black prisoners. Oconee King to Henry White, 11 May 1802, EF, bnd. 115K9, reel 43, PKY. In 1772, Creek warrior Emistesiguo argued "that they were men and must show themselves so" by turning out for war. Affidavit of Joseph Dawes, 4 August 1772, LOC, CO 5/589, PKY.

[61] Theda Perdue suggests that southern Indians mutilated women in war because women perpetuated clans and lineages. Perdue, *Cherokee Women*, 88.

[62] Governor of Florida to Conde de Gálvez, 12 June 1786, EF, bnd. 42C4, doc. 6, 39, reel 16, PKY.

extremely vicious – reflect these complex motivations. In November 1790, for instance, two Muskogees reportedly raped a woman near the Altamaha River.[63] Two years later, in June 1792, a number of Indians led by mestizo William Cannard allegedly gang-raped a Mrs. Tillet in Florida. According to Alexander Steele, a male guest who was run out of the victim's house, Cannard stated "in the most vulgar language what he intended with Tillet's wife." Steele, who returned with a rescue party, later reported that the Indians "had carried and dragged her a considerable distance into the fields." He and his companions "found her in the possession of about fourteen or fifteen Indians, and with one in such a position and others aholding her that we doubted not but they had ravished her."[64] In 1798, Tuskegee Tustanagee, a prominent Creek leader known also as Big Feared, allegedly raped a Mrs. Hilton in Jackson County, Georgia, but state officials contrived to have the charges dropped because of the "pressure of dificultys attendant on Indian affairs."[65] According to the accounts of Spanish officers, another gang rape nearly occurred on the St. Marys River in February 1802 when eight Creeks attacked a white settler and "made attempts to ravish this man's wife and daughter, pushing him and his son away with their guns, telling them that the land was theirs and that they had no business off the islands."[66]

Some documents also suggest that in war, Creek men mutilated the sexual organs of their female victims. In 1793, on the disputed fork of the Oconee and Apalachee rivers in Georgia, for instance, a Mrs. Thrasher was found "alive, scalped, wounded in both her thighs, her

---

[63] Richard Lang to the Governor of St. Augustine, 8 December 1790, EF, bnd. 195M15, doc. 1790–25, reel 82, PKY.

[64] Alexander Steele, 12 September 1792, EF, bnd. 122E10, reel 47, PKY; and Residents of the South Side of the St. Mary's River to Juan Nepomuceno de Quesada, 18 August 1792, EF, bnd. 122E10, doc. 1792–291, reel 47, PKY; John Forrester to Juan Nepomuceno de Quesada, 6 November 1792, EF, bnd. 122E10, doc. 1792–389, reel 47, PKY; John Forrester to Juan Nepomuceno de Quesada, 18 June 1792, EF, bnd. 122E10, doc. 1792–234, reel 47, PKY; John Forrester to Juan Nepomuceno de Quesada, 22 September 1792, EF, bnd. 122E10, doc. 1792–335, reel 47, PKY. John Forrester suggested that the rape was in retaliation for Tillet's violation of a Creek woman.

[65] Affidavit of John Hilton, 6 February 1798, "Letters of Benjamin Hawkins, 1797–1815," ed. Louise F. Hays (hereafter cited as LBH), 19, GDAH; Big Feared restored to his nation, 2 March 1798, File II, group 4-2-46, loc. 1432-02, box 76, folder 7, GDAH; Joseph Phillips, Charles Burk, and Zacaria Phillips to Benjamin Hawkins, 7 March 1798, "Indian Letters, 1782–1839," ed. Louise F. Hays (Typescript in the GDAH), 35; and James Durouzeaux to Vicente Folch, 18 April 1798, PC, leg. 215B, 716, reel 298, PKY.

[66] John McQueen to Enrique White, 9 February 1802, EF, bnd. 137G11, 1802–57, reel 56, PKY; Enrique White to Marqués de Someruelos, 12 February 1802, EF, bnd. 28B3, doc. 461, 85, reel 10, PKY. In the first half of the eighteenth century, historian Theda Perdue suggests, the abstention of warriors from sexual intercourse before, during, and immediately after battle prevented them from raping their victims. Perdue, Slavery and the Evolution of Cherokee Society, 6–7.

right breast, with balls, and stabbed in her left breast with a knife, her left arm cut nearly off, as is supposed with a tomahawk, of which wounds she died in about 24 hours."[67] A year later in a Creek raid on Colerain on the St. Marys, a Mrs. Rawlins "received a ball through her body, the Indians then scalped her and cut her in a most barberous manner and left her body on the field."[68]

Living with husbands, brothers, and fathers whose masculine pursuits often seemed at odds with the welfare of their households, Creek women greeted Benjamin Hawkins and his "plan of civilization" in early 1797 with far more interest than did most men. One woman, apparently dissatisfied with the state of gender relations, even professed she would never marry a "red man."[69] The civilization plan condemned warrior culture and seemed to promise access to much-needed goods such as food and clothing. Women also may have appreciated the agent's attention to their plight. (On at least one occasion, however, Hawkins's interest was sexual as well as professional.) "I visit them, take them by the hand and talk kindly to them, and I eat with them frequently," he wrote to a woman friend, "and this day I had four Indian women to dine with me with some Chiefs and white men, a thing they tell me unknown before to either of them."[70] Neighboring Cherokee women told Hawkins that, of the several Indian agents who visited them, he was the first who "thought it worth while to examine into the situation of the women." They were sure, they told him, that he "meant to better their condition."[71]

Among men, mestizo ranchers and planters most readily welcomed Hawkins. Warriors, by contrast, whose masculine identity rested heavily on the pursuits of hunting and warring, accused the Indian agent of wanting "to make slaves of them and their women and children."[72] Moreover, according to Hawkins, they were "apprehensive . . . that if their women could clothe and feed themselves, they would become independent of the degrading state of connexion between them."[73] Hawkins had observed that warriors rarely satisfied the material needs of their

---

[67] Affidavit of Michael Cupps and Nancy Smith, 23 April 1793, CIL, 1:288, GDAH.
[68] Affidavit of Benjamin Rawlins, 28 February 1794, CIL, 2:359, GDAH.
[69] Benjamin Hawkins to Elizabeth House Trist, 25 November 1797, LBH, 1:164–165.
[70] Ibid.
[71] Journal of Benjamin Hawkins, 2 December 1796, Letters of Benjamin Hawkins, 1796–1806, 21–22.
[72] James Durouzeaux to Vincent Folch, 27 May 1798, PC, leg. 208A, 592, reel 286, PKY.
[73] Benjamin Hawkins to James McHenry, 9 January 1799, LBH, 1:238.

families. In 1797 at a meeting in Kasihta on the Chattahoochee River, for example, when he suggested that Creeks cultivate and spin cotton, one man laughed aloud. Warriors, the Indian agent explained, feared that "if the women can cloathe themselves, they will be proud and not obedient to their husbands."[74] For their part, Hawkins and his assistants used this fear to encourage men to work in the fields. Richard Thomas, the agent at the Creek factory, explained, "The females of this nation approve much of Colonel Hawkins' plan of introducing the culture of cotton and the spinning wheel; it may, in the course of a few years, induce the young men to throw away the hungary flute." Thomas believed that when Creek women "are able to cloathe themselves by their own industry, it will render them independent of the hunter, who in turn will be obliged to handle the ax & the plough, and assist the women in the laborious task of the fields, or have no wife."[75]

Without the support of warriors, the development of Hawkins's plan rested on women and male planters and ranchers. These two groups did not work in concert, however, because most women embraced economic reforms yet rejected the tenets of patriarchy. One woman who married a white ironsmith at the Creek agency, for example, "took direction of the provisions, then the house and pay and finally the absolute government of every thing at the agency whether connected with the Smith or not." Hawkins thereafter forbade unions between his employees and Creeks.[76] Another woman, who proposed arranging a marriage for Hawkins in 1797, "would not consent that the women and children should be under the direction of the father, and the negotiation ended there."[77] Hawkins spelled out the differences between Creek and European American marriage customs, noting that Creek women were "in the habit of assuming and exercising absolute rule, such as it was, over their children, and not attending to the advice of their white husbands."[78] By 1803, perhaps in light of the failing crops that year, some women had reconsidered, according to Hawkins, offering to "submit themselves and

[74] Journal of Benjamin Hawkins, 5 January 1797, *Letters of Benjamin Hawkins, 1796–1806*, 55–56.
[75] Richard Thomas to Henry Gaither, 28 January 1798, *Letters of Benjamin Hawkins, 1796–1806*, 478. Hawkins stated the same opinion in his letter to Silas Dinsmoor, 7 June 1798, *LBH*, 1:199. He wrote, "The plan is not relished by the men, they are apprehensive that the women by being able to clothe themselves will become independent and compel the men to help them in their labour."
[76] Benjamin Hawkins to Thomas Jefferson, 11 July 1803, *LBH*, 2:454.
[77] Journal of Benjamin Hawkins, 16 February 1797, *Letters of Benjamin Hawkins, 1796–1806*, 83–84.
[78] Ibid.

children to be governed by white men" if he would rescind the ban on marriages at the Creek agency.[79]

Outside of the purview of the agency, Creeks fought over the same issue. Take the case of Alexander Cornels, the mestizo son of an English trader, and his wife, the daughter of Creek leader Efau Hadjo. Cornels readily adopted the model of the patriarchal, nuclear family, taking agricultural production out of the hands of his wife and daughters and using slaves in their place.[80] The women in his wife's lineage protested, however, demanding that Cornels's daughters receive payment for learning how to spin cotton.[81] Five or six of his wife's relatives also expected Cornels to feed them. Cornels objected under the belief that he was responsible solely for his own immediate family. From the perspective of these women, however, Cornels had married into their clan and lived in their household.[82] Cornels's wife and her female relatives refused to abide by the precepts of patriarchy.[83]

Like the family, the marketplace became a site of competition between women and men. Hawkins encouraged market production by purchasing agricultural products for his residence and model farm at Coweta Tallahassee, on the Chattahoochee near present-day Columbus, Georgia. In 1798, two years after his arrival, the Indian agent observed the effect of his efforts: "The women who are the labourers in this land experience the advantage of having corn for sale, as they have been many of them clothed by it this season."[84] Hawkins's intention, however, was "to introduce a regular husbandry," meaning plow agriculture practiced by men, and he expected the market at Coweta Tallahassee to serve as a "powerful stimulus" to the residents of Coweta, Coweta Tallahassee, and

---

[79] Benjamin Hawkins to Thomas Jefferson, 11 July 1803, *LBH*, 2:454. Hawkins reported that Creeks were starving in spring 1804, suggesting that crops the year before had failed. "Journal of Benjamin Hawkins," 15 July 1804, *LBH*, 2:476.

[80] Benjamin Hawkins, "A sketch of the Creek Country in the years 1798 and 1799," *LBH*, 1:291–293.

[81] Benjamin Hawkins, "Journal of Occurrences in the Creek Agency from January to the Conclusion of the Conference and Treaty at Fort Wilkinson by the Agent for Indian Affairs," *LBH*, 2:411–412.

[82] Karen Anderson points out, in her study of the matrilocal Hurons, that women derived a substantial amount of power from their control of domestic space. From this perspective, the conflict between Efau Hadjo and his wife's clan over control of the household had significant ramifications. Anderson, *Chain Her by One Foot: The Subjugation of Women in Seventeenth-Century New France* (London: Routledge, 1991), 119.

[83] Benjamin Hawkins, "Journal of Occurrences in the Creek Agency from January to the Conclusion of the Conference and Treaty at Fort Wilkinson by the Agent for Indian Affairs," *LBH*, 2:410.

[84] Benjamin Hawkins to Edward Price, 31 December 1798, *LBH*, 1:230.

Kasihta, three towns where men had seen the "advantages of the plough over the slow and laborious hoe."[85]

The slow but steadily declining fortunes of women farmers can be followed by counting the growing number of plows in Creek country. In 1800, there were fifty plows in use in the region. Two years later, that number had risen to seventy.[86] "I have to regret that our women, with the hoes, are behind us," Creek leader Efau Hadjo told Hawkins in 1802; "they and their children are likely to have poverty and hunger for their lot."[87] By 1809, a hundred families were using the plow.[88] These wealthy households wielded a power far greater than their small number would appear to indicate.

Women competed in agricultural markets as long as they could, but they also began spinning and weaving.[89] "The women approve much of the plan for introducing the culture of cotton & the spinning wheel," reported U.S. factor Richard Thomas, "and I have had several applications for cotton seed, cards & wheels." Soohahoey, for example, purchased two gallons of cotton seed in 1798 and wished to plant every seed herself. She reminded Thomas to procure for her a small spinning wheel and cotton cards (used to disentangle cotton fibers prior to spinning).[90] Hawkins reported in 1799 that women were spinning in Hilabee, Coweta, Coweta Tallahassee, and Palachuckaly where two Creek girls had prepared 100 yards of cotton fit for the loom. "Some of the Indian girls have showed much desire to be instructed and aptness to learn," he

[85] Benjamin Hawkins, "A sketch of the Creek Country in the years 1798 and 1799," LBH, 1:308–309, 311–313.

[86] Benjamin Hawkins, "A Sketch of the present state of the objects under the charge of the principal agent for Indian affairs south of the Ohio," March 1801, LBH, 1:353; Benjamin Hawkins, "Journal of Occurrences in the Creek Agency from January to the Conclusion of the Conference and Treaty at Fort Wilkinson by the Agent for Indian Affairs," LBH, 2:424.

[87] Report of Commissioners to the Secretary of War, May and June 1802, ASPIA, 1:668–681.

[88] Benjamin Hawkins, "A Sketch of the Affairs of the Creek Agency under the direction of Benjamin Hawkins, Agent for Indian Affairs up to the end of May, 1809," 31 May 1809, LBH, 2:551.

[89] Historical documents about women are clearly biased, as Theda Perdue points out. Hawkins was deeply interested in encouraging cotton production among the Creeks and consequently commented often on his success. Nevertheless, though he frequently remarked on the resistance of Creek men toward his program of civilization, he rarely noted resistance by women, suggesting that women were actually more accepting than men of the changes he was introducing. Joan Jenson finds that Seneca women were similarly enthusiastic when missionaries first introduced spinning and weaving. She suggests that they wanted a means to enter the market. Theda Perdue, "Cherokee Women and the Trail of Tears," Journal of Women's History 1 (1989), reprinted in Unequal Sisters: A Multi-Cultural Reader in U.S. Women's History, ed. Vicki L. Ruiz and Ellen Carol DuBois (New York: Routledge, 1994), 35; Joan M. Jenson, "Native American Women and Agriculture: A Seneca Case Study," in Unequal Sisters, 74. See also Diane Rothenberg, "The Mothers of the Nation: Seneca Resistance to Quaker Intervention," 78–79.

[90] Richard Thomas to Benjamin Hawkins, 28 January 1798, Letters of Benjamin Hawkins, 1796–1806, 476–477.

wrote.[91] That year 300 women and children clothed themselves in home-spun.[92] In spring 1801, Hawkins delivered 100 cotton cards to Musko-gee women, and the same year residents of Creek country shipped 1,500 pounds of cotton down the Tallapoosa to market in Mobile. "Three Indian women of one family who have been spinning for two years only," Hawkins noted, "have clothed themselves well, and acquired some hogs and cattle; are proud of the exertions they have made, and are, by their conduct, a stimulus to their country women."[93] Hawkins received other encouraging reports from Mr. Rhodes, a machinist and loommaker whom he had sent into the nation to assist the women "most active in spining and weaving." Rhodes related that he found them "very desirous of being instructed and determined to follow the orders of the agent."[94]

Creek mestizos and white residents who grew cotton soon asserted their control over women workers, however. In his initial tour through Creek country in December 1796, Hawkins noted with pleasure that Robert Grierson, a Scotsman who had settled with his Indian family near Hillabee Creek (north of present-day Alexander City, Alabama), "had his family around him ginning and picking cotton" on his thirty-acre farm. Grierson reported that he had no problem finding Creek women to pick cotton, paying them half a pint of salt or three strands of mock wampum per bushel, or half a pint of taffia (a type of rum) for two bushels. When the cotton was fully open, each woman could pick two to three baskets a day. Grierson had purchased a treadle-gin in Providence, Rhode Island, to separate the seed from the cotton and was probably one of the first inhabitants in Creek country to take advantage of the new invention. By the end of the decade, he employed eleven women, "red, white and black," as Hawkins put it, to spin and weave his product. To pick the cotton, he relied solely on Indian women, most of whom were unskilled at spinning.[95] Hawkins encouraged Grierson to serve as a model to other traders and Creek men, and several of them took up

---

[91] Benjamin Hawkins to James Jackson, 27 February 1799, LBH, 41, GDAH.
[92] Benjamin Hawkins to William Panton, 3 February 1800, *LBH*, 1:328.
[93] Benjamin Hawkins, "A Sketch of the present state of the objects under the charge of the prin-cipal agent for Indian affairs south of the Ohio," March 1801, *LBH*, 1:353; Benjamin Hawkins to William Panton, 7 February 1801, Cruzat Papers, PKY.
[94] Benjamin Hawkins, "Journal of Occurrences in the Creek Agency from January to the Conclu-sion of the Conference and Treaty at Fort Wilkinson by the Agent for Indian Affairs," *LBH*, 2:407.
[95] Journal of Benjamin Hawkins, 9–10 December 1796, *Letters of Benjamin Hawkins, 1796–1806*, 29–30; Benjamin Hawkins, "A sketch of the Creek Country in the years 1798 and 1799," *LBH*, 1:301.

cotton production. Trader Benjamin Steadham's two mestiza daughters who lived at Palachuckaly were reportedly "good spinners," and Alexander Cornels grew two acres of cotton in 1801.[96] Thomas Marshall, a trader located at the Coweta village called Hatcheuxau, also "set up a manufactory of cotton cloth at the recommendation of the agent."[97] He had a "negro" working for him who reportedly wove sixty yards of homespun per week.[98]

Spurred at different times by men and women, cotton production continued to expand. In 1802, Tuskeneah Chapco of Coweta asked Hawkins to send a weaver to teach Creek women to weave, "as they have already spun a good deal of cotton," and Tussekiah Micco made a similar request.[99] In February 1803, Hawkins learned from Creek leaders that in the fork of the Flint River "spinning, weaving was the general topic of conversation, more so than we have ever heard."[100] Vicente Folch, the commandant at Pensacola, received similar reports in 1804: "The Indians are all busy in planting their corn and other provisions and cotton which they spin and weave and make themselves clothes with."[101] By 1806 cotton was a commodity of such importance that the leading Creek representative, Hopoy Micco, requested of the Spanish crown that Forbes and Company, the main trading house operating in the Deep South, be allowed to ship cotton free of duty "for the benefit of the Creek nation." He hoped "his friend Govr Folch will be aiding and assisting to this good purpose which will be a great assistance to this nation as killing of deer is partly at an end." Those Creeks involved in shipping cotton to markets on the Gulf Coast were usually men who owned plantations. The market for homespun, in contrast, was only local.[102] As the cotton market expanded, wealthy Creek men would increasingly exploit the labor of African American and Creek women.

---

[96] Traders in the Upper Creeks, 1797, *Letters of Benjamin Hawkins, 1796–1806*, 168–174; Benjamin Hawkins, "A sketch of the Creek Country in the years 1798 and 1799," *LBH*, 1:291–293.

[97] Ibid., 308.

[98] Timothy Barnard to Benjamin Hawkins, 10 October 1802, LTB, 281G, GDAH.

[99] Report of Commissioners to the Secretary of War, May and June 1802, *ASPIA*, 1:668–681. See also Timothy Barnard to Benjamin Hawkins, 10 October 1802, LTB, 281G, GDAH.

[100] Report of Tuskegee Tustanagee to Benjamin Hawkins, 8 February 1803, PC, leg. 220B, 112, reel 308, PKY.

[101] James Durouzeaux to Vicente Folch, 8 May 1804, PC, leg. 2372, 19, reel 436, PKY. See also Durouzeaux to Folch, 16 April 1804, PC, leg. 2372, 17, reel 436, PKY.

[102] Daniel McGillivray to [John Forbes?], 28 August 1806, Forbes-Innerarity Papers, 67/30, reel 147P, PKY. According to Big Warrior, Upper Creek women were still anxious to become involved in cotton production in 1810: "we stand in need very much us upper towns for spinning wheels and our women are complaining bitterly they cannot get wheels. There is but few wheels in the upper towns, if our women had wheels spinning would go on finally, there is hardly one woman among us if they had wheels they spinn." Quoted in Doster, *Creek Indians*, 1:19–20.

Ranching also set women and men against each other. "The raising of stock is more relished by the Creeks than any other part of the plan devised for their civilization," Hawkins noted in 1799, but with his careless language he meant to refer to men.[103] Men, and especially mestizo men, were the most dedicated ranchers in Creek country, though a few women acquired cattle.[104] As their livestock multiplied, these ranchers moved out of densely settled towns in search of more grazing range for their animals. In the process, they established patriarchal settlements away from the town households controlled by women. In the 1770s, William Bartram had seen only a "very few instances" among the Creeks of farms or plantations "out of sight of the town." The one outlying plantation he visited was established by the mestizo rancher Boatswain.[105] Boatswain had followed the practice of ranchers in South Carolina and Georgia who established cowpens – isolated, fenced farms surrounded by thousands of acres of open grazing land.[106] Concentrated settlements discouraged residents from tending large herds of livestock because each cow needed between fifteen and twenty-five acres of grazing land to survive.[107] Moreover, ranchers required extra wood to construct the fences necessary to keep cattle out of their crops.[108]

By 1798, matrilocal towns were losing a steady if small stream of families to outlying patriarchal settlements. In that year, Benjamin Hawkins

---

[103] Benjamin Hawkins to James McHenry, 9 January 1799, *LBH*, 1:238. That same year, Moravian missionaries reported, "We saw a number of Creek Indians, who had drived cattle thither for the garrison. . . . The Creeks bring much cattle into this region, some it very fine." Quoted in Hatley, "Cherokee Women Farmers," 48. Theda Perdue finds that among the Cherokees, cattle did not have a significant impact on their lives. Instead, Cherokees adapted these animals to traditional hunting patterns. Perdue, "Women, Men and American Indian Policy: The Cherokee Response to 'Civilization,'" in *Negotiators of Change*, 97–100.

[104] Pope, *A tour through the southern and western territories*, 64–65; Swan, "Position and State of Manners," 260–261; Benjamin Hawkins, "A sketch of the Creek Country in the years 1798 and 1799," *LBH*, 1:290–301. For examples of women ranchers, see Affidavit of Ojoyasque and Sojoyane, 1 October 1791, EF, bnd. 114J9, reel 43, PKY; and Journal of Benjamin Hawkins, 24 December 1796, *LBH*, 1:24.

[105] William Bartram, "Observations," 156. Bartram mentioned that Boatswain traded in cowhides. Boatswain, according to the naturalist, was "a Chief of the Town of the Apalachucklas," who lived "about six miles from the Town." When Arturo O'Neill conferred on Boatswain a great medal, he identified Boatswain as being from Hitchiti. Arturo O'Neill, 31 May 1783, EF, bnd. 195M15, doc. 1783–1, reel 82, PKY.

[106] John S. Otto, "Open-Range Cattle-Herding in Southern Florida," *Florida Historical Quarterly* 65 (1987): 331–333; James C. Bonner, *A History of Georgia Agriculture, 1732–1860* (Athens: University of Georgia, 1964), 26.

[107] Otto, "Open-Range Cattle-Herding in Southern Florida," 333; Bonner, *A History of Georgia Agriculture*, 25.

[108] Ranching caused a similar dispersal among the Choctaws and Chickasaws. Daniel H. Usner, Jr., "American Indians on the Cotton Frontier: Changing Economic Relations with Citizens and Slaves in the Mississippi Territory," *Journal of American History* 72 (1985): 305–306.

reported, "A number of the Indian families seem to be attentive to raising Stock, and have moved and are moving out of the towns and settling in villages."[109] Creeks from Tuckabatche had "begun to settle out in villages for the convenience of raising stock, and having firewood." "Several of them," Hawkins noted, "have from 50 to 100 cattle."[110] In 1800, Hawkins proudly reported that Creeks brought 1,000 cattle to market.[111] Two years later, in the summer of 1802, the "Coweta towns" alone drove 2,000 head of cattle to market in Georgia.[112] In accumulating cattle, these men were following trends in neighboring white settlements. In the Natchez district on the Mississippi, for example, between 1784 and 1794, the number of cattle jumped from around 3,000 to over 18,000, doubling the ratio of cattle to people.[113]

Two Creek ranchers serve as examples of the divisive effect of cattle on women and men. Micco Thlucco moved away from his hometown Kasihta in the late 1790s to establish a settlement at the junction of Hitchiti Creek and the Chattahoochee River. There, at his "well-fenced" plantation, he had hogs, cattle, and horses, and his family learned "how to turn their corn to account by giving it to their hogs." Micco Thlucco had been to New York "and seen much of the ways of the white people," wrote Hawkins, and accordingly he plowed rather than hoed his plantation.[114] Similarly, in the 1790s Tussekiah Micco moved to an outlying Kasihta village called Auputtaue where the residents had cattle and hogs. After Hawkins hired a white farmer to tend a corn crop there in 1797, several villagers, including Tussekiah Micco, began plowing their fields.[115] Back in the hometown of both Micco Thlucco and Tussekiah Micco, according to Hawkins, the "Cussetuhs have some cattle, horses, and hogs, but they prefer roving idly through the woods and down on

[109] Benjamin Hawkins to Silas Dinsmoor, 7 June 1798, *LBH*, 1:199.
[110] Benjamin Hawkins, "A sketch of the Creek Country in the years 1798 and 1799," *LBH*, 1:292. Archaeological evidence confirms Hawkins's observation about Tuckabatche. Vernon J. Knight, *Tukabatchee: Archaeological Investigations at an Historic Creek Town, Elmore County, Alabama* (Office of Archaeological Research, Alabama State Museum of Natural History, University of Alabama, 1985), 59–64.
[111] Benjamin Hawkins to William Panton, 3 February 1800, *LBH*, 1:328.
[112] Timothy Barnard to Benjamin Hawkins, 10 October 1802, LTB, 281G, GDAH. For archaeological evidence of the consumption of pork and beef in the late eighteenth century, see Charles H. Fairbanks, "Excavations at Horseshoe Bend, Alabama," *The Florida Anthropologist* 15 (1962): 41–56. Excavations from an earlier Creek settlement (1735–1750), on the Chattahoochee River just north of the Florida border, reveal bird and deer bones, but no livestock remains. C. G. Holland, "A Mid-Eighteenth Century Indian Village on the Chattahoochee River," *The Florida Anthropologist* 27 (1974): 43.
[113] Clark and Guice, *Frontiers in Conflict*, 103.
[114] Benjamin Hawkins, "A sketch of the Creek Country in the years 1798 and 1799," *LBH*, 1:312.
[115] Ibid., 311–312.

the frontiers to attending to farming or stock raising."[116] Again, his language, so unspecific in gender, obscured the real point: In Kasihta, women still tended to the farm.

In two areas in the market, women had no real competition. The first was the production of nut oil, the only rivals being swine which ate many of the nuts before they could be gathered. Both Bernard Romans and William Bartram had noted before the Revolution that women made "milk" and "oil" from nuts.[117] In 1797, Edward Price, the storekeeper at the Creek factory at Fort Wilkinson on the Oconee, wrote, "We have been much perplexed with the small trade for groundnuts, chestnuts, and etc., but thought right to accommodate the poor women for their little matters[,] of consequence to them and not of any material amount."[118] The following year, the "material amount" rose to eight gallons and then thirty gallons the year after that. In 1800, when Hawkins raised the price of hickory-nut oil from 75 cents per quart to one dollar, women brought in 300 gallons, ample evidence that they were anxious to enter the market economy and were responding to its incentives.[119] Creek women earned $1,200 from their trade in hickory-nut oil in 1800, the equivalent value of 1,600 deerskins.[120]

The other area in the market free of competition was the exchange of sexual favors for goods.[121] Romans had observed that Creek women "will

---

[116] Ibid., 312.

[117] William Bartram, "Observations" 152; and Romans, *A Concise Natural History of East and West Florida*, 96. Bartram reported:

> I have seen above an hundred bushels of these nuts belonging to one family. They pound them to pieces, and then cast them into boiling water, which, after passing through fine strainers, preserves the most oily part of the liquid: this they call by a name which signifies hickory milk; it is as sweet and rich as fresh cream, and is an ingredient in most of their cookery, especially homony and corn cakes.

Bartram, *Travels*, 57.

[118] Edward Price to Benjamin Hawkins, 4 December 1797, p103, Records of the Creek Trading House, Letter Book, 1795–1816, reel 94-O, PKY.

[119] Henri, *The Southern Indians*, 120.

[120] The Creek factory paid one chalk, or 25 cents, per pound of deerskins, and an average undressed deerskin weighed about three pounds. It took in about 50,000 pounds of deerskins annually, paying out $12,500 to hunters. By selling hickory nut oil, women thus earned about one-tenth of the total income of Creek hunters. Wright, *Creeks and Seminoles*, 59. For the average harvest of deerskins per hunter, see Braund, *Deerskins and Duffels*, 70–71.

[121] As in Creek country, when the products of Native American women along the Pacific Northwest coast were displaced by European goods at the close of the eighteenth century, women turned to prostitution to enter the marketplace. When the Hudson's Bay Company forbade prostitution at their trading posts in the mid-1820s, native women reportedly said that "they would not conform to this innovation as it deprived them of a very important source of Revenue."

never scruple to sell the use of their bodies when they can do it in private; a person who wishes to be accommodated here can generally be supplied for payment, and the savages think a young woman nothing the worse for making use of her body, as they term it."[122] By 1802, after five full years of Hawkins's civilization program, women were clearly using their bodies to enter the male-dominated market economy. Hawkins complained of women who "think of no support but prostituting their granddaughters or daughters." "On this," he wrote, "they confidently rely for cloths and food and spoke of it as a cheap and easy way of acquiring both."[123] Two Moravian missionaries who visited Creek country in 1804 confirmed Hawkins's observations:

> A single woman is permitted to reach an agreement with a man, or with several men, if the parties concerned agree. For this she accepts pay. . . . In bargaining with the white men, Creek girls employ interpreters. All matters are discussed frankly and without hesitancy, as though it were the most innocent matter in the world.[124]

Prostitution was one of the surest ways women could obtain clothes and food in the market.

Creek men, who objected to the independence secured by women who cultivated cotton, also tried to control female sexuality. Though unmarried women had no restrictions on their sexual activities, Creek men appear to have associated female sexual independence with female economic independence, and they tried to limit both.[125] In 1802, the year in which Hawkins commented on the prevalence of prostitution, Abraham Mordecai, a Jewish man long involved in the deerskin trade, set up a cotton gin just below the confluence of the Coosa and Tallapoosa rivers.[126] One visitor to the Upper Creeks reported in 1803 that there

Mary C. Wright, "Economic Development and Native American Women in the Early Nineteenth Century," *American Quarterly* 33 (1981): 534–535; Jo-Anne Fiske, "Colonization and the Decline of Women's Status: The Tsimshian Case," *Feminist Studies* 17 (1991): 523–525, 527.

[122] Romans, *A Concise Natural History of East and West Florida*, 97.

[123] Benjamin Hawkins, "Journal of Occurrences in the Creek Agency from January to the Conclusion of the Conference and Treaty at Fort Wilkinson by the Agent for Indian Affairs," *LBH*, 2:412.

[124] Carl Mauelshagen and Gerald H. Davis, "The Moravians' Plan for a Mission among the Creek Indians, 1803–1804," *Georgia Historical Quarterly* 51 (1967): 363. John Swanton notes that these "temporary marriages" often involved women who had committed adultery and been abandoned by their husbands. Swanton, *Social Organization*, 384.

[125] Sattler, "Muskogee and Cherokee Women's Status," 218–9.

[126] Pickett, *History of Alabama*, 469–70. By 1813, there were at least two other cotton gins in the area. Mestizo Samuel Moniac owned one, probably located at his plantation on the Alabama River, and the Peirce brothers owned one at Tensaw. *United States Serial Set*.H.doc. 200 (20–1)

were 200 spinning wheels in the area, and he "saw a list of 100 more bespoken."[127] Many of Mordecai's suppliers were Creek women.[128] Soon after Mordecai completed his gin, a number of Creek warriors destroyed it in retaliation for the entrepreneur's relationship with a married Creek woman.[129] They were likely threatened as much by the sexual independence of the adulteress as by her growing economic autonomy. Some years earlier, a visitor to the Deep South had purportedly recorded the words of an old Creek "conjurer" who clearly linked (and condemned) economic and sexual freedom: "Our Women laugh at us and refuse to work: they are Prostitutes and suckle the Children of white Men!"[130]

Long-standing tensions between Muskogee women and men profoundly affected the reception in Creek country of Hawkins's "plan of civilization." Where the deer harvest had once proved bountiful, its decline and the rise of a trade dominated by young warriors impoverished Creek women. Hawkins's market economy allowed women to obtain much-needed goods for their households, but rather than resolving tensions between women and men it led to greater anxieties. Warriors resented the growing initiative of women, while women disapproved of the reluctance of warriors to take advantage of the economic changes wrought by the "plan of civilization." Yet despite their enthusiasm for many of Hawkins's reforms, women refused to abide by the rules of patriarchy, putting them at odds with the few men who engaged in planting and ranching. These were not the only tensions that the "plan of civilization" aggravated; as we shall see, it also provoked a violent confrontation between property-holders and the propertyless.

173:9 (hereafter cited as *USS*); Richard S. Lackey, ed., *Frontier Claims in the Lower South: Records of Claims Filed by Citizens of the Alabama and Tombigbee River Settlements in the Mississippi Territory for Depredations by the Creek Indians During the War of 1812* (New Orleans: Polyanthos, 1977).

[127] Stephen Folch, "Journal of a Voyage to the Creek Nation from Pensacola in the year 1803," 5 May 1803, PC, leg. 2372, 1, reel 436, PKY.

[128] Aside from deerskins, Mordecai traded for pink root and hickory-nut oil. These items were produced by women. Pickett, *History of Alabama*, 469–470.

[129] Ibid.; Dwight M. Wilhelm, *A History of the Cotton Textile Industry of Alabama, 1809–1950* (n.p., n.d.), 25.

[130] Pope, *A tour through the southern and western territories*, 60–62.

7

Creating a country of laws and property

"Every man who has understanding enough to acquire property and to know his own," Tustanagee Hopoy (Little Prince) and Tuskegee Tustanagee stated in 1809, "ought to know his neighbours property and in a country of Laws and property should be made to respect it."[1] Though these Lower Creek leaders, objecting to the theft of their cattle by Georgians, surely enjoyed addressing whites with rhetoric usually directed at Native Americans, they spoke only partially in irony. Their admonishment also reflected the lessons of hard-won experience, for Creeks themselves had recently begun to covet and acquire property. The words of Benjamin Hawkins neatly summed up the process: The Creeks "tasted the sweets of civilization" and "began to know the value of property and the necessity of defending it."[2] Some of them became desirous of its accumulation, uneasy about its security, and violent in its defense. In the last three years of the eighteenth century, these changes, whose early origins and subsequent development will be traced in this chapter, culminated when Creeks under the direction of Hawkins formed a national police force to make recalcitrant Muskogees respect their neighbors' property.

Understanding these developments clearly requires examination of the local dynamics of Creek history. But it also demands attention to more general and far-reaching changes in this period, when the Atlantic economy and U.S. government invaded once autonomous regions throughout North America.[3] From Georgia to Maine, land speculators,

---

[1] Chiefs of the lower towns to Benjamin Hawkins, 14 March 1809, LTB, 296, GDAH.
[2] "Journal of Benjamin Hawkins," 15 July 1804, *LBH*, 2:476.
[3] One historian has identified a "national pattern of backcountry resistance" to the encroachment of the Atlantic economy into peripheral regions occupied by white hunters and farmers. Alan Taylor, *Liberty Men and Great Proprietors: The Revolutionary Settlement on the Maine Frontier,*

international trading houses, and government authorities encroached on the lands of Native Americans and white hunters and farmers alike. In the eyes of many reformers who wished to educate the unruly about the dictates of law and property, Indians and white "crackers" were cut from the same cloth, and both demanded refashioning. Whites living in the piedmont of South Carolina, for example, were subject to an unofficial plan of civilization in the 1760s when vigilante "regulators," as they called themselves, enforced law and order on "strolling" hunters deemed "little more than white Indians."[4] One early historian, writing in 1809, described the antagonists in terms of the "old order and the new order of things," echoing Hawkins's recognition of conflict in Creek country between "age and old habits" and the "new order of things."[5] In 1769, South Carolina Lieutenant Governor William Bull complained about the "back inhabitants who chuse to live rather by the wandering indolence of hunting than the more honest and domestic employment of planting."[6] His remarks foreshadowed Hawkins's repeated condemnation of "idle" Creek hunters.

In neighboring states, leading citizens raised similar concerns.[7] In 1783, for example, one Georgia resident described the growing number of "Crackers" who "subsist in that vagrant way, which the Indians pursue . . . by driving off gangs of horses and cattle to Virginia." As the Indians "dwindle away before them," concluded the writer, "they certainly threaten ruin to the civilized parts of the rice Colonies."[8] Farther afield, in Maine in the years following the Revolution, reformers condemned "white Indians" who left society in "a kind of medium between barbarism and civilization."[9] Secretary of War Henry Knox, who owned

1760–1820 (Chapel Hill: University of North Carolina, 1990), 4. The transformation of Native American regions into countries of laws and property can be followed in William G. McLoughlin, *Cherokee Renascence in the New Republic* (Princeton: Princeton University, 1986); White, *The Roots of Dependency*, chap. 5; and David B. Guldenzopf, "The Colonial Transformation of Mohawk Iroquois Society" (Ph.D. diss., State University of New York at Albany, 1986).

[4] Quoted in Rachel N. Klein, *Unification of a Slave State: The Rise of the Planter Class in the South Carolina Backcountry, 1760–1808* (Chapel Hill: University of North Carolina, 1990), 51.

[5] Hatley, *The Dividing Paths*, 179–183, 189. For Hawkins's use of the phrase, see Benjamin Hawkins to William Panton, 22 November 1798, Forbes-Innerarity Papers, 83/1, reel 147P, PKY; and Benjamin Hawkins to Henry Dearborn, 1 June 1801, *LBH*, 1:359.

[6] Quoted in Klein, *Unification of a Slave State*, 51. The comment of Anglican minister Charles Woodmason, that both "Men and Women will do any thing to come at Liquor, Cloths, Furniture, etc. etc. rather than work for it," was directed at piedmont whites, but it expressed the common white view of Indians as well. Quoted in Klein, *Unification of a Slave State*, 54.

[7] Ibid., 53.

[8] Quoted in James Etheridge Callaway, *The Early Settlement of Georgia* (Athens: University of Georgia, 1948), 69.

[9] Quoted in Taylor, *Liberty Men and Great Proprietors*, 142.

a huge tract of land in Maine, noted in 1789 that the key to civilizing Indians was to encourage "love for exclusive property," a policy he extended to the white Indians squatting on his property as well.[10] When that failed, both in Maine and in Creek country, he led the move to survey lands in these regions and to evict the red and white inhabitants. In 1794, his house guest, the French statesman Charles Maurice de Talleyrand, visited Maine and complained about its people: "Indolent and grasping, poor but without needs, they still resemble too much the natives of the country whom they have replaced."[11] In many cases, poor whites even adopted the garb of local Indians, expressing a kinship, however shallow, with dispossessed Native Americans.[12]

From St. Augustine, where he served as governor of Florida, Vicente Manuel de Zéspedes perceived a schematic and repeated process of change in the Southeast. His 1790 description, though perhaps only vaguely resembling actual events, illustrates the highly visible and dramatic nature of the transformations that frontier regions were undergoing in the late eighteenth century. The first white residents to inhabit the interior of the southern states, he wrote, were "crackers," a "kind of white *cimarrones*." "These Crackers, wanderers like Arabs, are only different from the savages in color, language, and in a superiority in depraved cunning and dishonesty," he noted. They were "skilled like the Indians in hunting, in crossing large rivers in weak rafts, and in tracking men and animals through the thickest forests." According to Zéspedes, they constructed "Indian-style huts for the shelter of their women or children in the first unpopulated area where they find land suitable for planting corn."[13] When they abandoned their land, Zéspedes continued, another class of "crackers" moved in, more sociable, but nevertheless "enemies of all civil rule." They left when they felt the approach of a third class. These people obtained proper land grants, but state authority remained "scorned or unsteady." Finally, according to Zéspedes, a fourth class of people arrived who, "buying at low cost the lands granted to the third, are the first to become useful members of the state."[14]

[10] Ibid., 56.
[11] Quoted in ibid., 50.
[12] Ibid., 189. On the history of whites wearing Indian dress, see Philip J. Deloria, *Playing Indian* (New Haven: Yale University, 1998). Deloria suggests that by dressing as Indians, whites could lay claim to custom and moral economy even though they were recent immigrants to America (25).
[13] Vicente Manuel de Zéspedes to Domingo Cavello, 22 June 1790, EF, bnd. 22I2, 114, reel 8, PKY.
[14] Ibid. Zéspedes may have been familiar with J. Hector St. John de Crèvecoeur's 1782 description

In late 1796, when Hawkins assumed his post, the Indian agent could see the progress of an economic and social transformation as dramatic and uneven as the one described by Zéspedes. The twelve miles along the Alabama River below the confluence of the Coosa and Tallapoosa, for example, held stunning contrasts between the propertied and propertyless. One mile or so below the river junction, Charles Weatherford lived on a high bluff overlooking the Alabama River. Weatherford, an English trader married to McGillivray's half-sister Sehoy, bred horses and raced them on his property.[15] His residence stood across the river from Coosada, a small Creek village that, according to one report from the late 1790s, had some hogs, horses, and seventy to eighty cattle. While Weatherford worked his fenced estate with slave laborers, Coosada farmers toiled in common fields, sharing labor except at the time of harvest.[16] Three more villages – Pauwocte, Towassee, and Ecunchate – sat on the west bank, downstream. Only Ecunchate had any cattle, and only Towassee had any fenced garden plots.[17] On the east bank, in contrast, sat the establishment of Sehoy McGillivray, Weatherford's wife.[18] In the late 1790s, she reportedly owned thirty slaves, and her plantation may have rivaled the neighboring Indian villages in population.[19] About eleven miles below the confluence of the Coosa and Tallapoosa, near where the city of Montgomery is now situated, the social and economic divide across the river reached its deepest point. There, according to Hawkins, residents of Attaugee avoided contact with whites for fear of contamination. They disposed of leftover food touched by the rare white visitors and washed everything used by their unwelcome guests.[20] These contrasts illustrate that not every Creek had developed a taste for the

of the "half civilized, half savage" frontier inhabitants who preceded the "arrival of a second and better class." Crèvecoeur, *Letters from an American Farmer* (Dublin: John Exshaw, 1782), 45–46.

[15] Journal of Benjamin Hawkins, 20 December 1796, *Letters of Benjamin Hawkins, 1796–1806*, 42–43. Until 1799, when he moved a few miles downriver, Weatherford lived not far above Sehoy on the Alabama. Pickett, *History of Alabama*, 392; "The Hickory Ground Plantations," *Arrow Points* 14 (1930): 48–49; Benjamin Hawkins to James Seagrove, 9 August 1799, *LBH*, 1:256.

[16] Benjamin Hawkins, "A sketch of the Creek Country in the years 1798 and 1799," *LBH*, 1:295–296.

[17] Ibid., 296.

[18] Sehoy was Alexander McGillivray's half-sister by their mother's first marriage to a Scotsman named Malcolm McPherson. Alexander Beaufort Meek, *Romantic Passages in Southwestern History; including orations, sketches and essays* (New York: S. H. Goetzel and Co., 1857), 263–6.

[19] Benjamin Hawkins, "A sketch of the Creek Country in the years 1798 and 1799," *LBH*, 1:298–299. Hawkins wrote that Towassee, Ecunchate, Pauwocte, and Attaugee had a combined population of about 80 gunmen, or about 280 men, women, and children, making on average 70 people per village. Benjamin Hawkins, "A sketch of the Creek Country in the years 1798 and 1799," *LBH*, 1:296. [20] Ibid.

"sweets of civilization." Nor had all of the residents of Creek country come to what Tustanagee Hopoy and Tuskegee Tustanagee described as an "understanding" and "knowledge" of private property. The story of this development, then, is also one of conflict.

Three indicators of possessiveness mark the emergence of a new attitude toward private property among some Creeks: the conveyance of inheritance, the raising of fences, and the installation of locks. Throughout most of the eighteenth century, Creeks buried the deceased with their most important possessions. In the early 1700s, these included European goods made of iron, brass, and glass: iron strike-a-lights, axes, hoes, gun parts, scissors, and nails; brass arm bands, bells, bracelets, belt buckles, and gorgets; and glass beads and bottles, among other items.[21] By 1775, after iron, brass, and glass had lost its exotic appeal,[22] deceased men, according to Bernard Romans, were "furnished with a musket, powder and ball, a hatchet, pipe, some tobacco, a club, a bow and arrows, a looking glass, some vermilion and other trinkets, in order to come well provided in the world of spirits."[23] Women were buried with agricultural and cooking implements, as well as with jewelry.

    White observers, revealing their own preoccupations, expected ailing Creeks to fret about the fate of their possessions. Longtime trader James Adair, for example, too readily assumed that Coweta leader Malache had "bequethed all he possessed to his real, and adopted relations" before his death in January 1756. Malache, he wrote, was "sensible they would be much more useful to his living friends, than to himself during his long sleep."[24] The Creek leader, however, had done nothing of the kind. A little more than a year before dying, Malache had sent word to

---

[21] These items were found in graves, dated from 1650 to 1715, on Woods Island in the Coosa River, later flooded by the construction of a dam. L. Ross Morrell, "The Woods Island Site in Southeastern Acculturation, 1625–1800," *Notes in Anthropology* 11 (1965): 1–68. For a comparison with later burials, see David L. Dejarnette and Asael T. Hansen, "The Archaeology of the Childersburg Site, Alabama," *Notes in Anthropology* 4 (1960): 2–65.

[22] Vernon J. Knight, Jr., working primarily from the archaeological record, makes the point that Creeks initially valued European goods as luxuries. Other archaeological evidence shows that as early as the seventeenth century, some goods had lost their exotic status. Iron axes, for example, have been uncovered in midden areas rather than in graves. At the same time, however, some residents in the lower Mississippi valley stored firearms in their religious structures, suggesting that they believed guns had spiritual power. Knight, *Tukabatchee*, 169–183; Smith, *Aboriginal Culture Change*, 121–122.

[23] Romans, *A Concise Natural History of East and West Florida*, 98–99. See also the following sources: Bartram, *Travels*, 403; Fabel and Rea, "Lieutenant Thomas Campbell's Sojourn among the Creeks," 109; Pope, *A tour through the southern and western territories*, 59; Swan, "Position and State of Manners," 270; Adair, *Adair's History*, 186–187.

[24] Ibid., 187.

the governor of South Carolina that he was "in a very bad State of Health that I cannot come down, nor have I any Thing left me but my Body, having been obliged to give all I had to the Doctors."[25] Malache had distributed his goods to secure the healing powers of Creek doctors, not to ensure that his wealth remained above ground. He in fact died penniless.

Yet under the influence of European values, some Creeks did begin to deviate from established tradition regarding the posthumous disposition of their property. Adair noted that several Indian nations "used formerly to shoot all the live stock that belonged to the deceased, soon after the interment of the corpse."[26] According to a few accounts, Creeks continued to bury horses, cows, hogs, and dogs through the end of the eighteenth century, but such practices must have ceased rather quickly among individuals who accumulated large herds of livestock.[27] When Thomas Campbell visited Creek country in 1760, for example, he found that the Wolf King of Muclasa had given most of his 200 head of black cattle "to his children for fear they should be killed after he dies."[28] In 1793, *The Gentleman's Magazine* assumed that Alexander McGillivray was responsible for such changes among the Creeks, noting that it was "only since Mr. McGillivray had influence amongst them, that they have suffered the slaves of a deceased master to live."[29] The writers at this London newspaper had wildly imagined human sacrifices among their former allies, but they nevertheless rightly recognized that Creeks such as McGillivray would have no part in destroying their property.[30] "I have been in the nation all last month looking after McGillivray's affairs," William Panton reported soon after the Scots Indian's death, "and notwithstanding his sisters had divided the negroes among them, conformable to Indian usage, I got them to yield up all the negroes and a part of the cattle for his children and they are to be placed under a white man of my choosing to labour for their benefit."[31] Scotsman Adam Taitt, married to McGillivray's sister, also left his

[25] King Malachey to Governor Glen, 15 October 1754, *DIASC*, 2:29.

[26] Adair, *Adair's History*, 187.

[27] Pope, *A tour through the southern and western territories*, 59; William Hayne Simmons, *Notices of East Florida, with an Account of the Seminole Nation of Indians* (1822; reprint, Gainesville: University of Florida, 1973), 77; and Swanton, *Social Organization*, 392–393, 394, 396.

[28] Fabel and Rea, "Lieutenant Thomas Campbell's Sojourn among the Creeks," 108.

[29] Obituary notice in *The Gentleman's Magazine* (v63pt2), 767, August 1793, no. 213, *McGillivray of the Creeks*.

[30] Arturo O'Neill to Barón de Carondelet, 17 February 1793, PC, leg. 39, 1424, reel 162, PKY.

[31] Extract of a letter from William Panton to John Leslie, 28 August 1793, EF, bnd. 116L9, reel 44, PKY.

property to his son David, requesting in his will that the boy be educated in Scotland before reaching majority.[32]

A dispute over inheritance in 1799 illustrates just how much some
Creeks had come to value property.[33] In June of that year, Alexander
McGillivray's half-brother, McPherson, passed away.[34] Tinghyaby, his
oldest son, took control of his property, but McPherson's sister Janet
initially objected, consenting only "at last to his Son's . . . having the
management."[35] She later renewed her protests, however, this time
joined by another sister, Sehoy, and Sehoy's son, David Taitt.[36] William
Panton, of Panton, Leslie and Company, also became involved in the
affair, using trader Daniel McGillivray (no relation to Alexander) to
secure payment of McPherson's debts.[37] Eventually, Janet, Sehoy, and
a third sister, Sophia Durant, prevailed. They sent warriors from
Ecunhatke (White Ground) to take "all the cattle that was" along with

[32] C. H. Driesbach, "William Weatherford," *Arrow Points* 4 (1922): 112.

[33] Cherokee Indians were also beginning to become acquisitive. See the inheritance dispute
recounted in Gary E. Moulton, *John Ross: Cherokee Chief* (Athens: University of Georgia, 1978),
2–3.

[34] McPherson's sister, known as B. Crook's wife, was the sister of Mrs. Durant, who we know was
also the sister of McGillivray. McPherson thus must have been McGillivray's half-brother, the
son of Sehoy and Malcolm McPherson, the business partner of Alexander's father. Cashin,
Lachlan McGillivray, 73 and 333n28. Two sources in fact refer to McGillivray's brother, but do
not mention him by name. Timothy Barnard to Edward Telfair, 27 May 1786, LTB, 55, GDAH;
and William Panton to Barón de Carondelet, 1793, PC, leg. 2353, 706, reel 380, PKY. Hawkins
also mentioned meeting a cousin of McGillivray's named McFaisson. Cashin, *Lachlan
McGillivray*, 73–74.

[35] Daniel McGillivray to William Panton, 28 September 1799, Greenslade Papers, PKY.

[36] Daniel McGillivray to William Panton, 28 September 1799, Forbes-Innerarity Papers, 84/15,
reel 147P, PKY.

[37] Daniel McGillivray to William Panton, 18 October 1799, Cruzat Papers, PKY.
     The following is a family tree of the people involved in this dispute:

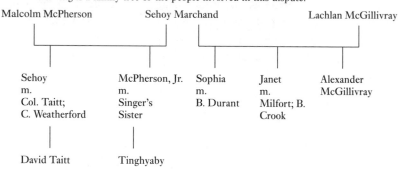

Pickett, *History of Alabama*, 229, 342–346; Thomas S. Woodward, *Woodward's Reminiscences of
the Creek, or Muscogee Indians, Contained in Letters to Friends in Georgia and Alabama* (Montgomery: Berrett & Wimbish, 1859), 111, 59–61, and 88–89; Milfort, *Memoir*, 135; Caughey,
McGillivray of the Creeks, 9–13; and Halbert and Ball, *The Creek War*, 164–166.

the "Negroes," "wenches," and "small Negroes." Despite Daniel
McGillivray's efforts to oppose them with a group of warriors from
Hickory Ground (Ocheaupofau), the trader eventually relented: "I am
of opinion they will have them all & make away with them."[38] The struggle after McPherson's death testifies to both the extent of his property
and the acquisitiveness of his heirs.

If inheritance posed trouble at the end of a lifetime, controlling property during one's life presented a more constant problem. The solution,
in large part, was fences. In the second half of the eighteenth century,
the growing number of fences in the Deep South reflected and contributed to the desire of certain Creeks to mark off and protect their
property. As late as the 1750s, no fences whatsoever had existed in the
region. In 1756, when Upper Creeks refused to permit the construction
of a fort on their land, despite the promise of South Carolina to offer
better trading prices, they explained that a fort would necessitate cattle
to feed the garrison. "We have no Fences to keep them out of our Corn,"
they stated, and "if any of them should be killed that will make Differences."[39] Similarly, James Adair related how, in 1767, Creeks feared that
cattle would "spoil their open corn-fields."[40] When more Creeks themselves began ranching, however, they began raising fences around their
farms.[41] Fences were often (though not always) a personal investment in
labor that gave Creeks a more permanent stake, literally and figuratively,
in the land they were using. Moreover, these improvements made settlements more permanent. Their effect, then, was twofold: Originally
constructed to keep cattle and hogs out of planted fields, fences also contributed to a growing sense of private land ownership. In the late 1790s,
for example, the fences and improvements on the land of mestizo
Alexander Cornels made his commitments clear. His fences were "well
made and straight, his garden 150 feet square, well spaded, laid off and
planted with the variety usual in good gardens." In addition, he had
planted a grove of peach trees, further establishing his roots in the land.[42]
His fences not only kept cattle out, but also testified visibly to his sense
of ownership.

[38] Daniel McGillivray to William Panton, 13 October 1800, Greenslade Papers, PKY.
[39] Headmen of the Upper Creek Nation to Governor Lyttelton, 9 August 1756, *DIASC*, 2:153–154.
[40] Adair, *Adair's History*, 138.
[41] For an illuminating discussion of the relationship between cattle and fences, see Cronon, *Changes in the Land*, 129–132.
[42] Benjamin Hawkins, "A sketch of the Creek Country in the years 1798 and 1799," *LBH*, 1:291–293.

The first Creek fences appeared in the 1760s. Made of forks, about two feet high, and cross-laid with poles, they were "just high enough to keep out horned Cattle." These constructions sufficiently obstructed small numbers of cattle, but the Creeks soon found that swine could easily pass underneath and that large herds of cattle required more secure barriers.[43] When Hawkins arrived in Creek country, "there did not exceed in the whole nation a half dozen fences made of rails," George Stiggins, a longtime Alabama resident, recalled in the 1830s.[44] Laws in South Carolina and Georgia required farmers to fence their crops,[45] but Hawkins had to rely on exhortation. Those who listened began building substantial worm fences – stacked rails that zigzagged around farms and reflected both a growing sense of property and the proliferation of cattle in the region.

According to the agent's own estimate, 400 Creek settlements were fenced in the four years preceding 1802.[46] In the late 1790s, for instance, Micco Emathla moved out of Kasihta and settled along the east side of the Chattahoochee where he built "a good worm fence" and "a comfortable house." His neighbors had already begun speculating in land, at least in the sense that they exclusively possessed tracts they could not yet use. According to Hawkins, they were "industrious, have forked fences, and have enclosed more land than they can cultivate."[47] Worm fences also delineated each of the five settlements at Auputtaue, a village twenty miles east of the Chattahoochee on Upatoi Creek. "We have made

---

[43] As early as 1772, Tallassee and Tuckabatche, both on the Tallapoosa River near the great bend, had about 150 cattle, but Creeks still were uncomfortable with having cattle among them. Taitt, "David Taitt's Journal," 504, 508. James Adair describes fencing practices among the Cherokees and Choctaws in *Adair's History*, 436. When poorly constructed fences were permitting swine to destroy crops in seventeenth-century Virginia, colonists passed a law ordering farmers to build hog-proof worm fences "foure feet and a half high [and] substantiall close downe to the bottome." Quoted in John Solomon Otto, *The Southern Frontiers, 1607–1860: The Agricultural Evolution of the Colonial and Antebellum South* (New York: Greenwood Press, 1989), 16.

[44] John Pope, *A tour through the southern and western territories*, 63; "A historical narration of the genealogy, traditions, and downfall of the Ispocoga or Creek tribe of Indians," PKY. For examples of the construction of worm fences, see Journal of Benjamin Hawkins, 3 February 1797, *Letters of Benjamin Hawkins, 1796–1806*, 70–71; Benjamin Hawkins, "A sketch of the Creek Country in the years 1798 and 1799," *LBH*, 1:311 and 314–315; and Benjamin Hawkins to Henry Gaither, 27 February 1799, *LBH*, 1:241.

[45] Otto, "Open-Range Cattle-Herding in Southern Florida," 329, 332.

[46] Benjamin Hawkins, "Journal of Occurrences in the Creek Agency from January to the Conclusion of the Conference and Treaty at Fort Wilkinson by the Agent for Indian Affairs," *LBH*, 2:424.

[47] Benjamin Hawkins, "A sketch of the Creek Country in the years 1798 and 1799," *LBH*, 1:311. Creeks borrowed the construction technique of the worm fence from colonists. Gregory A. Waselkov, "A Reinterpretation of the Creek Indian Barricade at Horseshoe Bend," *Journal of Alabama Archaeology* 32 (1986): 99.

it a rule to admit no neighbours who will not make fences," Tussekiah Micco explained.[48]

As Tussekiah Micco indicated, fences not only separated livestock from crops, but also divided Creeks from each other. Muskogees who did not fence also did not ranch. In Hitchiti, a town situated twenty miles south of present-day Columbus, Georgia, Hawkins, from his one-sided perspective, observed "much poverty and indolence." He noted significantly that the residents "have no fences." By contrast, the inhabitants of newer villages nearby impressed the agent as "honest and industrious" – demonstrated, of course, by their fencing. The village of Hitchetooche, he noted, had "good fences and stocks of cattle"; Tuttalosee had "good worm fences and large stocks of cattle, [and] some hogs"; and Cheauhooche was "beginning to fence."[49] A similar contrast existed between Okfuskee, on the Tallapoosa about ten miles below what is now Horseshoe Bend National Military Park, and its villages. Despite the presence of a few cattle, hogs, and horses, Okfuskee had no fences, and consequently, in the late 1790s, several residents began moving out. In one satellite village called Epeesaugee, forty Creeks fenced their fields in one year "for the benefit of their stock." This was a wealthy village where every resident owned cattle. Ecunchate Emathla, for example, had ten head, McCartney and Totechu Hadjo each had 100, and Tools King had 200.[50] In a town named Eufala, two miles below Okfuskee, a dismal hunting season over the winter of 1798–1799 "reduced to a certainty in the minds of many of the Indians that they cannot depend on hunting for their support," according to Hawkins, leading some hunters to fence their fields for the benefit of raising cattle.[51] Other Creeks, however, remained aloof from the fenced communities of the Deep South.

[48] Benjamin Hawkins, "A sketch of the Creek Country in the years 1798 and 1799," *LBH*, 1:312; Journal of Benjamin Hawkins, 3 February 1797, *Letters of Benjamin Hawkins, 1796–1806*, 70–71.
[49] Benjamin Hawkins, "A sketch of the Creek Country in the years 1798 and 1799," *LBH*, 1:315.
[50] Ibid., 303–304.
[51] Benjamin Hawkins to James Jackson, 27 February 1799, LBH, 41, GDAH. In 1802, when Efau Hadjo asked Hawkins for presents to assist him in his old age, Hawkins gave him a stern lecture:

> I am here to remedy the past, to assist the Indians as the game is gone to clothe and feed themselves by farming, spinning and stockraising & to help all who will help themselves but not to tollerate or support sturdy beggars. . . . I will assist you from my own funds on this condition and no other. Put your negros and family to work, make them pen and milk your cattle, let me see your fields enlarged and well fenced. I have furnished you with axes, grubing hoes, wedges and ploughs, make them use them. And you must bring the old Chiefs to consent to sell their waste lands for present use, and to meet their future wants. The young people as they grow up must be taught to farm, to raise stock and to spin. And you must

These significant changes in settlement patterns brought stress and conflict to Creek towns.[52] Every town had its "idlers," as Hawkins liked to call those who were not adhering to his program.[53] He offered a revealing if one-sided account of how property rapidly fragmented the town of Hoithlewaule:

> The increase of property among them, and the inconvenience attendant on their situation, their settlement being on the right side of the river, and their fields and stock on the left, brought the well-disposed to listen with attention to the plan of civilization, and to comment freely on their bad management. The town divided against itself; the idlers and ill-disposed remained in town, and the others moved over the river and fenced their fields.[54]

The dispersal caused by cattle separated the wealthy from the poor. When Hopoy Micco, the speaker of the nation, sent word to the commandant of Pensacola in 1803 asking for two kegs of rum "to give for making a cowpen to pin wild cattle," he was contributing to this process, separating himself from his neighbors. For their labor, his fencers would receive only alcohol, a property quickly consumed, while Hopoy Micco would increase the value of his land. And when the cowpen was finished, his "cow hunter," a black slave, would watch over it for him.[55]

---

think seriously of these things, turn your attention to them and make them the constant theme of conversation. When I hear and know this I shall take pleasure in helping you.

Hawkins thus used the spoils of the federal government to promote "civilization." Benjamin Hawkins, "Journal of Occurrences in the Creek Agency from January to the Conclusion of the Conference and Treaty at Fort Wilkinson by the Agent for Indian Affairs," *LBH*, 2:411.

[52] Historian Virginia DeJohn Anderson argues that livestock was a key point of contention between the Wampanoags and New England colonists in the late seventeenth century. The problems that cattle presented to the Wampanoags, such as the destruction of crops and the expansion of grazing land, were a major cause of Metacom's War in 1675. This same conflict came to the fore a century later in the Deep South, this time pitting Creek ranchers against Creek hunters and subsistence farmers. Virginia DeJohn Anderson, "King Philip's Herds: Indians, Colonists, and the Problem of Livestock in Early New England," *The William and Mary Quarterly* 51 (1994): 601–624.

[53] For examples of this epithet, see Benjamin Hawkins, "A sketch of the Creek Country in the years 1798 and 1799," *LBH*, 1:293–294; Benjamin Hawkins to James McHenry, 24 June 1798, *LBH*, 1:209; and Benjamin Hawkins, "Journal of Occurrences in the Creek Agency from January to the Conclusion of the Conference and Treaty at Fort Wilkinson by the Agent for Indian Affairs," *LBH*, 2:406. In one instance, he recorded the talk of a Creek Indian who labeled a faction of his fellow Creeks as "idlers." Extracts of occurrences in the agency for Indian affairs, August 1813, LBH, 238, GDAH.

[54] Benjamin Hawkins, "A sketch of the Creek Country in the years 1798 and 1799," *LBH*, 1:294.

[55] Opoymicco to the Governor of Pensacola, 31 August 1803, Forbes-Innerarity Papers, PKY, reel 147P. The "cow hunter" is mentioned in Daniel McGillivray to William Panton, 28 September 1799, Greenslade Papers, PKY.

Increasingly divided by fences, the propertied and propertyless lived in ever greater hostility. But well into the nineteenth century, Creeks remembered a time when private property had created few problems. In 1820, one Muskogee recalled when "there was no law against stealing; the crime itself being almost unknown." Away on hunting trips, he said, they had left their "silver trinkets and ornaments hanging in their open huts."[56] In the 1830s, Creeks described the past in similar terms. Formerly, stealing was "unknown to them," George Stiggins learned, "being raised poor and habituated to that life." They "felt no anxiety to perpetrate acts of thievery for the acquisition of a thing that they did not crave nor know the want of."[57]

In the 1790s, however, the changing relationship between Creeks and private property led to conflict. The discord had two sources. First, the declining deerskin trade and the reluctance of American and Spanish agents to dole out presents left many Creeks without a viable economic pursuit. Out of necessity and as political protest, these Muskogees took goods from their wealthier neighbors. Second, well-off Creeks redefined as theft what in the past had been construed as sharing. "Indians never say they steal, but they borrow," Alexander McGillivray complained to his Scottish trading partner in 1792.[58]

The proliferation of locks in the 1790s in Creek country attests to both of these sources of discord: Hungry Creeks took what they needed, and wealthy Creeks defined those actions as theft.[59] William Bartram had observed in the 1770s that Creeks then had "neither Locks nor Bars to their Doors,"[60] though archaeological and documentary evidence suggests that as early as the 1760s a very few Creeks were beginning to lock up their possessions. Excavations at Spalding's Lower Store, a trading post operating between 1763 and 1775 on the St. Johns not far from the

[56] Adam Hodgson, *Remarks during a journey through North America in the years 1819, 1820, and 1821* (New York, 1823), 267–268.
[57] "A historical narration of the genealogy, traditions, and downfall of the Ispocoga or Creek tribe of Indians," PKY.
[58] Alexander McGillivray to William Panton, 28 November 1792, ST, PC, leg. 204/27, PKY.
[59] Writing about eighteenth-century London, historian Peter Linebaugh observes:

> The control of space is the essence of private property, and its architecture became more complex: yards, fences, railings and gates formed an outer perimeter; stair-wells, doors, rooms and closets an inner one; bureaux, chests, cabinets, cases, desks and drawers protected the articles of private property themselves. Each space was controlled by locks, and access to each required a key.

Creeks could not control space as tightly as London merchants, but they too used yards, railings, doors, rooms, chests, and locks. Linebaugh, *The London Hanged*, 336.
[60] Bartram, "Observations," 160.

present-day city of Palatka, uncovered a padlock, a brass chestlock with a sliding latch, and five lock keys.[61] Records from the 1760s also indicate that trunks and locks were at least occasional trade items. One list of "goods proper for Indian presents for West Florida," for example, included eighty "gilt trunks" and seventy-two padlocks.[62]

By the end of the eighteenth century, the use of locks had become common among wealthy Creeks. In 1787, when trader Charles McLatchy died at his store in Apalache, an inventory revealed he had on hand nine dozen "common padlocks" as well as three dozen pairs of hinges.[63] McLatchy's patrons were evidently building lockable doors. So were the customers of mestizo trader Peter McQueen. In 1803, he requested six house locks from John Forbes along with more common merchandise such as looking glasses, earrings, and blankets.[64] One of his patrons may have been Samuel Moniac, among the wealthiest mestizos in the Deep South, who had twelve padlocks in the early nineteenth century to protect his substantial holdings.[65] The U.S. trading factory also dealt in locks. Factor John Halsted requested twenty-four double-bolted padlocks and an equal number of common padlocks in 1806 when the post was situated on the Oconee River, and in 1810, the factory, now relocated to the Flint River, received specific requests from Creek leaders for double and single-bolted padlocks. Halsted saw fit to order three dozen of each type and anticipated that he could sell them for a 50 percent profit to those men who received the annual cash stipend for the Creek nation.[66] As recipients of the stipend and beneficiaries of other federal largesse, these men indeed had more property to lock up than other Creeks.

Yet, despite such evidence, the majority of Creeks still did not have

[61] Kenneth Edmund Lewis, "The History and Archaeology of Spalding's Lower Store (PU-23), Putnam County, Florida" (M.A. thesis, University of Florida, 1969), 85–88.

[62] "An assortment of goods proper for Indian presents for West Florida," enclosed in George Johnstone to the Secretary of the Board of Trade, 29 January 1764, PRO 5/574, p. 11, reel 66K, PKY. These items must have been popular, for in a list of presents to be given out in 1766 in St. Augustine at a congress with Creeks, 72 padlocks and 120 gilt trunks were included. "State of presents wanting to compleat an assortment for a meeting proposed to be held with the Indians in 1766," enclosed in Grant to Board of Trade, 13 January 1766, PRO, CO 5/540, p. 501, in "British Colonial Office Records," 1:216, PKY.

[63] Luis de Bertucat to Arturo O'Neill, 14 October 1787, PC, leg. 37, bnd. 7, doc. 276–2, reel 169, PKY.

[64] See Peter McQueen to John Forbes, 18 February 1803, Cruzat Papers, PKY.

[65] USS.H.doc. 200 (20–1) 173:9.

[66] John Halsted to William Davy, 5 April 1806, p. 287; Halsted to General John Mason, 31 July 1810, p. 331, Records of the Creek Trading House, Letter Book, 1795–1816, reel 94-O, PKY; Invoice of merchandise . . . to be forwarded to the Factory at the Oakmulgee Old Fields, 26 September 1810, U.S. Bureau of Indian Affairs, Records of the Office of Indian Trade, Creek Factory Records, Vouchers, 1796–1821, Record Group 75, entry 51, National Archives.

locks on their doors. In 1791, for example, Caleb Swan noted that Creeks barricaded the doors of their houses with heavy pieces of wood before leaving on hunting trips.[67] In fact, Creeks who pursued the chase did not accumulate large amounts of property, nor had they developed the acute sense of attachment to their belongings that warranted the security of a bolt. As late as 1811, locks remained relatively rare even among the Indian and white residents at the Creek agency.[68] The uneven distribution of bolts and latches indicates that such hardware served to divide Creeks rather than unite them in defense of their property.

The conflict assumed greater dimensions when hunters took life and property from white Georgians. In a relationship defined partly by cooperation and partly by coercion, U.S. officials and Creek representatives condemned these warriors as "sturdy beggars" and tried to curb their actions.[69] Just as the "borrowing" of property grew more common and was defined more frequently as theft, so frontier conflicts increased absolutely and were interpreted more often as crimes. As deer herds dwindled and as Georgians continued to push into Creek hunting grounds, hunters who refused to ranch (or who did not have the means to do so) raided Georgia settlements out of desperation. In 1763, a Creek leader named Mortar had explained that, with the encroachment of Georgians on their hunting territory, warriors killed cattle to "fill their Bellies when they are hungry having nothing else to do it with."[70] The same motivation pertained in the 1790s. In addition, as Creeks explained in 1798, it "had always been customary when a great Chief or warrior was mad and threatened to go on the frontiers to do mischief, to pacify them with presents." Such gifts, they added, "were more necessary now than ever that the game was gone." The "people were naked," they said, "& had not any other resource but in the presents to be offered them by the white people."[71]

Before it became a crime, Creeks had understood frontier violence to be an integral and healthy part of their relationship with whites. They rightly believed that their red-hearted warriors had in the past obligated Europeans to regale them, and they were reluctant to concede that they had since lost that power.[72] In 1795, an angry Chickasaw leader sent word

---

[67] Swan, "State of Arts and Manufactures," 692–693.
[68] Mauelshagen and Davis, *Partners in the Lord's Work*, 49.
[69] Benjamin Hawkins, "Journal of Occurrences in the Creek Agency," *LBH*, 2:411.
[70] At a meeting of the head men of the Upper Creek nation, 5 April 1763, *CRG*, 9:71–72.
[71] Benjamin Hawkins to James McHenry, 24 June 1798, *LBH*, 1:209.
[72] In 1738, for example, after a Spanish agent had refused a request for gifts, a Creek warrior changed the agent's mind by explaining that "if they wished to stay in these lands, they had to

to Efau Hadjo asserting that frontier violence was for naught because there was no "prospect of killing and driving the white people back to where they came."[73] But as Hawkins noted, Creek warriors still remembered when they had done "a favour by receiving, when naked, clothes and comforts from the British agents."[74] Efau Hadjo reported in 1801:

> The old Chiefs and their associates in opposition are of opinion that if we reject the new order of things, order the agent with the Blacksmiths and ass't to leave the nation, stop traveling of all white people through their land, and let the horse thieves worry the frontiers for a while, the government will change its plan, revive the old mode of presents for the sake of peace and court, caress and accommodate their wants and those of their adherents as the British formerly did.[75]

By forging a social compact, a few Creek leaders had been trying to redefine border raids as national crimes since the end of the American Revolution, but by the end of 1796, they still had not succeeded. One Creek reformer told a well-known horse thief named Nauhonelubby Thlucco:

> I am directed to talk to you, and to inform you that if you cannot live without stealing, as you have been so long in the practice of it, you must steal from us, come and steal from us, even if you want fowls, come and steal them from us and let the white people and their property alone.[76]

This desperate appeal illustrates not only the lack of a central government capable of quelling dissension, but also the pressure Creeks were

---

give as much as they asked for." Alonso del Toro, diary of distribution of goods, 21 February 1738, enclosed in Governor of Havana to Secretary Torrenueva, 28 May 1738, ST, bnd. 5731, 87-1-3/48, SD 2593, PKY. Colonial governors denied that they were doing the Creeks favors by giving them presents, but they in fact knew that their Indian neighbors were in control of affairs. After describing the frequency with which Creeks murdered settlers and stole horses, Governor James Wright of Georgia complained in 1771 that, "as things are now circumstanced, there is no kind of Power or Controul whatever over the said Indians; all which they are too sensible of, also that they are Powerfull enough, and can whenever they please, greatly distress if not totally Ruin that most flourishing Province." Memorial of James Wright to the Lords of Trade, 1771, CRG, vol. 28, 2:769, GDAH.

[73] Opaymingo to James Seagrove, 1 September 1795, ST, PC leg. 203/49, PKY.

[74] Benjamin Hawkins to James McHenry, 19 November 1797, *LBH*, 1:156–160.

[75] Quoted in Benjamin Hawkins to Henry Dearborn, 1 June 1801, *LBH*, 1:360. Choctaw and Cherokee warriors behaved similarly. Carson, "Horses and the Economy and Culture of the Choctaw Indians, 1690–1840"; and William G. McLoughlin, "Cherokee Anomie, 1794–1809: New Roles for Red Men, Red Women, and Black Slaves," in *Uprooted Americans: Essays to Honor Oscar Handlin*, ed. Richard L. Bushman et al. (Boston: Little, Brown, and Company, 1979), 150–152.

[76] Journal of Benjamin Hawkins, 9 February 1797, *LBH*, 1:45.

under to create one. Spanish commandant Vicente Folch instructed his Creek agent to "find means to persuade the more reasonable chiefs that they ought to unite among themselves to oblige their warriors either by admonition or force, not to disturb in any manner whatsoever their neighbours the white people."[77] Hawkins similarly stated that Creek men, "bred in habits proudly indolent and insolent, . . . will reluctantly and with difficulty be humbled to the level of rational life."[78] Spanish and American agents and their Creek allies needed an instrument stronger than locks.

On assuming his post, Hawkins immediately began drawing up plans for a national council composed of representatives from each Creek town and led by a speaker. It was to meet annually to draft and enforce laws "for the welfare of the nation." "An establishment of this sort appears to me indispensable to enable the nation to fulfill its engagements with us," Hawkins wrote the secretary of war.[79] Creeks had long assembled to discuss important matters, but only in irregular and regional meetings. Extraordinary events occasionally demanded large discussions, and the more extraordinary the matter, the greater the attendance, but Creeks rarely gathered from all, or even most, of the Muskogee towns in the Deep South. "Your Excellency will please observe," one Indian agent had written to the governor of South Carolina in 1756, "as there is such a great Distance between the Upper and Lower Creek Nations they never come to one another's Talks, but upon very extraordinary Occasions."[80] Because Creeks did not have a centralized means of enforcing conformity, these large meetings provided forums solely for discussion and debate; each participant was free to leave with a different plan of action.[81] The regularity of Hawkins's council made it novel, but the real innovation lay in its pretensions to represent a nation and to wield executive powers.

From Hawkins's perspective, the national council allowed him to circumvent the hundreds of autonomous clan leaders who had long

[77] Governor of Florida to the King, 4 December 1797, EF, bnd. 46G4, 131, reel 18, PKY; Governor Folch to James Durouzeaux, 26 March 1798, PC, leg. 215B, 722, reel 298, PKY. In October 1798, Folch reported that the Spanish party within the Creek nation had nearly been destroyed due to the suspension of gifts. Vicente Folch to Marqués de Casa Calvo, 3 October 1799, PC, leg. 2355, 179, reel 382, PKY.
[78] Benjamin Hawkins to James McHenry, 19 November 1797, LBH, 1:156–160.
[79] Benjamin Hawkins, "A sketch of the Creek Country in the years 1798 and 1799," LBH, 1:316–317; Benjamin Hawkins to James McHenry, 6 January 1797, LBH, 1:63.
[80] Daniel Pepper to Governor Lyttelton, 18 November 1756, DIASC, 2:255.
[81] Benjamin Hawkins to James McHenry, 6 January 1797, LBH, 1:63.

stymied attempts by colonial officials to control the Muskogees. The hierarchy of the national council permitted Hawkins to bribe and cajole a limited number of prominent Creek politicians, and even without payoffs and threats, many national representatives were committed to reform because their power and wealth derived from "civilized" pursuits such as ranching and planting. Hopoy Micco (Muclasa Hopoy or Singer), for example, eventually became the speaker for the national council. Although he hunted, he also held slaves and cattle.[82] In November 1797, Hopoy Micco burned down the houses of three Indians accused of horse rustling and murdered two blacks presumed guilty of theft, giving notice that "he would put all to death who kept disturbing the property of the white people, and kept confusion in their land."[83] According to Hawkins, this Creek leader was "Intent on the plan of civilization, desirous to introduce a regular & efficient Government among his people, decisive in all his purposes, and a stranger to the ordinary habits and propensities of his kind."[84]

Advocates of reform such as Hopoy Micco helped promote Hawkins's program of "civilization," but before they could effectively control other Creeks, the national council had to become a coercive institution. The council's transformation from persuasion to force took place between 1797 and 1799 when a series of murders spurred Creek politicians to form a proto-police force, known as the "warriors of the nation" or "law-menders." The murders themselves were not extraordinary in the context of the violent relations between Creeks and Georgians, but Hawkins's presence and the gathering momentum of several years of partial reforms proved decisive.[85] Hawkins demanded justice: "Nothing I see will restrain the Creeks but the fear of punishment."[86] In spring 1798, he secured promises from the national council to execute the murderers.[87] At the same time, Creek representatives led by national speaker Efau Hadjo "passed a law" to punish horse rustling by "severe whipping."[88]

---

82   Daniel McGillivray to William Panton, 28 September 1799, Greenslade Papers, PKY.
83   Journal of Benjamin Hawkins, 25 November 1797, *Letters of Benjamin Hawkins, 1796–1806*, 259.
84   Benjamin Hawkins to Henry Dearborn, 17 July 1802, *LBH*, 2:450.
85   For details on the murders, see Affidavit of Jeremiah Oates, 10 April 1797, "Indian Depredations, 1787–1825," 3:77, GDAH; Benjamin Hawkins to James Jackson, 11 July 1798, *LBH*, 1:211; Benjamin Hawkins to Timothy Barnard, 13 July 1797, *LBH*, 1:120.
86   Benjamin Hawkins to Timothy Barnard, 13 July 1797, *LBH*, 1:120.
87   Benjamin Hawkins to William Panton, 20 May 1798, *LBH*, 1:194.
88   Journal of Benjamin Hawkins, 29 May 1798, *LBH*, 1:189; Benjamin Hawkins to Thomas Butler, 6 June 1798, *LBH*, 1:198; James Durouzeaux to Juan Nepomuceno de Quesada, 12 October 1795, EF, bnd. 115K9, reel 43.

Efau Hadjo hoped these coercive measures, symbolized by the sticks that warriors wielded to punish transgressors, would succeed:

> When we do make a law we believe we can execute it; we now address our talk to all our towns, and I believe when the sticks are cut and put into the hands of the warriors they will exert themselves. Now I will try the experiment, it is for the good of the land, you have long wished it; you have a regard for our land and wish to see us in peace and quietness.[89]

Despite his commitment, over the next four months, Creeks beat several horse thieves but did not execute one of the murderers.[90] In fact, the beatings were less a result of a new national council than of Hawkins's personal sway. Hawkins himself later observed that "with all my exertions I cannot get their laws carried into effect, but in the cases where my personal influence is exerted in a few towns."[91] The mixed results of the experiment indicated the reluctance of most Creeks to recognize any coercive authority among them, though some Muskogees remained committed to the reforms. "If beating will not tame them," one Creek said of horse rustlers, "something else must be done."[92]

Like locks, beatings addressed only the symptoms of a larger ailment, but Hawkins's single-minded crusade and the national council's experiment with force meant that as the condition worsened, Creek politicians foresaw greater violence as the only possible cure. Such was the case in September 1799 when dissident Creeks disrupted a boundary commission surveying the line between Spanish Florida and the United States. Creek leader Efau Hadjo had assured that the commission would proceed without incident, but other Muskogees, including many Seminoles, suspected that the new boundary would lead to the loss of their hunting grounds.[93] Though Andrew Ellicott, the U.S. surveyor, explained that it "was not a line of property, but of jurisdiction, a line between white people, and not intended in any way to affect the Indians

[89] Journal of Benjamin Hawkins, 27 May 1798, *LBH*, 1:186.
[90] Richard Thomas to [?], 17 July 1798, *Letters of Benjamin Hawkins, 1796–1806*, 488–489; Journal of Richard Thomas, 30 July 1798, *Letters of Benjamin Hawkins, 1796–1806*, 490–492; Benjamin Hawkins to Silas Dinsmoor, 24 August 1798, *LBH*, 1:218; Benjamin Hawkins to George Walton, 25 August 1798, *LBH*, 1:221–222; Benjamin Hawkins to William Panton, 22 November 1798, Forbes-Innerarity Papers, 83/1, reel 147P, PKY.
[91] Benjamin Hawkins to David Henley, 15 April 1799, *LBH*, 1:245.
[92] Journal of Richard Thomas, 30 July 1798, *Letters of Benjamin Hawkins, 1796–1806*, 490–492.
[93] Benjamin Hawkins to James McHenry, 23 May 1799, *LBH*, 1:249; James Durouzeaux to Vicente Folch, 28 September 1799, PC, leg. 1573, doc. 3, frame 20, reel 83.

in either their property, manners, customs, or religion,"[94] Creeks must have taken little comfort in finding that the line, following the thirty-first parallel from the Mississippi to the Chattahoochee River, ran directly through the town of Chisquitaluja on the west side of the Chattahoochee. (Curiously, Ellicott's map omitted this settlement.) Had the line proceeded as planned, the commissioners would have chained the distance from the mouth of the Flint to the head of the St. Marys, then blazed a trail, and finally constructed a series of mounds marking the boundary.[95] The commission disbanded precipitately in September, however, after Creeks and Seminoles stole surveying equipment and over thirty-five horses and threatened to commit more serious violence.[96]

When Hawkins called on nearby towns to supply fifty warriors to protect the commissioners, he received over 150 men.[97] On the urging of Hawkins, seventy-two warriors, carrying heavy sticks to beat their victims, gathered in Tuckabatche to punish the ringleaders of the thieves. Istelechu, or Mankiller, from Tallassee, was their first victim. They knocked down his house and burned it to the ground. A participant described the brutal punishment:

> We beat him with sticks until he was on the ground as a dead man, we cut off one of his ears with a part of his cheek and put a sharp stick up his fundament. We killed all his fowls and hogs and broke all his pots, pans, spoons and furniture of his house.[98]

Ieginne, or Chepaustunnuggee Futcheligee, received similar treatment. Another participant escaped his persecutors, and four others fled to the Cherokees. "The sticks are now in the hands of the warriors,

---

[94] Andrew Ellicott, *The Journal of Andrew Ellicott* (1803; reprint, Chicago: Quadrangle Books, 1962), 206.

[95] Stephen Minor to Governor Gayoso, 5 August 1799, PC, leg. 2355, 651, reel 382, PKY.

[96] Ibid.; Stephen Minor to Manuel Gayoso de Lemos, 16 August 1799, PC, leg. 2355, 666, reel 382, PKY; Stephen Minor to Nicolas Daunoy, 24 September 1799, PC, leg. 2355, 639, reel 382, PKY; James Durouzeaux to Vicente Folch, 28 September 1799, PC, leg. 216B, 372, reel 301, PKY; Tomás Portell to Vicente Folch, 1 October 1799, PC, leg. 2355, 697, reel 382, PKY; Andrew Ellicott to Benjamin Hawkins, 1 October 1799, ST, PC leg. 23/68, PKY; Lorenzo Vitrian to Juan Ventura Morales, 3 October 1799, PC, leg. 1574, doc. 28, frame 65, reel 86, PKY; Benjamin Hawkins to James McHenry, 5 October 1799, *LBH*, 1:260; Benjamin Hawkins to William Panton, 14 October 1799, Forbes-Innerarity Papers, 84/32, reel 147P, PKY; Ellicott, *The Journal of Andrew Ellicott*, 202–224.

[97] James Durouzeaux to Vicente Folch, 28 September 1799, PC, leg. 1573, doc. 3, frame 20, reel 83, PKY; Benjamin Hawkins to James McHenry, 5 October 1799, *LBH*, 1:260; Murdock McLeod to James Jackson, 6 October 1799, CIL, 2:582–3, GDAH.

[98] Report of Tustunnue Haujo and Robert Walton to Benjamin Hawkins, 4 November 1799, LBH, 44, GDAH.

and they will not lay them down 'till they punish every thief and mischiefmaker in the nation to fulfill the promises made to you and to carry the Laws into effect," a warrior told Hawkins.[99] To many Creek observers, however, the punishments must have seemed as arbitrary an imposition as the line of mounds to be constructed through their hunting grounds.

Tustunnue Hadjo, who participated in the beatings, revealed the magnitude of the event in a question he posed to Hawkins:

> As this is the first time the nation ever undertook to punish and cross people who violate their laws, we want your advice and opinion respecting those who die under the punishment we inflict. Can anyone be answerable for executing the orders of the nation in such case?[100]

In traditional Creek justice, Tustunnue Hadjo and his cohorts were murderers answerable to the injured clans. Hawkins's answer was predictable but significant. In cases of state-sanctioned executions, he said, the law is responsible, not "one man and one family." Creeks who demanded satisfaction were to be told that their relation was a "rogue and a mischiefmaker." It is "their pay," Hawkins said of the murdered. "It is the pay of the Nation."[101]

Soon after these severe beatings were administered, the national council adopted three hierarchical and systematic measures proposed by Hawkins, introducing a new discipline to Creek country.[102] The first

---

[99] Ibid.; Benjamin Hawkins to Vicente Folch, 17 November 1799, PC, leg. 216B, 392, reel 301, PKY.

[100] Report of Tustunnue Haujo and Robert Walton to Benjamin Hawkins, 4 November 1799, LBH, 44, GDAH.

[101] Ibid. Hawkins gave a similar but more extensive report of his conversation with Tustunnue Hadjo to Alexander Cornels. See Benjamin Hawkins to Alexander Cornells, [5 November 1799], LBH, 1:267. In the aftermath of the punishments, Vicente Folch, commandant of Pensacola, congratulated Hawkins:

> I must candidly confess to you that though I never thought it impossible to bring the Indians to a certain degree of subordination, supposing the two neighbouring powers in the good intelligence they are now, yet I was really convinced that this period was very distant, but the punishment the banditti underwent through your firmness proves to me that the greater part of the work is performed. Since you have the power to bring the mischief makers to punishment, good order will soon be established.

Vicente Folch to Benjamin Hawkins, 5 December 1799, PC, leg. 2355, 244, reel 382, PKY.

[102] According to Luis Milfort who lived among the Creeks for nearly two decades before Hawkins's arrival, "The maintenance of order on hunting expeditions is entrusted to each family chief, who is responsible for what is done in his family; and the great chief of the nation does not have the right himself to interfere in policing, which moreover presents no difficulty because no crimes are ever committed on these hunts." Milfort, *Memoir*, 45.

measure broke down the inhabitants of every Creek town into specific classifications and appointed a warrior over each class to "superintend the execution of the law." Hawkins took advantage of the so-called "warriors of the nation" almost immediately, directing a warrior of "class no. 1" to Cumberland to recover stolen horses, and sending others out among the hunters to keep order. The warriors were paid 25 cents per day plus provisions, while leaders of every group of ten warriors received 50 cents per day. The second measure absolved police of responsibility for their actions. And the third was directed against Bowles, who had recently landed again in Florida: It granted permission to the Indian agent to call on federal troops to apprehend and punish "mischiefmakers and thieves of any country of white people."[103]

In the daily lives of most Creeks, the national council and its police force probably had little impact, but on rare occasions, the police descended on Creek towns where, trespassing on the traditional authority of clans, they punished residents deemed guilty by Creek leaders. By July 1803, two and a half years after the formation of the police, the national council had executed two Indians and three blacks and publicly whipped at least twenty-four others.[104] Even if not directly affected, Creeks witnessed the handiwork of the police. In July 1804, for example, "warriors of the nation" sent the severed ears of a number of horse rustlers through Creek towns.[105] Perhaps the "guilty" had to be punished to "save the innocent," as a Creek named Ageyauhowlo believed. "Let us free our land from guilt to save it," he urged, aware that the United States would destroy them if they did not conform to the new order.[106] But others remained uncertain.

By 1800, the Deep South had become a country of laws and property,

---

[103] Regarding these measures, see Benjamin Hawkins, "A sketch of the Creek Country in the years 1798 and 1799," *LBH*, 1:306 and 316–317; Benjamin Hawkins to James McHenry, 4 December 1799, *LBH*, 1:275; Benjamin Hawkins to Vicente Folch, 8 December 1799, PC, leg. 216B, 400, reel 301, PKY; and Benjamin Hawkins to James Jackson, 20 December 1799, LBH, 48, GDAH.

[104] Benjamin Hawkins to James Madison, 11 July 1803, *LBH*, 2:458.

[105] "Journal of Benjamin Hawkins," 15 July 1804, *LBH*, 2:479. For other examples, see Doster, *Creek Indians*, 1:8–9.

[106] Benjamin Hawkins, "Journal of Occurrences in the Creek Agency from January to the Conclusion of the Conference and Treaty at Fort Wilkinson by the Agent for Indian Affairs," *LBH*, 2:422–423; Benjamin Hawkins to Henry Dearborn, 2 May 1802, *LBH*, 2:440. Efau Hadjo similarly embraced the distinction between guilt and innocence. When asked about the justice of punishing the innocent for the guilty, he responded:

> I believe our custom did not proceed from Essaugetuh Emissee [the master of breath], but from the temper of rash men, who do not consider consequences before they act. It is a bad custom.

Benjamin Hawkins, "A sketch of the Creek Country in the years 1798 and 1799," *LBH*, 1:325.

but only in principle, and only in the eyes of a small number of residents. This powerful Creek minority amassed large amounts of property and passed it down to their sons, creating a new class of wealthy families. They installed locks to protect their goods, and they erected fences around their farms and plantations. Because not all Creeks shared their understanding of property, they had to compel dissidents to conform. Dissent would continue to grow beyond the capabilities of the "law-menders," however, and Creek politicians would yet need to summon U.S. soldiers to secure the new order.

8

The power of writing

In Shakespeare's *The Tempest*, which draws heavily on New World imagery, the slave Caliban plots to overthrow his master, a European colonizer named Prospero. Caliban, whose name recalls the Indian "Cannibals" of the Caribbean, tells a co-conspirator:

> . . . thou mayst brain him,
> Having first seized his books, or with a log
> Batter his skull, or paunch him with a stake,
> Or cut his wesand with thy knife. Remember
> First to possess his books; for without them
> He's but a sot. . . .[1]

Shortly after giving this advice, Caliban again reminds his partner in crime, "Burn but his books."[2] Prospero's seemingly magical powers on this unmapped island clearly derive from his books; hence Caliban's repeated plea to destroy his master's library. In Caliban's preoccupation with the written word, Shakespeare underscored a link between writing and power in the New World, as numerous critics have observed in recent years. Not surprisingly, perhaps, Shakespeare's supposition is borne out by Creek history.

Like their fictional counterpart in *The Tempest*, Creeks were preoccupied by the literacy of European colonists.[3] In 1733, for example,

---

[1] *The Tempest*, 3.2.85–90.
[2] Ibid., 3.2.92.
[3] Literary theorists argue that the very division between speech and writing betrays a naive belief in Western metaphysics, but Creeks may have had their own ideological reasons for making such a distinction. For the statement of a literary critic on the subject, see Jacques Derrida, *Of Grammatology* (1967; first American edition, Baltimore: The Johns Hopkins University, 1976), 101–140. For a useful review of the ethnography on literacy and orality, see John Halverson, "Goody and the Implosion of the Literacy Thesis," *Man* 27 (1992): 301–317.

Oeekachumpa told Georgia newcomers that the Giver and Taker of Breath had "given more Wisdom to the White Men."[4] A Creek leader named Captain Aleck echoed those words in 1765, explaining that "he does not doubt but both red and White Men spring from the same God, but tho' the White People are more sensible and can write yet the red People are very sincere in what they say and speak from their hearts."[5] Creek leaders restated this sentiment in 1786. "The white people have instruction," they said, referring to the written word. "We have none at all. Nevertheless, we hope to fix things in such a way that both parties will be satisfied."[6]

By the beginning of the nineteenth century, the Creek preoccupation with writing had led to the development of a Muskogee creation story that explained why some people knew how to write while others did not. The story told how whites, Indians, and blacks, newly formed from clay, selected their tools of labor. Whites took pen, paper, and books, Indians weapons of war and hunting, and blacks agricultural instruments. A version of this tale recorded in the early twentieth century added that whites gained an "advantage" when one of their books directed them to a gold strike. They were "terrible people to take the lead," the narrator concluded.[7] Much like *The Tempest*, this story asks the audience to consider the role of writing in Creek history. Power, wealth, and literacy went hand in hand, it suggests.

If southeastern Native Americans had once viewed the written word with astonishment, they no longer did so by the eighteenth century.[8] As

[4] *SCG*, 2 June 1733. Creeks commonly equated literacy with "wisdom," as the English translators interpreted the Muskogee word.
[5] "At a Congress held at the Fort of Picolata in the Province of East Florida . . . ," 9 December 1765, PRO, CO 5/548, p. 113, in "British Colonial Office Records," 2:574, PKY.
[6] "Contextacion que al otro dia aa hicieron los Reyes, Hombres Principales, y guerreros de la nacion crique," 22 October 1786, EF, bnd. 114J9, reel 43, PKY.
[7] This creation story was recorded twice in the early nineteenth century and once in the early twentieth century. John R. Swanton, *Myths and Tales of the Southeastern Indians* (1929; reprint, Norman: University of Oklahoma, 1995), 75; Littlefield, *Africans and Creeks*, 146.
[8] In examining how literacy affected Native Americans in the colonial era, historians have generally focused on first encounters with the written word when Indians attributed magical qualities to alphabetic script. Some native peoples, according to European accounts, believed that books could speak and that their readers, in many cases missionaries, had supernatural powers. James Axtell documents some of these encounters in North America in "The Power of Print in the Eastern Woodlands," in *After Columbus: Essays in the Ethnohistory of Colonial North America* (New York: Oxford University, 1988), 86–99. See also Axtell, *The Invasion Within: The Contest of Cultures in Colonial North America* (New York: Oxford University, 1985); Peter A. Dorsey, "Going to School with Savages: Authorship and Authority among the Jesuits of New France," *William and Mary Quarterly*, 55 (1998): 416–420; Peter Wogan, "Perceptions of European Literacy in Early Contact Situations," *Ethnohistory* 41 (1994): 407–429; and Jill Lepore, *The Name of War: King Philip's War and the Origins of American Identity* (Knopf: New York, 1998), chap.

in the case of firearms, the magical qualities of this particular technology seem to have dissipated quickly. But even if writing lost its power to amaze, its more ordinary properties presented a serious, long-term problem of enormous historical significance to the Creeks. Eager to consolidate economic and political power, Creeks comfortable with the new order embraced the technology. Others, however, looked on pen and paper with mistrust. Not surprisingly, the struggle began in the era of Alexander McGillivray.

According to one early historian, an Indian tradition held that McGillivray's mother Sehoy "repeatedly dreamed of piles of manuscripts, of ink and paper, and heaps of books. . . . She was delivered of a boy, who received the name of Alexander, and who, when grown to manhood, wielded a pen which commanded the admiration and respect of Washington and his cabinet, and which influenced the policy of all Spanish Florida."[9] Not just an erstwhile counting-room clerk for a Savannah mercantile firm, McGillivray was also a student of Greek, Latin, English history, and literature.[10] He eventually derived much of his power from his ability to read and write. In fact, by the time of his death, power and literacy were inextricably linked in Creek country. In 1793, when Spanish Indian agent James Dearment asked Creek Indian John Cannard who would succeed McGillivray, the "mestizo replied that he knew nothing for certain; he knew that young Alexander Cornel was clever and able, but he was illiterate." When Dearment suggested that Cannard himself might replace McGillivray, Cannard answered that "he was illiterate also, although he did not know how well he would manage with the assistance of an amanuensis."[11] The close connection between literacy and power evolved over a period of less than a decade, a relatively short time for such a dramatic change. Before 1783, no Creek would have thought to make literacy a qualification for leadership. A decade later, Cannard considered it a prerequisite.

McGillivray, by exploiting the power of writing, had much to do with this change. "Please excuse the hurry in which I write," begged McGillivray in the fall of 1777, "I can scarce turn about for the number

---

1. On one of the more famous accounts of the astonishment of Native Americans over writing, see Patricia Seed, "'Failing to Marvel': Atahualpa's Encounter with the Word," *Latin American Research Review* 26 (1991): 7–33.

[9] Pickett, *History of Alabama*, 344.

[10] Caughey, *Alexander McGillivray*, 15–16; Watson, "Strivings for Sovereignty," 401; Cashin, *Lachlan McGillivray*, 75.

[11] Declaration of James Dearment, 18 April 1793, no. 209, *McGillivray of the Creeks*.

of Indians that surround."[12] By sending letters to American and Spanish officials, McGillivray established himself as spokesman for a Creek nation that seemed far more unified on paper than it was in reality.[13] These letters increased his power not just with government authorities, but with many Creeks as well. On numerous occasions, for example, Spanish officials distributed gifts to Creek visitors on the presentation of McGillivray's written requests.[14] Moreover, at a time when the ability to communicate fluently with literate neighbors was assuming ever greater importance in the lives of Muskogees, McGillivray positioned himself as the go-between. In 1788, for example, one Coweta Indian traveled from the Flint River to the Scots Indian's residence at the confluence of the Coosa and Tallapoosa rivers to deliver a "wretched dirty & scarce legible scrawl, on foul paper, which he found on a tree." In this instance, deciphering the letter proved to be urgent, for it relayed a threat from James Alexander, a well-known murderer of Indians.[15]

The new link between writing and power led many Creeks to devalue oral communication. In the 1780s, Creeks began attributing a special significance to letters, if only because whites recognized written documents as a means of validating talks. In 1783, Hoboithle Micco, after protesting to Georgia officials that he had not intended to cede lands beyond the Oconee, requested that his talk be "put down on paper that the beloved men might see what he had come for."[16] But such written evidence clearly had limitations for nonliterate peoples. The following year when he was in Augusta, Hoboithle Micco explained that his past efforts to record his talks in writing had failed. No one could read the letters, and when Hoboithle Micco had described their content, Creeks suspiciously demanded further evidence. This time, Hoboithle Micco explained to his white audience, "he has brought witnesses with him to hear the talk themselves."[17]

---

[12] Copy of a letter from Alexander McGillivray to John Stuart, 25 September 1777, Sir Guy Carleton Papers, doc. 677, reel 58A-4, PKY.

[13] See Jack Goody, *The Domestication of the Savage Mind*, 14–15, for a brief analysis of the difference between governments based on oral and written communication. For a discussion of the relationship between power and writing among the Catawba Indians, see James Merrell, *The Indians' New World: Catawbas and Their Neighbors from European Contact through the Era of Removal* (New York: Norton, 1989), 150–152.

[14] See the series of documents in PC, leg. 122A, 706–746, reel 395, PKY.

[15] Alexander McGillivray to William Panton, 20 September 1988, printed in Pickett, "McGillivray and the Creeks," 139.

[16] Memorial of the King's proposals and complaints, 1783, "Indian Treaties: Cessions of Land in Georgia, 1705–1837," 117, GDAH.

[17] A talk delivered by the Tallassie king to the governor and council, 20 September 1784, file II, group 4-2-46, loc. 1432-02, box 76, folder 8, GDAH. Scholars have found that in many oral

Despite their doubts, Creeks continued to appropriate writing. When Intipaya Masla delivered a talk to the governor of Florida in 1786 on behalf of the Lower Creeks, he asked for a copy written in English so it could be read to other chiefs in order that they "give credit to what I will tell them."[18] Five years later there was a more dramatic illustration of the power attributed to writing. When the adventurer William Augustus Bowles sent an Indian emissary to the Upper Creeks to meet with several chiefs including Hoboithle Micco and Efau Hadjo, the audience asked for Bowles's letters and for the "white man who had to read them." The Creek emissary responded that "he was the one who had to give them the talk." On hearing this, the chiefs laughed and answered that "they could hear from his mouth everyday, that they had come to see those letters and hear them read," and with this rebuff, most of them departed.[19] In this instance, mere speaking would not satisfy the Creeks; they wanted to hear written words.

All things being equal, Creeks might not have accorded such respect to the written word, but because whites insisted that writing legitimized and validated talks, Indians were encouraged to embrace the practices of their neighbors. In 1793, for example, Efau Hadjo explained to U.S. Indian agent James Seagrove, "When you see my talk, it is all the same as if you seen me, and, when I see your talks, it is all the same as if I seen you. I hope, when you see my belts, you will see an everlasting peace and friendship with our great father, General Washington."[20] Written words had a greater currency among whites than did wampum belts, however. In his message to Seagrove, Efau Hadjo also sent a written talk. In the 1790s, this obligatory gesture conceded in a small but important way the dominance of the written word. Seagrove, duly following the practice of his literate society, placed the document in his files and forwarded a copy to Washington, where it was

---

societies, even after writing has been in use for centuries, written documents are often mistrusted. Walter J. Ong, *Orality and Literacy: The Technologizing of the World* (Routledge: London, 1982), 96–97. Also see M. T. Clanchy, *From Memory to Written Record: England, 1066–1307* (Cambridge: Harvard University, 1979). Janet Ewald, writing about the kingdom of Taqali on the borders of Sudan, argues that "Taqali people rejected documents as they struggled to maintain their intellectual and political autonomy. They preferred face-to-face, oral communication because it was grounded in their cultural milieu and because it sustained the dynamics of their political life." Ewald, "Speaking, Writing, and Authority: Explorations in and from the Kingdom of Taqali," *Comparative Studies in Society and History*, 30 (1988): 202–203.

[18] "Talk of the Intipaya Masla, chief warrior of the Lower Creeks, named Toalatoche," 29 May 1786, EF, bnd. 114J9, reel 43, PKY.

[19] Mr. Middleton to Alexander McGillivray, 24 December 1791, PC, leg. 1436, 4973, reel 156, PKY.

[20] Upper Creek chiefs to James Seagrove, 8 April 1793, *ASPIA*, 1:384–385.

eventually put into print in the nineteenth century in the *American State Papers*.[21]

The acknowledgment by Intipaya Masla and Efau Hadjo that writing would "give credit" to what they said is all the more remarkable because of the importance that the Creeks (and other oral peoples) attributed to face-to-face communication and eyewitness accounts. Many Native American languages, including a Muskogean language called Koasati, allow a speaker to qualify verbs so that the audience knows whether he or she personally witnessed or only heard about the event in question. The "hearsay affix," as linguists call this part of speech, alerts listeners to the subjectiveness of the information being conveyed.[22] Hearsay could be unsubstantiated rumor – and rumors traveled quickly among southeastern Indians[23] – but personal testimony gave some assurance of accuracy. (English speakers similarly associate truth with eyewitness accounts, as reflected in the phrase "seeing is believing.") The declining authority of firsthand oral reports and the parallel rise of third-hand written accounts consequently reflected a significant reordering of Creek values.

Not surprisingly, even as Creek leaders began asking for copies of their talks as a way to confirm them to those who were not present, they also recognized that writing was a means of deceiving them. James Adair, who wrote his history of the American Indians while living among the Chickasaws in the mid-eighteenth century, noted that he was "obliged to conceal his papers, through the natural jealousy of the natives; the traders letters of correspondence always excited their suspicions, and

---

[21] There is also an element of "oralizing" in Efau Hadjo's actions, infusing written with oral communication. See Isabel Hofmeyr, *"We Spend Our Years as a Tale That Is Told": Oral Historical Narrative in a South African Chiefdom* (Portsmouth, NH: Heinemann, 1994), 61. Joanne Rappaport shows that, like the Creeks, native north Andean peoples in the sixteenth and seventeenth centuries also experienced a change in the ways they remembered the past. Where they had once depended on oral narrative and mnemonic devices, the legal ideology of the Spanish colonial administration forced them to recognize the primacy of alphabetic literacy. Joanne Rappaport, "Object and Alphabet: Andean Indians and Documents in the Colonial Period," in *Writing without Words: Alternative Literacies in Mesoamerica and the Andes*, ed. Elizabeth Hill Boone and Walter D. Mignolo (Durham: Duke University, 1994), 271–291.

[22] The hearsay affix is also used to report "another's desires, thoughts, or opinions, even if obtained firsthand," Geoffrey D. Kimball notes. In this case, the speaker "is unable to validate the reality of these subjective categories." Geoffrey D. Kimball, letter to the author, 28 July 1998; Geoffrey D. Kimball, *Koasati Grammar* (Lincoln: University of Nebraska, 1991), 203–206; Alan Kilpatrick, "A Note on Cherokee Theological Concepts," *American Indian Quarterly* 19:3 (1995): 398–400, 402n10; Buckner, *A Grammar of the Maskwoke, or Creek Language*, 79–80.

[23] See the discussion by Gregory Evans Dowd, "The Panic of 1751: The Significance of Rumors on the South Carolina-Cherokee Frontier," *The William and Mary Quarterly* 53 (1996): 527–560.

often gave offence."[24] In 1776, Timothy Barnard, a patriot Indian agent for Georgia, encountered a similar reaction among the Creeks. In a letter to another agent, he excused himself for not sending a talk he had promised: "I did not Chuse to put it in among my other papers but stuck it up in thes Clapboards in the Top of my House and as some of the Indians had got hold of it and not knowing what it was has made away with it."[25] Unread writing bred suspicion.

In the 1780s, that suspicion justifiably fell on McGillivray when he began sending letters as the "voice of the nation." According to a Spanish official, Upper and Lower Creeks agreed in assembly in 1788 that if "up to the present McGillivray has been given authority it was because he announced and interpreted as he wished the letters and orders that he distributed." McGillivray, they explained, had misled them by claiming to act in the name of Spanish officials. "Now it is clear," they reportedly concluded, that his authority "was not delegated by the Governor of Orleans and Pensacola."[26]

The extent of his duplicity did not become fully apparent to Creeks until 1796 when nearly 250 leaders and warriors met U.S. and Georgia agents in Colerain on the St. Marys River (the present-day boundary between Florida and Georgia). The two parties hoped to bring an end to the violence along the Georgia frontier. During the negotiations, Creeks discovered that McGillivray had used his knowledge of reading and writing to deceive them, and literacy became the theme of the proceedings. Two days into the meeting, Georgia commissioners read from a long list of claims against the Creeks for property destroyed since 1783.[27] Though the commissioners insisted that their written records were more valid than the memories of Creek men and women, Tustanagee Thlucco challenged this distinction. He asked whether "the commissioners could not furnish a roll of paper, somewhat longer than that exhibited by Georgia, as he could easily fill it up."[28] His request suggested that the paper measured the number of claims but did not testify to their accuracy.[29]

---

[24] Adair, *Adair's History*, xxxv.
[25] Timothy Barnard to David Taitt, 4 July 1776, LTB, 26, GDAH.
[26] Arturo O'Neill to Estevan Miró, 10 September 1788, PC, leg. 38, 388, reel 191, PKY.
[27] Treaty negotiations can be found in the Report of Commissioners to the Secretary of War, June 1796, *ASPIA*, 1:597–616.
[28] Report of Commissioners to the Secretary of War, June 1796, *ASPIA*, 1:598.
[29] Peter Wogan argues, in "Perceptions of European Literacy in Early Contact Situations," that historians have mistakenly assumed that nonliterate groups will attribute an "historical accuracy" to literacy. Such claims, he argues, are based more on literacy theory, which assumes automatic responses to writing, than on ethnographic evidence (417). In the case of the Indians in the Deep

His "somewhat longer" scroll, filled by memory, would be equally valid.[30]

Tustanagee Thlucco, however, had to treat by the terms of a literate society. "After consultation," wrote the U.S. commissioners, the Creeks "applied to Mr. Hawkins, and requested that he would have them furnished with a copy of the talk delivered them by the commissioners of Georgia, and all the papers referred to in it. They wished to have them in their own council, that they might understand every part, before they made up their minds to reply."[31]

Several days later, the Creek headmen submitted a *written* response to the commissioners, rejecting their claims on the basis that prior treaties with Georgia were invalid. "Why did not you say this face to face to us, in the square, where we spoke to you?" asked the commissioners. The Creeks answered that they could give no reason, but the threatened commissioners pressed the point: "Is this your usual custom, to carry on talks in writing," they asked, "or do you always give them from the voice, in the public square?" "There is no rule reduced to system," the Creeks answered:

> When they talk among themselves, it is usual to talk face to face, and to send beads to assist the memory. But, as we had, in this instance, a talk to deliver to white people, and having our linguisters all present, we chose to send our answer in writing.[32]

But the effort to challenge whites on their own terms proved fruitless, especially because the familiarity that Creek linguists exhibited with written words reflected a parallel intimacy with whites. As the

South, it is clear that the assumed historical accuracy of writing was not an "automatic response," but remained contested between the Creeks and their literate neighbors.

[30] We can imagine that Big Warrior's list would have differed significantly in nature from the one presented by the commissioners. Anthropologist Jack Goody notes that a written list "relies on discontinuity rather than continuity; it depends on physical placement, on location; it can be read in different directions, both sideways and downwards, up and down, as well as left and right; it has a clear-cut beginning and a precise end, that is, a boundary, an edge, like a piece of cloth. Most importantly, it encourages the ordering of the items, by number, by initial sound, by category, etc. And the existence of boundaries, external and internal, brings greater visibility to categories, at the same time as making them more abstract." *The Domestication of the Savage Mind*, 81. Big Warrior's list would likely have sounded like a narrative, the items connected by verbs and temporal markers. Ong, *Orality and Literacy*, 99–101.

[31] Report of Commissioners to the Secretary of War, June 1796, *ASPIA*, 1:598. A half-century before the Creeks in 1796, Delaware Indians in Pennsylvania had tried to treat with whites using the written word. Merritt, "Metaphor, Meaning, and Misunderstanding," 81–84.

[32] Report of Commissioners to the Secretary of War, June 1796, *ASPIA*, 1:604.

proceedings would reveal, Creeks could not always trust the literates among them.

During the meeting, Creeks also contested the location of the boundary along the Oconee River between Creek lands and Georgia. The boundary dated back to 1790 when McGillivray had negotiated the Treaty of New York. Now, as Creeks questioned this line, Fusache Micco argued that his own recollection of the agreement was more accurate than the written record. McGillivray was a "half-breed," he reminded the commissioners, and both his intentions and his actions were dubious: "He had more conversation with General Washington, and his great men, than we; but I heard, I will tell."[33] By memory, Fusache Micco recalled that the line ran up the north fork of the Oconee, not up the Apalachee, or south fork, as the written version of the Treaty of New York specified.[34] The commissioners explained that McGillivray should have carried copies of the treaty into the nation. Kasihta Micco answered, "McGillivray never collected the nation, or shewed the treaty at all; nor did the nation ever hear of this part of it till lately."[35]

The dispute over the boundary continued several days, whereupon the chiefs concluded:

> It has been understood by us, that the Little Oconee [or North Oconee] was the line; but we see that we have been imposed on, perhaps by our beloved man (McGillivray). . . . That land which McGillivray defrauded us out of, we know not if he had money for it; we never received a farthing for it – we mean that in the fork; but if you will keep it, we must lose it: we cannot help it.[36]

By deferring to the commissioners, the Creeks recognized that the literate record was backed by force of arms. Moreover, they came to the blunt realization that McGillivray had deceived them.[37] Fusache Micco

[33] Ibid., 599.
[34] Randolph C. Downes, in "Creek-American Relations, 1782–1790," suggests that Creeks, excluding McGillivray, had initially agreed to negotiate in 1790 under the mistaken impression that the Oconee lands would be returned to them (175). J. Leitch Wright suggests there were other deceptions and antagonisms, noting that though thirty Creeks had traveled to New York for the treaty, only twenty-four signed the final agreement. Wright, "Creek-American Treaty of 1790," 393–395.
[35] Report of Commissioners to the Secretary of War, June 1796, *ASPIA*, 1:602.
[36] Ibid., 606.
[37] The anthropologist William C. Sturtevant, in insightful but brief comments that he gave at a conference in 1976, called into question McGillivray's identity as an Indian. Regarding the 1790 delegation in New York, Sturtevant observed, "Only McGillivray could write: he signed boldly, with a grand rubric under his name. All the rest signed by making a mark, and they are all very

had heard the treaty and told what he had remembered, but it mattered little before the written record of the commissioners.

This disagreement between Creek leaders and U.S. commissioners reflects a larger conflict between two fundamentally different ways of thinking about oral and written communication. The Muskogee language has two main tenses, present and nonpresent, further qualified by what linguists call "aspect." One combination of tense and aspect stretches back only as far as the speaker can remember and, according to H. F. Buckner, a nineteenth-century linguist and missionary to the Creeks, it implies that the speaker has a "personal recollection or knowledge of whatever is implied in the verb." It seems likely that Fusache Micco, who had signed the Treaty of New York, responded to his antagonists in such a way. Another combination of tense and aspect, what for our purposes might be called the historic tense, "represents actions or events of which the person relating them has no personal knowledge or consciousness, but is dependent upon the *history* or testimony of others."[38] According to Buckner, in the historic tense, the source of the report must be explicit or "plainly implied." This tense applies to books or translations. In such applications, Buckner explained, "the third persons only are used, and then the document is represented as speaking by the authority of the writer or author." In a translation of the Bible, Buckner continued, a sentence from the Book of John such as "Jesus said to the Jews" would be understood by a Muskogee reader as "The evangelist John claims that Jesus said to the Jews." This apparent statement of fact in English thus rests upon the testimony of the evangelist in Muskogee.[39] Similarly, in the Muskogee translation of the Treaty of New York, the source and authority of the knowledge would have to be explicit. In English, a phrase such as "the line shall run from the south branch of the Oconee called Apalachee" carries an impersonal authority. But when translated into Muskogee, the same phrase would read, "We and the Americans agreed that . . ." or "The Americans promised that. . . ."[40] Creek linguists may have been even more explicit. Their

---

uncertain and poorly drawn X's, that look as though the signers had never held pens before." Sturtevant, "Commentary," 45.

[38] Buckner, *A Grammar of the Maskwoke, or Creek Language*, 79. Also see Kimball, *Koasati Grammar*, 207–208. In a letter to the author on 30 October 1996, Geoffrey D. Kimball, a scholar of Muskogee languages, writes, "Buckner realized that Creek tenses were not congruent with English tenses, but he was constrained by the grammatical descriptive apparatus available to him at the time." Buckner's observations are true, but his terminology is inaccurate.

[39] Buckner, *A Grammar of the Maskwoke, or Creek Language*, 79–80.

[40] Geoffrey D. Kimball, letter to the author, 28 July 1998.

translations may have implicated particular individuals, perhaps Alexander McGillivray or George Washington. In fact, Creeks soon concluded that McGillivray had deceived them.

On close examination, written records reveal the soundness of Creek suspicions.[41] Fusache Micco and the other chiefs could have easily been misled in New York. They likely were not present at the informal English-language negotiations between McGillivray and Secretary of War Henry Knox, and even if they had been, they would have understood little. Only the final signing of the treaty provided an opportunity to hear its terms. George Washington read the articles aloud, "which address was communicated sentence after sentence, by Mr. Cornell, sworn interpreter, to all of which the Creeks gave an audible assent."[42] But Joseph Cornels, closely allied with McGillivray, may have deliberately misinterpreted the treaty, perhaps simply replacing "Apalachee" with "north fork of the Oconee," in order to secure a deal.[43] The secret articles of the agreement, making McGillivray a brigadier general in the U.S. Army and establishing potential commercial ties between American traders and Creeks, show that deception was beyond neither McGillivray nor the United States.[44] Of the Creek signatures on the final treaty, all but McGillivray's were nonliterate marks, highlighting the disadvantage of the other Creek delegates.[45]

In April 1791, McGillivray met with Upper and Lower Creeks to explain the treaty, but after the congress, the Creeks understood that the line was to be run from Choty (the Cherokee town Echota) to the Oconee, and down the Altamaha, a line that follows the north branch of

[41] Historians have in general praised McGillivray's negotiations in New York. See, for example, Caughey, in *McGillivray of the Creeks*, 46; Braund, *Deerskins and Duffels*, 175–176; Dowd, *A Spirited Resistance*, 102; Green, "Alexander McGillivray," 55. Angie Debo and J. Leitch Wright are more circumspect. Debo, *The Road to Disappearance*, 49–51; Wright, *Creeks and Seminoles*, 137–140. Florette Henri suggests that it is "entirely probable that the talks at New York had been conducted in English, McGillivray's first language, and that the other chiefs did not know precisely what he had promised." Henri, *The Southern Indians and Benjamin Hawkins*, 54.

[42] Extract from the *Pennsylvania Packet and Daily Advertiser*, 18 August 1791, no. 147, *McGillivray of the Creeks*.

[43] Alternatively, Cornels himself, whose illiteracy was reflected by the mark he placed on his oath to translate faithfully, may not have had a clear understanding of the location of the border as stipulated in the treaty. Oath of Joseph Cornell, 7 August 1790, vol. 26, p. 126, Henry Knox Papers, Gilder Lehrman Collection, Pierpont Morgan Library, New York.

[44] Of the Creek representatives, only McGillivray signed the paper bearing the secret articles. *The Papers of George Washington: Presidential Series*, Dorothy Twohig, ed. (Charlottesville: University of Virginia, 1996), 6:253; Henry Knox to George Washington, rough copy, August 1790, vol. 26, p. 122, Henry Knox Papers, Gilder Lehrman Collection, Pierpont Morgan Library, New York.

[45] Doster, *Creek Indians*, 1:107. For a present-day parallel of such deception among the Huaorani of the Ecuadorian Amazon, see Kane, *Savages*, 204.

the Oconee, not the Apalachee. "It was all peace with the Indians and Americans," one Creek chief reported after learning that the line was to be run from Echota.[46] The Treaty of New York did not include any stipulations to modify the line, and so it appears that McGillivray must have misled his fellow Creeks, telling them the line followed the north fork instead of the Apalachee, as stated in the treaty.

Two letters from McGillivray to Henry Knox suggest that McGillivray colluded with the secretary of war to make the Apalachee the line in the written treaty, giving the United States legal title to the land. In the first, McGillivray wrote in 1791 that, as he expected, the Creeks would not cede the Apalachee fork but had unanimously agreed to a line down the north fork.[47] If they refused in 1791, then surely the Creek delegates would never have signed the treaty in 1790 had they fully understood its terms. A year later, after Knox had threatened, "Your reputation, and all dependent thereon, will be blasted forever if the line be not run,"[48] McGillivray wrote again to the secretary of war: "You will recollect, sir, that I had great objection to making the south fork the limit, and when you insisted so much, I candidly told you that it might be made an article, but I could not pledge myself to get it confirmed."[49] The division between the literate and nonliterate, exploited by McGillivray, allowed each side to come away with its own interpretation of the treaty. Literally, the United States obtained its claim, while orally the Creeks retained their claim as well. McGillivray served as the buffer between the two. In the long run, the two sides would collide, and the literal claims of the United States would emerge ascendant.[50]

The extent of McGillivray's deception was not lost on the Creeks. During negotiations in 1796, commissioners proposed that the United States assume responsibility for the education of some Creek children:

> When they became old men, and chiefs, and warriors, they could transact the affairs of the nation like the white people, without being subject to imposition from designing

---

[46] Richard Lang to Juan Nepomuceno de Quesada, 18 May 1791, EF, bnd. 121D10, doc. 1791–74, reel 46, PKY.

[47] Translation of a letter from Alexander McGillivray to General Knox printed in the *Charleston Gazette*, 8 June 1791, enclosed in Juan Nepomuceno de Quesada to Luis de las Casas, 4 January 1792, EF, bnd. 23J2, 11, reel 9, PKY.

[48] Quoted in Doster, *Creek Indians*, 1:112.

[49] Alexander McGillivray to the Secretary of War, 18 May 1792, *ASPIA*, 1:315–316.

[50] After the Treaty of New York, McGillivray methodically misled both the Spaniards and the Americans, privately pledging loyalty to each side while condemning the other. His deception of the United States and Spain can best be followed in Caughey, *McGillivray of the Creeks*, 315–353. Caughey is especially helpful by footnoting the inconsistencies and contradictions in McGillivray's statements.

characters, or interpreters; that they might keep a record of their transactions in their own tongue, or in English.[51]

After McGillivray's deception, the Creek response is not surprising:

> The Indians, when educated, turned out very worthless; became mischievous and troublesome, and involve the red and white people in difficulties. That they had many melancholy examples of this sort, without an exception.[52]

Indeed, according to a longtime friend of McGillivray's who lived in the Deep South for some twenty years, Creeks believed that "Natchoka," a word that referred to "books and all that is written," made Americans "so knavish and wicked."[53] The loss of their lands on the Oconee was a painful illustration of the trouble with writing.

After McGillivray's death in 1793, the struggle over the control and creation of a Creek nation often involved a concomitant struggle over the written word.[54] Some leaders asserted their authority nationwide by trying, like McGillivray, to become the sole mediators between nonliterate Creeks and Spanish and American authorities. These men complained about communications they deemed unofficial, inappropriate, or subversive. In 1794, for instance, White Lieutenant, Efau Hadjo, and Alexander Cornels accused William Panton of sending "bad talks" into the region, explaining that they would in the future only recognize letters from American and Spanish agents.[55] "From the Death of McGillivray to this time your commissaries in this land has

---

[51] Report of Commissioners to the Secretary of War, June 1796, *ASPIA*, 1:597–616.

[52] Ibid.

[53] Milfort, *Memoir*, 134. For a comparison to other nonliterate peoples, see Ewald, "Speaking, Writing, and Authority," 207–208. Claude Lévi-Strauss found a similar connection between literacy, power, and deceit among nonliterate peoples. In eastern Pakistan, the "scribe is rarely a functionary or employee of the group: his knowledge is accompanied by power, with the result that the same individual is often both scribe and money-lender; not just because he needs to be able to read and write to carry on his business, but because he thus happens to be, on two different counts, someone who *has a hold* over others." Among the Nambikwara in central Brazil, the anthropologist learned that "villagers who withdrew their allegiance to their chief after he had tried to exploit a feature of civilization . . . felt in some obscure way that writing and deceit had penetrated simultaneously into their midst." Lévi-Strauss, *Tristes Tropiques*, trans. John and Doreen Weightman (Paris: Librairie Plon, 1955; English ed., London: Jonathan Cape, 1973), 298, 300.

[54] Among Taqali people on the Sudanese border, historian Janet Ewald finds that orality promoted face-to-face, nonhierarchical relations, while writing fostered centralization and state formation. Ewald, "Speaking, Writing, and Authority," 208.

[55] White Lieutenant, Mad Dog, and Alexander Cornels to William Panton, 1794, EF, bnd. 114J9, reel 43, PKY.

always been at variance," Creek leaders told the governor of Florida that year; "the talks of one the other contradicted."[56] In 1795, Efau Hadjo asked the governor to refrain from sending letters suborning their warriors.[57]

By 1800, some Creek leaders, and probably many common Creeks as well, regretted the loss of stability that McGillivray had brought to their land. A leader named Molton expressed this sentiment to Vicente Folch, the commandant of Pensacola. In the past, he said, communication between "his good friend" McGillivray and the Spanish had allowed Spain and the Creeks to diffuse dangerous situations. "This is the intention of this talk," Molton explained to the Pensacola commandant.[58] But no one succeeded in monopolizing writing as completely as McGillivray had. Nearly all Creek leaders depended on amanuenses, and the few mestizos who could write had difficulty conveying information accurately. "I am an Indian and cannot explain myself on paper as my education will not allow," John Galphin wrote in 1800.[59]

Despite these difficulties, the association between writing and power remained firm. Hopoy Micco, for one, appreciated this connection. As speaker of the national council between 1802 and 1806, for example, he kept an archive of important papers and letters that reflected his intimate relations with Spanish and American officials.[60] Like McGillivray, he extended his power, presumably with the aid of an amanuensis, by rewarding friends with notes redeemable for presents in Pensacola. "The chiefs that received tickets from me to go to you," he wrote in 1803 to the Spanish commandant in Pensacola, "I hope you'll recieve them

---

[56] Mad Dog of Tuckabatche, Head Warrior of Tuckabatche, and Alexander Cornell to Enrique White, 28 May 1794, PC, leg. 208A, 665, reel 286, PKY.

[57] Mad Dog and Peck Cornel to the Governor of St. Augustine, 1 June 1795, PC, leg. 1438, doc. 14, frame 1348, reel 26, PKY.

[58] Opayemicco de Taskiki for Tusache Mico, Daniel McGillivray, et al. to Vicente Folch, 8 July 1800, PC, leg. 1573, doc. 24, frame 349, reel 83, PKY.

[59] Quoted in Vicente Folch to Marqués de Someruelos, 15 September 1800, PC, leg. 1551, 1095, reel 202–3, PKY.

[60] Daniel McGillivray to John Forbes, 24 December 1803, Cruzat Papers, PKY. As early as 1733, Creek leaders had begun preserving important documents. In that year, Creek leader Malache recalled in 1747, Oglethorpe met all the Creek headmen in Charleston. After promising "to be a Father to us Indians," Malache stated, he "gave us a Paper, which he said was for the Good of us all, our Wives and Children, but did not let us know the Contents of it, which we kept very carefully and thought it was all very good." A Speech made by Malatchi Opiya Mico to Alexander Heron, 7 December 1747, CRG, 36:315–325, GDAH. In 1746, during a land dispute with Georgia, Chigellie retrieved the paper as supporting evidence, but was told that the document stated the Creeks had indeed ceded their lands. Chickilli Tuskeestonnecah Mico to Mary Bosomworth, 4 December 1746, CRG, 36:303, GDAH. See also Corkran, The Creek Frontier, 1540–1783, 120. Cherokee leaders also kept an archive. John R. Alden, "The Eighteenth Century Cherokee Archives," American Archivist 5 (1942): 240–244.

friendly and [they will] return well satisfied."[61] His successor to the speakership of the national council, Tustanagee Thlucco, signed his name with a clear "BW," indicating his familiarity with the alphabet and his preference for his English name, Big Warrior.[62]

Other Creek leaders such as Alexander Cornels were also implicated in the deception perpetrated by literate Muskogees and Americans. In 1800, for example, shortly after the national council had brutally punished several Creeks for breaking up an American surveying party, John Galphin complained to rebel leader Hoboithle Micco about the relationship between Benjamin Hawkins and Cornels, who was on the payroll of the Creek agency:

> He pays men money to Deceve us, and Curnals he pays a large Sallerry to, becaus he has him fer his [toole?]. Curnels Can neither rede nor write therefore Every thing he tells him must be true you old men aut to no that a mans talk that has no Education the can be no Dependence put in him. What he Does is for money.[63]

Galphin had stated the problem carelessly. Hoboithle Micco too was uneducated, yet Galphin praised him. Unlike Hoboithle Micco, however, Cornels and other Creek leaders who were in the pocket of the United States mediated between the literate and the nonliterate.

Following in McGillivray's footsteps, some Creeks also used writing to engage in the market economy and enrich themselves by recording debt and credit and communicating with Panton, Leslie and Company in Pensacola.[64] Boatswain, for example, who lived as a "prince," according to William Bartram, discussed and recorded his commerce with Panton, Leslie and Company in words and numbers. Though Boatswain was not literate himself, when a dispute arose in the 1790s regarding his

---

[61] Opoymicco to the Governor of Pensacola, 31 August 1803, Forbes-Innerarity Papers, reel 147, PKY.

[62] The following three letters, for example, are signed "BW": Big Warrior to [John Forbes?], 23 November 1812, Forbes-Innerarity Papers, 74/56, reel 147P, PKY; Tustunnuggee Thlucco, Speaker of the nation council his talk to Col. Hawkins agent for I.A., 1 November 1812, Henry Wilson Papers, reel 150D, PKY; Chiefs of Upper Creeks to Benjamin Hawkins, 21 April 1813, State Department Territorial Papers, Florida Series, 1777–1824, 3:26, microcopy no.116/3, PKY.

[63] John Galphin to Tallessa King, 1800, PC, leg. 216B, 336, reel 300, PKY.

[64] Janet Ewald, in an article on the Taqali people on the Sudan border, suggests that there may be a relationship between the commercialization of gift exchange and the advent of literacy. Literacy provides the technology to eliminate face-to-face contact and thus to make trade an impersonal exchange. "As they enclosed their communities against the penetration of a regional commercial system and prevented the development of a bureaucratic state," writes Ewald, "Taqali people also rejected literacy." Ewald, "Speaking, Writing, and Authority," 216.

debt with the Pensacola trading company, he obtained the services of another trader to write to the firm complaining of his treatment. Boatswain concluded his letter, "I expect you to write me a few words."[65] The wealthy mestizo John Cannard also used writing to transact his business: "He cannot read or write," wrote a visitor, but "commonly has some mean person about his house to do it for him."[66] Most Creeks, unlike Boatswain and Cannard, had to travel to Pensacola personally to resolve disagreements, as White Lieutenant did in 1797. He "hopes as he is going to you himself," a trader explained to William Panton, "the matter will be settled to his satisfaction."[67] Writing and other systems of recording data such as the Incan knotted ropes known as *quipu* provide a substantial benefit to those engaged in exchanges involving debt and credit. Without them, the limits of human memory inevitably impede commercial engagement.[68]

The connection between writing and property could be seen on the hindquarters of many cattle and horses in Creek country. Unlettered horse rustlers, for example, carved the brands of stolen animals into trees to record their ownership against the claims of other Indians.[69] Wealthy Creek ranchers made the connection between writing and property even more explicit. They branded their stock with the same marks they drew on written documents.[70] On official documents, rancher Alexander Cornels inscribed an "AC" with a fleur-de-lys between the letters.[71] With the assistance of a blacksmith – another symbol of the new order – he likely branded his cattle with the same mark.[72] In fact, in the Muskogee language, "branded" and "written" are one and the same word, *cóke*.

[65] Bosen to [?], 13 December 1796, Forbes-Innerarity Papers, 64/5, reel 147P, PKY; List of debts due by traders, half breeds and Indian factors to Panton Leslie and Co. of Appalachy commencing October 1787 and ending September 1792, Greenslade Papers, PKY; and balance sheets from 30 April 1798, 30 April 1799, and 31 August 1799, in the Forbes-Innerarity Papers, reel 147P, PKY.

[66] Caleb Swan, "Position and State of Manners and Arts," 260–261. For an example of Cannard's use of writing to pursue business, see John Cannard to Robert Leslie, 21 January 1796, Forbes-Innerarity Papers, 81/13, reel 147P, PKY.

[67] Daniel McGillivray to William Panton, 24 April 1797, Cruzat Papers, PKY.

[68] Goody, *The Interface between the Written and the Oral*, 145.

[69] One Georgian described seeing this practice in 1788. Affidavit of William Melton, 20 July 1835, "Indian Depredations, 1787–1825," 2, pt. 3:845, GDAH. See also Merrell, *The Indians' New World*, 62.

[70] After four Creeks had marked one letter, for instance, the translator and letter writer referred to each mark as the "brand" of the signer. Payemicco, Cudgomicco, Pohosimicco, Tustoncos to [?], 21 October 1791, EF, bnd. 114J9, reel 43, PKY.

[71] For an example of Cornels's mark, see Tustunnuggee Thlucco, Speaker of the nation council his talk to Col. Hawkins agent for I.A., 1 November 1812, Henry Wilson Papers, reel 150D, PKY.

[72] Cornels's close friend Alexander McGillivray definitely branded his cattle. Pope, *A tour through the southern and western territories*, 49.

Privileged Creeks who received credit from Panton, Leslie and Company also signed their initials, or rather brands, on promissory notes.[73] And they made the same marks on treaties. Usually, an individual had occasion to leave his brand on all three media; ranchers, traders, and national leaders were often one and the same.[74]

In some respects, the greater the familiarity a Creek had with writing, the more committed he or she was likely to be to the new order. Most Creeks never communicated via written words, and when the necessity arose to convey information to whites, traditional Creek symbols sufficed. In 1799, for example, twelve warriors scratched a message on the cabin door of a Georgia settler near the Ohoopee River, southeast of the present city of Milledgeville, Georgia. Residents drafted nearby friendly Indians to interpret it for them. The two circles each enclosing twelve dots meant that twelve warriors intended to take twelve scalps in two moons.[75]

Even some Creeks involved in the country's national affairs continued to rely on and trust traditional means of remembering and transmitting talks. In 1802, for instance, a Creek Indian named Muclasa Hopoy, who held none of the beliefs of literate peoples in the exactness and accuracy of writing, requested that a message to the Seminoles be conveyed orally rather than by letter. The talk was an important one, he explained, and "should not depend so much on chance." The literal word could be misinterpreted from Muskogee to English, and it could be misunderstood if not delivered by someone who grasped its inten-

[73] See, for example: Cusitaw Tuskinia Promissory Note, 4 November 1793, Cruzat Papers, PKY; Promissory note from the Warrior King to Panton Leslie and Co., 7 December 1796, Forbes-Innerarity Papers, 81/6, reel 147P, PKY; Promissory Note of Nipeeholo, 28 March 1797, Cruzat Papers, PKY; Promissory Note of White Lieutenant, 1 May 1797, Cruzat Papers, PKY; Promissory Note of Tickalugie, 20 January 1798, Cruzat Papers, PKY; Promissory Note of George Cornels, 20 January 1798, Cruzat Papers, PKY; Promissory note from Kenhegee to Panton Leslie and Co., 29 May 1799, Innerarity-Hulse Papers, reel 147S, PKY; Promissory note from Tinghyhaby to Panton Leslie and Co., 8 August 1800, Forbes-Innerarity Papers, reel 147P, PKY.

[74] In her work on the Ndebele people in the Northern Transvaal, South Africa, in the twentieth century, anthropologist Isabel Hofmeyr proposes another possible connection between property and writing:

> While the most obvious role of fencing is to enforce dispossession and make private property a reality, it does also have a number of cultural functions that are not unrelated to the preconceptions of literacy. The notion of a boundary on a piece of paper, for example, is often seen by literate societies as having the same fixity as the printed text. As the referent of the text, the fence embodies the reality of the boundary and supposedly writes it permanently into the earth.

Hofmeyr, *"We Spend Our Years as a Tale That Is Told,"* 72–73, 77.

[75] George Sibbald to James Jackson, 31 August 1799, CIL, 2:561–563, GDAH.

tion. Moreover, as Muclasa Hopoy stated, after speaking to the Seminoles, the messengers "shall watch their eyes, their tongues, and lips, and
every feature of the countenance, whilst they are speaking, and report
to me in the square of the nation, what they have seen, what they have
heard, and what they have done."[76] No letter could do the same.

Yet whites openly disdained the oral technology of the Creeks.
Benjamin Hawkins wrote in 1808, "The doing of business with beads
might, if understood, do among Indians but not in their transactions
with white people. The beads may be forgotten, but an agreement
written by a faithful agent could never be forgotten, as it would remain
with the records of the government."[77] When Creeks confronted
this attitude in late June and July 1804, they revealed that years of
unequal relations with literate peoples had shaken their confidence in
memory. Commissioners from Georgia presented claims for damaged or
destroyed property, and the Creeks retired to their council with a written
copy of the speech and "a digest of the laws of Georgia containing
the treaties refered to." "They had some halfbreeds with them who could
read," Hawkins reported, "and they spent the day in deliberation of
thereon."[78] Afterward, Creek leaders told the commissioners that "we
are red people and not like you white people, are at a loss and just
can remember" the 1790 Treaty of New York. "You white people," they
continued, "have books in black and white where these things are
kept and you can know this."[79] The distinction between knowing and
remembering reveals that the primacy of literacy, once clearly dependent on the force of arms, was becoming "received wisdom" among the
Muskogees.[80]

---

[76] Report of Commissioners to the Secretary of War, May and June 1802, *ASPIA*, 1:668–681.
Scholars of literacy and orality call writing "context-free" language or "autonomous discourse."
It "cannot be directly questioned or contested as oral speech can be," writes Walter Ong, "because
written discourse has been detached from its author," Ong, *Orality and Literacy*, 78.

[77] Benjamin Hawkins to Henry Dearborn, 22 October 1808, *LBH*, 2:541. Compare the words of
the native commissioner of Potgietersrus in the Northern Transvaal to Chief Alfred Masibi of
Zebediela in 1923: "I do not as a rule take verbal messages – you must get your secretary to write
when transacting government business." Oral peoples throughout the Atlantic world confronted
the imperialism of literate bureaucracies. Hofmeyr, *"We Spend Our Years as a Tale That Is Told,"*
59.

[78] "Journal of Benjamin Hawkins," 1 July 1804, *LBH*, 2:474; John Clark, Jesse McCall, and David
Adams to the Kings, Chiefs, and warriors of the Creek nation, 2 July 1804, LBH, 87, GDAH.

[79] "Journal of Benjamin Hawkins," 2 July 1804, *LBH*, 2:475; Creek leaders to Georgia Commissioners, 3 July 1804, LBH, 92, GDAH; Proceedings of council at Tuckabatche, 3 July 1804,
LBH, 97, GDAH.

[80] Jack Goody witnessed the process in the 1970s of literacy coming to dominate the "wider social
system" in northern Ghana. He noted in 1987 that the "non-literate of yesterday has become
the illiterate of today." Goody, *The Interface between the Written and the Oral*, 147.

Because of its close association with Creeks who aspired to political and economic power, writing remained controversial. It was as unwelcome among some Indians as spinning wheels and plows. Without writing, every clan leader who traveled to Pensacola or Augusta spoke authoritatively, but with it, the voice of a Creek nation rested in the hands of a few leaders and their literate assistants. Familiar with words and numbers, they recorded their business transactions, signed treaties, and burned their initials onto the hindquarters of their cattle, thereby establishing exclusive ownership. Their commitment to the written word reflected a parallel commitment to the new order. Most Creeks remained excluded from the new order, however. In the years after 1800, their exclusion would become increasingly clear.

9

The hungry years

In the opening years of the nineteenth century, Seminoles mounted an organized resistance to the new order spreading across the Deep South. Buoyed by the return of William Augustus Bowles at the end of 1799 and by his renewed promises of British support, they joined with the adventurer to raid Spanish settlements. For a brief period in late May and June 1800, Seminoles succeeded in taking the Spanish fort on the St. Marks River below present-day Tallahassee. Thereafter, they raided plantations, stealing slaves and destroying property, until the Spanish captured Bowles in late May 1803. Though Bowles intended to establish and profit from a regular trade between British merchants in the Bahamas and Florida Indians, Seminoles had their own reasons for participating in his plans. According to Tuskegee Tustanagee, they believed that by harassing the Spanish and dividing the Creeks, "the United States or Spain will give them presents as the British formerly did for the sake of union among the Indians and a firm peace between them and the white people."[1]

The political ferment in Florida might have led directly to a conflict between dissidents and supporters of the new order except that an eight-year stretch of famine and disease intervened beginning in 1804. During the hungry years, as Muskogees called this period, wealthy Creeks continued to fare well, while hunters and hoers suffered without relief. In the 1770s, William Bartram had observed that Creeks seemed "as one Family or Community, and in fact all their possessions are in common." Rather than let someone go "necessitous," he had noted, a Creek "would divide with you the last grain of corn, or piece

---

[1] Benjamin Hawkins, "Journal of Occurrences in the Creek Agency from January to the Conclusion of the Conference and Treaty at Fort Wilkinson by the Agent for Indian Affairs," *LBH*, 2:412.

of flesh."[2] In the first decade of the nineteenth century, by contrast, wealthy Creeks, exhibiting their newly acquired possessiveness, often neglected their desperate neighbors. At the same time, Creek leaders ceded to the United States the very hunting grounds that most people depended on for survival during seasons of drought or flooding. The relative prosperity of these men and their self-interested and corrupt leadership during the years of famine stretched tensions between the wealthy and poor to a breaking point. When Creeks and Seminoles emerged from the hungry years in 1812, they had immediate reason to take action against the new order.

By the nineteenth century, Florida had become a point of resistance against the centralized power of the national council. Creek leaders had washed their hands of their Florida relatives, making Seminole settlements the place of refuge for political dissidents. In 1800, for example, Efau Hadjo, the first head of the national council, explained to Spanish commandant Vicente Folch, "We are not accountable for the conduct of the Seminoles, you must look to them yourself."[3] Though Creek leaders occasionally demanded that Seminoles obey them, these were idle threats, more indicative of their hubris, and of the Seminoles' independence, than of real political relationships. In 1804, for example, after Spain and the Seminoles had concluded a peace treaty, Hopoy Micco, Efau Hadjo's successor as speaker of the nation, bragged that if Kinache, the head of the Mikasuki Seminoles, did not "fulfill his promises, he would make him do so as one of his subjects."[4] That same year, Alexander Cornels suggested that he would try to bring the Seminoles "to reason," and if that failed, would resort to force.[5] Yet in 1805, only a year after Hopoy Micco threatened Kinache, the speaker of the nation explained to Vicente Folch that the Seminoles "were renegades and vagabonds" who "did not come to hear the talks of the headmen in the Nation, that you must correct them with confinement and your own laws."[6] Though they were "all one family," Tustanagee Thlucco, the head of the national council, admitted in 1812, the Seminoles "hold far off in a corner." They "never attend their House of Talks nor would they listen to the advice or counsel of the old Chiefs, but turned

[2] Bartram, "Observations," 160–161.
[3] Efau Hadjo to Vicente Folch, 3 June 1800, PC, leg. 108, 425, reel 163, PKY.
[4] Ignacio Balderas to Vicente Folch, 6 June 1804, PC, leg. 2355, 26, reel 381, PKY.
[5] "Journal of Benjamin Hawkins," 2 July 1804, LBH, 2:475.
[6] James Durouzeaux to Vicente Folch, 22 June 1805, PC, leg. 221B, 2, reel 310, PKY.

their backs upon them with disdain & would not at all be governed by them."[7]

The political independence of the Seminoles and their distance from Benjamin Hawkins – in 1812, the agent confessed that he did not even know who managed the Indian affairs of the Spaniards[8] – allowed Native American politics in the Florida peninsula to follow its own course. In addition to the Seminoles' indigenous movement against the power of the national council, an influx of Creek refugees contributed to the political ferment in the region. Creeks who "think much of times past and are constantly talking of them . . . look towards the Seminoles," Efau Hadjo warned in 1802.[9] After visiting the area in 1812, the Lower Creek warrior Tuskegee Tustanagee reported that "several [people] of the upper towns . . . have been there a long while. Some fled from crimes and some gone there from curiosity."[10] The fugitives included men such as Tussekiubbe whom Creek leaders had ordered "severely whipped" in 1800 for stealing two horses near Pensacola. He had experienced what for many Indians remained an abstract or remote problem: the concentration of power in the hands of the national council. Tussekiubbe furthered his political education by visiting Tecumseh, the Shawnee leader who strove to unite Native Americans against the expanding United States.[11] Other Creek dissidents, unnamed in the sources, were equally influential in shaping Seminole politics.

African American fugitives, who had personal stakes in resisting the expansion of power and property into Florida, also contributed significantly to the political ferment among the Seminoles. In part, they furnished manpower and skilled labor. Some blacks, such as Harry and Esten, who translated and negotiated for Seminole leader Payne and for Bowles, worked as linguists.[12] Others served as warriors. In early June

---

[7] "The Creek Nation, Debtor to John Forbes & Co., Successors to Panton, Leslie and Co.: A Journal of John Innerarity, 1812," *Florida Historical Quarterly* 9 (1930): 78.

[8] Benjamin Hawkins to David B. Mitchell, 7 September 1812, *LBH*, 2:617.

[9] Benjamin Hawkins, "Journal of Occurrences in the Creek Agency from January to the Conclusion of the Conference and Treaty at Fort Wilkinson by the Agent for Indian Affairs," *LBH*, 2:419.

[10] Tuskegee Tustunugee to Benjamin Hawkins, 18 September 1812, LOC, PKY.

[11] Benjamin Hawkins to Vicente Folch, 7 June 1800, PC, leg. 108, 425, reel 163; Benjamin Hawkins to Vicente Folch, 7 June 1800, *LBH*, 1:335; Tuskegee Tustunugee to Benjamin Hawkins, 18 September 1812, LOC, PKY; and Benjamin Hawkins to Kinache and Payne, 5 December 1812, *LBH*, 2:623; Doster, *Creek Indians*, 2:50.

[12] The following sources document Harry's involvement in negotiations: Benito de Pangua to Enrique White, 7 March 1802, EF, bnd. 137G11, 1802–140, reel 56, PKY; [Enrique White] to

1800, shortly after the Spanish surrendered to Bowles and his Seminole allies in Apalache, occupants of Fort San Marcos included nine blacks, thirty Indians, and twenty-one whites.[13]

African Americans in fact appeared prominently in the busy events after the sack of the fort. When four or five Indians traveled to the outskirts of St. Augustine to harass the Spanish, a black man accompanied them, and when Spanish officer Richard Lang received word from Bowles that the Seminoles had taken San Marcos and declared war on Spain, "a certain negro man named Cudjo, an inhabitant of the Creek nation," delivered the letter.[14] Accompanied by another African American from Alachua (Payne's Town), Cudjo then went to the American settlement of Colerain on the St. Marys River to trade for salt and ammunition, but was taken prisoner by local officials. In jail, he must have encountered three free blacks, also from Payne's Town, who had been imprisoned only a few days earlier. They too had gone to Colerain to trade, accompanied by a white outlaw named Robert Allen, who lived with about thirty Indians, blacks, and "infamous whites." One of these African Americans, a companion of Payne's for over twenty years, later drowned while trying to escape across the St. Marys, and local residents worried about the repercussions. St. Marys resident James Seagrove ominously reported that "there are several dreadful vagabonds with parties of Indians and negroes now out from Bowles for plunder and if opposed no doubt murder."[15] In November 1800, during a temporary

José Cordovy, 10 March 1802, EF, bnd. 137G11, 1802–147, reel 56, PKY; Henry White to Chief Payne, 11 March 1802, EF, bnd. 115K9, reel 43, PKY; Enrique White to Marqués de Someruelos, 13 March 1802, EF, bnd. 28B3, doc. 479, 111, reel 10, PKY; José Cordovy to Enrique White, 25 March 1802, EF, bnd. 137G11, 1802–182, reel 56, PKY; [Enrique White] to José Cordovy, 26 March 1802, EF, bnd. 137G11, 1802–183, reel 56, PKY; Enrique White to Marqués de Someruelos, 29 May 1802, EF, bnd. 28B3, doc. 538, 191, reel 10, PKY; Chief Payne to Henry White, 5 June 1802, EF, bnd. 115K9, reel 43, PKY; and Enrique White to Marqués de Someruelos, 30 July 1802, EF, bnd. 28B3, doc. 557, 22, reel 11, PKY. Regarding Esten, see Jacobo Dubreuil to Vicente Folch, 22 June 1803, PC, leg. 2355, 45, reel 381, PKY. For another example of the intelligence network of African Americans, see Trib. of Com. Jacobo Dubreuil, 22 February 1801, PC, leg. 163A, 873, reel 409, PKY.

[13] Vicente Folch to Marqués de Someruelos, 15 September 1800, PC, leg. 1551, 1095, reel 202–3, PKY.

[14] Enrique White to Marqués de Someruelos, 4 July 1800, EF, bnd. 28B3, doc. 296, 65, reel 10, PKY; Henry White to Prince Payne, Cholockochully, Opia, and other chiefs of the Seminoles, 18 July 1800, EF, bnd. 115K9, reel 43, PKY; and Brother Payne King to Henry White, 29 July 1800, EF, bnd. 115K9, reel 43, PKY. Regarding Cudjo, see Affidavit of Richard Lang, 26 June 1800, CIL, 2:589, GDAH. Bowles's letter to Richard Lang, dated 5 June 1800, can be found in PC, leg. 1556, doc. 3, frame 1204, reel 45, PKY.

[15] James Seagrove to John McQueen, 24 June 1800, EF, bnd. 109E9, doc. 1800–3, reel 42, PKY; Richard Lang to James Jackson, 26 June 1800, "East and West Florida, 1764 to 1850, and Yazoo Fraud, 1796," ed. Louise F. Hays (Typescript in the GDAH), 119; John McQueen to Enrique White, 4 July 1800, EF, bnd. 135E11, 1800–154, reel 55, PKY.

lull in hostilities, Bowles's immediate party consisted of eight whites and eight blacks, and one of the latter served as Bowles's captain.[16]

African Americans also contributed political leadership to the Seminoles during the political ferment of the early nineteenth century. Even more so than Tussekiubbe and other dissident Creeks, plantation slaves understood the nature of oppressive power, giving them special motivation to assist and encourage Seminole resistance. Moreover, it is possible that some of them knew about or had personal experience in the Haitian Revolution, the successful slave revolt of the 1790s that reverberated throughout the Americas.[17] Laurent and Dominique, two "French" slaves, may well be examples. In June 1800, Seminoles stole them from planter Francis Richards on the St. Johns River, leading them to the residence of Mitloque, the second chief of Mikasuki, who lived about twenty miles to the west of the main town. There, stories about the overthrow of colonial rule on the Caribbean island would have deeply interested the Seminole audience.[18] Other blacks with firsthand knowledge about the Haitian Revolution may have included five French slaves from Grenada whom Seminole leader John Cannard purchased in Savannah in 1798.[19]

The influence of African Americans, once established, rapidly grew when they encouraged other slaves to join them among the Seminoles. In the first week of July 1800, for example, two "hostile negroes" and four Indians stole four slaves from planter George Fleming. The "hostile negroes," according to one East Florida resident, "went voluntarily at first with the Indians and was with them as a guide when they took Capt. Fleming's negroes."[20] That same year, two of James Cashen's slaves, Peter and Tim, ran away to the Seminoles. Cashen's Harry followed soon after. Six years later, Harry was rooming in Alachua with Jacob,

---

[16] Manuel de Castilla to Enrique White, 10 November 1800, EF, bnd. 135E11, 1800–387, reel 55, PKY.

[17] In "The Common Wind," Julius S. Scott documents the spread of revolutionary ideas among slaves in the era of the Haitian Revolution.

[18] Fernando de la Puente to Enrique White, 29 June 1800, EF, bnd. 135E11, 1800–133, reel 55, PKY; Andrew Atkinson to Enrique White, 30 June 1800, EF, bnd. 135E11, 1800–137, reel 55, PKY; James Hall to Andrew Atkinson, 30 June 1800, EF, bnd. 135E11, 1800–139, reel 55, PKY; undated document, EF, bnd. 197B16, doc. 1801–33, reel 83, PKY.

[19] The slaves were shipwrecked along the North American coast while being transported to western Cuba. They were taken to Savannah where mestizo John Cannard purchased them. William Laurence to William Panton, 15 August 1798, Cruzat Papers, PKY; and Tomás Portell to Vicente Folch, 20 September 1798, PC, leg. 57, 885, reel 223, PKY.

[20] Nathaniel Hall to Enrique White, 8 July 1800, EF, bnd. 135E11, 1800–172, reel 55, PKY; Andrew Atkinson to Onofre Gutierrez, 8 July 1800, EF, bnd. 135E11, 1800–173, reel 55, PKY; John Forrester to Henry White, 16 July 1800, EF, bnd. 115K9, reel 43, PKY.

another fugitive from Cashen's plantation, and Peter and Tim resided nearby. Peter had changed his name to Augustine, and Jacob also "probably goes by another name," Cashen noted with disapproval.[21] A similar pattern of repeated flights and raids occurred at the plantation of Josiah Dupont. Since settling on the St. Johns a decade earlier, he complained in 1802, "he had two negro men which ran from him and took refuge amongst the Indians and an Indian Negro stole a wench and child and since she has been amongst the Indians she had a second."[22] In January 1802, Dupont lost ten more slaves when Seminoles sacked his plantation.[23] These slaves proceeded to Mikasuki where they saw several white prisoners being guarded by armed blacks, a sight that must have suggested to them that their prospects were better among Seminoles than on the St. Johns River.[24]

The actions of a slave named Billy perhaps best exemplify the importance of African Americans to Seminole resistance. The commandant of San Marcos, Jacobo Dubreuil, identified Billy as "a famous negro rogue" who belonged to mestizo William Cannard. A fierce partisan of Bowles's, Billy reportedly made "plenty of trouble for the Spanish" during the siege and occupation of San Marcos.[25] After the Spanish retook the fort in July 1800, Billy negotiated a deal with them, agreeing to kill Bowles in return for his freedom, plus 2,000 pesos and permission to settle where he desired, but his apparent turnabout perhaps only concealed efforts to gather intelligence.[26] In February 1801, according to Dubreuil, Billy continued to cause trouble by "relating to Bowles everything that was happening here."[27] That month, Spanish officials arrested Billy for

[21] John McQueen to Enrique White, 18 April 1801, EF, bnd. 136F11, 1801–115, reel 55, PKY; Enrique White to Marqués de Someruelos, 1 May 1801, EF, bnd. 28B3, doc. 363, 162, reel 10, PKY; James Cashen to John Hampton, 27 November 1806, EF, bnd. 197B16, doc. 1806–1, reel 83, PKY. Peter Wood writes that black slaves sometimes took direct English translations of their African names. "Negroes were called *Monday* or *Friday*, as well as other temporal names such as *March* and *August*, *Christmas* and *Midday*." Wood, *Black Majority*, 182.

[22] The remonstrance of Josiah Dupont, 24 January 1802, EF, bnd. 197B16, doc. 1802–7, reel 83, PKY.

[23] [Enrique White] to John McQueen, 23 January 1802, EF, bnd. 137G11, 1802–16, reel 56, PKY; the remonstrance of Josiah Dupont, 24 January 1802, EF, bnd. 197B16, doc. 1802–7, reel 83, PKY; Enrique White to Marqués de Someruelos, 1 February 1802, EF, bnd. 28B3, doc. 459, 79, reel 10, PKY.

[24] Jacobo Dubreuil to Manuel Juan de Salcedo, 8 April 1802, PC, leg. 2355, 92, reel 381, PKY.

[25] Jacobo Dubreuil to Vicente Folch, 28 March 1801, no. 19, in letterbook Correspondencia de officio con el S.or Governador de Panzacola, PC, leg. 225B, reel 431, PKY. Dubreuil identified Billy's owner as John Cannard, but other sources indicate that it was actually William Cannard. John Cannard to Jacobo Dubreuil, 16 December 1802, PC, leg. 2372, 54, reel 436, PKY.

[26] Zenon Trudeau to Marqués de Casa Calvo, 5 October 1800, PC, leg. 71A, 879, reel 247, PKY; Jacobo Dubreuil to Vicente Folch, 7 October 1800, PC, leg. 58, 801, reel 39–0, PKY.

[27] Jacobo Dubreuil to Vicente Folch, 28 March 1801, no. 19, in letterbook Correspondencia de officio con el S.or Governador de Panzacola, PC, leg. 225B, reel 431, PKY.

selling horses and corn to Bowles. "It would be very dangerous to allow him to go free," Dubreuil concluded, noting that he had offered to purchase the "negro rogue" from Cannard and would send him on to Pensacola as soon as possible.[28] Billy went in chains to Pensacola and on to New Orleans, but Cannard refused to sell him. More than a year later, in June 1803, the Spanish returned Billy, expecting this gesture of goodwill would favorably influence Cannard toward the Spanish and would appease Kinache whose town, Mikasuki, had in the past purchased corn from the slave.[29] Billy clearly garnered respect and honor from his Mikasuki neighbors. He appears occasionally in the sources over the next several years selling goods to the Spanish. Most intriguing is a reference in 1816 to the "negro Billy . . . who enjoys among [the Mikasuki] Indians the title of great warrior." He perhaps had earned it sixteen years earlier during the occupation of Fort San Marcos.[30]

Despite the convergence of Native and African American refugees in Florida, Seminoles were not waging a war of liberation. They did not share the liberal ideology of emancipationists and did not profess special concern for the fate of black plantation slaves. Nor were their reasons for stealing slaves uniform. Some Seminoles used slaves as they would any other war booty. In January 1801, for instance, several Indians sailed to Nassau at Bowles's direction to exchange black slaves for ammunition.[31] Later that year, Seminoles stole thirty-eight slaves from Francisco Fatio's plantation on the St. Johns to exchange for the imprisoned Mikasuki leader Mitloque.[32] The arrival of these strangers in Mikasuki

[28] William Bowles to [John Cannard], 1801, PC, leg. 211B, 541, reel 291; Jacobo Dubreuil to Vicente Folch, 28 March 1801, no. 19, in letterbook Correspondencia de officio con el S.or Governador de Panzacola, PC, leg. 225B, reel 431, PKY.
[29] John Cannard to Jacobo Dubreuil, 16 December 1802, PC, leg. 2372, 54, reel 436, PKY; Manuel de Salcedo to Jacobo Dubreuil, 13 January 1803, PC, leg. 76, 362, reel 250, PKY; Manuel de Salcedo to Jacobo Dubreuil, 23 June 1803, PC, leg. 76, 385, reel 250, PKY.
[30] Expenses attending the Cession of a Tract of Land by the Creek Indians to the House of John Forbes and Co. of Pensacola, 4 February 1810 to 31 July 1811, Greenslade Papers, PKY; A List of Outstanding Debts at Prospect Bluff, Appal.a, 31 July 1811, Innerarity-Hulse Papers, reel 147-S, PKY; Francisco Caso y Luengo to Mauricio de Zuñiga, 12 July 1816, PC, leg. 79, 664, reel 479, PKY.
[31] James Seagrove to John McQueen, 31 January 1801, EF, bnd. 136F11, 1801–33, reel 55, PKY.
[32] For details of this raid, see John Forrester to Henry White, 31 August 1801, EF, bnd. 115K9, reel 43, PKY; John McQueen to Enrique White, 1 September 1801, EF, bnd. 136F11, 1801–204, reel 56, PKY; [Enrique White] to John McQueen, 3 September 1801, EF, bnd. 136F11, 1801–207, reel 56, PKY; Governor of St. Augustine to Jack Cannard, 4 September 1801, EF, bnd. 197B16, doc. 1801–17, reel 83, PKY; [F].P. Fatio to [?], 4 September 1801, "Creek Letters, 1800–1819," ed. T. J. Peddy, vol. 1, GDAH; John Forrester to Henry White, 10 September 1801, EF, bnd. 115K9, reel 43, PKY; James Seagrove to John Cannard, 10 September 1801, EF, bnd. 197B16, doc. 1801–19, reel 83, PKY; Enrique White to Marqués de Someruelos, 11 September 1801, EF, bnd. 28B3, doc. 384, 199, reel 10, PKY; Enrique White to Vicente Folch, 12 September 1801, PC, leg. 104B, doc 333., frame 876, reel 4, PKY; John Forrester to Henry White, 16 September 1801, EF, bnd. 115K9, reel 43, PKY; Timothy Barnard to Henry White, 27

divided the town, for it was already short of provisions, and many residents accused the raiders of trying to starve them.[33] For Kinache, the head of the town, the taking of slaves, like the destruction of other property, struck at the heart of Spanish colonization. When Fatio's son came to Mikasuki to reclaim his property, Kinache expressed his surprise that he "would come on so simple an errand." The Spaniards, he said sarcastically, "had taken their horses, their negroes, their goods, and even one of their people, but . . . he never had any thoughts of asking them to be returned."[34]

The fate of Fatio's slaves suggests that Seminoles, like their ancestors, often killed or sold troublesome or old male captives and adopted young women and children. The Mikasukis returned seventeen who were "old and infirm [or] nursing children." Of the fifteen remaining in Mikasuki, two were mature men, two were women in their twenties, one with a nursing child, and the other ten were children from six to twelve years old.[35] Without regular patrols, locks, and chains, Seminoles could not easily control men who wished to escape. One of Fatio's slaves, for example, fled Mikasuki with his family, reaching the Spanish fort in Apalache after a violent encounter with two Seminoles that left him with several knife wounds and his wife with a severe bullet wound.[36] The man reported that other captives would try to escape as well. Precaution may explain why Seminoles killed a free black named Antonio Perpall, yet kept his wife and four children.[37]

Despite the often violent relations between blacks and Indians, the political ferment in the region attracted more and more fugitive slaves, the most important historical legacy of the Seminole raids on Spanish settlements. When the Mikasukis laid siege again to Fort San Marcos in January 1802, for example, around forty fugitive blacks from Pensacola and St. Augustine accompanied 300 to 500 Seminole warriors, thus com-

September 1801, EF, bnd. 115K9, reel 43, PKY; John Cannard to Henry White, 2 October 1801, EF, bnd. 115K9, reel 43, PKY; Enrique White to Marqués de Someruelos, 2 December 1801, EF, bnd. 28B3, doc. 394, 214, reel 10, PKY.

[33] F. P. Fatio, Jr. to F. P. Fatio, Sr., 2 October 1801, EF, bnd. 197B16, doc. 1801–23, reel 83, PKY.

[34] F. P. Fatio, Jr., ". . . Trifling observations made during a journey through the Indian country . . . ," 12 November 1801, EF, bnd. 197B16, doc. 1801–26, reel 83, PKY.

[35] Jacobo Dubreuil to Manuel Juan de Salcedo, 11 May 1802, PC, leg. 2355, 99, reel 381, PKY; John Forrester to Henry White, 7 September 1802, EF, bnd. 115K9, reel 43, PKY; Noticia de los Individuos Blancos, Negros Esclavos y Libres que se hallan detenidos por los Indios de Miccosukee cuya devolución se solicita, 27 January 1803, EF, bnd. 115K9, reel 43, PKY; for quote see East Florida slave owners to Henry White, 1 July 1803, EF, bnd. 115K9, reel 43, PKY.

[36] Jacobo Dubreuil to Manuel Juan de Salcedo, 11 May 1802, PC, leg. 2355, 99, reel 381, PKY.

[37] Noticia de los Individuos Blancos, Negros Esclavos y Libres que se hallan detenidos por los Indios de Miccosukee cuya devolución se solicita, 27 January 1803, EF, bnd. 115K9, reel 43, PKY.

posing around 10 percent of the fighting force.[38] In the coming years, Florida Indians would continue to harbor fugitive slaves and to welcome Creek dissidents into their towns, though Bowles's imprisonment in 1803 and subsequent death in a Havana prison brought a halt to the open hostilities between Spain and the Seminoles. Crop failures in 1805 and 1806 also quieted the unrest.[39] The convergence of black and Indian interests in the opening years of the nineteenth century presaged events to come; it also pointed to the divergence of Seminoles from the new order promoted by many Creek leaders.

The dynamics of the food shortage among the Seminoles remain obscure, but such was not the case among the Upper and Lower Creeks. Among these Indians, a severe scarcity, which began in 1804, brought the growing inequalities in their towns into sharp focus. Creeks had weathered occasional years of poor harvests in the past, and in extreme situations, some had even succumbed to starvation or opportunistic diseases. But in these instances, all Creeks had suffered together, sharing food until supplies were exhausted. In 1756, for example, several people "dyed for Want," but only after "Stock and every Thing" were consumed.[40] Again in 1760, crops failed along the Chattahoochee, and in November of that year, the "whole body" of Lower Creeks "left the nation in search of provisions in the woods."[41] In 1777, when Creeks were "really starving for want of provisions," even the British Indian agent was reduced to eating dogs and horses.[42]

By the beginning of the nineteenth century, Creeks no longer worked together in times of adversity. During the hungry years, some Creeks

---

[38] Jacobo Dubreuil to Manuel Juan de Salcedo, 20 January 1802, PC, leg. 2355, 84, reel 381, PKY; Manuel de Salcedo to Marqués de Someruelos, 24 February 1802, PC, leg. 1553, 282, reel 36, PKY.

[39] Seminole leaders asked repeatedly for a trading store to be reestablished in Apalache and also requested supplies of powder and shot from the Spanish fort. Enrique White to Marqués de Someruelos, 23 June 1804, EF, bnd. 29C3, doc. 765, 50, reel 11, PKY; Ignacio Balderas to Vicente Folch, 7 July 1806, PC, leg. 61, 721, reel 493, PKY; Ignacio Balderas to Carlos Howard, 15 December 1807, no. 9, in letterbook Correspondencia de oficio con el S.or Don Vicente Folch y Juan, Gobernador de la Florida Occidental, PC, leg. 226B, reel 432, PKY. On the crop failures, see Ignacio Balderas to Vicente Folch, 2 August 1805, no. 128, in letterbook Correspondencia de oficio con el S.or Don Vicente Folch y Juan, Gobernador de la Florida Occidental, PC, leg. 226B, reel 432, PKY; Ignacio Balderas to Juan Ventura Morales, 6 July 1806, PC, leg. 260, 1313, reel 240, PKY; Ignacio Balderas to Vicente Folch, 7 July 1806, PC, leg. 61, 716, reel 493, PKY.

[40] Daniel Pepper to Governor Lyttelton, 18 November 1756, DIASC, 2:255.

[41] SCG, 29 November 1760.

[42] David Taitt to Patrick Tonyn, 24 August 1777, enclosed in Tonyn to Germain, 18 September 1777, PRO 5/557, p. 699, reel 66C, PKY; Bernardo de Gálvez to Joseph de Gálvez, 13 October 1777, ST, bnd. 6614-A, 87-1-6/63, SD 2596, PKY.

starved to death while their neighbors ate well. Crops first failed in 1803, and by early spring 1804, the hunt had provided so little meat that some Creeks were already starving and many others, weakened by hunger, were falling to disease.[43] "Food could rarely be bought at any price because of famine conditions throughout the Creek country," reported two Moravian missionaries.[44] The food shortage exposed an extraordinary degree of inequality. In summer 1804, addressing Hopoy Micco (the speaker of the nation), Benjamin Hawkins stated that from "our continuing to cultivate the old towns from year to year where the land was tired we had scanty crops." Now, he continued, "some of our women and children were actually starved and many so reduced by hunger as to be unfit for any business and a prey to disease."[45] Hawkins located the severe famine in the old towns, where women farmed with hoes and men continued to hunt. In outlying fenced communities, by contrast, ranchers and planters still had food reserves. Usiche Emathla, for example, "has informed us that while we are starving he is surrounded with plenty of bread and meat."[46]

In subsequent years, famine continued to aggravate inequalities in the Deep South. In July 1807, Benjamin Hawkins reported, "We have had a greater scarcity of corn than was ever known in this country." It is "emphatically named the *hungry year*," he wrote.[47] Though everyone felt the effects of the failed crops, Creeks who had livestock, according to Hawkins, "have lived on their beef and milk." Those who did not lived "by theft or on China briar root, by Potatoe, Blackberries and whortleberrys." "Some have actually starved," Hawkins wrote.[48] Creeks received a yearly cash payment of $16,000 from the federal government, which could have alleviated the famine, but according to Hawkins, the "rich will not let their stipend go for wheat or anything else to accommodate [the poorer part of the nation] nor anybody else who can get cards, wheels, etc. under the plan for their civilization."[49] In the eyes of wealthy Creeks, warriors and women farmers who refused to use plows and spinning wheels apparently deserved their suffering.

[43] "Journal of Benjamin Hawkins," 15 July 1804, *LBH*, 2:476.
[44] Mauelshagen and Davis, "The Moravians' Plan for a Mission among the Creek Indians, 1803–1804," 361.
[45] "Journal of Benjamin Hawkins," 15 July 1804, *LBH*, 2:477.
[46] Ibid., 476–477.
[47] Benjamin Hawkins to Henry Dearborn, 9 July 1807, *LBH*, 2:521.
[48] Ibid.; Benjamin Hawkins to Henry Dearborn, 16 September 1807, *LBH*, 2:524.
[49] Benjamin Hawkins to Henry Dearborn, 8 October 1807, *LBH*, 2:527; Benjamin Hawkins to James Forbes, 29 May 1806, Henry Wilson Papers, reel 150D, PKY.

In 1808, Creeks again experienced a poor harvest. That year Micco Achulee sent word to Hawkins, "I am the first Chief who ploughed and adopted the plan of civilization and am clothed and fed by it."[50] The following year, Hoboithle Micco, whom Hawkins had recently considered putting to death because he found his "conduct and talks so subversive of the Laws he had in contemplation,"[51] complained of the growing poverty of his warriors in a letter addressed to Thomas Jefferson. "Our goods are so very dear," he stated, "we cannot cloath ourselves." "Such as have stocks of cattle and hogs can clothe themselves," he continued, but "others must and do go naked."[52] Ranchers not only had clothes, but also a ready food source. The string of misfortunes continued in 1810 when a severe spring hurricane delayed planting for two months, and then a long drought destroyed most of the crops. Weakened by hunger, many Creeks succumbed to an epidemic, identified by Spanish doctors as yellow fever.[53] The following year, a Moravian missionary at the Creek agency reported that "the ground is so hard from the steady heat of the sun that everything within range of its rays is burned." "I found hardly a house where several [Indians] were not ill with fever and some were in bed," the missionary reported on visiting the towns on the Chattahoochee.[54]

Creeks certainly could have used attentive political leadership during the hungry years, but their leaders instead scrambled to secure their own interests.[55] One year before the initial crop failure of 1803, for example, the Creeks relinquished two tracts of land in the Treaty of Fort Wilkinson, one south of the Altamaha River and the other along the west side of the Oconee. The cession was the first since Alexander McGillivray's

[50] James Durouzeaux to Vicente Folch, 25 May 1809, PC, leg. 221B, 10, reel 310, PKY; Benjamin Hawkins to Henry Dearborn, 16 October 1808, *LBH*, 2:540.

[51] Stephen Folch, "Journal of a Voyage to the Creek Nation from Pensacola in the year 1803," 5 May 1803, PC, leg. 2372, 1, reel 436, PKY.

[52] Quoted in Doster, *Creek Indians*, 2:17.

[53] Benjamin Hawkins to Reverend Christian Benzien, 7 October 1810, *LBH*, 2:569; Mauelshagen and Davis, *Partners in the Lord's Work*, 29–30; Vicente Folch to Marqués de Someruelos, 1 October 1810, PC, leg. 1568B, doc. 972, frame 630, reel 76, PKY.

[54] Mauelshagen and Davis, *Partners in the Lord's Work*, 55 and 61.

[55] Creeks had valid reasons to condemn the wealthy among them, a fact that some historians have not recognized. Mary Young suggests, for example, that the Creeks might have done well to follow the example of their Choctaw, Chickasaw, and Cherokee neighbors. These groups, she says, traced the origins of their troubles to "meddlesome intruders, coercive state governments, and faithless friends in Washington" rather than to corrupt leaders. If the Creeks had done the same, Young suggests that they might have avoided the violent conflicts of the early nineteenth century. Mary Young, "Conflict Resolution on the Indian Frontier," *Journal of the Early Republic* 16 (1996): 13–14.

deceptive Treaty of New York twelve years earlier. Young Creek warriors objected to the cession, and Seminoles, who frequented the area south of the Altamaha, boycotted the treaty in protest. Creek leaders nevertheless disregarded the interests of their Florida relatives and ignored the objections of young people. Micco Thlucco of Kasihta, a wealthy planter, dismissed the treaty's Seminole opponents as "wild and double tongued."[56] Despite this opposition, Creek representatives embraced the treaty and its cash proceeds. The Creek nation received a yearly stipend of $3,000 for ten years, and "the chiefs who administer the government agreeable to a certificate under the hands and seals of the commissioners of the United States" shared $1,000 a year over the same period. The $1,000 annuity was divided according to the wishes of the U.S. commissioners: The speaker of the national council received $150, the first three chiefs $70 each, and sixteen other chiefs $40 each. Even the lowest payment of $40 was sufficient to purchase four cows every year. U.S. agents also distributed $10,000 in presents at the treaty signing.[57] In the past, these presents would have sealed the agreement by establishing ties of mutual obligation between fictive fathers and children, but the discord the treaty generated among Muskogees suggests that the presents now functioned to bribe Creek leaders. Creeks unhappy with the treaty threatened to kill at least one of their representatives.[58]

A more flagrant instance of corruption occurred in 1805 when six Muskogees traveled to Washington and signed away the remaining Creek land between the Oconee and Ocmulgee rivers. Despite express instructions to the contrary from the representatives in the national council, they also granted permission for the construction of a post road across Creek lands from the Ocmulgee River to Mobile to facilitate the passage of U.S. mail and troops.[59] For signing the Treaty of Washington, each

---

[56] Micco Thlucco of Cussita to Benjamin Hawkins, 3 February 1804, LTB, 287, GDAH; Benjamin Hawkins to Henry Dearborn, 17 July 1802, *LBH*, 2:447. For treaty proceedings, see Report of Commissioners to the Secretary of War, May and June 1802, *ASPIA*, 1:668–681; and "Journal of Occurrences at Fort Wilkinson during the Conference and Treaty with the Creek Indians there, by Benjamin Hawkins," *LBH*, 2:425–432.

[57] In addition, the treaty provided for $10,000 to go to the Creek factory to pay debts and $5,000 to satisfy the claims of Georgia residents against Creek raids. Treaty at Fort Wilkinson with the Creek Indians, 1802, "Indian Treaties: Cessions of Land in Georgia, 1705–1837," 336, GDAH.

[58] "Journal of Benjamin Hawkins," 30 June 1804, *LBH*, 2:472.

[59] For a history of the post road, see Henry Deleon Southerland, Jr., and Jerry Elijah Brown, *The Federal Road through Georgia, the Creek Nation, and Alabama: 1806–1836* (Tuscaloosa: University of Alabama, 1989).

representative received part of $500 from the Creek annuity of 1806.[60] In addition, the treaty provided that Creek chiefs operate lucrative ferries and inns, or stages, along the road, and at least two of the Creek signers, Alexander Cornels and William McIntosh, intended to profit from this business. Cornels, a salaried assistant to the Creek agency, knew that the road would pass by his house just south of the Tallapoosa River,[61] and McIntosh planned to run a ferry across the Chattahoochee.[62] McIntosh also attempted to direct the post road by his plantation and two-story log house, but after a crew had cut the four-foot-wide path past his residence, swampy ground forced them to abandon this route.[63] Years later, dissident Creeks would recall in anger that McIntosh had been bribed in Washington.[64] Eventually, several other wealthy Creeks entered the tavern business, including Tustanagee Hopoy and Tustanagee Thlucco, prominent members of the national council.[65] The "possession of the stages was a principal inducement on the part of the Chiefs to permit the free use of a path thro' their country," Benjamin Hawkins concluded.[66]

Mounting discontent over the corrupt proceedings of the Treaty of Fort Wilkinson and the Treaty of Washington led two Kasihta dissidents to murder Hopoy Micco, the speaker of the national council, over the winter of 1805–1806.[67] In addition, Creeks removed McIntosh and Tuskeneah Chapco (Long Lieutenant) from office for their roles in approving the construction of the post road and for embezzling the stipend.[68] But these measures did little to improve the quality of Creek leadership, largely because Hawkins recognized the effectiveness of money in securing U.S. interests. In 1803, he had told three prominent Creeks that "it is impossible for them to go on in their plans of civilization without an augmentation of their salary," suggesting the need for

[60] Benjamin Hawkins to Henry Dearborn, 24 November 1805, *LBH*, 2:500.
[61] Southerland and Brown, *The Federal Road*, 26; *Letters of Benjamin Hawkins, 1796–1806*, 326.
[62] Benjamin Hawkins to Henry Dearborn, 22 January 1807, *LBH*, 2:511; Benjamin W. Griffith, *McIntosh and Weatherford, Creek Indian Leaders* (Tuscaloosa: University of Alabama, 1988), 60.
[63] Southerland and Brown, *The Federal Road*, 25.
[64] Resolution of the Muscogee Nation, 10 March 1815, LOC, PRO, Foreign Office (hereafter FO) 5/139, PKY.
[65] Southerland and Brown, *The Federal Road*, 76 and 82–90; John Spencer Bassett, "Major Howell Tatum's Journal, while acting Topographical Engineer (1814) to General Jackson, Commanding the Seventh Military District," *Smith College Studies in History* (1921–22): 35–36.
[66] Treaty of Washington, *ASPIA*, 1:698–699; Benjamin Hawkins to Henry Dearborn, 22 January 1807, *LBH*, 2:510.
[67] Benjamin Hawkins to John Milledge, 9 June 1806, *LBH*, 2:505.
[68] Benjamin Hawkins to David Meriwether, 1 October 1807, *LBH*, 2:526.

an additional $10,000 to "raise the salaries of certain chiefs" and to add fifty more warriors to the payroll of the national council.[69] The Treaty of Fort Wilkinson had already tripled the annual stipend to $4,500, and the Treaty of Washington in 1805 granted Creeks an additional $12,000 every year. From the point of view of most Muskogees, the cash payments became little more than bribes, promoting corrupt leadership.

Hawkins cultivated the allegiance of a number of warriors by drawing orders on the annuity (usually with the approval of the national council) in the names of Creeks who assisted the agency.[70] A few examples will illustrate the point. In 1798, Tussekiah Micco received $50 for his "faithful and persevering exertions in the service of his country," and Tustanagee Hopoy and Tuskegee Tustanagee each earned $12.50 for their "faithful service" and "fidelity."[71] All three actively helped Hawkins implement the "plan of civilization."[72] The same year, George Cornels, a "chief of Tuckabatche," pocketed $100 for "the use of the chiefs of the Creek nation."[73] From his own budget, Hawkins purchased goods and services from "civilized" Creeks, thereby promoting the welfare of ranchers, planters, and others committed to the new order. Yahoola Micco sold $35 of pork and $33 of beef to the Creek agency in 1797 and 1798, and in the latter year Framautlau and Sauwaulee earned $7.25 and $11, respectively, for guiding U.S. and Spanish boundary commissioners.[74] Yahoola Micco again did business with Hawkins in 1799, selling 1,500 fence rails for $7.50.[75] Considering that the average deerskin sold for 75 cents at the Creek factory, even a few dollars represented a significant amount. Tustanagee Hopoy and Tuskegee Tustanagee each garnered the equivalent of about sixteen deerskins ($12.50) at a time when many hunters killed not a single deer in a season.[76] Even Framautlau, with the small sum of $7.25, might have purchased 100 pounds of flour and 22 pounds of bacon.

In addition to funding Hawkins's carefully directed rewards, the

---

[69] Stephen Folch, "Journal of a Voyage to the Creek Nation from Pensacola in the year 1803," 5 May 1803, PC, leg. 2372, 1, reel 436, PKY.

[70] See the various orders on the stipend in *Letters of Benjamin Hawkins, 1796–1806*, 324–339.

[71] Creek Stipend for 1798, *Letters of Benjamin Hawkins, 1796–1806*, 331.

[72] These Creeks performed many services for Hawkins. For three examples, see Journal of Richard Thomas, 30 July 1798, *Letters of Benjamin Hawkins, 1796–1806*, 490–492; Benjamin Hawkins, "A sketch of the Creek Country in the years 1798 and 1799," *LBH*, 1:306; and "Journal of Benjamin Hawkins," 30 June 1804, *LBH*, 2:472.

[73] Creek Stipend for 1798, *Letters of Benjamin Hawkins, 1796–1806*, 330.

[74] *Letters of Benjamin Hawkins, 1796–1806*, 327, 329, 333.

[75] Ibid., 332.

[76] Henri, *The Southern Indians and Benjamin Hawkins*, 119; Benjamin Hawkins to Henry Gaither, 27 February 1799, *LBH* 1:241.

stipend promoted corruption by dint of its informal administration
by the national council. Creeks had a long tradition of redistributing
resources such as surplus corn. But by the nineteenth century, the priorities of many of their leaders had changed. These Creeks sought not
to share wealth, but to accumulate it. When the national council determined each town's share of the annuity, for example, rather than working
toward equitable distribution, representatives fought for control of the
money. After the assassination of Hopoy Micco, a feud erupted between
Upper and Lower Creek leaders over the distribution of the stipend,
preventing the appointment of a new speaker. In 1807, Hawkins reported
that Upper Creek leaders were "avaricious and desirous of engrossing
as much of the stipend as they can." The agent concluded that each
leader was "intent on his own gain, regardless of the public."[77] Three
years later, the Indian agent again accused a faction of Upper Creek representatives of trying to secure possession of the annuity.[78] "The great
men" among the Upper Creeks, he wrote, "are contending for office and
to embezzle their stipend and they leave the people to shift for themselves after misleading them by falsehoods."[79] "They each wish to have
it all," Spanish Indian agent James Durouzeau said of the Upper and
Lower towns.[80] By 1810, Upper Creek leader Tustanagee Thlucco had
consolidated his power and promoted himself as the new speaker of the
national council, apparently with the aim of monopolizing the annuity.[81]
An acquaintance would later describe Tustanagee Thlucco as "a lover of
wealth."[82]

The distribution of the stipend favored the locales of prominent
and powerful men attached to the "plan of civilization." In 1811, the

[77] Benjamin Hawkins to Henry Dearborn, 16 September 1807, *LBH*, 2:524; Benjamin Hawkins to
David Meriwether, 1 October 1807, *LBH*, 2:526.
[78] Benjamin Hawkins to William Eustis, 8 April 1810, *LBH*, 2:562.
[79] Benjamin Hawkins to Reverend Christian Benzien, 7 October 1810, *LBH*, 2:569.
[80] James Durouzeaux to Vicente Folch, 9 October 1810, PC, leg. 147A, 227, reel 451, PKY.
[81] Tallassee King (Hoboithle Micco) had for a time acted as the head of the Upper Creeks. Benjamin Hawkins to William Eustis, 8 April 1810, *LBH*, 2:562; Doster, *Creek Indians*, 2:8–25. On
Tustanagee Thlucco and the discord he created between the Upper and Lower Creeks, see the
following documents: Benjamin Hawkins to Vicente Folch, 27 September 1809, PC, leg. 221B,
32, reel 310, PKY; Benjamin Hawkins to William Eustis, 8 April 1810, *LBH*, 2:562; Benjamin
Hawkins to William Eustis, 21 July 1810, *LBH*, 2:564; Governor Maxent to James Durouzeaux,
26 July 1810, PC, leg. 221B, 30, reel 310, PKY; Benjamin Hawkins to Reverend Christian
Benzien, 7 October 1810, *LBH*, 2:569; James Durouzeaux to Vicente Folch, 9 October 1810, PC,
leg. 147A, 227, reel 451, PKY; Benjamin Hawkins to William Eustis, 5 November 1810, *LBH*,
2:575; Benjamin Hawkins to William Eustis, 9 November 1810, *LBH*, 2:577; Benjamin Hawkins
to William Eustis, 22 May 1811, *LBH*, 2:588.
[82] Absalom Harris Chappell, *Miscellanies of Georgia; Historical, Biographical, Descriptive, etc.*
(Columbus, GA: Gilbert Printing Company, 1928), 72.

representatives of seven Upper Creek settlements on the northern and western periphery of Creek country complained to Hawkins, "Our stipend being delivered by order of the Chiefs to certain Great Chiefs to share out and grow ritch out of it, we have received no part of it." The Indian agent explained that "you do not all attend to your affairs, and when you do not, those who attend will not attend to you." Divided among all the towns in Creek country, he stated, the stipend would amount to nothing,[83] indicating that the annuity served to reward and purchase obedience, not to compensate Creeks for the loss of their lands. The Seminoles also never received any part of the annuity. "Our hold on [the Seminoles] is by a slender thread," Hawkins concluded in 1812.[84]

Funneling money toward favored towns amounted to one form of embezzlement. Creek leaders also used the stipend to purchase goods that favored adherents of the "plan of civilization." In 1802, for example, Hawkins proclaimed that the "philanthropist & the friend of humanity" would "rejoice" at the news that the Creeks had appropriated $1,000 for axes, grubbing hoes, and salt. With axes, Creeks would clear new fields, and with grubbing hoes they would remove tree roots and stumps in preparation for plowing. Salt went to nourish livestock and cure "domestic meats."[85] Hoboithle Micco, a staunch opponent of Hawkins's program, expressed a different view of such purchases. In 1803, he said he did not want a "Blacksmith in the nation or weavers to bring them into slavery, no plough or any plantation tools."[86] In 1807, as the Creeks entered the worst famine in living memory, the national council budgeted for blankets, corn hoes, bullets, flints, cash, iron, and steel, but not for food.[87] Even Hawkins failed to rejoice over these purchases. Four years later, the national council bought similar goods: blankets, cowbells, cotton cards, iron and steel for agricultural implements, and sheet iron for cotton gins.[88]

[83] Benjamin Hawkins to William Eustis, 24 February 1811, *LBH*, 2:583.
[84] Benjamin Hawkins to David B. Mitchell, 7 September 1812, *LBH*, 2:617.
[85] Benjamin Hawkins to Henry Dearborn, 17 July 1802, *LBH*, 2:448; Benjamin Hawkins, "Journal of Occurrences in the Creek Agency from January to the Conclusion of the Conference and Treaty at Fort Wilkinson by the Agent for Indian Affairs," *LBH*, 2:411. The axe was a symbol of "civilization." Richard Thomas to Henry Gaither, 28 January 1798, *Letters of Benjamin Hawkins, 1796–1806*, 478. For information on the agricultural practices of southern farmers such as the Creeks would have witnessed, see Otto, *The Southern Frontiers, 1607–1860*, 13–14.
[86] James Durouzeaux to Vicente Folch, 5 October 1803, PC, leg. 220A, 489, reel 307, PKY.
[87] Benjamin Hawkins to Henry Dearborn, 24 February 1807, *LBH*, 2:513.
[88] See, for example, Stipend to be paid by the U.S. to the Creeks in 1811, "Creek Letters, 1800–1819," vol. 1, GDAH.

Some documents suggest, but do not prove, that Creek leaders may have directly pocketed part of the annuity when it was paid in cash. In 1810, the year before Hawkins heard complaints about "certain Great Chiefs" embezzling the stipend, Creeks received the entire payment of $16,500 in cash.[89] The following year, they accepted half in cash.[90] The informality of these transactions encouraged corruption. In 1811, for example, two "young men" from Upper Creek towns collected distributions from U.S. factor John Halsted in two wooden boxes, each containing $1,000.[91] Other Creek representatives spent their people's cash allotments in advance or at the time of delivery by purchasing goods at the U.S. factory.[92] In 1799, for example, Tustanagee Thlucco of Kasihta spent $25 of his town's stipend of $250 on a musket.[93] Other Creek representatives purchased ribbon, blankets, padlocks, knives, and cotton cards, according to a list from 1810.[94] Ribbon, blankets, and knives may have been distributed widely among Creeks, but padlocks and cotton cards were of interest to only a select few. Though it is impossible to prove without a doubt that Creek politicians stole cash payments, the dismissal of William McIntosh and Tuskeneah Chapco from the national council and the complaints of some Upper Creeks about the actions of "certain Great Chiefs" indicate at the very least that Muskogees distrusted their representatives; the fight for control of the stipend suggests that they had good reason to be suspicious.

Stipends and bribes were not the only ways in which Creek leaders profited during the hungry years. Between 1804 and 1812, Forbes and Company, the successor to Panton, Leslie and Company and the main trading house operating in the Deep South, extinguished all debts owed by the Creek nation.[95] This process involved three major agreements: a land cession in 1804, another in 1811, and cash payments out of the annuity in 1812. These agreements favored the wealthy inhabitants of

[89] John Halsted to General John Mason, 31 July 1810, p. 331, Records of the Creek Trading House, Letter Book, 1795–1816, reel 94-O, PKY.
[90] Stipend to be paid by the U.S. to the Creeks in 1811, "Creek Letters, 1800–1819," vol. 1, GDAH.
[91] John Halsted to Benjamin Hawkins, 2 May 1811, p. 337, Records of the Creek Trading House, Letter Book, 1795–1816, reel 94-O, PKY.
[92] Charles Magnan to John Mason, 26 July 1813, p. 358, ibid.
[93] Letters of Benjamin Hawkins, 1796–1806, 336.
[94] John Halsted to General John Mason, 31 July 1810, p. 331, Records of the Creek Trading House, Letter Book, 1795–1816, reel 94-O, PKY.
[95] Forbes and Company pursued a similar policy with the Choctaws and Chickasaws. Usner, "American Indians on the Cotton Frontier," 301–304.

Creek country by canceling their debts at the expense of other Muskogees. Like the controversy over stipends, these agreements also contributed to Creek discontentment and anger.[96]

In 1804, Seminole and Lower Creek leaders ceded to Forbes a tract
of land between the Apalachicola and St. Marks rivers, nearly 1.4 million
acres situated southwest of present-day Tallahassee.[97] Bribes may have
sealed the agreement. In a book published in 1804, John Forbes discussed his desire to secure a stretch of land next to Pensacola: "At first
the Indians will object to losing it," he wrote, "but if the necessary
amounts were placed in the hands of the people who conduct this business, there would be no doubt of its success."[98] The cession extinguished
a debt of just under $66,534. (In the following discussion, figures are
rounded off to the nearest dollar.) Of that sum, debts due by "different
Indian dealers" at the Panton store in Apalache before May 1800
accounted for $19,157, accruing to $23,346 by August 1804 due to 6
percent annual interest. The damage sustained by the store in Bowles's
raids of 1792 and 1800 accounted for another $27,970, and interest on
this debt added $13,073. Expenses incurred at congresses relative to the
cession itself comprised the remaining $2,137.[99]

Though the debt appears to have been shared widely by the
Seminoles, the character of the debt that they incurred when warriors
damaged Panton's property in Apalache differed significantly from
the debt of the "Indian dealers" (responsible for 35 percent of the
total). For the most part, Seminoles who participated in Bowles's
raids destroyed property and stole goods to assert their superiority
and dominance over the Spanish. Because the raids were ultimately
ineffective, each dollar of debt represented a total loss; Seminoles
had nothing to show for the "investment" of their warriors. Indian
dealers, or traders, in contrast, had gone into debt to purchase goods
from Panton, Leslie and Company which they then resold to hunters
for a profit. In 1801, Efau Hadjo suggested to John Leslie, a partner
in the company, "Our traders have property enough in negroes, cattle,
horses; and it may be that the skins have been given for these things

---

[96] The attitudes of southeastern Indians regarding debt had changed significantly over the previous
half-century. Cf. Tom Hatley on pre-Revolutionary Cherokee debt in *The Dividing Paths*, 48.

[97] William S. Coker and Thomas D. Watson, *Indian Traders of the Southeastern Spanish Borderlands: Panton, Leslie and Company and John Forbes and Company, 1783–1847* (Pensacola: University of West Florida, 1986), 251–255.

[98] John Forbes, *John Forbes' Description of the Spanish Floridas, 1804* (1804; reprint, Pensacola:
Perdido Bay Press, 1979), 30–31.

[99] *American State Papers: Public Lands* (Washington: Gales and Seaton, 1859), 4:161–163. An
accounting error by Forbes and Co. explains the difference between the total debt and the sum
of its parts.

which ought to have paid your debt." He noted that both white and Indian factors "have accumulated property and they certainly could pay off some."[100]

Table 1, reflecting data reported in 1787 by William Panton of Panton, Leslie and Company, illustrates the extent of the profits earned by traders. According to Panton, though traders made a gross profit of 100 percent, their net profit was notably smaller. A trader, he explained, was "always obliged to give away Some part to His Headmen of the Town for Protection." Additional expenses included the salaries of "hirelings," damage to skins, the loss of horses, and bad debts. At the end of the year, Panton concluded, a trader was "not much richer than when it began."[101] But Panton, in making his case to the Spanish crown for monopoly rights, had reason to underestimate the profitability of the deerskin trade. Despite the expenses he mentioned, it is difficult to imagine that traders did not come out ahead.[102] By the beginning of the nineteenth century, many traders such as James Burgess, Thomas Perryman, and John Cannard were headmen in their own right and did not have to pay for protection or the attendant expenses that burdened outsiders. Indian and mestizo factors were becoming ever more common.[103] Moreover, with their profits, they could purchase goods for personal use at half the price of other Creeks.

Creek hunters, by contrast, clearly fared poorly in the trade. Each needed five pounds of shot and twelve pounds of powder just to sustain a year's hunt. The cost of these necessities amounted to fourteen deerskins, at least half of an individual's annual harvest. In a good year, a hunter might have been able to purchase two plain shirts, one shag-end blanket, and a felling axe with his remaining skins.[104]

---

[100] Talk from Efau Hadjo to John Forbes, 31 May 1801, Greenslade Papers, PKY. He repeated these thoughts in 1803. Stephen Folch, "Journal of a Voyage to the Creek Nation from Pensacola in the year 1803," 5 May 1803, PC, leg. 2372, 1, reel 436, PKY.

[101] William Panton, 2 June 1787, PC, leg. 200, 914, reel 277, PKY.

[102] Braund, *Deerskins and Duffels*, 98–99.

[103] Daniel McGillivray complained in 1800 to William Panton. Daniel McGillivray to William Panton, 28 September 1799, Forbes-Innerarity Papers, 84/15, original in Mobile Public Library, Mobile, Alabama, microfilm copy in the PKY, reel 147 P; and Efau Hadjo to John Forbes, 31 May 1801, Greenslade Papers, PKY. Indian and mestizo factors also appear on lists of debtors kept by Panton, Leslie and Company. See, for example, List of debts due by traders, half breeds and Indian factors to Panton Leslie and Co. of Appalachy commencing October 1787 and ending September 1792, Greenslade Papers, PKY.

[104] In the 1760s, John Stuart suggested trade regulations that limited the credit of each hunter to 5 lbs. of powder and 12 lbs. of shot per hunting season. Assuming these amounts to be the average needed, a hunter would pay 5 lbs./112 lbs.·150 skins + 12 lbs./112 lbs.·70 skins = 14 skins. William Panton, 2 June 1787, PC, leg. 200, 914, reel 277, PKY; "Regulations for the better carrying on the trade with the Indians in the Southern district," enclosed in Stuart to Gage, 10 March 1767, Thomas Gage Papers, American series, reel 140F, PKY.

Table 1. *The deerskin trade out of Pensacola*

Item	Trader's price	Hunter's price in skins	Trader's profit	Profit (%)
Three-point blanket	$2.50	6	$2.17	87
Two and one half-point blanket	$2.00	5	$1.89	94
Shag-end blanket	$2.00	5	$1.89	94
Ruffled white shirt	$1.83	6	$2.84	155
Plain white shirt	$1.50	4	$1.61	107
Limbourg/blanket	$2.55	6	$2.12	83
Hundredweight (2,800) balls	$10.00	70	$44.44	444
Handkerchief	$0.47	1.5	$0.70	148
Hundredweight of gunpowder	$40.00	150	$76.67	192
Large felling axes/ dozen	$15.00	36	$13.00	87

Source: Based on data found in William Panton, 2 June 1787, PC, leg. 200, 914, reel 277, PKY. Panton stated that the average skin weighed three pounds and that traders sold skins for 14 pence per pound, or $0.26 per pound. Profit is $S \cdot 3 \cdot \$0.26 - T$, where S is the number of skins and T is the trader's price. In Panton's complete list of trade goods, the average profit is just over 100%. For comparative data on the deerskin trade compiled in 1793 by Francisco Montreuil, the Spanish officer at Fort San Marcos in Apalache, see Montreuil's relation dated 25 July 1793, ST, PC leg. 123/6, PKY.

An examination of debts due by Indian traders and factors at the store in Apalache reveals that the cession of 1804 extinguished the obligations of the wealthiest men in the region, a reflection of the profitability of trading as well as of the injustice of the agreement. James Burgess, for example, who worked until 1799 as an assistant and interpreter to the Creek agency for an annual salary of $400, owed $4,232, according to the accounting of Panton, Leslie and Company. Assuming a profit of 100 percent, Burgess would have been able to turn this amount into a net gain of about $4,000, equivalent to the market value of eight slaves, or 350 head of cattle.[105] Edward Forrester, a former storekeeper for Panton,

---

[105] Tomás Portell to Vicente Folch, 3 June 1798, PC, leg. 57, 873, reel 223, PKY; James Burgess to James Seagrove, 15 June 1799, PC, leg. 216B, 414, reel 301, PKY. *Letters of Benjamin Hawkins, 1796–1806*, 326. Portell reported that Burgess's salary was $600, but the payments disbursed by

Leslie and Company, similarly profited. He owed $3,510 in 1800. White traders were not the only people to benefit from the cession. Ninny-wageechee, the Little Black Factor, owed $239, John Cannard $1,338, his brother William $783, Kinache $1,673, Thomas Perryman $250, and John Galphin $404, to name just a few.[106] These wealthy men benefited disproportionately from the cession while hunters lost twice, once because they made no profit on their debt and a second time because they depended on the ceded land for survival.

Thomas Perryman, who among the Creeks most actively pushed for the cession, had additional plans to profit from the land grant. When he first proposed the cession in 1803, he suggested a detailed plan of development. One Spaniard left an account of Perryman's project:

> If Spain would allow him to form an establishment in that quarter of 60 or 80 families of Loyalists from the Bahamas, he could afford to pay the Crown for the support of a Governor the sum of three thousand dollars annually upon being exempted from Duties of importation and Exportation for ten years and liberty to trade directly with England during that period. They could by these means lay the foundation of a Colony that would effectually bridle the Indians, and render the Spanish name in that quarter respectable. Every man's property would be a sufficient Guarantee for his good behavior.[107]

Perryman intended to profit from the colony by exporting timber from Creek lands.[108] His proposal to "bridle the Indians" reflects how frag-

---

factor Edward Price reveal that his salary was actually $400. For an accounting of the deerskin trade before 1775, see Alden, *John Stuart*, 16–17.

[106] "List of debts due by Indian traders and factors to Panton Leslie and Co. at their store at Appalachy . . . ," Forbes-Innerarity Papers, 85/15, reel 147P, PKY. It is unclear whether this list enumerates the exact debts extinguished by the cession. In one case, it clearly does not. William Perryman's debt is listed as just over $102 while another document makes clear he had nearly $288 extinguished by the cession. Statement of Recoveries made on the Outstanding Debts of the Concerns W.P., I.F., and I.L., 1812, Cruzat Papers, PKY. In any case, we can assume that most of the debts listed in 1800 were extinguished by the cession.

[107] Stephen Folch, "Journal of a Voyage to the Creek Nation from Pensacola in the year 1803," 5 May 1803, PC, leg. 2372, 1, reel 436, PKY.

[108] As early as 1785, Perryman had proposed the settlement of Apalache by British citizens. Doster, *Creek Indians*, 1:54. On two later occasions in the second decade of the nineteenth century, he requested the creation of a port of entry on the Apalachicola in order to export timber. Thomas Perryman and 15 other Chiefs to Vicente Folch, 23 April 1810, PC, leg. 1568A, doc. 918, frame 1124, reel 74, PKY; Francisco Maximiliano de San Maxent to Marqués de Someruelos, 12 May 1810, PC, leg. 1568A, doc. 918, frame 1121, reel 74, PKY; Vicente Folch to Marqués de Someruelos, 10 June 1810, PC, leg. 1568B, 12, reel 75, PKY; Francisco Maximiliano de San Maxent to Juan Ruiz de Apodaca, 9 June 1812, PC, leg. 1797, 79, reel 121, PKY. That Perry-

mented and divided the Creeks had become over the preceding quarter century.

Part of the agreement of 1804 provided for the establishment of a trading post on the Apalachicola River at Prospect Bluff. By 1810, traders owed another $19,388 at this store, and again Seminole leaders agreed to cede land to cover the debts. This agreement complemented the original cession of 1804, adding St. Vincent Island and the adjacent coast at the mouth of the Apalachicola as well as land between the Wakulla and St. Marks rivers and a tract at the northwestern corner of the original cession.[109] An examination of the debts recovered by Forbes in this agreement again reveals that, though not all debtors were among the wealthy inhabitants of the region, those who held large debts occupied privileged positions, either as Seminole leaders (Thomas and William Perryman) or as white traders (James Lovett, George Cousins, and Thomas Carr).[110]

Many Seminoles challenged the justice of this cession. In January 1811, as Seminole leaders were meeting in Pensacola to finalize the agreement, lower towns, especially Mikasuki, threatened to kill those men most active in pushing for the cession, including Thomas Perryman.[111] Perryman again worked for the establishment of a British settlement on the Forbes grant, sending his son Billy to the Bahamas "on purpose to see Mr. Forbes and to induce settlers to come over to a tract of land granted to the house of John Forbes and Co. and in which it is understood this halfbreed has an interest."[112] By September 1811, Edmund Doyle, the storekeeper at Prospect Bluff, reported that "if some Satisfactory measures are not entered into" with Perryman, Seminoles would destroy the store. The result of Perryman's embassy, he wrote, "will turn the scales one way or the other."[113] Doyle believed Perryman would be able to control young Creek and Seminole warriors, but he was mistaken. These warriors were angry because Perryman and others had ceded land against their wishes, not because Perryman had yet to profit by his scheme.

After successfully securing the repayment of debts in Apalache,

man intended to profit from the Forbes grant is clear in the events surrounding the second cession to Forbes in 1811.

[109] Coker and Watson, *Indian Traders*, 268–270.

[110] Statement of Recoveries made on the Outstanding Debts of the Concerns W.P., I.F., and I.L., 1812, Cruzat Papers, PKY.

[111] Innerarity to John Forbes, 9 February 1811, Greenslade Papers, PKY.

[112] John McKee to James Monroe, 25 March 1812, State Department Territorial Papers, Florida Series, 1777–1824, 2:76, microcopy no. 116/2, PKY.

[113] Edmund Doyle to John Forbes, 1 September 1811, Greenslade Papers, PKY.

Forbes and Company turned its attention to the Upper Creeks, who held the remaining outstanding debt. In late October 1812, John Innerarity arrived in Tuckabatche to collect about $40,000 owed to the firm. On hearing the list of debtors read aloud, Creek leaders complained that "several of them were dead that some had property, negroes etc. that some were not regular Traders had no rights but merely settled among them for a short time."[114] After extensive negotiations, Innerarity agreed to cancel the interest – Creeks insisted that their language did not even have a word to describe the strange accrual of debts common among whites. In turn, Creek leaders agreed to pay the principal of $21,916. The schedule of repayment called for Forbes and Company to receive $5,000 of the Upper Creek annuity in 1812, all of the annuity of $8,500 the following year, and the remaining balance the third year.[115]

The Upper Creeks, despite Innerarity's insistence otherwise, did not have "the sole and entire benefit" of the goods Forbes and Company had distributed to deceased or "insolvent" traders.[116] Often, children inherited the property of their fathers, keeping the wealth in the hands of specific families.[117] Sehoy and Charles Weatherford, for instance, accounted for $2,974, or about 14 percent of the total debt of the Upper Creeks. Their children John and William Weatherford, along with David Taitt, Sehoy's son by another man, were likely the primary beneficiaries of the profits gleaned from their parents' debts.[118] John owned a lucrative ferry on the road from Fort St. Stephens, on the Tombigbee River, to Georgia, and in 1813, he had at least $1,200 in property.[119] William and David, plantation owners, both held a substantial number of

[114] "The Creek Nation, Debtor to John Forbes and Co., Successors to Panton, Leslie and Co.: A Journal of John Innerarity, 1812," *Florida Historical Quarterly* 9 (1930): 80. A summary of the lives of John Innerarity and his brother James can be found in Thomas C. Kennedy, "Sibling Stewards of a Commercial Empire: The Innerarity Brothers in the Floridas," *Florida Historical Quarterly* 67 (1989): 259–289.

[115] "Obligation of the chiefs and headmen of the upper towns of the Creek nation to John Forbes and Co., November 1, 1812," *Florida Historical Quarterly* 9 (1930): 83, 87–89; Upper Creeks to Benjamin Hawkins, 26 April 1813, *ASPIA*, 1:841.

[116] Cash Statements, 31 October 1812, Greenslade Papers, PKY.

[117] The list of debts canceled by the agreement can be found in "List of debts due by the traders and factors of the Upper Creek towns to the firm of Mssrs. Panton, Leslie and Co., and John Forbes and Co. of Pensacola, adjusted to 1st Novemr. 1812," *Florida Historical Quarterly* 9 (1930): 86.

[118] See Benjamin W. Griffith, *McIntosh and Weatherford, Creek Indian Leaders* (Tuscaloosa: University of Alabama, 1988), for an account of William Weatherford's life.

[119] John Spencer Bassett, "Major Howell Tatum's Journal, while acting Topographical Engineer (1814) to General Jackson, Commanding the Seventh Military District," *Smith College Studies in History* (1921–22): 35–36; *USS.H.doc.* 200 (20–1) 173:29.

slaves.[120] Another trader named George Cornels, who may also have been deceased, owed $699; his brother James had at least $2,000 in possessions in 1813, and Scurgey and Slaugey Cornels, perhaps his heirs, had property worth a minimum of $975.[121] Similarly, deceased traders Robert and Alexander Grierson (Grayson) owed $233, yet their heirs possessed at least $4,500 in goods.[122] Joseph Stiggins also had his debt of $218 canceled by the agreement in 1812, though in 1813 his son George claimed possessions worth $1,100.[123] Three other deceased traders, Daniel McGillivray, John Clark, and Francis Tuzant, together owed $5,241, or 24 percent of the total debt. Clark's presumed heirs had a minimum of $617 in 1813.[124] Tuzant's and McGillivray's beneficiaries are unknown, but McGillivray, before his death, had parlayed his debt into a plantation on the Coosa River from which he exported corn, cotton, and cattle to Pensacola.[125] Those "insolvent" debtors still alive included James Quarles (Qualls), who owed $632 yet retained at least $1,800 in goods in 1813, and John O'Kelley, who owed $172 but possessed property worth at least $2,000.[126] From these debtors alone (out of a total of 48), it appears that at least 25 percent of the debt could have been recovered. The Creeks' resolution to "compel payment" from individuals who had "sufficient property to pay their respective debt" reflects their anger at being held responsible for the obligations of these and other traders.[127] After examining the accounts of Robert Grierson's son and grandson in April 1813, for example, Creek leaders threatened to "go and take property to satisfy the debt."[128] But before they could act, Muskogees would take matters into their own hands.

Benjamin Hawkins had hoped that hunger would compel Creeks to adopt his "plan of civilization." (It must not have helped his cause when

---

[120] J. D. Dreisbach to Lyman Draper, July 1874, Draper Mss. 1V62, State Historical Society of Wisconsin, reel 146I, PKY; C. H. Driesbach, "William Weatherford," *Arrow Points* 4 (1922): 112–113; Bassett, "Major Howell Tatum's Journal," 41.

[121] *USS*.H.doc. 200 (20–1) 173:29–30.

[122] Ibid., 23.

[123] Ibid., 29.

[124] Ibid., 23.

[125] "Journal of Benjamin Hawkins," 20 December 1796, *Letters of Benjamin Hawkins, 1796–1806*, 42–43; Daniel McGillivray to William Panton, 28 September 1799, Greenslade Papers, PKY; Daniel McGillivray to [John Forbes?], 28 August 1806, Forbes-Innerarity Papers, 67/30, reel 147P, PKY.

[126] *USS*.H.doc. 200 (20–1) 173:26, 33.

[127] "Obligation of the chiefs and headmen of the upper towns of the Creek nation to John Forbes and Co., November 1, 1812," *Florida Historical Quarterly* 9 (1930): 83, 87–89; Upper Creeks to Benjamin Hawkins, 26 April 1813, *ASPIA*, 1:841.

[128] Upper Creeks to Benjamin Hawkins, 26 April 1813, *ASPIA*, 1:841.

the agent's crops withered under the hot sun in summer 1811.)[129] But as the hungry years drew to a close, Creeks who looked back over the preceding decade must have been struck by the failure of "civilization" to provide for them. Crop failure may have temporarily quieted unrest, but the controversial treaties of Fort Wilkinson and Washington, the efforts of Creek leaders to engross the annual stipend, and the objectionable debt payments to Forbes and Company added to the Creeks' disaffection. At the end of the hungry years, rather than embracing Hawkins's plan, they renewed their efforts to destroy it.

[129] Mauelshagen and Davis, *Partners in the Lord's Work*, 55.

PART IV

The new order challenged, 1812–1816

10

Seminole resistance

In September 1811, sixteen Shawnees, nineteen Choctaws, forty-six Cherokees, and two or three unidentified native groups met Creek leaders and warriors in the square ground of Tuckabatche, the Upper Creek town on the Tallapoosa River. Led by the Shawnee warrior Tecumseh, the delegation had come with important news. Among literate peoples, the weight of the information might have been conveyed with official documents, perhaps marked by seals. Tecumseh instead carried a pipe whose purpose, Benjamin Hawkins explained, was "to unite all the red people in a war against the white people."[1] Tecumseh hoped to form a military alliance between the Creeks and the Shawnees, Delawares, and other Indians of the Old Northwest.

The Shawnees had long occupied a position between the native peoples of the Old Northwest and the Southeast. Scattered many times by their enemies, they had fled in the seventeenth century from the Ohio to the Cumberland River, and from there, breaking into two groups, to the lower Susquehanna River in Pennsylvania and the head of the Savannah River in Georgia and South Carolina.[2] By the middle 1700s, Shawnee settlements stretched from the Susquehanna west down the Ohio to the mouth of the Cumberland. Some Shawnees also lived among the Upper Creeks in a town called Sawanogee on the Tallapoosa.[3] These peregrinations encouraged the Shawnees to act as go-betweens, and as early as the 1760s, they were brokering Indian alliances against the British and carrying "long belts and great talks from all the Northward

---

[1] Benjamin Hawkins to William Eustis, 21 September 1811, *LBH*, 2:591. Tecumseh's visit is treated in detail in John Sugden, *Tecumseh: A Life* (New York: Henry Holt, 1997), 243–251.
[2] R. David Edmunds, *Tecumseh and the Quest for Indian Leadership* (Boston: Little, Brown, and Company, 1984), 3.
[3] Ibid., 4; Swanton, *Early History of the Creeks*, 317–320, 415–16; Benjamin Hawkins, "A sketch of the Creek Country in the years 1798 and 1799," *LBH*, 1:295.

Nations" to the South.[4] After the Revolution, they continued to convey talks and negotiate alliances between the Indians of the Old Northwest and the Creeks, most notably in 1793 when a group of Shawnees successfully encouraged some of the Lower Creeks and Seminoles to join them against the Americans.[5]

By the end of 1805, Indians in the Old Northwest had ceded most of Ohio and southern Indiana to the United States, and they were struggling to maintain viable communities amidst growing poverty and alcoholism. At this time, Tecumseh's brother, known as the Shawnee Prophet and as Tenskwatawa, had a dream that inspired him to seek spiritual renewal. Preaching in a long tradition of native prophets, he told Indians to stop drinking and to revive the ways of their ancestors. Eliminate cattle, swine, and poultry, he urged, and avoid European foods, including wheat. Indian women, he stated, should abandon their white husbands and mestizo children and return to their native towns. Tenskwatawa also condemned leaders who had ceded land to the United States. The Shawnee Prophet's pan-Indian message attracted thousands of Native Americans, including Ottawas, Wyandots, and Potawatomis. After the United States carved out another section of Indiana in 1809, the religious movement took on a military component. Survival now seemed to depend not only on a spiritual rejection of U.S. colonialism, but also on armed victory over American troops.[6]

---

[4] Hatley, *The Dividing Paths*, 110–111; John Stuart to Thomas Gage, 14 December 1771, Thomas Gage Papers, American series, reel 140H, PKY. John McIntosh to Peter Chester, 3 September 1772, enclosed in Chester to the Earl of Hillsborough, 16 November 1772, PRO 5/579, p. 305, reel 66M, PKY; David Taitt to John Stuart, 19 October 1772, enclosed in Stuart to Gage, 24 November 1772, Thomas Gage Papers, American series, reel 140H, PKY; John Stuart to Thomas Gage, 14 September 1774, Thomas Gage Papers, American series, reel 140H, PKY; Alexander Cameron to Henry Clinton, 18 July 1780, Sir Guy Carleton Papers, doc. 2919, reel 58A-10, PKY; Patrick Tonyn to Guy Carleton, 23 December 1782, Sir Guy Carleton Papers, doc. 6476, reel 58A-19, PKY.

[5] Alexander McGillivray to Arturo O'Neill, 20 June 1787, PC, leg. 200, 946, reel 277, PKY; John Forrester to Juan Nepomuceno de Quesada, 18 February 1793, EF, bnd. 123F10, doc. 1793–25, reel 48, PKY; Timothy Barnard to Major Henry Gaither, 18 February 1793, LTB, 125, GDAH, also in *ASPIA*, 1:418; James Seagrove to the chiefs and headmen of the Cussita and Coweta towns, 20 February 1793, *ASPIA*, 1:375; James Seagrove to Timothy Barnard, 24 February 1793, LTB, 127, GDAH, also in *ASPIA*, 1:377; Timothy Barnard to Henry Gaither, 4 March 1793, LTB, 130, GDAH, also in *ASPIA*, 1:418; Timothy Barnard to James Seagrove, 26 March 1793, LTB, 136, GDAH, also in *ASPIA*, 1:381; John Forrester to Juan Nepomuceno de Quesada, 8 April 1793, EF, bnd. 123F10, doc. 1793–67, reel 48, PKY; Timothy Barnard to [James Seagrove], 9 April 1793, LOC, PKY; Timothy Barnard to Henry Gaither, 10 April 1793, LTB, 145, GDAH, also in *ASPIA*, 1:419; Juan Nepomuceno de Quesada to Luis de Las Casas, 26 April 1793, PC, leg. 1436, 5614, reel 158, PKY; Benjamin Hawkins to James McHenry, 26 October 1799, *LBH*, 1:263. For early connections between the Creeks and Shawnees, see Sugden, *Tecumseh*, 57–60, 69–70, 73–76, 80.

[6] Sugden, *Tecumseh*, 113–120, 182–190; Dowd, *A Spirited Resistance*, 123–147.

Tecumseh, whose Shawnee, Creek, and white ancestry made him the embodiment of his people's history of dislocation and migration, journeyed to the Deep South in 1811 to urge the Muskogees to join this armed movement. Speaking in Tuckabatche in the presence of Benjamin Hawkins, he claimed he had followed the war pipe southward to urge all to reject it in favor of peace with their white neighbors.[7] But out of Hawkins's earshot, he pressed Creeks to accept the war pipe, explaining that the "Northward" Indians had the firm support of the British.[8] Creek leaders refused to join the alliance, though many young warriors were receptive to Tecumseh's overtures. Unsuccessful, the Shawnee leader moved on to Coweta and Kasihta on the Chattahoochee River, and perhaps traveled into Florida to speak to the Seminoles.[9] No matter the exact destinations of his visit, his message spread far and wide through the Deep South.

Tecumseh came at a turbulent time for the Creeks and Seminoles. A meteor blazed across the sky during his visit and a series of violent quakes, including a tremendous one centered at New Madrid, Missouri, shook the earth soon thereafter, portents to Muskogees of the magnitude of events to come.[10] In addition, the Shawnee warrior arrived at the end of the hungry years during which Creek leaders had ceded lands to the United States and transferred annuities to Forbes and Company. In 1811, too, the federal road opened from the Flint River to Fort Stoddert above Mobile, directing settlers through Creek lands to the fast-growing colonies on the Mobile, Tombigbee, and Alabama rivers.[11]

---

[7] Benjamin Hawkins to William Eustis, 21 September 1811, *LBH*, 2:591. On Tecumseh's early history, see Edmunds, *Tecumseh*, chap. 2; and Sugden, *Tecumseh*, 13–66.

[8] Benjamin Hawkins to William Eustis, 3 October 1811, *LBH*, 2:592. Edmunds, *Tecumseh*, 148–153.

[9] Tecumseh's biographers R. David Edmunds and John Sugden both conclude that the Shawnee leader's visit to the Seminoles is uncertain. Even if Tecumseh did not visit Florida, Seminoles may have been present at some of his talks. In the late nineteenth century, Creeks recalled that two Seminole leaders had attended Tecumseh's talk in Tuckabatche. Edmunds, *Tecumseh*, 220; Sugden, "Early Pan-Indianism; Tecumseh's Tour of the Indian Country, 1811–1812," *American Indian Quarterly* 10 (1986): 283. Sugden, "The Southern Indians in the War of 1812: The Closing Phase," *Florida Historical Quarterly* 60 (1982): 275.

[10] Griffith, *McIntosh and Weatherford*, 76–77. Sugden, "Early Pan-Indianism: Tecumseh's Tour of the Indian Country, 1811–1812," 289–290. Sugden notes that Tecumseh's name means "shooting star" in Shawnee. For a brief examination of how the Creeks might have interpreted these cosmological and geological phenomena, see Martin, *Sacred Revolt*, 114–116, and 122–124; and Sugden, *Tecumseh*, 249–251.

[11] Benjamin Hawkins to Governor Mitchell, 29 April 1811, LBH, 143, GDAH; Hoboheithle to the President of the United States, 15 May 1811, "Creek Letters, 1800–1819," vol. 1, GDAH; Benjamin Hawkins to William Eustis, 3 October 1811, *LBH*, 2:592; Halbert and Ball, *The Creek War of 1813 and 1814*, 29–39; Henry Deleon Southerland, Jr., and Jerry Elijah Brown, *The Federal Road through Georgia, the Creek Nation, and Alabama: 1806–1836* (Tuscaloosa:

All of these events coincided with the mounting resentment of many Creeks toward wealthy leaders who pretended to wield national judicial and political power. This anger, growing since the early days of Alexander McGillivray's self-promotion, needed only a small spark to explode into war.

For the Seminoles, that spark came in March 1812 when an invading band of 150 self-styled patriots, organized and backed by the United States, crossed the St. Marys River into Spanish Florida to foment a "revolution." American planters and land speculators had long been anxious to extend U.S. sovereignty over the pine barrens and swamps that lay to the south of Georgia. Once the invasion began, American troops stood ready to take control of the territory at the request of "local authorities," and regular U.S. soldiers followed the insurrectionists into Florida, beginning a year of sedition and despoliation of Spanish settlements. Led by Payne of Alachua town, near present-day Gainesville, Florida, Seminoles opposed the invasion and engaged their enemies in several significant battles. Federal troops pulled out in May 1813, but insurgents continued occupying parts of Florida for a year afterward.[12]

From one perspective, Payne's War from 1812 to 1814 has a familiar and predictable outline: Indians reflexively defended their lands from aggressors. But the substance of the war – how and why Seminoles became involved and who fought the battles – reveals that a deep-seated hostility to the new order spreading through Creek country underlay the actions of Florida Indians. Without that antipathy there would have been no war. Seminoles ignored the admonitions of the national council to remain at peace and they drew inspiration from the opponents of "civilization": Creek dissidents, Tecumseh, and, most especially, fugitive slaves.

African Americans participated in every step of the Seminole decision to go to war. They had good reasons to do so, for as Brigadier General John B. Floyd revealed just after the invasion had begun in late March

University of Alabama, 1989), 35–38. Tecumseh in fact spoke to the Creeks during the same meeting in which they debated the opening of the federal road. After three days of debate, Hawkins told them that "he did not come there to ask their permission to open a road, but merely to inform them that it was now cutting." Sugden, "Early Pan-Indianism: Tecumseh's Tour of the Indian Country, 1811–1812," 285.

12 Rembert Wallace Patrick provides a detailed account of American attempts to annex Florida in *Florida Fiasco: Rampant Rebels on the Georgia-Florida Border, 1810–1815* (Athens: University of Georgia, 1954).

1812, the United States hoped for a pretext to penetrate Seminole lands and destroy black settlements, "an important evil *growing* under their patronage," he explained.[13] In the long run, no white slaveholder could tolerate a settlement of free blacks and Indians one day's journey from plantations. Thomas Perryman, a Seminole leader, described Floyd's scenario from the other side, stating that "Amrica want take negro belong to the Indans and send to the Indans bad nuse thay whould come and kill all the men and take the women for thier owen use."[14]

When Florida Indians moved against the insurgents in July 1812, they did so because of the "talks of a negro."[15] By the end of March 1812, the invading forces had taken Picolata, a fort that guarded the crossing of the St. Johns River to St. Augustine, cutting off communication between the Spaniards and Seminoles. The Spanish loss allowed insurrectionist leader and U.S. agent George Mathews, the former governor of Georgia, to negotiate freely with the Florida Indians.[16] In need of a linguist, he kidnapped a slave named Tony, a translator at trading stores at least since 1801 and "known to be the best interpreter of Indian languages in the province," according to the governor of Florida, Sebastián Kindelán.[17] On arriving in Alachua with the unsuspecting Mathews, Tony explained his situation and convinced them that Mathews's promises were false.[18] "These fine talks are to amuse and deceive you," he reportedly said:

> They are going to take your country beyond St John's. The old people will be put to sweep the yards of the white people, the young men to work for them and the young females to spin and weave for them.[19]

[13] John Floyd to William H. Crawford, 26 March 1812, LOC, State Department, Miscellaneous, PKY.

[14] Thomas Perryman to the Governor of Pensacola, 20 August 1812, PC, leg. 2356, 125, reel 172, PKY.

[15] Benjamin Hawkins to Kinache and Payne, 5 December 1812, *LBH*, 2:623.

[16] José de Estrada to Marqués de Someruelos, 26 March 1812, EF, bnd. 31E3, doc. 101, 4812, reel 12, PKY; Patrick, *Florida Fiasco*, 180–182, 325n11.

[17] Nathaniel Hall to [Andrew Atkinson and John McQueen], 11 August 1801, EF, bnd. 136F11, 1801–191, reel 56, PKY; John Forrester to Henry White, 19 June 1804, EF, bnd. 116L9, reel 44, PKY.

[18] Sebastián Kindelán to Juan Ruiz de Apodaca, 13 August 1812, EF, bnd. 31E3, doc. 39, 4931, reel 12, PKY.

[19] Tuskegee Tustunugee to Benjamin Hawkins, 18 September 1812, LOC, GDAH. Alexander Cornels gave a slightly different version:

> There was a negro went from Alachua to work amongst the whites and when he returned he told the Seminoles that there was a young officer told him that when they finished at Augustine that they was agoing to

It perhaps was not by chance that Tony, who had known Payne and his people for over ten years, painted a picture of the future characterized by the taming of mad warriors and the domestication of women, a future closely resembling the new order emerging among the Upper and Lower Creeks.

Shortly after the meeting, the African American linguist escaped from Mathews's camp, returned to Alachua, and persuaded the Indians to send an embassy to the Spanish to convey their willingness to offer military support. (The governor later manumitted Tony in reward for his service.)[20] Despite Payne's wish to remain neutral, the Seminoles chose war by popular consensus – the traditional Muskogee means of decision-making that had been abandoned by the national council. African Americans composed a significant part of the majority. Lower Creeks stated that there were 200 Seminole and forty "negro" warriors involved in the hostilities.[21] General John Floyd claimed that at least 500 blacks, including men, women, and children, lived under the "patronage" of the Seminoles, and his fellow officer Thomas Flournoy estimated that between 400 and 600 Seminole and black warriors were attached to the Spanish interest.[22] African Americans, composing a significant but undetermined percentage of the population, may have tipped the balance in favor of war.

The active participation of blacks in Payne's War illustrates their resolve to combat the new order promoted by Hawkins and his Creek allies. Shortly after meeting with Governor Kindelán to confirm their alliance, Seminoles "carried off" seventy or eighty slaves from American and Spanish plantations, and sent the governor eight of "their negro

sweep the red people. He did not mind him but another officer asked him when he was going home that he expected he would see him there for he wanted to eat some of their beef at Seminoles. This was the commander told him, and when he came home he told the red people and they said if they were to be destroyed that they would begin first.

Alexander Cornells to Benjamin Hawkins, 19 September 1812, LOC, State Department, Miscellaneous, PKY.

[20] Sebastián Kindelán to Juan Ruiz de Apodaca, 13 August 1812, EF, bnd. 31E3, doc. 39, 4931, reel 12, PKY; Edward Wanton to Juan José de Estrada, 5 July 1812, EF, bnd. 148E12, 1812–222, reel 61, PKY.

[21] Tuskegee Tustunugee to Benjamin Hawkins, 18 September 1812, LOC, PKY.

[22] John Floyd to William H. Crawford, 26 March 1812, LOC, State Department, Miscellaneous, PKY; and Extract of a letter from Brigadier General Flournoy to Major General Pinckney, enclosed to the Secretary at War, 12 December 1812, enclosed in a message of the President of the United States transmitting a report of the Secretary of State on the subject of East Florida, received 14 January 1813, in the Territorial Papers of the United States Senate, 1789–1873, Florida, 2 December 1806 to 7 February 1825, microcopy no.200/9, PKY.

slaves" to fight the insurgents.[23] Then a party of blacks and Indians murdered a lieutenant in the invasion forces. He was "left lying in the road,
he had been flogged, his nose, one ear, & – cut off," a U.S. commander
reported. The "blacks assisted by the Indians," the officer noted, "have
become very daring & from the want of a proper knowledge of the
country the parties which I have sent out have always been unsuccessful."[24] The attack presaged a more serious blow to the invaders. In early
September, between fifty and seventy blacks and six Seminoles, led by a
free black man named Prince, destroyed a wagon train headed to Fort
Stallings, effectively cutting the American supply line and forcing a
retreat to the St. Johns.[25]

The success of the joint Seminole and black force led to the most
significant battle in Payne's War, again revealing the prominent place of
African Americans in the hostilities. On 24 September, Colonel Daniel
Newnan led 117 soldiers across the St. Johns toward Alachua to "destroy
their towns, provisions and settlements." The expedition ended in disas-
ter for the United States, despite American claims to have surprised a
body of Seminole warriors six or seven miles from the Alachua towns.[26]
Spanish sources reveal that the Alachuas and Mikasukis were in fact fore-
warned of the coming attack and were scouting U.S. troop movements.[27]
After a brief charge against the Seminoles, Newnan ordered a breastworks constructed and there his troops remained for eight days, besieged
by blacks and Indians painted and prepared for battle by the war dance.

[23] Patrick, *Florida Fiasco*, 185; Lt. Col. Smith to Maj. Gen. Pinckney, 30 July 1813, T. Frederick Davis, "United States Troops in Spanish East Florida, 1812–13, Part II," *Florida Historical Quarterly* 9 (1931): 106; Edward Wanton to Juan José de Estrada, 26 July 1812, EF, bnd. 148E12, 1812–227, reel 61, PKY; Sebastián Kindelán to Juan Ruiz de Apodaca, 29 July 1812, EF, bnd. 31E3, doc. 26, 4906, reel 12, PKY.

[24] Lt. Col. Smith to Gov. Mitchell, 21 August 1812, Davis, "United States Troops in Spanish East Florida, 1812–13, Part II," 111.

[25] Patrick, *Florida Fiasco*, 191–194; Payne and his principals to the Governor of East Florida, 8 September 1812, EF, bnd. 115K9, reel 43, PKY; Governor Kindelán to Chief Payne and other principals of the Seminole Nation, n.d., EF, bnd. 115K9, reel 43, PKY; Lt. Col. Smith to Gov. Mitchell, 22 September 1812, Lt. Col. Smith to Col. Newnan, 26 August 1812, T. Frederick Davis, "United States Troops in Spanish East Florida, 1812–13, Part III," *Florida Historical Quarterly* 9 (1930): 138; Lt. Col. Smith to Capt. Massias, 22 September 1812, Davis, "United States Troops in Spanish East Florida, 1812–13, Part III," 140–141.

[26] Extract of a letter from an officer of rank in the southern army, 7 October 1812, *Niles' Weekly Register*, 14 November 1812, p. 171; Account of Newnan's late expedition, 19 October 1812, *Niles' Weekly Register*, 12 December 1812, pp. 235–237; and Lt. Col. Smith to Gen. Floyd, 30 September 1812, Davis, "United States Troops in Spanish East Florida, 1812–13, Part III," 143. A brief overview of Daniel Newnan's life can be found in John K. Mahon, "Daniel Newnan: A Neglected Figure in Florida History," *Florida Historical Quarterly* 74 (1995): 148–153.

[27] Marcos de Villiers to Maurizio de Zuñiga, 28 October 1812, PC, leg. 79, 619, reel 479, PKY; and Sebastián Kindelán to Juan Ruiz de Apodaca, 20 November 1812, EF, bnd. 31E3, doc. 106, 5051, reel 12, PKY.

Reduced to eating horses, the hungry troops hastily retreated eight miles on the night of 4 October, again constructing breastworks around their camp. On 5 October, a fever-ridden Newnan ordered another retreat, but had to halt after four of the advance guard were wounded, three mortally, by Seminole fire from behind pine trees recently toppled by a hurricane. There the soldiers remained, subsisting on alligators, gophers, and palmetto stalks until relief arrived a few days later.

Newnan wrote that the Indians, "including negroes, who are their best soldiers," numbered at different times from between fifty and 200, and claimed that his soldiers had killed fifty of them.[28] A Spanish report, however, put the number of Seminoles killed at three along with four wounded, including Payne, who died of his wounds several months later.[29] Newnan himself only listed eleven specific cases in which Seminoles fell. He reported eight of his own men dead and nine wounded, though the actual number may have been higher.[30] One Florida resident who observed Newnan's troops returning from defeat wrote that they concealed the true number of casualties. He noted with certainty that Newnan had lost many people; the survivors, who had been reduced to eating horses and cartridge belts, were "burdened with misery and grief" (*cargados de miserias y pesadumbre*).[31] Despite Newnan's blunder, newspapers around the country proclaimed him a hero, and Newnansville, Florida (an early capital of Alachua County), and Newnan, Georgia, honored his name.[32] Shortly after the Seminole victory, perhaps in response to the contributions of African Americans, insurrectionist leader Buckner Harris, presiding as a judge for the nominal Republic of Florida, executed two free blacks, a father and son who had been free for over fifty years. According to one Spanish citizen, "they were guilty of no other crime than being free blacks." The insurgents, he explained, "say that they will not leave free any black or colored person who falls into their hands."[33]

[28] Account of Newnan's late expedition, 19 October 1812, *Niles' Weekly Register*, 12 December 1812, pp. 235–237.

[29] Marcos de Villiers to Maurizio de Zuñiga, 28 October 1812, PC, leg. 79, 619, reel 479, PKY; Benjamin Hawkins to James Monroe, 18 January 1813, *LBH*, 2:627.

[30] Account of Newnan's late expedition, 19 October 1812, *Niles' Weekly Register*, 12 December 1812, pp. 235–237.

[31] George Clarke to Juan José de Estrada, 16 October 1812, EF, bnd. 198C16, doc. 1812–62, reel 84; George Clarke to Juan José de Estrada, 25 October 1812, EF, bnd. 198C16, doc. 1812–65, reel 84, PKY.

[32] Davis, "United States Troops in Spanish East Florida, 1812–13, Part III," 155.

[33] Jorge Clarke to Juan José de Estrada, 5 December 1812, EF, bnd. 198C16, doc. 1812–69, reel 84, PKY.

The willingness of Seminoles to trust and join with fugitive slaves set them apart from many of their Creek relatives, and they rebuffed the efforts of the national council to reverse their decision. In August 1812, a delegation of "distinguished chiefs" of the Lower Creeks had set out for Alachua to deliver a "strong talk of peace and neutrality from the national council."[34] Two months later, Tustanagee Thlucco (Big Warrior), the speaker of the nation, complained of the Seminoles' defiance:

> They do not follow our rules and dont go by our orders. They will not be governed by us. Our wish is for peace and friendship [with the U.S.]. – When we asked them to come and visit us at our council house, and to hear the talks of the nation, they would not come and will not accept with my rules and orders; They will not be governed by the Chiefs of the nation. They turned their backs to us, have taken up the sharp hatchett and are Spilling the blood of our white friends.[35]

The path of action chosen by the national council in 1812 differed significantly from the one chosen by Seminoles. Some Upper Creeks responded favorably to Tecumseh's call to arms, but Creek leaders brutally punished the dissidents. In May 1812, for example, forty-three warriors went in pursuit of some Creeks who had killed four of Benjamin Hawkins's cattle. Cropping the rustlers' noses and ears was "in accord with Creek law for theft," according to two Moravian missionaries living at the Creek agency, but they neglected to mention that the personal ownership of cattle in the Deep South had a history of scarcely fifty years, and that punishment by an anonymous group of warriors had an even shorter history.[36] Several days later, four Creeks murdered two Americans traveling through the Deep South to settle in Mississippi Territory, and others killed a third American riding on the post road.[37] Around the same time, a party of Upper Creeks murdered two white families at the mouth of Duck River on the Tennessee, fifty miles west

[34] Benjamin Hawkins to David Mitchell, 24 August 1812, LBH, 166, GDAH.
[35] Tustanagee Thlucco to Benjamin Hawkins, 29 October 1812, LTB, 301, GDAH.
[36] Mauelshagen and Davis, *Partners in the Lord's Work*, 70.
[37] Benjamin Hawkins to William Eustis, 6 April 1812, *LBH*, 2:605; Benjamin Hawkins to William Eustis, 25 May 1812, *LBH*, 2:609; Benjamin Hawkins to the chiefs of the Creek nation, June 1812, LBH, 156, GDAH; Chiefs of the Creek nation to Benjamin Hawkins, 17 June 1812, LBH, 159, GDAH; Benjamin Hawkins to William Eustis, 22 June 1812, *LBH*, 2:610; C. Limbaugh to Benjamin Hawkins, 27 July 1812, LBH, 164, GDAH; Benjamin Hawkins to the Governor Mitchell, 7 September 1812, LOC, PKY.

of present-day Nashville.[38] The political protests continued when two
Indians broke into the Creek factory and stole furs worth $216.[39] All of
these actions came on the heels of Tecumseh's visit to the Creeks. The
site at Duck River is particularly significant, for it lay on the path that
Tecumseh had followed on his journey to the Southeast.[40]

Creek leaders responded with brutality.[41] Lower Creek warriors loyal
to the national council promptly whipped and cropped the ears of the
Indians involved in the robbery of the Creek factory, and they promised
to assist Upper Creek leaders in punishing those involved in the
murders.[42] "If we could begin when we hear of crimes and punish the
guilty, the innocent would never suffer," Hawkins instructed the Creeks.
Meeting in council in Tuckabatche, Creek leaders "unanimously agreed
that satisfaction shall be given without delay for the murders committed
in our land" and appointed several parties to pursue the culprits.[43]

By the end of July 1812, shortly after Seminoles had committed themselves against U.S. troops, Creek police had executed six of the murderers. In addition, five thieves suffered whippings and cropped ears.[44]
After narrowly escaping from his pursuers, one Creek warrior charged
with murder fled to Tallassee, traditionally a "white" Creek town where
accused Indians often found asylum for their crimes.[45] There, he took
sanctuary in the square ground on the honored seat of Hoboithle Micco,
but the leader of the proto-police force "shot him on the seat through
the head and body," a violent reminder that Creek leaders intended to
establish a new political order without regard for older practices.[46] By
the end of August, Creek warriors had whipped and cropped the ears of

[38] Benjamin Hawkins to William Eustis, 25 May 1812, *LBH*, 2:609; Benjamin Hawkins to William
Eustis, 22 June 1812, *LBH*, 2:610; Chiefs of the Creek nation to Benjamin Hawkins, 17 June
1812, LBH, 159, GDAH; Extract of a letter from William Henry to John J. Henry, 26 June 1812,
ASPIA, 1:814; Benjamin Hawkins to William Eustis, 13 July 1812, *LBH*, 2:612.
[39] Benjamin Hawkins to William Eustis, 9 June 1812, *LBH*, 2:609; John Halsted to [?], 1812, p. 346,
Records of the Creek Trading House, Letter Book, 1795–1816, reel 94-O, PKY.
[40] Sugden, "Early Pan-Indianism: Tecumseh's Tour of the Indian Country, 1811–1812," 279.
[41] Ross Hassig argues that it was the Redstick disregard for traditional Creek political structures
that led to the war, but it in fact appears to be the reverse. Hassig, "Internal Conflict in the Creek
War of 1813–1814," 266.
[42] Benjamin Hawkins to William Eustis, 9 June 1812, *LBH*, 2:609.
[43] Chiefs of the Creek nation to Benjamin Hawkins, 17 June 1812, LBH, 159, GDAH.
[44] Benjamin Hawkins to William Eustis, 3 August 1812, *LBH*, 2:613.
[45] William Bartram wrote of Apalachicola, another white town, that it was "sacred to peace; no captives are put to death or human blood spilt here. And when a general peace is proposed, deputies
from all the towns in the confederacy assemble at this capital, in order to deliberate upon a subject
of so high importance for the prosperity of the commonwealth." Bartram, *Travels*, 313.
[46] Benjamin Hawkins to Governor Mitchell, 13 July 1812, LBH, 163, GDAH; Benjamin Hawkins
to William Eustis, 13 July 1812, *LBH*, 2:612.

two more thieves, and had tracked down Hilabee Hadjo, the leader of
the murderers at Duck River. They shot him at the council house in
Hickory Ground and threw his body into the Coosa River. The police
later executed two of Hilabee Hadjo's accomplices as well.[47]

This violent persecution of political dissenters contrasts markedly
with the Seminoles, who freely drew inspiration from the same people
condemned by Creek leaders. According to Payne and Kinache, the
leaders of Alachua and Mikasuki towns, a Creek refugee and prophet
named Tussekiubbe played a decisive role in convincing them to defy
the national council and attack American invaders. Other "disorderly
young men from the upper Creeks," as one U.S. officer put it, also contributed to the movement.[48]

These dissidents encouraged Seminoles to meet the invading U.S.
forces with war dances inspired by Tecumseh. After their initial armed
foray against U.S. insurgents in July 1812, for example, warriors reportedly retired to their villages to "celebrate." They would return to battle
in ten to twelve days, they promised the Spanish governor, "elated with
the triumphs of that celebration" whose principal object reportedly was
"to inspire the warriors of the other towns or villages that have not yet
taken up arms."[49] Kindelán, the governor of Florida, did not fully understand the behavior of his Seminole allies, but Upper Creeks explained,
"There has arisen a prophet among the Seminoles and all of them have
taken his talks."[50] Later, the governor realized that the refusal of Seminole warriors to follow his military plans derived not from their desire
for booty but from their religious inspiration. "They are so supersti-
tious," he reported, "that after they take the extravagant medicines with
which they prepare themselves for battle, they neither eat nor permit

---

[47] Benjamin Hawkins to William Eustis, 24 August 1812, *LBH*, 2:615; Benjamin Hawkins to David
B. Mitchell, 31 August 1812, *LBH*, 2:616; Benjamin Hawkins to the Governor Mitchell, 7 September 1812, LOC, PKY.

[48] Benjamin Hawkins to Kinache and Payne, 5 December 1812, *LBH*, 2:623; Extract of a letter
from Brigadier General Flournoy to Major General Pinckney, enclosed to the Secretary at War,
12 December 1812, enclosed in message of the President of the United States transmitting a
report of the Secretary of State on the subject of East Florida, received 14 January 1813, in the
Territorial Papers of the United States Senate, 1789–1873, Florida, 2 December 1806 to 7 February 1825, microcopy no.200/9, PKY; Doster, *Creek Indians*, 2:50. By the end of 1812, Tussekiubbe reportedly had to flee Florida when angry Seminoles, recovering from attacks by U.S.
troops, threatened his life. Historian John Sugden suggests that Tussekiubbe was a Creek prophet
known as Seekaboo who had lived with Tecumseh. Sugden, *Tecumseh*, 320–321; Doster, *Creek
Indians*, 2:57. See also Tuskegee Tustunugee to Benjamin Hawkins, 18 September 1812, LOC,
PKY.

[49] Sebastián Kindelán to Juan Ruiz de Apodaca, 29 July 1812, EF, bnd. 31E3, doc. 26, 4906, reel
12, PKY.

[50] Benjamin Hawkins to the Governor Mitchell, 13 September 1812, LOC, PKY.

any white person to talk to or approach them, and even their slaves separate from them, so that they cannot be commanded or made to remain in the same place for two days."[51]

Colonel Daniel Newnan witnessed a performance of the Seminoles' prophetic dance when his troops, marching against Alachua, fell under siege:

> Having obtained a considerable reinforcement of negroes and Indians from their towns, they commenced the most horrid yells imaginable, imitating the cries and noise of almost every animal of the forest, their chiefs advancing in front in a stooping serpentine manner, and making the most wild and frantic gestures.[52]

Compare the dance of the Shawnee delegation in Tuckabatche one year earlier:

> [They] leaped up with one appalling yell, and danced their tribal war-dance, going through the evolutions of battle, the scout, the ambush, the final struggle, brandishing their warclubs, and screaming in terrific concert an infernal harmony fit only for the regions of the damned.[53]

One Creek reported that Tecumseh had introduced into the Southeast the practice of performing a dance before rather than after battle.[54] Newnan learned as much. When the Seminoles finished dancing, they "commenced firing," killing two and wounding one of the colonel's soldiers.[55]

The victory of Seminoles and their black allies over Newnan initiated a crisis among Georgia slaveholders. Governor David Mitchell complained of the "murderous excursions" of Seminoles and St. Augustine

---

[51] Sebastián Kindelán to Juan Ruiz de Apodaca, 13 September 1812, EF, bnd. 31E3, doc. 54, 4965, reel 12, PKY. In the coming civil war between the Creeks, warriors inspired by Tecumseh would similarly consecrate certain lands against white intruders. Robert Breckinridge McAfee, *History of the Late War in the Western Country* (1816; reprint, Bowling Green, OH: Historical Publications Co., 1919), 507; and Meek, *Romantic Passages*, 278–279.

[52] Account of Newnan's late expedition, 19 October 1812, *Niles' Weekly Register*, 12 December 1812, pp. 235–237.

[53] John F. H. Claiborne, *Life and Times of Gen. Sam Dale, the Mississippi Partisan* (New York: Harper and brothers, 1860), 61–62.

[54] Deposition of Sam Moniac, in Halbert and Ball, *The Creek War of 1813 and 1814*, 91–93. See, for example, Nimrod Doyell to Benjamin Hawkins, 3 May 1813, *ASPIA*, 1:843–844. For a general discussion of the significance of the dance, see Martin, *Sacred Revolt*, 145–149.

[55] Account of Newnan's late expedition, 19 October 1812, *Niles' Weekly Register*, 12 December 1812, pp. 235–237.

blacks. "[M]ost of our male negroes on the sea board are restless and make many attempts to get off to Augustine, and many have succeeded," wrote Mitchell, "which, considering the disproportion between our white and black population in the same part of the state, renders it necessary to have constant guards and patrols, which harass our people accordingly."[56] After Payne's victory over Newnan, Mitchell warned that if American regulars withdrew from Florida, "nothing short of the whole military strength of the state [of Georgia] being brought to act against the Indians and negroes would in my opinion save her from the very worst evils imaginable."[57] Mitchell, in short, feared that Georgia would become another Haiti.[58] Some months earlier, in January 1813, insurrectionist leader John McIntosh had expressed such fears in a letter to Secretary of War James Monroe:

> Our slaves are excited to rebel. . . . St. Augustine, the whole province will be the refuge of fugitive slaves; and from thence emissaries . . . will be detached to bring about a revolt of the black population in the United States.[59]

For "local reasons," fearful Georgia newspaper editors deleted mention of "negroes" from accounts of the armed struggle in Florida.[60]

After the inflammatory rhetoric of southern newspapers had fostered anti-Spanish sentiment and fueled a sense of crisis, President James Madison redoubled efforts to take the Spanish colony, ordering more

---

[56] Extract of a letter from Governor Mitchell to James Monroe, 19 September 1812, enclosed in message of the President of the United States transmitting a report of the Secretary of State on the subject of East Florida, received 14 January 1813, in the Territorial Papers of the United States Senate, 1789–1873. Florida, 2 December 1806 to 7 February 1825, microcopy no.200/9, PKY.

[57] D. B. Mitchell to James Monroe, 13 October 1812, State Department Territorial Papers, Florida Series, 1777–1824, 2:133 microcopy no.116/2, PKY.

[58] George Clarke, observing affairs from Fernandina on Amelia Island, described the critical situation of the United States:

> Without ships, without money, and without union among its people, its coasts covered with English vessels and its ports at the mercy of those vessels; its back infested by Indians who are harassing it from Canada to Florida, and its center ready to become a second Saint Domingue, as for the English, they are inclined to disembark one or two of the black regiments that they have in these Indies!

George Clarke to Juan José de Estrada, 25 October 1812, EF, bnd. 198C16, doc. 1812–65, reel 84, PKY.

[59] Quoted in Kenneth W. Porter, "Negroes and the East Florida Annexation Plot, 1811–1813," *Journal of Negro History* 30 (1945): 24.

[60] Patrick, *Florida Fiasco*, 318n40.

troops to the Florida–Georgia line in December 1812.[61] Perhaps aware of the soldiers amassing on the border, the Seminoles sued for peace, but the invasion came anyway.[62] At four in the morning on 8 February 1813, a joint force of Tennessee volunteers and U.S. regulars numbering almost 500 entered Payne's town in Alachua, finding it deserted.[63] Benjamin Hawkins reported that the Alachua Seminoles had abandoned their villages in January 1813, but a report from the governor of Florida adds further detail. He learned that the Indians had left a party of blacks to ambush the troops, but, tired of waiting, they dropped their guard, fleeing into the woods when the aggressors caught them unprepared.[64] American reports triumphantly noted that the troops had killed thirty-eight Indians, taken seven prisoners, burned 386 houses, destroyed several thousand bushels of corn, and taken 400 cattle and the same number of horses.[65] Governor Kindelán gave a different assessment of the invasion, noting that the destruction of the huts "truly was not worth the show of an entire expedition."[66] After the razing of Alachua, American troops withdrew from Florida, ending for a time their efforts to annex the Spanish colony.[67] A band of freebooters remained in Alachua between January and May 1814 when a party of blacks and Indians killed the leader, Buckner Harris.[68]

[61] Ibid., 207, 213–217, 220–221. Ramón Romero Cabot suggests that Florida was a proving ground for propaganda techniques that the U.S. used later in Texas and California. Cabot, "Ideología y Propaganda Expansionista Norteamericana y la Florida Española," *Revista de Indias* 51 (1991): 132–142.

[62] *Niles' Weekly Register*, 9 January 1813; Governor Mitchell to Benjamin Hawkins, 8 February 1813, LOC, PKY.

[63] Patrick, *Florida Fiasco*, 231.

[64] Sebastián Kindelán to Juan Ruiz de Apodaca, 27 March 1813, EF, bnd. 32F3, doc. 183, 5157, reel 12, PKY. One week earlier, Marcos de Villiers, the commandant of Apalache, wrote a similar report, though without the details provided by Kindelán. Marcos de Villiers to Maurizio de Zuñiga, 19 March 1813, PC, leg. 146, 37, reel 452, PKY.

[65] Extract of a letter from a gentleman in St. Marys, 27 February 1813, *Niles' Weekly Register*, 27 March 1813, p. 67. One soldier reported slightly different numbers. He wrote, "I think we have killed about twenty of the enemy, wounded many . . . burnt three hundred and eighty six houses, took about five hundred head of cattle and horses, fifteen hundred bushels of corn, and about two thousand deer skins." William Cocke to [?], 24 February 1813, LOC, State Department, Miscellaneous, PKY. Thomas Smith gave another set of numbers: 386 houses burned, about 1,500 to 2,000 bushels of corn consumed and destroyed, 300 horses and 400 cattle collected, and 2,000 deerskins taken or destroyed. Col. Smith to Gen. Flournoy, 24 February 1813, T. Frederick Davis, "United States Troops in Spanish East Florida, 1812–13, Part IV," *Florida Historical Quarterly* 9 (1931): 273.

[66] Sebastián Kindelán to Juan Ruiz de Apodaca, 27 March 1813, EF, bnd. 32F3, doc. 183, 5157, reel 12, PKY.

[67] See Patrick, *Florida Fiasco*, chap. 20, for an account of the U.S. retreat.

[68] Patrick, *Florida Fiasco*, 278–282. See also Sebastián Kindelán to Juan Ruiz de Apodaca, 18 February 1814, EF, bnd. 33G3, doc. 409, 24, reel 12, PKY; Sebastián Kindelán to Juan Ruiz de Apodaca, 14 April 1814, EF, bnd. 33G3, doc. 476, 103, reel 12, PKY; Sebastián Kindelán to Juan

Despite the strong resistance mounted by blacks and Indians in Payne's War, the American invasion of 1812–1814 definitively forced the Seminoles and their African American allies to recognize each other as distinct peoples. Hawkins and other U.S. officials indicated that there could be no peace until Seminoles returned fugitive slaves.[69] Governor Mitchell explained in February 1813, "I will venture to say if they are collected and delivered up, it will be considered by Georgia as one of the best evidences of the sincerity of their present proposition for peace."[70] In fact, John Cannard and Kinache proposed to the governor just such a plan, but U.S. troops, to Mitchell's chagrin, had attacked before negotiations could be completed.[71] When the Seminoles abandoned Alachua, then, their black allies went their own way. In May 1813, Hawkins reported that the "negroes were now separated and at a distance from the Indians on the Hammocks or the Hammock not far from Tampa Bay." From their "unguarded mode of speaking" about the politics of slavery, he said, they "have acquired information which they avail themselves of more frequently lately than at any former period."[72] African Americans, Hawkins implied, understood U.S. intentions. Alerted by other blacks, they chose temporarily to separate themselves from the Seminoles, and the Seminoles perhaps chose to let them go, recognizing that along with their military skills they also brought a certain risk. Though blacks and Seminoles remained close and fought as allies in the First and Second Seminole wars, they did so with distinct identities, and when they removed to Oklahoma, two separate communities formed with different interests.[73] By the end of Payne's War, someone visibly of

Ruiz de Apodaca, 4 May 1814, EF, bnd. 33G3, doc. 481, 110, reel 12, PKY; Sebastián Kindelán to Juan Ruiz de Apodaca, 6 June 1814, EF, bnd. 33G3, doc. 490, 127, reel 12, PKY; Francisco Caso y Luengo to Mateo González Manrique, 1 July 1814, PC, leg. 1797, 277, reel 121, PKY; Sebastián Kindelán to Juan Ruiz de Apodaca, 7 July 1814, EF, bnd. 33G3, doc. 520, 3, reel 12, PKY; and Sebastián Kindelán to Juan Ruiz de Apodaca, 20 August 1814, EF, bnd. 33G3, doc. 536, 41, reel 12, PKY.

[69] Benjamin Hawkins to Kinache and Paine, 5 December 1812, *LBH*, 2:623.

[70] Governor Mitchell to Benjamin Hawkins, 8 February 1813, LOC, PKY.

[71] Ibid.; Thomas Pinckney to David B. Mitchell, 5 March 1813, CIL, 3:769, GDAH; Governor Mitchell to John Floyd, 12 April 1813, LOC, PKY.

[72] Benjamin Hawkins to Governor Mitchell, 31 May 1813, LOC, PKY.

[73] On black and Seminole relations following 1816, see the collection of Kenneth Wiggins Porter's articles in *The Negro on the American Frontier* (New York: Arno Press, 1971), in particular "Negroes and the Seminole War, 1817–1818," "Negroes and the Seminole War, 1835–1842," "Florida Slaves and Free Negroes in the Seminole War, 1835–1842," and "The Negro Abraham." Porter speaks of a "common resistance to exploitation and oppression" that united blacks and Indians (293). George Klos, in "Blacks and the Seminole Removal Debate, 1821–1835," *Florida Historical Quarterly* 68 (1989): 55–78, shows how African Americans, much as in the invasion of 1812–1814, counseled the Seminoles not to remove to Oklahoma and thus were responsible for the outbreak of the Second Seminole War. For a view of the relationship between blacks and

African descent could rarely if ever become a Seminole, as Philatouche and Ninnywageechee had done a generation earlier.

The invasion of 1812–1814 also forced the Seminoles to move further down the Florida peninsula. This retreat continued a pattern that extended throughout the nineteenth century. Successive invasions forced Seminoles deeper into swamps and farther south, until in the Third Seminole War from 1855–1858, the ocean prevented further flight. In 1794, Payne had used a metaphor to describe his country. White settlers in Florida were birds "going to build a nest in some sequestered point of land, where nobody is likely to find them," but the Seminoles were boys, ready to "dispossess them."[74] Where the fragile and tenuous colonies of their enemies in Florida had made the metaphor apt in the 1790s, the invasion of 1812–1814 established the presence of a new and foreign power in a once sequestered land.

Seminoles different from the one presented here, see Kevin Mulroy, *Freedom on the Border*, 186n38. See also Rebecca B. Bateman, "Africans and Indians: A Comparative Study of the Black Carib and Black Seminole," *Ethnohistory* 37 (1990): 1–24.

[74] The Oconee King called Payne, Tulachiche, Chackoslie, Ockisee, Tiwassie, Sihoyie, Cawasiccie, Ayamie, Mellowie, Mahopankie, and Lachchichie to Juan Nepomuceno de Quesada, 31 January 1794, EF, bnd. 115K9, reel 43, PKY.

11

The Redstick War

While the Seminoles were at war in 1812, Creek leaders had worked to crush dissent, punishing and executing warriors involved in a series of political crimes inspired by Tecumseh. Their actions not only imposed law on an unwilling people but also steered the nation away from the religious renewal sweeping through Indian peoples in the early nineteenth century.[1] The conflict between national leaders and Creek dissidents remained circumscribed within the limited compass of crime and punishment until April 1813 when victims of the national council's police force struck back at their persecutors, killing a number of the nation's warriors. The attack marked the beginning of a violent and devastating civil war in which the United States would play a pivotal role. On one side, Redstick Creeks, named for the red clubs that they wielded, challenged the power and property of Creek leaders.[2] On the other, Creek leaders and their U.S. allies defended the new order. By March 1814, when Andrew Jackson struck a decisive blow against the Redsticks at Tohopeka (Horseshoe Bend), many Creek towns had been completely destroyed and the Muskogee peoples permanently divided.

A year before the conflict, in March 1812, national leaders had assured Hawkins that their people were "now more occupied than ever in our domestic concerns, spining, weaving and farming." They looked forward to the arrival of a new blacksmith and to the delivery of spinning wheels

---

[1] Dowd, *A Spirited Resistance*. See also Reginald Horsman, *The War of 1812* (New York: Knopf, 1969); Sugden, *Tecumseh*; and Edmunds, *The Shawnee Prophet*.

[2] Redsticks described themselves after the red clubs they carried. See, for example, Josiah Francis, the Old Interpreter, and others to the Governor of Pensacola, August 1813, PC, leg. 221B, 335, reel 311, PKY. Historians H. S. Halbert and T. H. Ball interviewed Creeks in 1895 and found that they used "redstick" as a positive appellation and referred to the conflict of 1813–14 as the Redstick War. Halbert and Ball, *The Creek War of 1813 and 1814*, 134; I. G. Vore to Lyman Draper, 15 December 1881, Draper Mss. 4YY20, reel 147E, PKY.

and cotton cards. "Our people who use these things think not of war," the leaders concluded.[3] But they either dismissed or failed to recognize the extent of the division between Muskogees.[4] Thirty years of dramatic change had set the Creeks against one another. The story of the war, read for its symbols and significance, illustrates that the preceding three decades of strife over power and property caused the internecine violence of 1813–1814.

At the outbreak of the war, Creek dissidents appropriated the red stick of justice. "Redstick" was a doubly significant name for the dissidents: Not only did it signal allegiance to Tecumseh's cause, but, as the traditional Creek emblem of punishment, it represented the reappropriation of justice and power from wealthy leaders. The adoption of the name reflects the war's origins in a dispute over the power and authority of the national council. In February 1813, a party of Creeks led by Little Warrior, who had lived among the Shawnees for over a decade, headed back from the Great Lakes carrying "hairs and beads with talks from the Prophet and the northern tribes . . . to take up the hatchet against the United States."[5] Passing by the mouth of the Ohio River in early March 1813, he and his companions murdered and mutilated seven white people.[6] On arriving in Tuckabatche, Little Warrior spoke before Creek leaders in council, urging them to take up arms against Americans, but he was "severely reprimanded by the rest of the Chiefs and ordered immediately to leave the council house as a man unworthy to have a seat in it."[7]

By amassing power in their hands over the preceding years, Creek leaders had in effect already committed themselves against the growing

[3] Benjamin Hawkins to William Eustis, 30 March 1812, *LBH*, 2:604.

[4] Extracts of occurrences in the agency for Indian affairs, August 1813, LBH, 238, GDAH.

[5] Benjamin Hawkins to Upper Creek Chiefs, 25 March 1813, *LBH*, 2:631. J. C. Warren, sent by Governor Mitchell of Georgia to the Creek agency, reported that Little Warrior had been living among the Shawnees for 15 years, but he is mentioned along with other Creeks in a source dated 1801. "Report of J. C. Warren to his Excellency D. B. Mitchell," 13 May 1813, LOC, PKY; and Cussita King, Little Prince, and Little Warrior to Mad Dog and other chiefs of the Upper Towns, 26 September 1801, "Creek Letters, 1800–1819," vol. 1, GDAH. Little Warrior's visit with Tecumseh is treated in Sugden, *Tecumseh*, 349–350. For Tecumseh's use of the red club of war, see Benjamin Hawkins to the Big Warrior, Little Prince, and other chiefs, 16 June 1814, *ASPIA*, 1:845.

[6] Benjamin Hawkins to Upper Creek Chiefs, 25 March 1813, *LBH*, 2:631; Chiefs of Upper Creeks to Benjamin Hawkins, 21 April 1813, State Department Territorial Papers, Florida Series, 1777–1824, 3:26, microcopy no. 116/3, PKY; Extract of a letter from William Henry to John J. Henry, 26 June 1812, *ASPIA*, 1:814; Extracts of occurrences in the agency for Indian affairs, August 1813, LBH, 238, GDAH.

[7] Benjamin Hawkins to John Armstrong, 29 March 1813, *LBH*, 2:632.

prophetic movement, yet they had also made the movement viable. Dissident Creeks defined themselves in part by their distance from these men, their actions, and their vision. "Those people that committed the murder on the white people do not come in our old towns," several leaders observed, "but keep out on our frontiers, in the woods, that gives the old chiefs a great deal of trouble."[8] The geographic marginality of the murderers reflected their relationship to the social compact. By centering political and economic power around Coweta, Kasihta, and Tuckabatche, prominent national leaders such as Tustanagee Thlucco and William McIntosh had created "frontiers" where Muskogees who lived under their own authority became renegades from the new nation. In the past, given the conditional and negotiable nature of the white path, Creeks would have tolerated serious political differences, but now Creek leaders undertook to compel conformity.

In April 1813, after a contentious debate, Upper Creek leaders organized a force of warriors to execute Little Warrior and his companions. Fifty to 100 Lower Creeks under William McIntosh assisted them.[9] Little Warrior had successfully recruited four new supporters, but the larger force surrounded part of his band at Hickory Ground. The Creek dissidents barricaded themselves inside a house, gave the "war whoop," and began a dance, defending themselves by firing through holes they knocked in the chinking of the cabin. When the besieged men ran out of ammunition, the warriors of the nation set fire to the house. One dissident was burned alive, and two wounded men crawled to the door and pleaded for help. They were dragged twenty yards away and dispatched with tomahawks. The remaining two broke for the river, where one was overtaken and executed. When the other escaped, Creek leaders instead executed his aunt.[10] The warriors of the nation also murdered three other dissidents in Hoithlewaule. "Every one, to the very last, called on the Shawanee General Tecumseh," reported Nimrod Doyle, an assistant

[8] Chiefs of Upper Creeks to Benjamin Hawkins, 21 April 1813, State Department Territorial Papers, Florida Series, 1777–1824, 3:26, microcopy no. 116/3, PKY.

[9] Statement of John Lawson and Mr. McDuffie relative to the hostile conduct of the Creek Indians, 15 April 1813, CIL, 3:778–9, GDAH; Chiefs of Upper Creeks to Benjamin Hawkins, 21 April 1813, State Department Territorial Papers, Florida Series, 1777–1824, 3:26, microcopy no. 116/3, PKY.

[10] Chiefs of Upper Creeks to Benjamin Hawkins, 21 April 1813, State Department Territorial Papers, Florida Series, 1777–1824, 3:26, microcopy no. 116/3, PKY; Benjamin Hawkins to David B. Mitchell, 26 April 1813, LBH, 2:633; Nimrod Doyle to Benjamin Hawkins, 3 May 1813, ASPIA, 1:843–844; Upper Creeks to Benjamin Hawkins, 26 April 1813, ASPIA, 1:841; I. G. Vore to Lyman Draper, 15 December 1881, Draper Mss. 4YY20, reel 147E, PKY.

to Benjamin Hawkins.[11] Only Little Warrior remained alive, and he was soon flushed out of a swamp near the Coosa River and murdered.[12]

Emboldened by Tecumseh's pan-Indian movement, the "friends" of the "mischiefdoers" took revenge on the chiefs "active in having them punished," and here the Creek red stick of justice and Tecumseh's weapon of war began to converge.[13] Dissidents first burned down the house of Captain Isaacs and killed at least two of his allies, appropriate targets because Isaacs had directed the murder of Little Warrior. Their actions placed them in league with Tecumseh. Hawkins explained that those Creeks who welcomed the pan-Indian leader "have been strengthened by the families of those executed last year and in the present year for murder."[14] Yahoola Chapco, for example, whose son was executed by the national council, became a leading Creek prophet.[15] Similarly, near the fork of the Coosa and Tallapoosa, where 250 warriors were reportedly "armed in favor of the murderers," many participated in a war dance, carrying red sticks in support of Tecumseh.[16] Around the same time, Creek prophets scalped a messenger from the national council for his participation in the execution of the Ohio River murderers.[17] Local issues – the consolidation of power in the hands of the national leaders – had merged with pan-Indian prophetism.

The red stick of justice was not the only icon of the enemy that Creek prophets appropriated for their own symbolic and practical purposes. So too they appropriated the written word.[18] At the outbreak of the war, a

[11] Nimrod Doyell to Benjamin Hawkins, 3 May 1813, *ASPIA*, 1:843–844.

[12] Big Warrior and Alexander Cornells to Benjamin Hawkins, 26 April 1813, *ASPIA*, 1:843.

[13] "Report of J. C. Warren to his Excellency D. B. Mitchell," 13 May 1813, LOC, PKY. Even before the executions, a party had formed to oppose the policy of punishing the guilty. Statement of John Lawson and Mr. McDuffie relative to the hostile conduct of the Creek Indians, 15 April 1813, CIL, 3:778–779, GDAH.

[14] Big Warrior and Alexander Cornells to Benjamin Hawkins, 26 April 1813, *ASPIA*, 1:843; Benjamin Hawkins to David Mitchell, 21 June 1813, LBH, 202, GDAH; Benjamin Hawkins to John Armstrong, 22 June 1813, *LBH*, 2:641. Hawkins, in his letters to Mitchell and Armstrong, reported that the Redsticks had killed Isaacs, his nephew, and three others. Alexander Cornels, however, reported that the Redsticks had only killed two of Isaacs's allies. Cornels's report is clearly the more accurate one, for Captain Isaacs appears later on in several other documents and was among the signers of the Treaty of Fort Jackson in 1814. "Report of Alexander Cornells to Benjamin Hawkins," 22 June 1813, LOC, PKY; and Treaty at Fort Jackson, *ASPIA*, 1:826–827.

[15] Benjamin Hawkins to the chiefs of the Creek nation, June 1812, LBH, 156, GDAH; "Report of Alexander Cornells to Benjamin Hawkins," 22 June 1813, LOC, PKY.

[16] Statement of John Lawson and Mr. McDuffie relative to the hostile conduct of the Creek Indians, 15 April 1813, CIL, 3:778–779, GDAH; Juan Nepomuceno de Quesada to Luis de las Casas, 26 April 1793, EF, bnd. 24, 84, reel 9, PKY.

[17] "Report of Alexander Cornells to Benjamin Hawkins," 22 June 1813, LOC, PKY.

[18] Linguist Walter Ong writes, "There is hardly an oral culture or a predominately oral culture left in the world today that is not somehow aware of the vast complex of powers forever inaccessi-

leading Redstick prophet named Hillis Hadjo (Josiah Francis) received an order from the Giver and Taker of Breath to meet him every day at "a certain place." According to a resident of the Deep South who relied on notes, personal memory, and oral sources to recall the story fifteen years after the event, the Giver and Taker of Breath intended to teach Hillis Hadjo "the different languages that he would want to use, and writing so as he would be able to transact his own and the national council affairs without applying for such assistance from another person."[19]

By using writing, Hillis Hadjo did not become his enemy. Rather, the very method by which he acquired the technology, the oral communication of a dream, distanced him from believers in the written word. National leaders disparaged the prophetic inspiration of their enemies. "Now we want to see and hear what you say you have seen and heard," they told the prophets. "Let us have the same proof you have." Redsticks killed and scalped the bearer of the request.[20] In itself, the demand for rational evidence of miracles precluded any reconciliation between Creek leaders and Redsticks.[21] In 1811, Alexander Cornels had affirmed that Creeks knew the word of God without a book. They "dream much of God," he explained, "therefore they know it." But two years later, during the Redstick War, he condemned prophetic revelations as "fooleries," and other Creek leaders dismissed them as "a sort of madness, and amusement for idle people."[22]

---

ble without literacy," listing such "powers" as science, history, and philosophy. Ong, *Orality and Literacy*, 15. For the present-day example of the Huaorani in the Ecuadorian Amazon, see Kane, *Savages*, 137–138.

[19] "A historical narration of the genealogy, traditions, and downfall of the Ispocoga or Creek tribe of Indians," PKY. This story may be apocryphal, or more likely embellished. In any case, it reveals a truth about the relationship between Creeks and writing in the early nineteenth century. On George Stiggins's method of composition, see J. N. Stiggins to Lyman Draper, 5 February 1874, Draper Mss. 1V65, reel 146I, PKY.

[20] "Report of Alexander Cornells to Benjamin Hawkins," 22 June 1813, LOC, PKY.

[21] Jean and John Comaroff, "Conversion and Conversation: Narrative, Form, and Consciousness," in *Of Revelation and Revolution: Christianity, Colonialism, and Consciousness in South Africa* (Chicago: University of Chicago, 1991), 1:208–212.

[22] Mauelshagen and Davis, *Partners in the Lord's Work*, 53; "Report of Alexander Cornells to Benjamin Hawkins," 22 June 1813, LOC, PKY. Jack Goody writes about the creation of literate religions:

> Once writing was introduced the voice of God was supplemental to His hand; scriptural authority is the authority of the written (scriptural) word, not the oral one. Written religion implies stratification. The written word belongs to the priest, the learned man, and enshrined in ritualistic religion; the oral is the sphere of the prophet, of eastern religion, messianic cults, of innovation.

> Goody, *The Interface between the Written and the Oral*, 161.

After learning "the branches of writing and languages far perfect enough to converse, write, and do his own business," Hillis Hadjo reportedly wrote a "lengthy letter" in Spanish to the commandant of Pensacola, requesting arms and munitions for his struggle against the Americans. Hillis Hadjo, who not only did not know how to write, but also did not know a word of Spanish, then gave "his envoys a circumstantial and full detail of the contents of his letter, by reading and interpreting the substance of it to them in a precise manner." But when the Pensacola commandant received the document, he asked the messengers "why such a paper of marks was sent him."[23] The messengers later revealed that it "looked more like a paper full of crooked marks than writing." (After losing the war, Hillis Hadjo would send his son to England to learn to read and write "that in the future they may not be deceived.")[24] By appropriating the red stick of justice and the technology of writing, dissidents revealed a major theme of the war: power.

Both as a symbol and as a literal manifestation of hostility, Redstick violence further elucidates the causes of the conflict. Redsticks destroyed forges, spinning wheels, and cattle, leading their enemies to describe the two warring sides in terms of "civilization" and "tradition." "The Prophets are enemies to the plan of civilization and advocates for the wild Indian mode of living," claimed Alexander Cornels, the wealthy mestizo on the payroll of the U.S. government.[25] But like "American" and "communist" in the 1950s, Cornels's terms exalted one side and disparaged the other without actually describing the difference between them.[26] By requesting and expecting assistance from Spain and Britain, Redsticks illustrated that they did not envision a return to a mythic "wild Indian mode of living," a phrase meaningful only to those who deemed themselves "civilized."[27] Rather, the hostility evident in their violence

[23] "A historical narration of the genealogy, traditions, and downfall of the Ispocoga or Creek tribe of Indians," PKY.

[24] Edward Nichols to J. P. Morier, 25 September 1815, LOC, PRO, WO 1/143, PKY. Hillis Hadjo's response to writing is not unique. Edmund Carpenter, an anthropologist interested in the effect that new media of communication exert on "primitive" peoples, documents similar actions among inhabitants of Papua New Guinea. "In remote areas," he writes, "one encounters men who, after only the most fleeting exposure to writing, develop their own systems. They proudly exhibit such efforts, with others crowding around, their faces eager. Strange notes are sent to patrol officers & missionaries or left for them in villages." Many of the notes contain "nonrepeated markings, translatable only by their authors." Edmund Carpenter, *Oh, What a Blow That Phantom Gave Me!* (New York: Holt, Rinehart and Winston, 1972), 73–74.

[25] "Report of Alexander Cornells to Benjamin Hawkins," 22 June 1813, LOC, PKY.

[26] Wright, *Creeks and Seminoles*, 156–157.

[27] Archaeological evidence does reveal, however, that Redsticks stopped using many common goods,

suggests that they intended to destroy the concentration of power in the national council and the property that supported it. Henry Toulmin, U.S. judge for the Tombigbee district of the Mississippi Territory, observed that a "low spirit of envy and jealousy of the growing wealth and prosperity" of some Creeks led the Redsticks to attack "those chiefs who so far outstripped them in solid advantages."[28] Toulmin's perceptions were colored by European American conceptions of society and economy, yet a Creek Indian reporting to Benjamin Hawkins made a similar comment, explaining that on one side "those who were industrious attended to spining weaving had stock and plenty of food"; on the other were "a great many idlers" who "had nothing" and were "finding fault and ready for mischief."[29]

As these observations suggest, Redstick attacks focused on Creek leaders and their property.[30] After executing Captain Isaacs's allies, the Redsticks "gave out they would destroy Tuckabatche and Coweta with every person in them, then kill Mr. Cornells the interpreter, Tustunugee Thlucco, Col. Hawkins, and all the old chiefs who had taken his talks."[31] They intended to destroy Cornels's property as well. Significantly, Tuckabatche and Coweta were the seats of the national council, and Cornels, Hawkins, and Tustanagee Thlucco, the speaker of the nation, had great influence in the Creek government. After these murders, Cornels reported, the Redsticks "would be ready for white people."[32] When

---

such as silver and brass ornaments and glass beads, during the war. Roy S. Dickens, Jr., "Archaeological Investigations at Horseshoe Bend National Military Park, Alabama," *Alabama Archaeological Society, Special Publication* 3 (1979); and Charles H. Fairbanks, "Excavations at Horseshoe Bend, Alabama," *The Florida Anthropologist* 15 (1962): 41–56.

[28] Henry Toulmin to Thomas B. Robertson, 23 July 1813, LOC, State Department, Miscellaneous, 61:2 M, PKY.

[29] Extracts of occurrences in the agency for Indian affairs, August 1813, LBH, 238, GDAH.

[30] Ethnohistorian Ross Hassig describes the hostility toward the elite as a product of the conflict between established chiefs and young, ambitious warriors. But Gregory Waselkov and Brian Wood suggest that "there may be a correlation between Red Stick converts and those individuals who received few economic and political benefits because they lacked social ties to micos supported by the U.S." Ross Hassig, "Internal Conflict in the Creek War of 1813–1814," 265; and Gregory A. Waselkov and Brian M. Wood, "The Creek War of 1813–1814: Effects on Creek Society and Settlement Pattern," *Journal of Alabama Archaeology* 32 (1986): 7.

[31] "Report of Alexander Cornells to Benjamin Hawkins," 22 June 1813, LOC, PKY.

[32] Ibid. Cornels later repeated:

> It appears they are first to put to death every chief and warrior who aided to execute the murderers, then the old chiefs, friends to peace who have taken the talks of Col. Hawkins from whom the orders for punishing the murderers came, then Mr Cornells because he was the interpreter, and if they could at the same time to put Col Hawkins to death. But being killed all the others if he escaped them it would be of no consequence as then none would be left alive to receive and communicate his talks and the nation could fix their affairs their own way. After this they would be ready for the white people, who could do them no injury if they came among them.

Redsticks moved toward Tuckabatche, Cornels fled to Hawkins's residence and Creek leaders and their supporters assembled to defend themselves.[33]

By July 1813, Tustanagee Thlucco and 300 of his supporters lay under siege in Tuckabatche. Redsticks had converted nearly every Upper Creek town to their cause. They now numbered about 2,500 warriors (out of a total of perhaps 3,000 among the Upper Creeks), plus women and children. In all, of thirty-four towns, fewer than six supported Tustanagee Thlucco and his party.[34] Most Lower Creeks, many of whom lay ill from an epidemic, remained neutral, but eventually warriors from Kasihta and Coweta came to the aid of the besieged, dispersing the Redsticks and escorting the residents to Coweta.[35] Redsticks burned down Tuckabatche after the evacuation.[36]

Wealthy and powerful Creeks came under attack in towns outside of Tuckabatche as well. In Autossee, inhabitants who were "converted" to the Redstick party drove off their chiefs.[37] In Okfuskee, residents "killed five Chiefs and destroyed almost all the cattle in town." And in Kialeegee, Redsticks killed several wealthy inhabitants along with their cattle, swine, and fowl.[38] Redsticks also burned down the houses of Alexander Cornels and drove off or slaughtered his livestock.[39] The assault on these chiefs, considering the overwhelming support in Upper Creek towns for the Redstick movement, illustrates that a great schism existed between leaders and their people. In effect, leaders had ceased to lead, despite their assertions otherwise.

[33] "Report of Alexander Cornells to Benjamin Hawkins," 22 June 1813, LOC, PKY; Halbert and Ball, *The Creek War*, 88–90.
[34] Affidavit of James Moore, 13 July 1813, CIL, 3:785, GDAH; Big Warrior, Little Prince, and Tustunugee Opoy to Robert Walton, 24 July 1813, CIL, 3:786–787, GDAH; Tustanagee Thlucco to Benjamin Hawkins, 26 July 1813, CIL, 3:790–792, GDAH; Big Warrior and Tustanagee Hopoy to Benjamin Hawkins, 4 August 1813, CIL, 3:806–807, GDAH; Benjamin Hawkins to John Armstrong, 13 September 1813, *LBH*, 2:660; Robert Grierson to Benjamin Hawkins, 23 September 1813, LBH, 254, GDAH; Benjamin Hawkins to David B. Mitchell, 9 August 1813, *LBH*, 2:653.
[35] Benjamin Hawkins to John Armstrong, 6 July 1813, *LBH*, 2:643; James Durouzeaux to Benjamin Hawkins, 7 July 1813, LBH, 211, GDAH; Benjamin Hawkins to David B. Mitchell, 7 July 1813, *LBH*, 2:644; Cussita Micco to Benjamin Hawkins, 10 July 1813, LBH, 214, GDAH; Benjamin Hawkins to David B. Mitchell, 11 July 1813, *LBH*, 2:645; Benjamin Hawkins to Governor Mitchell, 20 July 1813, LBH, 219, GDAH; Benjamin Hawkins to David B. Mitchell, 22 July 1813, *LBH*, 2:648; Big Warrior, Little Prince, and Tustunugee Opoy to Robert Walton, 24 July 1813, CIL, 3:786–787, GDAH; Big Warrior and Tustanagee Hopoy to Benjamin Hawkins, 4 August 1813, CIL, 3:806–807, GDAH; Benjamin Hawkins to David B. Mitchell, 9 August 1813, *LBH*, 2:653.
[36] Tustanagee Thlucco to Benjamin Hawkins, 26 July 1813, CIL, 3:790–792, GDAH.
[37] Benjamin Hawkins to John Armstrong, 28 June 1813, *LBH*, 2:643.
[38] Ibid., 651; Tustanagee Thlucco to Benjamin Hawkins, 26 July 1813, CIL, 3:790–792, GDAH.
[39] Benjamin Hawkins to John Armstrong, 20 July 1813, *LBH*, 2:647.

Though Redsticks attacked all forms of wealth, they singled out live-stock, slaughtering swine, fowl, and especially cattle.[40] At the grazing range of Tuckabatche, the stench of dead cattle and hogs reportedly carried for fifteen miles.[41] One infantry officer later testified that "some time before the war ended, not a track of a cow or hog was to be seen in the Creek country; and I marched through the greater part of it."[42] Cattle, in particular, symbolized the innovations of the new order. Men accumulated great numbers of these animals, and unlike hogs, which in the Deep South were half-feral and half-domesticated, cattle had dis-tinct owners.[43]

For Redsticks, cowtails apparently served the same function as human scalps, encouraging and rallying men in battle.[44] Many warriors, for example, met the enemy with these appendages tied to their arms.[45] At one battle, a prophet appeared waving a staff with a cowtail attached, and at another, a "prophet was seen in the midst of the Creek bowmen, frantically rushing to and fro, waving a red-dyed cow's tail in each hand and uttering most appalling yells."[46] These descriptions suggest that Creeks perceived cattle as semiautonomous beings who had invaded and destroyed their hunting grounds, New World versions of Sir Thomas More's sheep that "turned into man-eaters" by prompting the conver-

---

[40] For examples, see Talesco to Benjamin Hawkins, 5 July 1813, LBH, 209, GDAH; Benjamin Hawkins to John Armstrong, 20 July 1813, LBH, 2:647; Benjamin Hawkins to John Armstrong, 28 July 1813, LBH, 2:651; Benjamin Hawkins to John Armstrong, 28 July 1813, LBH, 2:651; Big Warrior and Tustanagee Hopoy to Benjamin Hawkins, 4 August 1813, CIL, 3:806–807, GDAH; Extracts of occurrences in the agency for Indian affairs, August 1813, LBH, 238, GDAH; Benjamin Hawkins to Philip Cook, 3 October 1813, LBH, 2:669; Nimrod Doyell to Benjamin Hawkins, 20 November 1813, LBH, 271, GDAH. Whites and mestizos living along the Tombigbee and lower Alabama rivers put in claims after the war for the loss of almost 8,000 cattle and hogs. Waselkov and Wood, "The Creek War of 1813–1814: Effects on Creek Society and Settlement Pattern," 6.

[41] Benjamin Hawkins to John Armstrong, 28 July 1813, LBH, 2:651.

[42] USS.H.doc. 200 (20–1) 173:12. Joel Martin notes that the destruction of livestock was an act of renunciation and purification from colonialism. Martin, Sacred Revolt, 142–143.

[43] Benjamin Hawkins, "A Sketch of the present state of the objects under the charge of the principal agent for Indian affairs south of the Ohio," March 1801, LBH, 1:352; Timothy Silver, A New Face on the Countryside: Indians, Colonists, and Slaves in South Atlantic Forests, 1500–1800 (Cambridge: Cambridge University, 1990), 174–175; Bonner, A History of Georgia Agriculture, 30, 145–147. In relation to New England, see Cronon, Changes in the Land, 135–137.

[44] Like the Choctaws, who in their ball play in the early nineteenth century wore horsetails instead of the tails of wild animals, Creeks may have used cowtails in place of other less common animal tails associated with masculine power. James Taylor Carson, "Horses and the Economy and Culture of the Choctaw Indians, 1690–1840," 504 and 507. On Creeks and scalping, see Bartram, "Observations," 154; Swan, "Position and State of Manners and Arts," 264–266, 280; Adair, Adair's History, 415–416.

[45] Halbert and Ball, The Creek War, 187.

[46] Ibid., 189 and 251.

sion of English farmland into pasture in the sixteenth century.[47] More-over, Redsticks may have held cattle partially responsible for disruptive social changes such as the dispersal of Creek towns and accumulation of wealth. Their attribution of agency to livestock would not have been without precedent in the Southeast. In 1767, Choctaws had slaughtered cattle they deemed responsible for an unusual illness.[48]

Like livestock, salt was a symbol as well as defining material of the new order, and Redsticks purged themselves of this substance during the war.[49] Before the expansion of cattle raising in the Deep South, Creeks had obtained the required dietary sodium chloride through trade, at salt springs, and in the meat they consumed.[50] Cattle need large amounts of salt added to their feed, however, and consequently, by 1791, the demand for the mineral among some Creeks had risen to such a level that Alexander McGillivray requested the supply be supplemented by imports from the Bahamas.[51] Creeks also began using salt to preserve domestic meats, a process less labor-intensive than smoking.[52] The use of salt by

[47] More's comment referred to the eviction of tenants and the enclosure of lands for pasture in sixteenth-century England. Thomas More, *Utopia*, trans. Paul Turner (1516; reprint, New York: Penguin, 1965), 46. His observation is more nearly literal in North America after the introduction of livestock following contact. Swine competed with Creek women for acorns, and cattle ate cane and grasses, destroying the habitats of bear and deer. California probably witnessed the most devastating competition in North America between livestock and humans. See Sherburne F. Cook, *The Conflict between the California Indian and White Civilization* (originally published in *Ibero-Americana*, 1940–1943; reprint, Berkeley: University of California, 1976).

[48] Adair, *Adair's History*, 138–139. In Metacom's War in New England in 1675, Indians "began their hostilities with plundering and destroying cattle," a contemporary observed. According to historian Virginia DeJohn Anderson, "Because livestock had come to symbolize the relentless advance of English settlement, the animals were special targets of native enmity during the war." She notes too that the violence reserved for cattle resembled "the tortures more often inflicted on human victims and perhaps similarly served a ritual purpose." Virginia DeJohn Anderson, "King Philip's Herds," 622–623.

[49] Redsticks treated alcohol in a similar fashion. When 280 Redsticks traveled to Pensacola in 1813 to ask for munitions, John Innerarity of Forbes and Company commented, "It is remarkable that of the whole band of Indians not a single one would taste a drop of liquor, or anything else but water." Compare Nimrod Doyle's plea to Benjamin Hawkins, made from Coweta, the stronghold of Redstick enemies: "Don't let anymore rum come here for it is a bad thing, there was a great drunk here the other day and they kicked up hell for a while." Extract of a letter from John Innerarity to James Innerarity, 27 July 1813, CIL, 3:795–802, GDAH; and N. Doyle to Benjamin Hawkins, 4 October 1813, CIL, 3:826–827, GDAH.

[50] Ian W. Brown, *Salt and the Eastern North American Indian: An Archaeological Study, Lower Mississippi Survey*, Bulletin no. 6 (Peabody Museum, Harvard University, 1980), 4, 8–10; Swanton, *Indians of the Southeastern United States*, 300–304, and map 13 facing 254; M. Thomas Hatley, "The Three Lives of Keowee," 231.

[51] Alexander McGillivray to Estevan Miró, 26 February 1791, PC, leg. 204, 733, reel 283, PKY. McGillivray was surely motivated in part by the consideration that his friend and business partner Robert Panton was part owner of the salt works on New Providence Island. Pope, *A tour through the southern and western territories*, 44–45.

[52] Journal of Benjamin Hawkins, 2 December 1796, *Letters of Benjamin Hawkins, 1796–1806*, 21–22; Benjamin Hawkins to Henry Dearborn, 17 July 1802, LBH, 2:451.

Americans proved equally troublesome. In 1808, Creek hunters had found large numbers of cattle on their hunting grounds along with salt logs where settlers salted their livestock.[53]

The symbolic and real association between salt and the new order perhaps explains the behavior of a Redstick prophet upon touching an enemy or someone who ate salted meat: He "instantly commenced trembling and the defilement subsided by gradual jerking and evoaking of all his muscles, not excepting his face, which jerking of his muscles concluded in a tremble of all his flesh."[54] Redsticks tried to purify themselves of sodium chloride, just as they usually did during the *Poskita*, the annual ceremony of renewal.[55] When warriors destroyed the house of Redstick leader Peter McQueen, for example, they found "a good deal of salt."[56] By collecting and removing it, they had cleansed themselves.

In July 1813, after three months of hostilities between Creeks, a band of Redstick warriors on their way to Pensacola for supplies sacked the residences of three mestizo settlers. When the warriors returned from the Spanish town, militia from the mestizo and white settlements along the Alabama and Tombigbee rivers attacked them at Burnt Corn Creek (where it now crosses the boundary between Escambia and Conecuh counties). The attack precipitated a retaliatory strike by Redsticks against Fort Mims, a redoubt sheltering local residents on the eastern bank of the Alabama River just north of its confluence with the Tombigbee. In response, U.S. troops entered into the war. The encounters on the road to Pensacola, at Burnt Corn Creek, and at Fort Mims reveal a meaningful pattern: Redsticks targeted the legacy of Alexander McGillivray, mestizos who supported the new order.

This series of encounters began in early July 1813 when Redstick leader Peter McQueen set out for Pensacola with 280 warriors to request arms from the Spanish commandant. They camped briefly at Burnt Corn Spring, the head of a path to Pensacola about ten miles east of present-day Monroeville, Alabama. There they sacked the house of mestizo James Cornels and took his wife prisoner. A smaller group pro-

---

[53] Tuskegee Tustanagee to Benjamin Hawkins, 21 December 1808, LBH, 121, GDAH.
[54] "A historical narration of the genealogy, traditions, and downfall of the Ispocoga or Creek tribe of Indians," PKY.
[55] Martin, *Sacred Revolt*, 142–143; Waselkov and Wood, "The Creek War of 1813–1814," 5.
[56] Extracts of occurrences in the agency for Indian affairs, August 1813, LBH, 238, GDAH; Benjamin Hawkins to John Armstrong, 23 August 1813, *LBH*, 2:658; Benjamin Hawkins to David B. Mitchell, 28 August 1813, *LBH*, 2:659.

ceeded to Little River – where Alexander McGillivray had established one of his plantations in the 1780s – and burned down the "river plantation" of mestizo Samuel Moniac. They also destroyed the house of one Leonard McGee.[57] Moniac himself explained the nature of Redstick hostility: The "halfbreeds" were not "objects of their animosity originally, but merely on account of their attachment to the white people."[58]

Moniac and Cornels were neither entirely Creek nor entirely American. Both held far more property than other Muskogees. In the Redstick attack, for example, Moniac lost 700 cattle, 200 hogs, 48 goats and sheep, valued at $5,060, plus a cotton gin, 2,000 pounds of cotton, 36 slaves, and several houses.[59] To escape, he had to promise to "sell [his] property and buy ammunition, and join them," but he later served in two campaigns against the Redsticks.[60] Like Moniac, James Cornels also lost his "cattle, hogs, horses, sheep and goats."[61] His plantation was a source of resentment, just as his father Joseph's plantation, next to Alexander McGillivray's, had rankled Creeks in 1783.[62] Both Moniac and the Cornels family had accumulated wealth while living among the Creeks, and then had retired to the mestizo and white community along

---

[57] Meek, *Romantic Passages*, 244–247; "A historical narration of the genealogy, traditions, and downfall of the Ispocoga or Creek tribe of Indians," PKY; Halbert and Ball, *The Creek War*, 126; Henry Toulmin to Thomas B. Robertson, 23 July 1813, LOC, State Department, Miscellaneous, 61:2 M; Deposition of Samuel Moniac, in Halbert and Ball, *The Creek War*, 91–93; William and John Pierce to Harry Toulmin, 18 July 1813, in Lackey, ed., *Frontier Claims in the Lower South*, 9–11; William and John Pierce to Harry Toulmin, 18 July 1813, in Lackey, *Frontier Claims in the Lower South*, 9–11; Henry Toulmin to Thomas B. Robertson, 23 July 1813, LOC, State Department, Miscellaneous, 61:2 M, PKY. The location of Moniac's plantation can be pinpointed with the assistance of Howell Tatum's survey of the Alabama River, undertaken on Andrew Jackson's orders in 1814. John Spencer Bassett, "Major Howell Tatum's Journal, while acting Topographical Engineer (1814) to General Jackson, Commanding the Seventh Military District," *Smith College Studies in History* (1921–22): 40.

[58] Henry Toulmin to Thomas B. Robertson, 23 July 1813, LOC, State Department, Miscellaneous, 61:2 M, PKY.

[59] Benjamin Hawkins, "A sketch of the Creek Country in the years 1798 and 1799," *LBH*, 1:297–298; Henry Toulmin to Thomas B. Robertson, 23 July 1813, LOC, State Department, Miscellaneous, 61:2 M; Benjamin Hawkins to John Armstrong, 28 July 1813, *LBH*, 2:651; Deposition of Samuel Moniac, in Halbert and Ball, *The Creek War*, 91–93. Moniac was later reimbursed $12,597.25 by the U.S. government for his losses. A complete list of Moniac's claim can be found in *USS*.H.doc. 200 (20–1) 173:8–10.

[60] Deposition of Samuel Moniac, in Halbert and Ball, *The Creek War*, 91–93. Regarding his military service, see *USS*.H.doc. 200 (20–1) 173:7.

[61] Benjamin Hawkins to John Armstrong, 20 July 1813, *LBH*, 2:647.

[62] Memorial of the King's proposals and complaints, 1783, "Indian Treaties: Cessions of Land in Georgia, 1705–1837," 117, GDAH. Joseph Cornel died in 1795. Enrique White to Barón de Carondelet, 1 June 1795, PC, leg. 31, 1288, reel 418, PKY; Journal of Benjamin Hawkins, 15 December 1796, *Letters of Benjamin Hawkins, 1796–1806*, 36–37; Woodward, *Woodward's Reminiscences*, 111.

the Alabama River and its feeders.[63] Leonard McGee, too, apparently had accumulated wealth as a trader and then moved to these river-bottom settlements.[64]

James Cornels and Samuel Moniac also were implicated in translating the talks of "white people." Hawkins had hired James to serve as interpreter at the Creek factory in 1799, James's father Joseph had served as a linguist for McGillivray, and James's cousin, Alexander Cornels, worked as an agent for Hawkins. Samuel Moniac, too, had interpreted for McGillivray.[65] As the Redsticks explained, should Hawkins escape after they had killed the interpreters, "it would be of no consequence as then none would be left alive to receive and communicate his talks and the nation could fix their affairs their own way."[66]

Ties of marriage further bound the families of Cornels and Moniac to McGillivray's legacy. One of James Cornels's sisters had married McGillivray, and another had married a son of Tustanagee Thlucco, the current speaker of the national council. James's cousin Alexander had married a woman who was at once the half-sister of Tustanagee Thlucco's son and the daughter of Efau Hadjo, McGillivray's main ally.[67] Samuel Moniac had married McGillivray's niece.[68] The Redstick attack

[63] Juan Nepomuceno de Quesada to Luis de las Casas, 26 April 1793, EF, bnd. 24, 84, reel 9, PKY. For a brief description of settlers on the Mobile, Tensaw, and Little River, see T. H. Ball, *A Glance into the Great South-East or, Clarke County, Alabama, and its Surroundings from 1540 to 1877* (Grove Hill, Alabama: 1882), 55 and 61.

[64] In 1799, McGee was listed as a witness to the Talk by Chiefs of Creek Nation to Benjamin Hawkins, 25 November 1799, PC, leg. 216B, 406, reel 301, PKY. Joel Martin dubs the mestizo Indians living along the Tombigbee and Alabama rivers "river bottom métis." Martin, *Sacred Revolt*, 104.

[65] Regarding Moniac, see Henri, *The Southern Indians and Benjamin Hawkins*, 354n37. Regarding Joseph Cornels and Samuel Moniac, see Copy of a letter from Alexander McGillivray to John Stuart, 25 September 1777, Sir Guy Carleton Papers, reel 58A-4, doc. 677, PKY; Alexander McGillivray to [Arturo O'Neill?], 21 February 1786, PC, leg. 199, 770, reel 383, PKY; Alexander McGillivray to Estevan Miró, 26 January 1787, PC, leg. 200, 939, reel 277, PKY; Alexander McGillivray to Estevan Miró, 26 January 1787, PC, leg. 200, 939, reel 277, PKY; Extract from the *Pennsylvania Packet and Daily Advertiser*, 18 August 1791, no. 147, *McGillivray of the Creeks*; Alexander McGillivray to Henry White, 6 May 1792, PC, leg. 205, 696, reel 283A, PKY. Juan Nepomuceno de Quesada to Luis de las Casas, 26 April 1793, EF, bnd. 24, 84, reel 9, PKY; and Woodward, *Woodward's Reminiscences*, 111–112.

[66] "Report of Alexander Cornells to Benjamin Hawkins," 22 June 1813, LOC, PKY.

[67] William Panton to Lachlan McGillivray, 10 April 1794, no. 214, in Caughey, *McGillivray of the Creeks*; Benjamin Hawkins, "Journal of Occurrences in the Creek Agency from January to the Conclusion of the Conference and Treaty at Fort Wilkinson by the Agent for Indian Affairs," *LBH*, 2:410; Halbert and Ball, *The Creek War*, 165–166; "Tukabachi Chiefs," *Arrow Points* 14 (1930): 33; Woodward, *Woodward's Reminiscences*, 111–112. Woodward in particular reveals how elite mestizo and Creek families intermarried. Woodward, *Woodward's Reminiscences*, 109–117.

[68] Cashin, *Lachlan McGillivray*, 77; Woodward, *Woodward's Reminiscences*, 89. The son of Samuel Moniac and Betsy was the first Indian to graduate at West Point. Tellingly, he fought in the

on the way to Pensacola, then, struck at significant participants in the new order, people who occupied a position between Creek and American lifeways.

After arriving in Pensacola, Redsticks requested arms, munitions, and other provisions from the Spanish government. The resulting report of the Spanish commandant, Mateo González Manrique, makes clear what English-language sources do not: The Redsticks intended to attack Americans as well as their Creek opponents. Redstick leader Peter McQueen told the Spanish governor that the continual incursions of Americans upon their lands had forced them to declare war, and that Spain had to support either the Indians or the United States. After receiving scanty gifts, angry Redsticks violently searched through houses, looking for one or two Americans who had taken refuge in the Spanish settlement.[69]

When McQueen's party left Pensacola, a party of mestizo and white militia from the Tensaw and Tombigbee settlements cut them off. A three-hour battle at Burnt Corn Creek ensued, during which the Redsticks lost most of their supplies.[70] The militia had a history of beating innocent Indians and provoking hostilities, but to emphasize this aspect of the conflict is to ignore internal Creek dynamics.[71] When Tustanagee Thlucco recounted his version of events, for example, he described a fight between Redsticks and mestizos, not Creeks and Americans.[72] The composition of the militia bears out Tustanagee Thlucco's narrative. In addition to Cornels, the militia reportedly included other mestizos, including David Taitt and Dixon Bailey, who served as one of the officers.[73]

Second Seminole War for the United States. Benjamin W. Griffith, "Lt. David Moniac, Creek Indian: First Minority Graduate of West Point," *Alabama Historical Quarterly* 43 (1981): 99–110.

[69] Mateo González Manrique to Juan Ruiz de Apodaca, 23 July 1813, PC, leg. 1794, 1417, reel 112, PKY. English-language sources imply as well that the Creeks intended to attack American settlers, but some historians have discounted these as biased. See, for example, Henry Toulmin to Thomas B. Robertson, 23 July 1813, LOC, State Department, Miscellaneous, 61:2 M, PKY; and Ferdinand L. Claiborne to David B. Mitchell, 14 August 1813, CIL, 3:810–813, GDAH. For another firsthand account of the Redstick visit to Pensacola, see Extract of a letter from John Innerarity to James Innerarity, 27 July 1813, CIL, 3:795–802, GDAH. John Innerarity reported that the Redsticks told him, "They were all now like one fire, that they were determined to make the land clear of the Americans or to lose their lives."

[70] Meek, *Romantic Passages*, 244–247; "A historical narration of the genealogy, traditions, and downfall of the Ispocoga or Creek tribe of Indians," PKY.

[71] Leland L. Lengel, "The Road to Fort Mims: Judge Harry Toulmin's Observation on the Creek War, 1811–1813," *The Alabama Review* 29 (1976): 22.

[72] Big Warrior to Benjamin Hawkins, 4 August 1813, CIL, 3:808, GDAH.

[73] Meek, *Romantic Passages*, 244–247; Stiggins, "A historical narration of the genealogy, traditions, and downfall of the Ispocoga or Creek tribe of Indians," PKY; Halbert and Ball, *The Creek War*, 130.

The battle at Burnt Corn Creek, which left between two and six Redsticks dead, including an African American, precipitated another clash between Redsticks and mestizo and white settlers.[74] In response to the loss, relatives of the slain Redsticks redirected warriors from Coweta to the Tombigbee and Tensaw settlements, where many of the mestizos involved in the attack lived.[75] Residents along the Alabama River had constructed a series of forts over the summer and fall of 1813,[76] and one of them, Fort Mims, caught in a state of unreadiness, fell to a Redstick attack in late August. Perhaps as many as 250 settlers died in the fighting, as did 50 of the 500 or so Redstick warriors.[77] Many of the victims were either married to wealthy Creek mestizos or were mestizos themselves.[78] Dixon Bailey, his wife and children, and two of his brothers and their families, for example, were killed. Tustanagee Thlucco reported that the "cutting of him to pieces has encouraged [the Redsticks] that they now think themselves above all the world."[79] Peter Randon, "a friendly active half breed Indian," according to one officer in the U.S. Army, also lost his entire family with the exception of two younger brothers and a

---

[74] "A historical narration of the genealogy, traditions, and downfall of the Ispocoga or Creek tribe of Indians," PKY; Big Warrior to Benjamin Hawkins, 4 August 1813, CIL, 3:808, GDAH; Extracts of occurrences in the agency for Indian affairs, August 1813, LBH, 238, GDAH.

[75] Meek, *Romantic Passages*, 247–253; Benjamin Hawkins to General Floyd, 30 September 1813, LOC, PKY; Benjamin Hawkins to Judge Toulmin, 23 October 1813, *ASPIA*, 1:857.

[76] Halbert and Ball, *The Creek War*, 107–110.

[77] Judge Toulmin to the editor of the *Raleigh Register*, 7 September 1813, *Niles' Weekly Register*, 16 October 1813, pp. 105–107; Article from *Mobile Register*, September 1884, Draper Mss. 10U10, reel 146E, PKY. Sources give varying accounts of the number dead. For the settler party, the estimates range from 250 to 533, and for Redsticks, from 30 to 350. See Owsley, *Struggle for the Gulf Borderlands: The Creek War and the Battle of New Orleans, 1812–1815* (Gainesville: University of Florida, 1981), 38–39; Josiah Francis and the Old Interpreter et al. to the Governor of Pensacola, August 1813, PC, leg. 221B, 335, reel 311, PKY; "A historical narration of the genealogy, traditions, and downfall of the Ispocoga or Creek tribe of Indians," PKY; Meek, *Romantic Passages*, 253; Halbert and Ball, *The Creek War*, 148; Robert Breckinridge McAfee, *History of the Late War in the Western Country* (1816; reprint, Bowling Green, OH: Historical Publications Co., 1919), 499–501; Extract of a communication from the chiefs at Coweta to Benjamin Hawkins, 16 September 1813, LBH, 248, GDAH; and Benjamin Hawkins to John B. Floyd, 26 September 1813, *LBH*, 2:667.

[78] Tom Tate Tunstall, "Tom Tate Tunstall Defends the Name of Weatherford," *Arrow Points* 9 (1924): 6.

[79] Extract of a Communication from the Chiefs at Coweta to Col. Hawkins, 16 September 1813, enclosed in Hawkins to Armstrong, 21 September 1813, *LBH*, 2:664; Big Warrior and Little Prince to Benjamin Hawkins, 24 September 1813, CIL, 3:820–821, GDAH; Halbert and Ball, *The Creek War*, 161–162; Margaret Bailey Loses [sic] by the Hosstile Indians, in Lackey, ed., *Frontier Claims in the Lower South*, 50–51. Halbert and Ball claim that both of Bailey's sisters escaped (164–165), though Hawkins reported that one of Dixon's sisters had been killed. It is unclear how many brothers Dixon had, but at least one of them survived to fight against the Creeks in 1818. Report of Benjamin Hawkins, 17 September 1813, enclosed in Hawkins to Armstrong, 21 September 1813, *LBH*, 2:665; "Fort Dale, Now and Then," *Arrow Points* 15 (1929): 33–34.

sister.[80] Burnt Corn Creek and Fort Mims were battles largely between "halfbreeds" and Redsticks, Benjamin Hawkins concluded.[81]

After the attack, Redsticks razed the surrounding mestizo and white plantations, the same settlements promoted by McGillivray thirty years earlier.[82] They slaughtered over 5,000 head of cattle, destroyed crops and houses, and murdered or stole slaves.[83] Mestizo Peter Randon, who lived on the creek that bears his surname, about twenty miles north of the confluence of the Alabama and Little rivers, lost over $5,000 worth of goods in Redstick attacks, including 300 head of cattle, 10,000 pounds of seed cotton, 50 hogs, and 100 sheep.[84] Dixon Bailey's family, which had a river plantation just below Randon's, lost 260 head of cattle, 60 hogs, and 12,286 pounds of seed cotton, among other goods.[85] His father Richard had made his Creek neighbors "uneasy" by "keeping stock among them" in 1798.[86] Dixon himself had studied in Philadelphia with the support of the U.S. government, and Dixon's sisters, one of whom was literate, had both married white men and were active in cotton production.[87] After returning from Philadelphia, Dixon, who married Alexander McGillivray's niece, reportedly had "brought with him into

---

[80] Schedule of losses sustained by John Randon Dec.d, in Lackey, ed., *Frontier Claims in the Lower South*, 49; Bassett, "Major Howell Tatum's Journal," 38.

[81] Benjamin Hawkins to General Floyd, 30 September 1813, LOC, PKY; Benjamin Hawkins to Judge Toulmin, 23 October 1813, *ASPIA*, 1:857. Hawkins later reported that several of the "halfbreeds" lost all their property and even their lives at Fort Mims. After the war, he wrote, "I am of opinion these people will never be suffered by their Chiefs to return again into the nation, unless they will in all things conform to the Indian habits, which from their practical knowledge of the plan of civilization is impossible." Benjamin Hawkins to William H. Crawford, 19 January 1816, *LBH*, 2:768. For a list of "Halfbreeds" whom Hawkins considered worthy of remuneration for their losses, see Petition of Sundry Halfbreeds, enclosed in Hawkins to the Secretary of War, 19 January 1816, U.S. Bureau of Indian Affairs, Letters Received by the Office of the Secretary of War relating to Indian Affairs, 1800–1823, Record Group 75, M271, National Archives.

[82] Alexander McGillivray to Arturo O'Neill, 5 February 1784, PC, leg. 197, 742l, reel 273, PKY. One early historian of Alabama writes that John Linder, a white settler on Lake Tensaw, had become acquainted with McGillivray in Charleston. During the Revolution, the Creek leader assisted in bringing Linder's "family and large negro property" to the Tensaw settlement. Pickett, *History of Alabama*, 417.

[83] See the claims in Lackey, ed., *Frontier Claims in the Lower South*.

[84] Schedule of losses sustained by John Randon Dec.d, in Lackey, ed., *Frontier Claims in the Lower South*, 49.

[85] Dickson Bailey Losses at the time, in Lackey, ed., *Frontier Claims in the Lower South*, 50–51. James Bailey, Dixon's brother, would lose an additional $1,110 worth of goods. James Bailey's Account, in Lackey, ed., *Frontier Claims in the Lower South*, 50–51.

[86] Journal of Benjamin Hawkins, 18 December 1796, *Letters of Benjamin Hawkins, 1796–1806*, 39–41; Benjamin Hawkins to Edward Price, 29 May 1798, *LBH*, 1:195; Halbert and Ball, *The Creek War*, 130.

[87] Journal of Benjamin Hawkins, 18 December 1796, *Letters of Benjamin Hawkins, 1796–1806*, 39–41; Halbert and Ball, *The Creek War*, 164–5.

the nation so much contempt for the Indian mode of life that he has got himself into discredit with them."[88]

Other mestizos who lost property included Dixon's sister, who had settled a few miles below Dixon with a white man named Arthur Sizemore, the owner of three separate plantations on the Alabama River.[89] Some five miles lower lived Mary Dyer, "a half-breed Indian woman of the friendly party," according to a U.S. officer, who also had a "valuable plantation" with at least three slaves and 340 head of cattle.[90] The plantations continued to Moniac's lands at the mouth of the Little River. Seven miles below Moniac lived David Taitt, who had a "large plantation," and just above the Alabama Cutoff, the current border between Clarke and Baldwin counties, a Mrs. Dunn, "a half-breed woman," owned a plantation that extended nearly a full mile along the western bank of the Alabama.[91] At nearby Lake Tensaw stood a cotton gin and the first school in Alabama, where descendants of McGillivray and other Creek mestizos learned to read and write.[92] After the war, these mestizo residents or their heirs would claim nearly $22,000 in property destroyed by the Redsticks.[93]

Hoboithle Micco, who had organized the resistance to McGillivray in the 1780s and 1790s, explained in early July 1813 that he looked on his Creek enemies "as people of the United States," even if their genetic backgrounds were in part Native American.[94] If Redsticks believed their enemies were "people of the United States," national leaders did little to convince them otherwise. Tustanagee Thlucco, the speaker of the national council who "cultivated a fine plantation" with seventy or eighty slaves near Tuckabatche, turned immediately to Georgia for support in facing the dissidents.[95] "We want as many of your people as the enemy

[88] Benjamin Hawkins, "A sketch of the Creek Country in the years 1798 and 1799," *LBH*, 1:293. On Bailey's marriage to McGillivray's nephew, see Pickett, *History of Alabama*, 419.

[89] Bassett, "Major Howell Tatum's Journal," 39.

[90] Ibid.; An Estimate of loss sustained by Theophilus Powell in the late Indian War, in Lackey, ed., *Frontier Claims in the Lower South*, 48–49. Powell was the administrator of Dyer's estate. Her claims amounted to $4,680.

[91] Bassett, "Major Howell Tatum's Journal," 40–42.

[92] Pickett, *History of Alabama*, 469.

[93] Schedule of losses sustained during the war, in Lackey, ed., *Frontier Claims in the Lower South*, 29.

[94] Tallassee Fixico to Benjamin Hawkins, 5 July 1813, LBH, 209, GDAH. See Russell Thornton, "Boundary Dissolution and Revitalization Movements: The Case of the Nineteenth-Century Cherokees," *Ethnohistory* 40 (1993): 360–362, for an article about the struggle by Native Americans in the colonial era and nineteenth century to maintain cultural boundaries between themselves and newcomers.

[95] Chappell, *Miscellanies of Georgia*, 72. By his death, Tustanagee Thlucco had accumulated 300 slaves. Peter A. Brannon, "Fort Bainbridge," *Arrow Points* 5 (1922): 23.

has with his 2,500 men and we Indians that are will join them and then we shall have a superior force against them," he wrote in late July, before U.S. troops had entered the war.[96] In mid-November, he requested aid from General John Floyd of the Georgia militia, despite that two weeks earlier, American troops had killed at least 186 Creek men and captured 84 women and children in Little Tallassee on the Coosa River.[97]

As remarkable as it may seem for a Native American leader to call on U.S. soldiers to kill his own people, Georgia officials did not express surprise. Instead, they drew Tustanagee Thlucco and other influential Creeks closer to their interests by constructing a series of forts near their property holdings. In 1814, Fort Bainbridge and Fort Hull were built next to land owned by Tustanagee Thlucco, and Fort Mitchell was situated next to the residence of Lower Creek leader Tustanagee Hopoy.[98] These forts not only housed soldiers, but later served as stages for settlers traveling through the Deep South. Nearby landowners profited by supplying provisions and Tustanagee Thlucco even acted as a silent partner in the operation of the inn at Fort Bainbridge and perhaps at Fort Hull as well. His daughters would later marry the proprietors at both stages.[99]

The pattern of violence against mestizos stands out vividly in accounts of the war. Another less perceptible pattern suggests that the "civilized" gender roles that had been imposed on the Creeks also provoked Redstick hostility. Warriors who had increasingly found their manliness compromised by the new order showed special anger toward women. The murders on the Ohio River that precipitated the war, for example, were a warrior's response to "civilization," an assertion of Creek masculinity against the relatively sedentary and pacific identity imposed by U.S. Indian agents. There, Redstick warriors had disemboweled a pregnant woman and impaled her fetus.[100] According to one account, a participant

[96] Big Warrior, Little Prince, and Tustunugee Opoy to Robert Walton, 24 July 1813, CIL, 3:786–787, GDAH. See also Tustanagee Thlucco to Benjamin Hawkins, 26 July 1813, CIL, 3:790–792, GDAH; Big Warrior to David B. Mitchell, 2 August 1813, CIL, 3:803, GDAH;

[97] Big Warrior, William McIntosh, Little Prince, and Alexander Cornels to J. Floyd, 18 November 1813, CIL, 3:839, GDAH; McAfee, *History of the Late War in the Western Country*, 504; J. Coffee to Andrew Jackson, 4 November 1813, *Niles' Weekly Register*, 27 November 1813, pp. 218–219.

[98] Brannon, "Fort Bainbridge," 26; Brannon, "Fort Hull of 1814," *Arrow Points* 14 (1930): 6–11. The land next to Fort Hull later belonged to Alexander Cornels, a gift from Tustanagee Thlucco.

[99] Brannon, "Fort Bainbridge," 26; Brannon, "Some Early Taverns in Alabama," *Arrow Points* 5 (1922): 52 and 54; Brannon, "Fort Hull of 1814," 7.

[100] Benjamin Hawkins to Upper Creek Chiefs, 25 March 1813, *LBH*, 2:631.

later boasted that "he had killed and eaten white people, and he had killed and cut open the white woman near the mouth of the Ohio."[101]

In subsequent battles, the behavior of Redstick warriors reflected their antipathy toward the gender roles of "civilization," an antipathy that stemmed from anxiety about their own compromised masculinity and from the threat that independent women posed. In Hilabee, for instance, Redsticks stripped Mrs. Grayson of her clothing and destroyed all of her property, including a stock of cotton, a loom, and a bolt of finished cloth. Grayson had been hired by Creek leaders to instruct women to spin and weave.[102] Several mestizo women also came under attack. In the late nineteenth century, one woman would recall that during the war, U.S. troops had rescued her wealthy grandmother Sophia Durant after Creek dissidents had bound her to a tree in preparation for burning.[103] And the two daughters of Alexander McGillivray were "induced to join" the Redsticks to "save their property." They both hoped to escape at the earliest opportunity.[104] At Fort Mims, the attacks on women may have reflected the warriors' fears about changing gender roles, although it is difficult to distinguish accurate descriptions of the violence from biased exaggeration. After the destruction of the fort, one witness reported that "he saw 250 dead bodies and the women in a situation shocking to behold or relate."[105] Another witness, an officer sent to bury the dead, noted that "the females of every age, were butchered in a manner which neither decency nor language will permit me to describe."[106] Even if Creeks attacked and mutilated their male victims with equal force, the violence against women violated white codes of warfare, and Creeks knew it. These were the actions of warriors anxious to reestablish their masculinity.

Mirroring the behavior of Redstick warriors, some women reasserted an earlier femininity in the war. They became prophets, preaching against the plows and looms that had upset older gender roles.[107] Others reassumed their traditional identity as "food makers" by gathering berries and nuts to support Redstick adherents.[108] In addition, they

[101] Nimrod Doyell to Benjamin Hawkins, 3 May 1813, *ASPIA*, 1:843–844.
[102] Benjamin Hawkins to John Armstrong, 28 July 1813, *LBH*, 2:652.
[103] I. G. Vore to Lyman Draper, 11 August 1886, Draper Mss. 4YY6, State Historical Society of Wisconsin, reel 147E, PKY.
[104] Deposition of Samuel Moniac, in Halbert and Ball, *The Creek War*, 93; Woodward, *Woodward's Reminiscences*, 65.
[105] Benjamin Hawkins to John B. Floyd, 26 September 1813, *LBH*, 2:667.
[106] Quoted in Pickett, *History of Alabama*, 542.
[107] Meek, *Romantic Passages in Southwestern History*, 271.
[108] Martin, *Sacred Revolt*, 145.

repositioned themselves at the heart of the Creek economy by rejecting most European-made goods.[109] They likely also condoned the Redsticks' wholesale slaughter of livestock in Creek country because ranching had encouraged the creation of patriarchal settlements. Yet we do not know how they perceived Redstick attacks on women such as Mrs. Grayson. Some may have participated, but perhaps others were troubled by the humbling of someone who had taught nearly every woman in Hilabee to spin and more than twenty of them to weave. Benjamin Hawkins, whose testimony must be taken cautiously in this case, noted that Grayson was "universally esteemed before."[110]

Whites interpreted the assertions of Creek masculinity and femininity as direct assaults on "civilization." In December 1813, in the heat of the war, *Niles' Weekly Register* published a letter from one resident who lived on the Tombigbee River, not far from some of the fiercest fighting in central Alabama:

> Many of [the Creeks] were regular farmers; the men labored in the field, the women plied the wheel and the shuttle at home. . . . they are without excuse, for they had nothing to complain of. They listened to the serpent, and became the murderers of their benefactors – the horrible assassins of women and children.[111]

According to this observer, Redsticks had overturned the proper order – one characterized by male farmers and female weavers – and had committed unnatural acts by murdering their benefactors and slaughtering women and children. Andrew Jackson, who led American troops against the Creek dissidents, used similar rhetoric, condemning the leading Redstick prophets as a "matricidical band." It "is not on defenseless women and children that retaliation will be made," he stated, distinguishing civilized from savage war.[112] Perhaps with the same contrast in mind, U.S. officers self-consciously reported in published letters that they had spared Creek women and children.[113] After the war, relatives of one half-hearted mestizo Redstick leader would revive his

[109] Roy S. Dickens, Jr., "Archaeological Investigations at Horseshoe Bend National Military Park, Alabama," *Alabama Archaeological Society, Special Publication* 3 (1979); Fairbanks, "Excavations at Horseshoe Bend, Alabama," *The Florida Anthropologist* 15 (1962): 48.

[110] Benjamin Hawkins to John Armstrong, 28 July 1813, *LBH*, 2:652.

[111] Letter to the editor, *Niles' Weekly Register*, 18 December 1813, pp. 270–271.

[112] Andrew Jackson to Mateo González Manrique, 25 August 1814, enclosed in Manrique to Juan Ruiz de Apodaca, 6 September 1814, PC, leg. 1795, 1006, reel 116, PKY.

[113] For example, see J. Coffee to Andrew Jackson, Nov. 4, 1813, *Niles' Weekly Register*, 27 November 1813, pp. 218–219; Andrew Jackson to General Pinckney, 28 March 1814, *Niles' Weekly*

reputation as a respectable planter in part by insisting that he had urged warriors to attack only men.[114] Though the repeated comments by whites on the savagery of the Creeks betray a one-sided perspective, they also highlight a real part of the conflict: Redsticks refused to abide by European ideals of masculinity and femininity.

If the violence that Redstick warriors directed toward mestizos and women indicates how unsettling the changing economy and gender roles were, the friendship they accorded African Americans is equally significant. Blacks embraced the Redstick cause and offered much-needed assistance. Before the battle at Fort Mims, they carried intelligence to the Redsticks on the state of the garrison, and when the attack began, a black man named Siras "cut down the Pickets."[115] The "Master of Breath has ordered us not to kill any but white people and half breeds," one warrior assured a black man hiding in the corner of a house at Fort Mims.[116] By one account, when Redstick morale began to wane during the battle, their black allies urged them on "by reciting that they thought it interested them to have the Fort people destroyed."[117] Hillis Hadjo, a leading prophet, recalled a year later that in the Fort Mims attack, "the blacks were the first in" and that one African American had single-handedly "killed seven Americans in that affair."[118] In the 1850s, some Creeks remembered that Alexander McGillivray's former slaves had helped set fire to the fort.[119]

Though Redsticks scalped some blacks at Fort Mims, they carried off 243 from the stockade and surrounding countryside.[120] These slaves were brought to Eccanachaca (Holy Ground), near present-day Montgomery,

Register, 23 April 1814, pp. 130–131; Benjamin Hawkins to Kendal Lewis, 16 February 1814, LTB, 305c, GDAH.

[114] J. D. Dreisbach to Lyman Draper, July 1874, Draper Mss. 1V62, State Historical Society of Wisconsin, reel 146I, PKY.

[115] "A historical narration of the genealogy, traditions, and downfall of the Ispocoga or Creek tribe of Indians," PKY; Extract of a communication from the chiefs at Coweta to Benjamin Hawkins, 16 September 1813, LBH, 248, GDAH.

[116] Report of Benjamin Hawkins, 17 September 1813, enclosed in Hawkins to Armstrong, 21 September 1813, *LBH*, 2:665.

[117] "A historical narration of the genealogy, traditions, and downfall of the Ispocoga or Creek tribe of Indians," PKY.

[118] Colonel Nicolls to Alexander Cochrane, August through November 1814, Cochrane Papers, MS 2328, p. 59, reel 65 M, no. 1, PKY.

[119] Woodward, *Woodward's Reminiscences*, 99.

[120] Mateo González Manrique to Juan Ruiz de Apodaca, 2 October 1813, PC, leg. 1794, 1821, reel 113, PKY; Extract of a communication from the chiefs at Coweta to Benjamin Hawkins, 16 September 1813, LBH, 248, GDAH; Benjamin Hawkins to John B. Floyd, 26 September 1813, *LBH*, 2:667.

Alabama, where they later assisted in its defense.[121] "It was customary with the hostile Indians to make the negro men with them fight against the white people," an infantry officer testified.[122] At Eccanachaca, the "negroes were the last to quit the ground," according to another U.S. officer, and ten or twelve were killed.[123] The convergence of Redstick and African American interests at Fort Mims laid the groundwork for the black–Indian alliance the following year in Florida. Jim and Tom, two slaves belonging to Samuel Moniac, could testify to this connection. They abandoned their master's plantation to fight with the Redsticks and soon found themselves headed for the Apalachicola River on the Gulf Coast.[124]

Between November 1813 and March 1814, American soldiers razed Upper Creek towns, killing more than 1,500 Redsticks, including as many as 800 in a single battle in March 1814 at Tohopeka, or Horseshoe Bend, on the Tallapoosa River. Of U.S. regulars and volunteers, about 120 were killed in the war, not including those at Fort Mims.[125] On 9

---

[121] Article from Mobile Register, September 1884, Draper Mss. 10U10, reel 146E, PKY.

[122] U.S.S.H.doc. 200 (20–1) 173:12.

[123] Ibid. These African Americans may have been inspired by the slave uprising in Louisiana in 1811 when 200 to 500 blacks marched on New Orleans. Other revolts in North America inspired by the Haitian Revolution include the Pointe Coupée uprising in Louisiana in 1795 and Gabriel's Rebellion in 1800. Scott, "The Common Wind," 264–274, 292; and Douglas R. Egerton, "Gabriel's Conspiracy and the Election of 1800," *Journal of Southern History* 56 (1990): 191–214. In April 1813, only a few months before the battle at Fort Mims, a number of "French" contraband slaves were reportedly transported through the Deep South from Pensacola to Savannah. Their example illustrates the potential for the exchange of revolutionary ideas between slaves in the Caribbean and Southeast. Extract from executive minutes of Georgia Assembly, 9 April 1813, CIL, 3:773–774, GDAH.

[124] U.S.S.H.doc.200 (20–1) 173:11.

[125] For an account of military operations during the war, see Owsley, *Struggle for the Gulf Border-lands*, and Halbert and Ball, *The Creek War*. The estimate of the number of Redsticks and U.S. soldiers killed is drawn from the following sources: J. Coffee to Andrew Jackson, 4 November 1813, *Niles' Weekly Register*, 27 November 1813, pp. 218–219; Extract of letter from Andrew Jackson to William Blount, 11 November 1813, *Niles' Weekly Register*, 18 December 1813, p. 267; James White to John Cocke, 24 November 1813, *Niles' Weekly Register*, 25 December 1813, pp. 282–283; John Floyd to Thomas Pinckney, 4 December 1813, *Niles' Weekly Register*, 25 December 1813, pp. 283–284; Ferdinand L. Claiborne to the Secretary of War, 1 January 1814, *Niles' Weekly Register*, 19 February 1814, p. 412; John Floyd to Thomas Pinckney, 27 January 1814, *Niles' Weekly Register*, 19 February 1814, p. 411; Andrew Jackson to General Pinckney, 29 January 1814, *Niles' Weekly Register*, 26 February 1814, pp. 427–429; Andrew Jackson to General Pinckney, 28 March 1814, *Niles' Weekly Register*, 23 April 1814, pp. 130–131; Andrew Jackson to Willie Blount, 31 March 1814, *Niles' Weekly Register*, 30 April 1814, pp. 146–148; General Coffee to Andrew Jackson, 1 April 1814, *Niles' Weekly Register*, 30 April 1814, p. 148; James Moore and James Taylor to David Adams, 20 May 1814, CIL, 3:859, GDAH. Because of their authorship by American military officers who wanted to inflate the magnitude of their victories, the preceding documents likely exaggerate the numbers of Redsticks killed. Green, in *The Politics of Indian Removal*, estimates that as many as 3,000 Creeks lost their lives in the war (42), while Martin puts the number closer to 2,000. Martin, *Sacred Revolt*, 163.

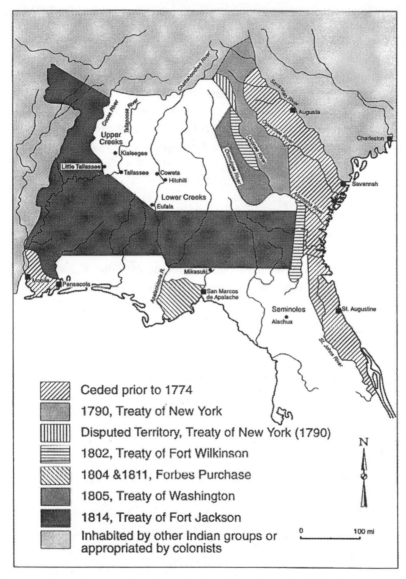

Figure 5. Creek land cessions through 1814. Map drawn by Mike Feeney, Campus Graphics and Photography, University of Georgia.

August 1814, the Treaty of Fort Jackson formally concluded hostilities between the Creeks and United States, though negotiations involved only the United States and its Creek allies. Surviving Redstick warriors had fled with their wives and children into Spanish territory between

Pensacola and the Apalachicola River.[126] The signers of the treaty, who
with one exception had remained loyal to the United States, nevertheless were forced to cede more than half of all Creek territory (see Fig.
5).[127] During the negotiations, Tustanagee Thlucco, the speaker of the
national council, offered a section of land to Andrew Jackson in appre-
ciation for his role in destroying the Redsticks.[128]

Despite the harsh, punitive nature of the treaty, Creek leaders
objected principally to its failure to remunerate them for personal losses
suffered during the war.[129] Their sustained efforts to recoup damaged or
destroyed property resulted in a partial payment of $85,000 from the
U.S. government in 1817, and in 1852, the survivors and heirs of the
claimants received the remaining balance of $110,417.90. These claims
provide a fitting end to a war driven by inequalities in power and property. As the violence of the conflict indicates, Redsticks directed their
hostility toward the people and things of the new order: national leaders,
wealthy Creeks, cattle, and cotton. The claims paid out in 1817 allow us
to quantify in some sense these social and economic divisions. They
reveal that the top 20 percent of Muskogees owned between 60 and 70
percent of the assessable wealth in Creek country, goods such as cattle,
cotton, and spinning wheels. The bottom 50 percent, in contrast, owned
only between 8 and 15 percent of the wealth.[130] This astounding degree
of inequality among a people who only thirty years earlier had disdained
the accumulation of property and the centralization of power explains
to a great extent why Redsticks took up arms in 1813.

---

[126] Benjamin Hawkins to Thomas Pinckney, 17 May 1814, *LBH*, 2:680; Benjamin Hawkins to
Joseph Graham, 5 July 1814, *LBH*, 2:688; George Woodbine to Vice Admiral Cochrane, 25 July
1814, Cochrane Papers, MS 2328, p35, reel 65M, no. 1, PKY.

[127] Treaty at Fort Jackson, *ASPIA*, 1:826–827; Benjamin Hawkins to George Graham, 1 August
1815, *LBH*, 2:743.

[128] For a discussion of this gift, see Saunt, "Taking Account of Property: Social Stratification
among the Creek Indians in the Late Eighteenth Century," forthcoming journal article.

[129] I have written elsewhere in detail about this treaty. See ibid.

[130] For more information on this quantitative data, see ibid.

12

The Negro Fort

Some forty miles west of Tallahassee, Florida, the Apalachicola River runs gently through a flat, sandy floodplain. The surrounding land lies nearly level with the water table, and during the rainy months between January and April, the river extends up to five miles across. Today, this swampy stretch of the Gulf Coast is largely unpopulated, but for the periodic invasion of loggers.[1] The region has not always been so quiet, however. Between 1814 and 1816, thousands of Redsticks, Seminoles, and fugitive slaves fled to the area where they built a fort, a final challenge to the new order spreading across the Deep South.

White Americans called the stronghold the Negro Fort, a name that reveals the symbolic as well as real threat that it represented to them. Farther upriver, on the banks of the Flint and Chattahoochee, the United States would soon establish other forts whose appellations testified to the dominance of American authority in that region: Fort Gaines, Fort Mitchell, Fort Scott, Fort Lawrence, and others, named in honor of American military officers and state governors. And in the heart of Upper Creek territory at the junction of the Coosa and Tallapoosa rivers, Andrew Jackson and his troops had already constructed Fort Jackson, where Creek leaders negotiated the treaty officially concluding the Redstick War. The Negro Fort stood in stark opposition to these military outposts and represented a challenge to their authority. To white Americans, the Negro Fort was an affront, a place where racial boundaries between black, white, and red threatened to dissolve, just as the familiar demarcation between dry land and running water disappeared in the region's distinctive wetlands. Whites feared that the fort represented the

---

[1] Carol A. Couch et al., "Influences of Environmental Settings on Aquatic Ecosystems in the Apalachicola-Chattahoochee-Flint River Basin," USGS, National Water-Quality Assessment Program, Water Survey Investigations Report, 95-4278.

dissolution of civilization into untamed nature. John Innerarity of
Forbes and Company called it an "accursed hornet's nest," and his
employee William Hambly spoke of routing the Negroes out of their
"nest."[2] To Francisco Caso y Luengo, the Spanish commandant at San
Marcos de Apalache, the fort was a "lair of Negroes."[3]

Redsticks, Seminoles, and African Americans came to the area to take
refuge from and organize against the new order. Redsticks had recently
been driven from their homes along the Tallapoosa and Coosa rivers, and
Seminoles were still recovering from the invasion of U.S. troops in 1812
and 1813. African Americans fled to the vicinity to escape from the rigid
racial hierarchy expanding across the land. These fugitives received
logistical support from Britain, which was then engaged in the War of
1812. For a time, until December 1814 when Britain signed the Treaty
of Ghent with the United States, Indians, blacks, and the British empire
found the alliance mutually advantageous despite their differences.[4] The
Negro Fort rallied dissidents in the Deep South and gave the Royal Navy
a toehold in Florida. Today, on a low bluff about sixteen miles up the
Apalachicola River, all that remains of this once formidable construction
is a depression in the earth.

It has left an even slighter impression on our historical consciousness.
By itself, the story of the fort appears anomalous, a bizarre and unim-
portant sideshow to the main events in American history, located on
firmer ground and in more hospitable climes. But placed in the context
of the dramatic changes that had occurred in the Deep South over the
preceding three decades, its construction marks a symbolic turning point
in American and Creek history, a last desperate stand against the new
order.[5] Where power had once been persuasive and negotiable, dramatic
inequalities between the powerful and the powerless now predominated
throughout the Deep South. And among the Creek people, who had long
doubted the value of wealth and hierarchy, property and coercion were
now the rule.

The story of the fort begins in September 1813 when a party of Seminoles visited Pensacola at the invitation of the Spanish commandant. By

---

[2] John Innerarity to John Forbes, 15 November 1815, Greenslade Papers, PKY; William Hambly
to John Innerarity, 14 May 1816, Forbes-Innerarity Papers, 74/20, reel 147Q, PKY.
[3] Francisco Caso y Luengo to Mauricio de Zuñiga, 12 July 1816, PC, leg. 79, 664, reel 479, PKY.
[4] It took several months for the Treaty of Ghent to be transmitted and turned from words to actions.
British support on the Apalachicola did not cease until spring 1815. Details of the British involvement with the Seminoles can be found in Sugden, "The Southern Indians in the War of
1812."
[5] One attempt to place the Negro Fort in a larger context is Frank Owsley, Jr., and Gene A. Smith,
Filibusters and Expansionists: Jeffersonian Manifest Destiny, 1800–1821 (Tuscaloosa: University of
Alabama, 1997), chap. 6.

chance, a British officer was in port at the same time to assess his country's alliance with southeastern Indians, and the Seminoles requested the assistance of his country against the United States.[6] In response, Britain drew up ambitious plans to take New Orleans with the help of Indians. Creeks and Choctaws, furnished with British arms, would prevent U.S. troops from marching overland to the aid of the city, while the Royal Navy would block access by sea. British forces would then capture Baton Rouge and cut off travel down the Mississippi, thereby rendering New Orleans indefensible.[7]

Implementation of these plans began in May 1814, barely a month after the massacre at Tohopeka (Horseshoe Bend), when Captain Hugh Pigot appeared off the Apalachicola coast with ammunition and 2,000 muskets for the assault. Pigot unloaded his men and drilled them onshore for three weeks, hoping to attract the attention of neighboring Indians. Near the end of the month, ten Seminole leaders from the surrounding area met with Pigot and welcomed British assistance.[8] George Woodbine, who had embarked from the Bahamas as a Creek interpreter, volunteered to stay on the Apalachicola River to aid them, and a sergeant and corporal from the Royal Marines also agreed to remain behind to instruct and drill the Seminoles in the use of the bayonet.[9]

Woodbine delivered two proclamations to the Indians. One of them promised logistical support. The second, directed at American slaves, offered three options "to all those who may be disposed to emigrate from the United States . . . with their families": induction into the British armed forces, freedom and settlement in British North America, or a similar arrangement in the West Indies. Woodbine reported his intention to send the second proclamation to Tennessee, Georgia, and New Orleans, and though the details of its distribution remain obscure, a copy of this explosive document did make its way into the papers of a Spanish surveyor in Pensacola.[10] Other copies appeared in the Atlantic coast

[6] Owsley, *Struggle for the Gulf Borderlands*, 27–28.
[7] Ibid., 96–98, 101–102.
[8] Ibid., 96–98; Hugh Pigot to George Woodbine, 5 May 1814, Cochrane Papers, MS 2328, p. 5, reel 65M, no. 1, PKY; Captain Pigot to Alexander Cochrane, 6 June 1814, Cochrane Papers, MS 2326, p. 149, reel 65M, no. 1, PKY; J. Wheeler to John Innerarity, 6 June 1814, Cruzat Papers, PKY.
[9] Captain Pigot to Alexander Cochrane, 6 June 1814, Cochrane Papers, MS 2326, p. 149, reel 65M, no. 1, PKY; Hugh Pigot to George Woodbine, 5 May 1814, Cochrane Papers, MS 2328, p. 5, reel 65M, no. 1, PKY. On Woodbine's embarkation in the Bahamas, see Owsley, *Struggle for the Gulf Borderlands*, 98.
[10] On Cochrane's proclamations, see Alexander Cochrane to the chiefs of the Creek nation, 28 March 1814, Cochrane Papers, MS 2346, p. 3, reel 65M, no. 5, PKY; "By the Honorable Sir Alexander Cochrane . . . ," 2 April 1814, Pintado Papers, reel 3, frame 776, PKY; A Proclamation, 2 April 1814, PC, leg. 147B, 460, reel 483, PKY; George Woodbine to Hugh Pigot, 25 May 1814, Cochrane Papers, MS 2328, p. 12, reel 65M, no. 1, PKY.

settlement of Fernandina. There, at the mouth of the St. Marys River on the boundary between Georgia and Florida, the proclamation was posted throughout the town.[11] Its circulation would have an important effect on events on the Apalachicola in the coming months. In the meantime, at Prospect Bluff, about sixteen miles up the river, Seminoles and British officers completed construction of a large storehouse and an octagonal powder magazine, with walls thirty feet long.[12]

By early June 1814, Redstick leaders, including Hillis Hadjo (Josiah Francis) and Peter McQueen, had learned of the British landing and sent word of their plight.[13] About 2,000 men, women, and children, virtually the entire surviving population of Redsticks, had fled to Spanish territory between the Apalachicola River and Pensacola. Conditions were poor in this huge encampment of weary refugees, and in their weakened state, many died of starvation or succumbed to disease.[14] Their request for carbines or fusils reflected their desperation. Muskets, the Redsticks explained, were too heavy for children, whom "the chiefs represent as being of infinite service." According to one report, the Redsticks were living "on the spontaneous produce of the earth."[15]

In addition to famine and disease, Redsticks faced relentless harass-

[11] Regarding Fernandina, see Mary Ricketson Bullard, *Black Liberation on Cumberland Island in 1815* (DeLeon Springs: M. R. Bullard, 1983), 55. Bullard's self-published book gives a superb account of concurrent events at the mouth of the St. Marys. When the British evacuated that region in 1815, they removed perhaps as many as 1,500 slaves, most to Halifax. Bullard, *Black Liberation on Cumberland Island*, 96–102.

[12] George Woodbine reported that the powder magazine was 40 feet by 24 feet, but archaeological excavations have determined that it was an octagon with walls 30 feet long. George Woodbine to Hugh Pigot, 25 May 1814, Cochrane Papers, MS 2328, p. 12, reel 65M, no. 1, PKY; Stephen R. Poe, "Archaeological Excavations at Fort Gadsden, Florida," *Notes in Anthropology* 8 (1963): 15. The Spanish name for the bluff was Loma de Buenavista. The Creeks called it Ackaikwheithle.

[13] Chiefs of the Red Stick Nation to Commanding Officer of His Britannick Magesty's at George's Island, 9 June 1814, Cochrane Papers, MS 2328, p. 28, reel 65M, no. 1, PKY.

[14] Captain Pigot to Alexander Cochrane, 6 June 1814, Cochrane Papers, MS 2326, p. 149, reel 65M, no. 1, PKY; George Woodbine to Alexander Cochrane, 9 August 1814, Cochrane Papers, MS 2328, p. 56, reel 65M, no. 1, PKY; Captain Lockyer to Alexander Cochrane, 12 August 1814, Cochrane Papers, MS 2328, p. 67, reel 65M, no. 1, PKY; Edward Nicolls to Alexander I. Cochrane, 1 March 1816, LOC, PRO, WO 1/144, PKY; and Edward Nicolls to Alexander I. Cochrane, 1 March 1816, LOC, PRO, WO 1/144, PKY. On the famine, see George Woodbine to Vice Admiral Cochrane, 25 July 1814, Cochrane Papers, MS 2328, p. 35, reel 65M, no. 1, PKY; George Woodbine to Alexander Cochrane, 9 August 1814, Cochrane Papers, MS 2328, p. 56, reel 65M, no. 1, PKY; Colonel Nicolls to Alexander Cochrane, August through November 1814, Cochrane Papers, MS 2328, p. 59, reel 65M, no. 1, PKY; Resolution of the Muscogee Nation, 10 March 1815, LOC, PRO, FO 5/139, PKY; Josiah Francis and Peter McQueen to Alexander Cochrane, [1815?], Cochrane Papers, MS 2328, p. 183, reel 65M, no. 1, PKY; Edward Nicolls to J. P. Morier, 25 September 1815, LOC, PRO, WO 1/143, PKY.

[15] Captain Pigot to Alexander Cochrane, 6 June 1814, Cochrane Papers, MS 2326, p. 149, reel 65M, no. 1, PKY.

ment and even murder at the hands of Colonel Joseph Carson and William Weatherford, a wealthy mestizo and half-hearted Redstick who had surrendered to Andrew Jackson.[16] Weatherford had since joined Carson, his former antagonist, to kill Redsticks.[17] One American officer commented on Weatherford's "integrity and great usefulness" during an expedition down the Alabama River against surviving dissidents.[18] Carson and his companion reportedly were "pursuing the Creek Indians and . . . Killing them wherever they meet them." In June 1814, for instance, Carson and Weatherford oversaw the murder of seven or eight refugees about sixteen miles outside of Pensacola, and then they attacked a Redstick camp on the Conecuh River above Pensacola, killing "all the Indians they could lay hands on."[19] (Weatherford would later establish a plantation in the area with about 300 slaves.)[20]

Without ammunition and supplies, Redsticks might have surrendered or fled down the Florida peninsula, but support from Britain provided a rallying point for the refugees to continue their struggle. On receiving the desperate appeal of the Redsticks, George Woodbine sailed to Pensacola with relief supplies. At the same time, 300 Seminoles, accompanied by a British sergeant, marched overland from the Apalachicola to join Woodbine in the Spanish town. Redsticks and Seminoles, Woodbine hoped, would join forces to attack American troops at Mobile.[21]

When Woodbine arrived in Pensacola in late July 1814, about 2,000 Creek men, women, and children, including 800 warriors, flooded into the settlement in search of clothing and food.[22] They received

---

[16] A document in the papers of British admiral Alexander Cochrane puts to rest the myth that Weatherford traveled as a guest of Jackson's to the Hermitage. (For one version of the myth, see Griffith, *McIntosh and Weatherford*, 155.) Weatherford instead was guiding U.S. troops against his former Redstick allies. [?] to Lieutenant Jackson of the Cockchafer, 9 June 1814, Cochrane Papers, MS 2328, p. 32, reel 65M, no. 1, PKY.

[17] Carson and Weatherford had once faced each other in the battle of Eccanachaca (Holy Ground). Griffith, *McIntosh and Weatherford*, 128–129.

[18] Edmund Bryan to [?], 1 June 1814, box 1, folder 1, Bryan and Leventhorpe Papers, Southern Historical Collection, Wilson Library, University of North Carolina, Chapel Hill.

[19] [?] to Lieutenant Jackson of the Cockchafer, 9 June 1814, Cochrane Papers, MS 2328, p. 32, reel 65M, no. 1, PKY. A Spanish source confirms the attacks but does not mention Carson or Weatherford. Mateo González Manrique to Juan Ruiz de Apodaca, 23 July 1814, PC, leg. 1795, 733, reel 115, PKY.

[20] Griffith, *McIntosh and Weatherford*, 252.

[21] George Woodbine to Sergeant Smith, 22 July 1814, Cochrane Papers, MS 2328, p. 33, reel 65M, no. 1, PKY; George Woodbine to Vice Admiral Cochrane, 25 July 1814, Cochrane Papers, MS 2328, p. 35, reel 65M, no. 1, PKY; Owsley, *Struggle for the Gulf Borderlands*, 101–105.

[22] George Woodbine to Alexander Cochrane, 9 August 1814, Cochrane Papers, MS 2328, p. 56, reel 65M, no. 1, PKY. For a different report that underestimates the number of women and

provisions, and Woodbine assembled a force of Redsticks, whites, mulattos, and blacks to ward off an attack by Andrew Jackson on Pensacola.[23] Colonel Edward Nicolls soon arrived by sea with 100 Royal Marines to assist them.[24] Nicolls carried word urging the Redsticks to encourage "by every means the emigration of Negroes from Georgia and the Carolinas," and Redstick leaders Hillis Hadjo and Peter McQueen responded that they would honor the request and "get all the black men we can to join your warriors."[25] "Indians and blacks are very good friends and cooperate bravely together," Nicolls observed.[26]

By early September 1814, some 500 armed and uniformed Redsticks were patrolling Pensacola while 100 African Americans manned the principal fort, San Miguel.[27] José de Soto, the Spanish commandant, noted the disapproval of local slaveowners and reported that slaves escaped continually because of the disruption and the "shelter that they find, be it from our [British] assistants or from the Indians."[28] African Americans, alerted by the British proclamations offering freedom, also began arriving from Georgia. In late October 1814 at Fort Hawkins on the Ocmulgee River, for example, Benjamin Hawkins reported hearing a cannon shot from the south and guessed that African Americans, Seminoles, and the British had agreed on "some signal of this sort." The following day, fourteen slaves ran off, including five belonging to Hawkins.[29] A few weeks later, Hawkins learned that a party of fourteen Redsticks and an equal number of blacks were out harassing their Creek enemies,

children, see Captain Lockyer to Alexander Cochrane, 12 August 1814, Cochrane Papers, MS 2328, p. 67, reel 65M, no. 1, PKY.

[23] José de Soto to Juan Ruiz de Apodaca, 8 August 1814, PC, leg. 1795, 822, reel 115, PKY; George Woodbine to Alexander Cochrane, 9 August 1814, Cochrane Papers, MS 2328, p. 56, reel 65M, no. 1, PKY.

[24] Alexander Cochrane to the chiefs of the Creek nation, 29 June 1814, Cochrane Papers, MS 2346, p. 7, reel 65M, no. 5, PKY; Colonel Nicolls to Alexander Cochrane, August through November 1814, Cochrane Papers, MS 2328, p. 59, reel 65M, no. 1, PKY; Owsley, Struggle for the Gulf Borderlands, 103–105.

[25] Alexander Cochrane to the chiefs of the Creek nation, 29 June 1814, Cochrane Papers, MS 2346, p. 7, reel 65M, no. 5, PKY; John Francis and Peter McQueen to Alexander Cochrane, 1 September 1814, LOC, PRO, FO 5/139, PKY.

[26] Colonel Nicolls to Alexander Cochrane, August through November 1814, Cochrane Papers, MS 2328, p. 59, reel 65M, no. 1, PKY.

[27] José de Soto to Juan Ruiz de Apodaca, 10 September 1814, PC, leg. 1795, 1082, reel 116, PKY.

[28] José de Soto to Juan Ruiz de Apodaca, 21 October 1814, PC, leg. 1795, 1189, reel 116, PKY.

[29] Benjamin Hawkins to Peter Early, 26 October 1814, LBH, 2:698. Nicolls later mentioned that "several of Colonel Hawkins' negroes" were among the African American soldiers at Prospect Bluff on the Apalachicola. Colonel Nicolls to Alexander Cochrane, August through November 1814, Cochrane Papers, MS 2328, p. 59, reel 65M, no. 1, PKY. In 1815, the Creek factory could not find any blacks to hire; apparently most had gone to Prospect Bluff. Henri, The Southern Indians and Benjamin Hawkins, 307.

and soon after, Redsticks, perhaps accompanied by their black allies, stole a number of slaves from wealthy mestizos.[30] These events troubled Creek leaders and American officials alike.

On 7 November, Andrew Jackson attacked and overran Pensacola, sending Seminoles, Redsticks, and at least 136 fugitive slaves on a hasty retreat to the Apalachicola.[31] By the beginning of 1815, there were 1,600 men, 455 women, and 755 children, for a total of 2,810 people, settled at Prospect Bluff.[32] Of these, more than 250 were black.[33] In addition to the Pensacola fugitives, other African Americans had enlisted when Woodbine traveled across the Florida peninsula in December 1814 to visit St. Augustine. There, eleven slaves along with two free black soldiers joined Woodbine.[34] News of Woodbine's visit also encouraged ninety slaves from the Mosquito River on the east coast of Florida to flee in February 1815 for Prospect Bluff.[35] In addition, on his way across

[30] Benjamin Hawkins to Andrew Jackson, 11 November 1814, *LBH*, 2:704; Benjamin Hawkins to John Houston McIntosh, 26 November 1814, *LBH*, 2:706; Benjamin Hawkins to Edward Nicolls, 24 March 1815, *Niles' Weekly Register*, 24 June 1815, p. 285.

[31] Colonel Nichols to Alexander Cochrane, August through November, Cochrane Papers, MS 2328, p. 59, reel 65M, no. 1, PKY; Mateo González Manrique to Juan Ruiz de Apodaca, 17 November 1814, PC, leg. 1795, 1289, reel 116, PKY; John Innerarity to James Innerarity, 11 November 1814, Greenslade Papers, PKY; Owsley, *Struggle for the Gulf Borderlands*, 112–119; John Innerarity to James Innerarity, 29 November 1814, John Innerarity Papers, reel 150D, PKY. For examples of how individual slaves were drafted into British and Creek forces, see "File of witnesses that may be examined by Commissioners in Pensacola in the suit via Woodbine," [1815?], Cruzat Papers, PKY; and "Narrative of the operations of the British in the Floridas," 1815, Cruzat Papers, PKY.

[32] Robert Henry to Captain William Rawlins, 18 December 1814, Cochrane Papers, MS 2328, p. 123, reel 65M, no. 1, PKY; Robert Henry to Alexander Cochrane, 22 December 1814, Cochrane Papers, MS 2328, p. 126, reel 65M, no. 1, PKY; Colonel Nicholls to Admiral Cochrane, 3 December 1814, Cochrane Papers, MS 2328, p. 117, reel 65M, no. 1, PKY, and Alexander Cochrane to John Lambert, 3 February 1815, LOC, PRO, WO 1/143, PKY.

[33] Vicente Sebastián Pintado to José de Soto, 29 April 1815, PC, leg. 1796, 590, reel 117, PKY; Deposition of Samuel Jervais, 9 May 1815, enclosed in documents to accompany the message of the President in response to a resolution of the Senate of 15 December 1818, in the Territorial Papers of the United States Senate, 1789–1873. Florida, 2 December 1806 to 7 February 1825, microcopy no. 200/9.

[34] Colonel Nicholls to Admiral Cochrane, 3 December 1814, Cochrane Papers, MS 2328, p. 117, reel 65M, no. 1, PKY; George Woodbine to the Governor of Florida, 30 December 1814, EF, bnd. 199D16, doc. 1814–17, reel 84, PKY; Copy of letter from Sebastián Kindelán to George Woodbine, 30 December 1814, Forbes-Innerarity Papers, 92/11, reel 147Q, PKY; Sebastián Kindelán to Juan Ruiz de Apodaca, 31 December 1814, EF, bnd. 33G3, doc. 577, 122, reel 12, PKY; Governor of St. Augustine to George Woodbine, 31 December 1814, EF, bnd. 199D16, doc. 1814–18, reel 84, PKY; "Narrative of the operations of the British in the Floridas," 1815, Cruzat Papers, PKY; Francisco Caso y Luengo to Mateo González Manrique, 30 January 1815, PC, leg. 1796, 300, reel 117, PKY; Francisco Caso y Luengo to Mateo González Manrique, 30 January 1815, PC, leg. 1796, 307, reel 117, PKY; Vicente Sebastián Pintado to José de Soto, 29 April 1815, PC, leg. 1796, 590, reel 117, PKY; and Testimony of De Lisle, enclosed in William Laurence to John Forbes, 25 February 1816, Cruzat Papers, PKY.

[35] Sebastián Kindelán to Juan Ruiz de Apodaca, 22 February 1815, EF, bnd. 33G3, doc. 612, 41, reel 13, PKY. Two days later, sixty-seven slaves fled to the British on Cumberland Island from

the peninsula, according to a report by two Indians, Woodbine "not only bribed and carried off the fugitive negroes who were established among those [Indian] nations as free people, but also the slaves belonging to the same Indians."[36] A number of these African Americans had fled from the United States years before and now lived "under the protection of the Simanole King" known as Bowlegs, to whom they paid "a small tribute in grain."[37] Bowlegs resented the disruption caused by Creek and British outsiders, and he protested to no avail the migration of black settlers to Prospect Bluff.[38] According to Nicolls, several of Hawkins's slaves who had joined the troops reported that at the first gun fired in Georgia, "a thousand or upwards of black men" would join them. Hawkins's slaves added that 200 were already on their way, an optimistic estimate that turned out to be untrue.[39]

As the assemblage of Indians and blacks continued to grow at Prospect Bluff, Redstick leaders encouraged the refugees and fugitives to construct a fort.[40] Kinache sent seventy of his warriors from nearby Mikasuki to assist in the work, and by the beginning of December 1814, they had dug a moat ten feet wide and four feet deep around the site.[41] By April 1815, the fort featured a parapet, built of hewn timber and earth

their plantation on San Pablo Creek, south of the St. Johns River. Sebastián Kindelán to Juan Ruiz de Apodaca, 24 February 1815, EF, bnd. 33G3, doc. 615, 45, reel 13, PKY.

[36] Sebastián Kindelán to Juan Ruiz de Apodaca, 21 January 1815, EF, bnd. 33G3, doc. 599, 24, reel 13, PKY.

[37] Colonel Nicolls to Alexander Cochrane, August through November 1814, Cochrane Papers, MS 2328, p. 59, reel 65M, no. 1, PKY.

[38] Governor Kindelán to the Governor of Pensacola, 6 February 1815, EF, bnd. 115K9, reel 43, PKY; Mateo González Manrique to Sebastián Kindelán, 13 March 1815, EF, bnd. 115K9, reel 43, PKY; [?] to Bowlegs, 1815, EF, bnd. 115K9, reel 43, PKY; Juan José de Estrada to Bowlegs and other chiefs and warriors of the Seminole nations, 5 July 1815, EF, bnd. 115K9, reel 43, PKY; Juan José de Estrada to Juan Ruiz de Apodaca, 10 July 1815, EF, bnd. 33G3, doc. 691, 3, reel 13, PKY.

[39] Colonel Nichols to Alexander Cochrane, August through November, Cochrane Papers, MS 2328, p. 59, reel 65M, no. 1, PKY.

[40] Colonel Nichols to Alexander Cochrane, August through November 1814, Cochrane Papers, MS 2328, p. 59, reel 65M, no. 1, PKY; Francisco Caso y Luengo to Mateo González Manrique, 1 December 1814, no. 24, in letterbook Correspondencia con el Govierno, PC, leg. 225B, reel 431, PKY. See also James W. Covington, "The Negro Fort," *Gulf Coast Historical Review* 5 (1990): 78–91. As early as 1789, Creeks had proposed that the British construct a fort on the Apalachicola River that they themselves would defend against the Spanish and Americans. Minutes of a Creek Council, *The Papers of George Washington*, 6:291. Another fort, little more than an earthen redoubt with a moat and palisade, was built one mile below the confluence of the Flint and Chattahoochee rivers.

[41] Reports on the size of the moat vary. See Colonel Nicholls to Admiral Cochrane, 3 December 1814, Cochrane Papers, MS 2328, p. 117, reel 65M, no. 1, PKY; Covington, "The Negro Fort," 79; and Vicente Sebastián Pintado to José de Soto, 29 April 1815, PC, leg. 1796, 590, reel 117, PKY. Archaeological excavations show that the moat was about ten feet wide and 3.7 feet deep. Poe, "Archaeological Excavations at Fort Gadsden, Florida," 4.

and standing fifteen feet high and eighteen feet thick. Cannons, howitzers, and mortars were mounted on the ramparts. Inside sat a considerable number of barracks and stone cabins, a well, and the powder
magazine. In all, the fort enclosed two full acres. A surrounding swamp
made the stronghold nearly invulnerable to attack by land.[42]

Despite the difficult conditions, blacks who had the opportunity to
return to Pensacola chose to remain at Prospect Bluff. When Spanish
officer José Urcullo arrived at the end of December 1814 to secure the
return of the fugitive slaves, a British officer wrote that "it would be dangerous and imprudent to force those People into a Vessel without a
strong Guard." After learning the purpose of Urcullo's mission,
explained the worried officer, "they expressed their sentiments of dis-
approbation in strong terms."[43] Urcullo himself reported that only
twenty-five slaves agreed to return voluntarily. When it came time to
board the launch, however, "the greater part" refused, stating that "if
they returned to Pensacola they would be slaves and here they were
free."[44] Ten women returned in the end, most with children.[45] Redsticks,
Seminoles, and African Americans still held out hopes for a successful
attack against Creek and American forces.

The progress of the War of 1812 soon dashed the military aspirations
of settlers at Prospect Bluff. At the request of Nicolls, a small number
of Redstick and Seminole leaders sailed to New Orleans in late December where they witnessed the disastrous British assault on the city.[46] The
fatal attack must have broken their faith in Britain's armed forces. Then
in late February, word reached Prospect Bluff that the United States and
Britain had concluded the Treaty of Ghent in the closing days of 1814.[47]
An American agent, who visited the site perhaps just days after the
Creeks had learned of the peace, reported that only 500 blacks and
Indians remained at the fort. Several of the fugitive slaves described a

---

[42] Vicente Sebastián Pintado to José de Soto, 29 April 1815, PC, leg. 1796, 590, reel 117, PKY;
Edmund Pendleton Gaines to Andrew Jackson, 14 May 1816, *The Papers of Andrew Jackson*, 4:31;
Covington, "The Negro Fort," 79.

[43] Robert Henry to Mateo González Manrique, 12 January 1815, Cruzat Papers, PKY.

[44] Copy of report of José Urcullo, 20 January 1815, Forbes-Innerarity Papers, reel 147Q, PKY;
Doster, *Creek Indians*, 2:139.

[45] Copy of report of José Urcullo, 20 January 1815, Forbes-Innerarity Papers, reel 147Q, PKY;
Pensacola residents to the Governor of West Florida, 8 March 1815, Cochrane Papers, MS 2328,
p. 148, reel 65M, no. 1, PKY.

[46] Alexander Dickson, "Journal of Operations in Louisiana," *Louisiana Historical Quarterly* 44
(1961):13; Benson Earle Hill, *Recollections of an Artillery Officer* (London, 1836), 1:299–300. I
am indebted to Adam Rothman for these references.

[47] Owsley, *Struggle for the Gulf Borderlands*, 177.

larger force of 450 blacks and between 800 and 900 Indians in arms. "Provision is very scarce," the agent noted, "and the Indians in the country are living altogether on alligators."[48] Another visitor reported that the refugees were partly subsisting on "old stinking cowhides."[49]

The scarcity of provisions forced Indians and blacks to disperse, and the rising waters of the Apalachicola River, a seasonal event, also drove the refugees to seek dry land elsewhere. Seminole leaders described their plight to the British in March 1815: "Famine is now devouring up our-selves and our children by reason of our upper town bretheren being driven down upon us at the time the Corn was Green." Starving Red-sticks, they said, were digging up the seed of their future crops. Yet the Seminoles refused to castigate their relatives: "[T]hey have seen their children dying in the woods for want and who can blame them when pressed by such cruel necessity."[50] Prospect Bluff was "nearly in a state of starvation and wretchedness," a British officer confirmed soon after.[51] When the Royal Navy finished evacuating in May 1815, it left behind a large stockpile of arms, including cannons and howitzers, but by the fol-lowing month, the Indian presence at the fort had been reduced to a small group of Choctaws.[52]

Though many as fifty African Americans may have embarked with the British, probably settling in Halifax, Nova Scotia, a significant number remained at the fort.[53] Like their Native American allies in nearby towns, they planted corn and pumpkins, and according to the

---

[48] Benjamin Hawkins to Peter Early, 21 April 1815, *LBH*, 2:724; General Gaines to the acting Sec-retary of War, 22 May 1815, enclosed in documents to accompany the message of the President in response to a resolution of the Senate of 15 December 1818, in the Territorial Papers of the United States Senate, 1789–1873. Florida, 2 December 1806 to 7 February 1825, microcopy no. 200/9. See also Benjamin Hawkins to Peter Early, 20 February 1815, CIL, 3:871, GDAH.

[49] Benjamin Hawkins to James Monroe, 7 January 1815, *LBH*, 2:713.

[50] Resolution of the Muscogee Nation, 10 March 1815, LOC, PRO, FO 5/139, PKY.

[51] R. L. Spencer to Vicente S. Pintado, 30 March 1815, Pintado Papers, reel 4, frame 254, PKY; Captain Spencer and Robert Gamble to John Forbes and Co., 2 May 1815, Cruzat Papers, PKY.

[52] Vicente Sebastián Pintado to José de Soto, 29 April 1815, PC, leg. 1796, 590, reel 117, PKY; Deposition of Samuel Jervais, 9 May 1815, enclosed in documents to accompany the message of the President in response to a resolution of the Senate of 15 December 1818, in the Territorial Papers of the United States Senate, 1789–1873. Florida, 2 December 1806 to 7 February 1825, microcopy no. 200/9; Owsley, *Struggle for the Gulf Borderlands*, 179–180; Francisco Caso y Luengo to José de Soto, 18 June 1815, PC, leg. 1796, 972, reel 118, PKY; Francisco Caso y Luengo to Joseph de Soto, 30 June 1815, PC, leg. 147B, 556, reel 479, PKY. On the origins of these Choctaw dissidents, see Sugden, *Tecumseh*, 351–352.

[53] Mateo González Manrique to Juan Ruiz de Apodaca, 30 October 1814, PC, leg. 1795, 1216, reel 116, PKY; Vicente Sebastián Pintado to José de Soto, 29 April 1815, PC, leg. 1796, 590, reel 117, PKY; John Innerarity to James Innerarity, 3 June 1815, Forbes-Innerarity Papers, 73/17, reel 147Q, PKY; J. D. Gaunaurd to John Forbes, 8 November 1815, Forbes-Innerarity Papers, 98/8, reel 147Q, PKY; Bullard, *Black Liberation on Cumberland Island*, 96–102.

report of one U.S. officer, their fields extended nearly fifty miles up the river.[54] They "are very violent and say they will die to a man rather than return," a surveyor named Vicente Sebastián Pintado learned after an unsuccessful visit to the fort in April to secure the return of Pensacola slaves.[55] Pintado "encouraged, threatened, [and] advised" the fugitives, but according to John Innerarity of Forbes and Company, the slaves "had an opportunity of seeing the latent causes, the underplot: perpetual freedom, lands in Canada or Trinidad, the assurances that the British government would pay their masters for their value, [Nicolls's] return, abundance of provisions to support them, a well-constructed fort to defend them in the interim."[56] Only twelve succumbed to Pintado's threats. The slaves who remained behind intended to establish themselves at Tampa Bay where many black Seminoles lived, Pintado reported.[57]

In the meantime, they organized themselves for defense. Felipe Prieto, a Spanish officer from Fort San Marcos in Apalache, described the military structure of the stronghold when he traveled up the Apalachicola to Prospect Bluff in early June 1815 in order to request rations for his struggling Spanish outpost. He was met "imperiously" by a "negro official" named Garzon, a thirty-year-old carpenter from Pensacola. Garzon shared the role of commanding officer with two other fugitive slaves, Cyrus and Prince. Cyrus was a twenty-six-year-old carpenter and cooper who was literate, and Prince was a master carpenter of the same age.[58] At the time of Prieto's visit, William Hambly, a former employee of Forbes and Company, was charged by the British with the command of

[54] Colonel Clinch to Colonel R. Butler, 2 August 1816, in Forbes, *Sketches*, 200; Edmund Doyle to John Innerarity, 23 November 1816, Forbes-Innerarity Papers, 74/53, reel 147Q, PKY.

[55] R. L. Spencer to Vicente Sebastián Pintado, 30 March 1815, Pintado Papers, reel 4, frame 254, PKY.

[56] John Innerarity to John Forbes, 22 May 1815, Forbes-Innerarity Papers, 98/3, reel 147Q, PKY; Vicente Sebastián Pintado to José de Soto, 29 April 1815, PC, leg. 1796, 590, reel 117, PKY.

[57] Ibid.; John Innerarity to John Forbes, 22 May 1815, Forbes-Innerarity Papers, 98/3, reel 147Q, PKY. Recall the news that Hawkins had learned about black Seminoles in May 1813 from Creeks: "They told me the negroes were now separated and at a distance from the Indians on the Hammocks or the Hammock not far from Tampa Bay." Benjamin Hawkins to Governor Mitchell, 31 May 1813, LOC, PKY.

[58] Benjamin Hawkins to Andrew Jackson, 12 August 1815, *LBH*, 2:748; Francisco Caso y Luengo to Joseph de Soto, 18 September 1815, PC, leg. 147B, 568, reel 479, PKY; Felipe Prieto to Francisco Caso y Luengo, 17 June 1815, PC, leg. 1796, 964, reel 118, PKY; José de Soto to Juan Ruiz de Apodaca, 13 May 1815, PC, leg. 1796, 751, reel 118, PKY. This Prince may have been the same Prince in Pensacola to whom Woodbine offered a lieutenant's commission and wages to persuade "all sorts of Negroes whether Freemen or Slaves to enter into his . . . corps." Indictment of William Augustus Baker, 1816, Cruzat Papers, PKY.

the fort. But Prieto found him absent. In fact, he soon abandoned the fort, "not wishing to stay any longer at the head of a band of uppity rogues [*pícaros levantados*] like the negros." According to Garzon, an Indian had assumed charge.[59] During Prieto's brief visit, he encountered a number of uniformed African American officials, including a twenty-five-year-old former cook and house servant named Hilario who served as a sergeant of the guard. To prevent Prieto from undertaking a reconnaissance of the fort, Hilario forbade him to leave his canoe. Finally, the black officers instructed Prieto to depart immediately. The Indians, they explained, were angry with the Spanish for allowing U.S. troops to storm Pensacola and take Indian prisoners.[60]

Francisco Caso y Luengo, the commandant at San Marcos in Apalache, concluded from Prieto's account that there was "the beginnings of an accumulation of negros, among them some slaves already decorated with higher grades, which might bring unfortunate consequences."[61] A mestizo who was spying for the Americans visited the fort around the same time. He noted that the fugitives "keep sentrys & the negros are saucy and insolent, and say they are all free."[62] By July 1815, the fugitive slaves at Prospect Bluff had armed a schooner and punt with cannons and were patrolling Apalachicola Bay, ready to take any boat that was not English.[63] The slaves "are now *organized as Pirates*," a worried James Innerarity reported, "have Several Small Vessels well armed, & some piracies that lately occurred in the lakes are supposed to have been committed by them."[64]

As rumors of an imminent invasion by Upper Creek and American slaveowners grew, however, and as it became more apparent that the British would not soon return, blacks, including Prince, one of the three African American commanding officers, began moving inland into Seminole towns.[65] They went in large numbers by canoe and pirogue to black and Seminole towns on the Suwannee River and farther south to black

[59] Felipe Prieto to Doyle, 17 September 1815, Cruzat Papers, PKY; Francisco Caso y Luengo to Joseph de Soto, 18 September 1815, PC, leg. 147B, 568, reel 479, PKY.

[60] Felipe Prieto to Francisco Caso y Luengo, 17 June 1815, PC, leg. 1796, 964, reel 118, PKY. For Hilario's age and occupation, see José de Soto to Juan Ruiz de Apodaca, 13 May 1815, PC, leg. 1796, 751, reel 118, PKY.

[61] Francisco Caso y Luengo to José de Soto, 18 June 1815, PC, leg. 147B, 552, reel 479, PKY.

[62] Quoted in Doster, *Creek Indians*, 2:149.

[63] Francisco Caso y Luengo to José de Soto, 5 July 1815, PC, leg. 1796, 1057, reel 118, PKY; Francisco Caso y Luengo to José de Soto, 14 July 1815, PC, leg. 1796, 1061, reel 118, PKY.

[64] James Innerarity to John Forbes, 12 August 1815, Greenslade Papers, PKY.

[65] Francisco Caso y Luengo to José de Soto, 14 July 1815, PC, leg. 1796, 1061, reel 118, PKY; Felipe Prietto to Doyle, 17 September 1815, Cruzat Papers, PKY; Francisco Caso y Luengo to Joseph de Soto, 18 September 1815, PC, leg. 147B, 568, reel 479, PKY.

settlements near Tampa Bay.[66] Others traveled the overland trail to the Seminole town of Mikasuki. Two blacks who gave their names as Juan Blanco and McFaly followed this latter route, but not before making an unsuccessful attempt to pass themselves off at Fort San Marcos as free Jamaicans and secure a passage to Pensacola. Blanco in truth was a convict who had escaped from Pensacola, and McFaly had fled from St. Augustine. Caso y Luengo, the commandant at San Marcos, described Mikasuki at the time as a "refuge for those who don't belong elsewhere."[67] His was an accurate description. In September 1815, a visitor to the town would have met Mikasukis, Redsticks, and blacks from the Caribbean, Africa, and North America and would have heard Spanish, English, Hitchiti, Muskogee, Alabama, and perhaps even several African languages spoken.

Despite the withdrawal of the British, blacks continued to flee to the Apalache region, settling in Mikasuki or at the Negro Fort. In November 1815, "a considerable number of Negroes" fled from Georgia to Prospect Bluff, and three months later, Hawkins wrote, "An invitation has come up from the Seminoles to invite the negros in the Creek nation and frontiers of Georgia to come down and be free." Hawkins knew of twenty-four slaves who took up the offer.[68] Mikasuki was growing so fast, Caso y Luengo wrote, that he feared for the security of his fort.[69]

In the first half of 1816, blacks at Prospect Bluff continued to expand their ties to towns on the Suwannee and at Tampa Bay, establishing a regular trade by water with the Seminole, Redstick, and African American settlements in those areas. Blacks not only often traveled by canoe along the coast between Prospect Bluff and the Suwannee settlements, noted the Spanish commandant at Fort San Marcos, but they also frequented Mikasuki. "Nothing is ever said to them," complained the officer, suggesting that Seminoles did not object to the intercourse.[70] On the Suwannee, some blacks set up a red pole to perform the Redstick

---

[66] Francisco Caso y Luengo to Joseph de Soto, 28 September 1815, PC, leg. 147B, 513, reel 479, PKY; Francisco Caso y Luengo to José de Soto, 14 July 1815, PC, leg. 1796, 1061, reel 118, PKY.

[67] Francisco Caso y Luengo to Joseph de Soto, 28 September 1815, PC, leg. 147B, 513, reel 479, PKY.

[68] John Innerarity to John Forbes, 15 November 1815, Greenslade Papers, PKY; Benjamin Hawkins to William H. Crawford, 3 February 1816, *LBH*, 2:771; Benjamin Hawkins to William H. Crawford, 16 February 1816, *LBH*, 2:773.

[69] Francisco Caso y Luengo to Joseph de Soto, 1 March 1816, PC, leg. 148, 126, reel 485, PKY.

[70] Francisco Caso y Luengo to Joseph de Soto, 10 March 1816, PC, leg. 147B, 582, reel 479, PKY; Francisco Caso y Luengo to Mauricio de Zuñiga, 28 April 1816, PC, leg. 79, 635, reel 479, PKY; Francisco Caso y Luengo to Mateo González de Manrique, 14 March 1816, PC, leg. 147B, 583, reel 479, PKY.

dance.[71] Blacks were "settled all about," Seminole leader Bowlegs observed in September 1816.[72]

Forces soon gathered to destroy these settlements. In 1816, John Innerarity of Forbes and Company renewed efforts to secure the return of his firm's property. Using the only leverage he had, Innerarity made the return of the slaves a precondition for the reestablishment of a store in the area.[73] Innerarity's agents Edmund Doyle and William Hambly had mixed success. Affairs looked promising when Doyle learned that Kinache had gone to the Suwannee to secure some of the slaves who had fled there, but the free passage of Apalachicola blacks to and from Mikasuki suggests that the Seminole leader did not intend to use force.[74] When Hambly attempted to hold a conference with Seminole and Lower Creek towns, Seminoles led by Kinache threatened his life. Hambly hastily took refuge at Fort Gaines "from the Fury of the Blacks and Lower Towns."[75] Doyle fled soon afterward, and Tustanagee Hopoy, a Lower Creek leader sent to the meeting by Hawkins, barely escaped with his life.[76]

During these farcical negotiations, the United States geared up for war. The construction of Fort Gaines on the Chattahoochee and Camp Crawford (later renamed Fort Scott) at the head of the Apalachicola made the Seminoles uneasy and encouraged them to remain allied with the black refugees at Prospect Bluff.[77] By May 1816, Seminoles near Camp Crawford were preparing for war, "drinking their war physic and dancing for several days."[78] Upper and Lower Creeks, at the urging of Hawkins and Hambly, responded by gathering warriors to attack the settlement at Prospect Bluff. Tustanagee Hopoy told the Indian agent that the "Chiefs

---

[71] Letter of Timothy Barnard to Benjamin Hawkins, quoted in Doster, *Creek Indians*, 172.

[72] Bowlegs to José Coppinger, 10 September 1816, EF, bnd. 115K9, reel 43, PKY.

[73] John Innerarity to James Innerarity, 20 January 1816, Forbes-Innerarity Papers, 72/5, reel 147Q, PKY; Governor of Pensacola to the Chiefs, Warriors, and others of the Seminole nation, 17 February 1816, Innerarity-Hulse Papers, reel 147S, PKY; Authorization given by José de Soto, 20 February 1816, Cruzat Papers, PKY.

[74] Francisco Caso y Luengo to Joseph de Soto, 10 March 1816, PC, leg. 147B, 582, reel 479, PKY.

[75] Francisco Caso y Luengo to Mateo González de Manrique, 14 March 1816, PC, leg. 147B, 583, reel 479, PKY; Francisco Caso y Luengo to Mauricio de Zuñiga, 28 April 1816, PC, leg. 1796, 1827, reel 120, PKY; Mauricio de Zuñiga to Juan Ruiz de Apodaca, 2 May 1816, PC, leg. 1796, 1821, reel 120, PKY; William Hambly to John Forbes, 17 May 1816, Forbes-Innerarity Papers, 68/5, reel 147Q, PKY.

[76] Francisco Caso y Luengo to Mauricio de Zuñiga, 20 May 1816, PC, leg. 79, 639, reel 479, PKY; Doster, *Creek Indians*, 2:167–168.

[77] Mauricio de Zuñiga to Juan Ruiz de Apodaca, 2 May 1816, PC, leg. 1796, 1821, reel 120, PKY.

[78] Benjamin Hawkins to the Governor of Georgia, 10 May 1816, *Niles' Weekly Register*, 1 June 1816, p. 231.

are coming to see him to hold a great council, and are determined to take the negro fort."[79] At the same time, U.S. troops at Fort Gaines made their own preparations for war.[80] "I don't fear the Americans," Kinache reportedly said, "but rather the many Indians who are coming with them, resolved to take at any cost their portion of slaves in that fort."[81] Accordingly, Kinache and his warriors set out to forestall the Creek and American troops, and they successfully secured a temporary truce.[82]

Under the threat of an attack by U.S. soldiers and hundreds of Creek warriors, Seminole leaders agreed to assist in securing the sixty African American men remaining in the fort along with the women and children.[83] The sincerity of their promise remains uncertain, for before the Spanish could send boats to transport the slaves, American troops began advancing on the fort. On 10 July 1816, two gunboats and two schooners arrived at Apalachicola Bay, supposedly to transport arms up the river to Camp Crawford.[84] A week later, 116 troops from Camp Crawford began descending the Apalachicola River. By chance, they met William McIntosh and 150 warriors, on their way to capture the blacks at Prospect Bluff. A day later, they were joined by another large group of warriors under Koteha Hadjo (Mad Tiger) of Coweta and Captain Isaacs, whose execution of Little Warrior had set off the Redstick War.[85] In all, the Creek warriors perhaps numbered 500.[86] By 20 July, the joint forces were camped outside the fort. A delegation of Indians visited and demanded its surrender. Met by Garzon, the former Pensacola carpenter who was acting as commander, they "were abused, and treated with the utmost contempt," a U.S. officer reported. Garzon "heaped much

[79] Hawkins reported that Mikasuki was divided as to what action to take, Kinache for peace, his head warrior for war. In any case, Kinache supported the war, perhaps reflecting his role as a traditional Creek leader, one who ruled by consensus rather than coercion. Benjamin Hawkins to James McDonald, 22 May 1816, *LBH*, 2:786.

[80] William Hambly to John Innerarity, 14 May 1816, Forbes-Innerarity Papers, 74/20, reel 147Q, PKY; William Hambly to John Forbes, 17 May 1816, Forbes-Innerarity Papers, 68/5, reel 147Q, PKY.

[81] Francisco Caso y Luengo to Mauricio de Zuñiga, 20 May 1816, PC, leg. 79, 639, reel 479, PKY.

[82] Francisco Caso y Luengo to Mauricio de Zuñiga, 12 July 1816, PC, leg. 79, 664, reel 479, PKY.

[83] Alexander Durand to Juan de la Rua, 8 July 1816, PC, leg. 1873, 104, reel 128, PKY; Governor of Pensacola to the Chiefs Kienhogee, Wm Perryman, Yawaly, Houche Emathle, Thlewaly, and Alex.r Durant, 23 July 1816, Innerarity-Hulse Papers, reel 147S, PKY; *Niles' Weekly Register*, 27 June 1816, p. 368.

[84] Covington, "The Negro Fort," 83; Colonel Clinch to Colonel R. Butler, 2 August 1816, in James Grant Forbes, *Sketches, Historical and Topographical, of the Floridas; More Particularly of East Florida* (New York: C. S. Van Winkle, 1821), 200.

[85] Colonel Clinch to Colonel R. Butler, 2 August 1816, in Forbes, *Sketches*, 200; Koteha Hadjo is mentioned in Talesco [Talosee Fixico] to Benjamin Hawkins, 5 July 1813, LBH, 209, GDAH.

[86] Benigno García Calderón to Mauricio de Zuñiga, 8 August 1816, PC, leg. 1873, 114, reel 128, PKY.

abuse on the Americans, and said he had been left in command of the fort by the British government, and that he would sink any American vessels that should attempt to pass it; and would blow up the fort if he could not defend it." His black troops then defiantly hoisted a red flag from atop their stronghold.[87]

A week later, at daybreak on 27 July, after troops had proved to be useless before the well-defended fort, gunboats moved within shot of its walls. The two sides exchanged fire for fifteen minutes. Then a cannonball, intentionally heated red-hot and fired from one of the American gunboats, landed in the powder magazine. The fort exploded at once.[88] As U.S. troops withdrew, they razed Redstick settlements in the area.[89]

Though American officers reported that nearly 300 people died in the fiery explosion, probably no more than forty lost their lives. Most of the inhabitants had fled to nearby Seminole towns at the approach of U.S. troops.[90] Resistance to the new order would continue in the swamps of Florida, but it would be defensive rather than offensive, meant to protect rather than to challenge. Increasingly pushed into the recesses of malarial swamps, the Seminole settlements in Florida would become, in the words of Spanish commandant Caso y Luengo, the "refuge of every

---

[87] Colonel Clinch to Colonel R. Butler, 2 August 1816, in Forbes, *Sketches*, 200. Garzon's response was consonant with his earlier pronouncements. When American troops had previously threatened the fort, Garzon sent word to the commander that "he was waiting for him and regretted his delay." In early June, Kinache reported that the fugitives at Prospect Bluff "were determined to perish before surrendering." Francisco Caso y Luengo to Mauricio de Zuñiga, 20 May 1816, PC, leg. 79, 639, reel 479, PKY; and Francisco Caso y Luengo to Mauricio de Zuñiga, 12 July 1816, PC, leg. 79, 664, reel 479, PKY.

[88] Colonel Clinch to Colonel R. Butler, 2 August 1816, in Forbes, *Sketches*, 200; J. Loomis to Benigno García Calderón, 2 August 1816, PC, leg. 1873, 117, reel 128, PKY; Covington, "The Negro Fort," 84–86. Some historians argue that the occupants of the fort may have destroyed it themselves. See, for example, Riordan, "Seminole Genesis," 256–258, 269–270.

[89] Francisco Caso y Luengo wrote that on 3 August, a Tallapoosa chief with 23 men and women arrived at Fort San Marcos fleeing from American troops who, "entering in his town, had razed cornfields and everything they had sown." Caso y Luengo's description of the chief as a "Tallapoosa" suggests that he was a Redstick who had fled to Florida after the war. Francisco Caso y Luengo to Mauricio de Zuñiga, 15 August 1816, PC, leg. 79, 667, reel 479, PKY.

[90] Accounts that exaggerate the number of people killed in the destruction of the Negro Fort include Colonel Clinch to Colonel R. Butler, 2 August 1816, in Forbes, *Sketches*, 200; *Niles' Weekly Register*, 31 August 1816, pp. 14–15; and J. Loomis to Benigno García Calderón, 2 August 1816, PC, leg. 1873, 117, reel 128, PKY. More reliable accounts, which suggest that most slaves had already fled the fort before its destruction, include John Innerarity to James Innerarity, 13 August 1816, Forbes-Innerarity Papers, 72/11, reel 147Q, PKY; John Innerarity to James Innerarity, 5 October 1816, Forbes-Innerarity Papers, 72/14, reel 147Q, PKY; Edmund Doyle to John Innerarity, 10 December 1816, Forbes-Innerarity Papers, 98/17, reel 147Q, PKY; Residents of Pensacola to Governor of Pensacola, May 1817, Innerarity-Hulse Papers, reel 147S, PKY.

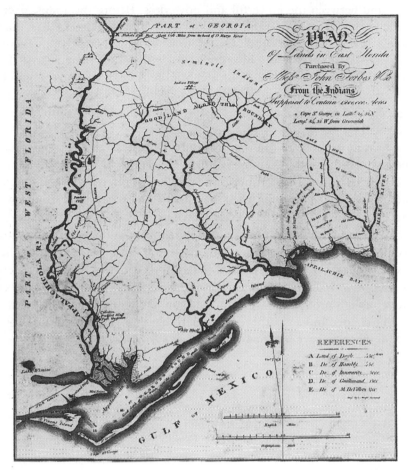

Figure 6. Drawn around 1821 to document the cessions of 1804 and 1811 to Forbes and Company, this map represents a country in the midst of dramatic change. The Indian paths and villages yet remain on the land, but the square tracts surveyed for prospective colonists mark the incursion of a new order. Fort Gadsden sits on Prospect Bluff, where only five years earlier the Negro Fort had offered hope to Redstick, Seminole, and black dissidents. Courtesy of the Hargrett Rare Book & Manuscript Library, University of Georgia Libraries.

fugitive."[91] The destruction of the fort marked the end of the movement against the new order (see Fig. 6).

In the thirty years following the American Revolution, a great transformation had introduced dramatic divisions between the wealthy and

[91] Francisco Caso y Luengo to Joseph Masót, 12 March 1817, no. 108, in letterbook Correspondencia con el Govierno, PC, leg. 225B, reel 431, PKY.

poor and between the powerful and powerless. Before the 1780s, deer-skins were, with few exceptions, the "best Thing" Creeks had, and Creeks maintained "very little Distinction" among themselves.[92] Power was persuasive, and leaders used rhetoric to compel their people. By 1816, in contrast, some Creeks owned hundreds of slaves and thousands of cattle, although their neighbors owned none.[93] National leaders as-signed guilt and administered punishment, calling on police to enforce their will.

Precisely because of the rise of Indian planters and ranchers, and because of the development of national governments with written laws and salaried police, white Americans soon began referring to the Creeks and Seminoles, along with their neighbors, the Cherokees, Choctaws, and Chickasaws, as the "five civilized tribes." Yet the racism and greed of whites prevented these Indian peoples from reaching the destination promised by American liberalism, inclusion into the new republic. Instead, in the 1830s, the United States forced native southeasterners to relocate to Indian Territory (now Oklahoma). Even the fulfillment of the republic's promise, however, would not have erased the difficult and violent change Indians suffered to reach that end. The promised desti-nation may not have justified the journey.

[92] SCG, 2 June 1733; Thomas Causton to his wife, 12 March 1733, CRG, 1982 ed., 20:15–18.
[93] Saunt, "Taking Account of Property."

Index